IT'S NEWS TO ME

IT'S NEWS TO ME

THE MAKING and UNMAKING of AN EDITOR

EDWARD KOSNER

THUNDER'S MOUTH PRESS
NEW YORK

IT'S NEWS TO ME:
The Making and Unmaking of an Editor

Published by
Thunder's Mouth Press
An Imprint of Avalon Publishing Group, Inc.
245 West 17th Street, 11th floor
New York, NY 10011

AVALON
publishing group incorporated

Library of Congress Cataloging-in-Publication Data is available.

ISBN-10: 1-56025-907-8
ISBN-13: 978-1-56025-907-7

9 8 7 6 5 4 3 2 1

Book design by Maria E. Torres

Printed in the United States of America
Distributed by Publishers Group West

For Julie, and for John, Anthony, and Lily

CONTENTS

Introduction by Pete Hamill • ix

1 CAROUSEL 1

2 THE LITTLE FUGITIVE 5

3 NEWS BOY 49

4 APRIL FOOL 59

5 WINNER AND SINNER 79

6 "I SALUTE YOU ON THE BEGINNING
OF A GREAT CAREER" 87

7 DEVIL'S ISLAND 91

8 GOOD-BYE, DOLLY 113

9 "RELAX, KID, IT'S ONLY A
TWENTY-FIVE-CENT MAGAZINE" 125

10 MADAM DRAGON 161

11 "THE DOGS LIKE THE DOG FOOD!" 169

12 "POOR CLAY" 177

13 THE FALLING WALLENDA 187

14 DEUS EX MURDOCH 203

15 MORT 'N' FRED 223

16 GODS AND MONSTERS 229

17 AMATEUR HOUR 241

18 EDSQUIRE 257

19 SUNDAY, BLOODY SUNDAY 271

20 ZUCKERMAN UNBOUND 281

21 THE BIG SCREW 301

22 THE MARCH OF FOLLY 307

23 ARROWS TO TOYLAND 319

Acknowledgments • 323
Index • 325

INTRODUCTION

by PETE HAMILL

IN THE FIRST HOUR of June 1, 1960, I walked into the city room of the old *New York Post* and started my life as a newspaperman. I knew nothing about this unruly craft except that I wanted desperately to learn it. I had never gone to journalism school. I had not served an apprenticeship anywhere. I was three weeks short of twenty-five and had been offered a tryout by an editor who was impressed by my letters. That was all.

I remember standing that night in the doorway of the shabby, high-ceilinged city room. The windows were open to the river air. There were dozens of empty desks, and a few gray middle-aged men wandering around, all of them smoking, glancing at fresh stories from the clacking AP ticker in the unseen wire room. One young man sat at a desk opening mail. The *Post* was then an afternoon paper, and this shift began at 1:00 AM and went until eight in the morning. I was early. One of the gray men came to me and asked if I needed directions. I told him my name and said I was to report to the city desk. He directed me, in a weary way, to a cluster of desks in the center of this emptiness.

At one desk, with his back to me, was a young man poring over fresh copy. He was as alone as I was. I went to him, and he looked up through horn-rimmed glasses. I told him my name.

"Hi," he said, and smiled. "I'm Ed Kosner."

He shook my hand as I explained why I was there, and he led me to a desk that had an old Remington typewriter snug in a well, and I started my education. My first teacher was Ed Kosner. "You worked at a newspaper before, I assume," he said. No, I told him. Never. He then explained, without condescension and only a slight suggestion of pity, the very basics of the craft. Those sheets of copy paper, separated by carbons, were called "books." Each one needed to carry a "slug," a short word that described the story and allowed Kosner and other editors to keep track of it, and later place it on the page.

"If it's a murder, don't slug it 'KILL,'" he said. "The printers will think we want to kill the story."

Then he hurried back to his place at the city desk, where he was doing the work as assistant night city editor that he describes so well in this book. More people arrived, carrying sandwiches and coffee. A young man named Don Forst. Another named Bill Rudy. A woman named Betsy Luce. An older man named Phil Kanter. And around ten minutes after one, Kosner called me over and handed me a press release from B'nai B'rith.

"Give me a one head on this," he said. "About three grafs."

I sat down, read the two-page release, tried to locate its essence, rolled a book into the machine, and started typing. It took me about thirty minutes and three cigarettes to write those three paragraphs. I don't remember anything about the content, but when I brought it over to Kosner, and he read it quickly, I awaited judgment with a certain fatalism. Perhaps he would just tell me to go home. Ah, well. . . .

"Fine," he said, and then handed me a small wad of clippings from the morning papers, held together by a paper clip, and said: "Get this into six grafs."

I was on my way. In the summer months that followed, Kosner was infinitely patient, the point man on a project that initially involved saving me from humiliation. He was two years younger than I was, and married, which I wasn't, but he brought to his task great intensity and a gift for laughter. He wasn't my only teacher. The faculty included tough copy editors, and fluent rewrite men, and those photographers who helped teach me to see revealing details when we went together to fires and homicides. The night city editor, for whom Kosner worked, was a lovely, sardonic man named Johnny Bott.

For several months I was on an official tryout, a provisional condition permitted under the rules of the Newspaper Guild. If I didn't work out, they would just let me go. At first, most of my stories did not carry a byline, as happened to most people on tryouts. Then one night, Kosner sent me out to cover the tale of a man and his family evicted from their flat in Brooklyn. "It might be nothing," he said. "Take a look, and call me." I found the family sitting on top of their belongings in the rain. I wrote about them, and how rain and tears were running together down the face of the humiliated father. The story ran on page four of the next day's paper, and city officials started moving to find shelter for that wounded family. Late in the morning, I got a call from Kosner at home.

"Congratulations," he said. "They just hired you."

When I hung up, I had to choke back tears. Until then, I had been working, without passion, as a graphic designer. My hands and my eyes were in the work, but not my heart. Now I would do work that had some meaning. That could make the world more knowable to strangers. That could get a humiliated man and his children out of the rain. I would do work in the best of company.

In the years that followed, Kosner and I went down separate paths, he to *Newsweek,* where he became editor in 1975, I to Europe for the *Saturday Evening Post,* while remaining, at heart, a newspaperman. I started writing a column for the *Post* in 1965. I would see Kosner from time to time, at political conventions or various social upheavals, where each of us had ringside seats. We always joked about the night he explained to a green young man how to slug a story. But we didn't work together again until he took over *New York* magazine in 1980.

In many ways, that was the best of times, because Kosner had become a superb editor, sensing ideas behind, or ahead of, the news. He did not edit a writer's work to prove his own superiority, as too many bad editors often do; he edited, always, to make the piece better. To make it, in fact, the best possible version of the story. He never looked down at the reader, or tried to make that reader dumber. At *New York,* and later when he edited *Esquire* and finally, the *New York Daily News,* we communicated in shorthand. He'd say "John Lennon" and I didn't have to ask what he wanted me to do. I knew that the result would not be three grafs. I didn't have to tell him in any detail what I would write on the September morning that the Twin Towers were reduced to rubble and dust. I was there. I would write it. He would edit it.

During the decades in which I worked with Kosner, I never knew much about his own background and didn't ask. That was part of my tabloid education. It wasn't, in the end, who you were, but what you did. That is, what you wrote. Or whether you put out that paper, or that magazine, without having to apologize.

About personal lives, the old codes were always in effect. No self-pity, please. Be a stoic when things go bad. Don't bother telling me why you broke up with your wife. Suck it up, pal, and get out the edition. That's why so many parts of this book have revealed Ed Kosner to me in ways that I never suspected at the time. The account of his New York childhood is superb, and explains why he was kind to other people trying to find their way. There is some anger here, but few tears. In these pages, Kosner re-creates several lost journalistic worlds, reveals some of the pain beneath the scar tissue inflicted by publishers, and yet expresses the sheer joy that can come to people who are working at a trade they truly love.

Kosner loved that life. So did I. It was my privilege to play solos in the same band.

Clean copy.
Hard work.
Better to know the truth than not.
—*Stanley Walker*

1

CAROUSEL

AS I CROSSED THE threshold to Kay Graham's small office at *Newsweek* that early spring evening, I knew I was leaving my life behind. Kay was sitting behind her desk wearing one of those Halston ultrasuedes she favored, and she looked teary. I was alert and numb—like somebody in a near-death experience watching himself from some serene remove.

"Oh, Ed," she said in her husky mezzo, "I feel so awful about this, but it's just not working."

I'd known I was gone that Monday morning when I turned to the business pages of the *New York Times*. The news magazines were more important in June 1979 than they are today, and *Time* and *Newsweek* would take ads in the *Times* at the start of each week showcasing their covers. In one corner, there was the cover I'd chosen for *Newsweek*: A send-up of those old pulp sci-fi magazines with a beautiful gasping girl and the headline in camp type,

HOLLYWOOD'S SCARY SUMMER!

Across the page, a benevolent Pope John Paul II waved to the ecstatic Polish homecoming crowds from *Time*'s cover.

It was nearly sixteen years since I'd first set foot in *Newsweek*'s Madison Avenue offices, a skinny twenty-six-year-old kid from the scruffy *New York Post* given a one-week tryout. Over the years, I'd scrambled to the top of the masthead, and now my *Newsweek* sold more copies each week than ever before and was thick with glossy ads. But I had lost favor with Kay, who ruled her magazine and newspaper, the *Washington Post*, with a twitchy, autocratic hand. *Time*'s smiling Pope had sealed my doom.

As much as I had anticipated her words, I was still stunned—at least by their timing. I was supposed to lead a *Newsweek* delegation to China in a week, a rare journey in those days. Like Nixon's pilgrimage to China in the midst of Watergate, the trip, I'd hoped, would buy me more time.

Being cast out of *Newsweek* was the worst thing that ever happened to me. I had never really failed at anything before. Although I'd spent five years at the *Post*, *Newsweek* was where I had grown up and transformed myself from a Washington Heights provincial to a reasonably polished journalist who could have dinner with Henry Kissinger or King Hussein of Jordan one night and Liv Ullmann the next, and effortlessly chat up each one. I had invested all my energy and intellect in the magazine and my heart, too. It was my identity. Or so I thought.

That night, I swallowed my second Valium ever and made a decision: I may have been fired, but I wasn't going to slink off from *Newsweek*. Next morning, I had an announcement distributed to everyone on the editorial and business floors asking them to join me at Top of the Week, the penthouse meeting place I. M. Pei had designed for the magazine. Kay Graham, I heard later, was alarmed when she saw the memo, sure that I planned some tirade or ugly scene, but of course I had nothing like that in mind.

Soon Top of the Week was jammed with hundreds of *Newsweek* staffers. As I reached the small lectern, I saw Kay standing against the wall, her arms folded across her chest, looking tauter than ever. It was over in an instant. I told them how honored I was to have been their editor, thanked them for all their good work, and wished them and *Newsweek* good fortune, the appropriate script. They applauded, as people always do at such grim rituals, and I walked through the crowd and rode down in the elevator to the street, where Julie was waiting in a car to take me away from the life I loved.

Later, I heard that Mrs. Graham, finding the elevators jammed, decided to hoof it down the stairwell thirty floors to her office. Midway, she suddenly stopped and turned to one of my ex-colleagues.

"Did I make a mistake?" she asked.

He reassured her that I had to go.

"No, not about *Ed*," she replied. "I mean about taking the stairs!"

As it happened, Kay Graham liberated me that day. Driven out of *Newsweek*, I was forced to fashion a new career as the editor of two iconic magazines, *New York* and *Esquire*, and of America's biggest tabloid newspaper, the *New York Daily News*. I wound up working with the most accomplished writers of our time, from Norman Mailer to Pete Hamill and Gay Talese, and toiling for other press lords as mighty as Rupert Murdoch and as mercurial as Mort Zuckerman.

It was my good fortune as a journalist to live in the most tumultuous era of modern American history—the frenzied decades that ran from the assassination of John F. Kennedy through the civil-rights uprising, Vietnam, Watergate, and on to September 11 and the war in Iraq. I was at *Newsweek* on November 22, 1963, when JFK was murdered in Dallas, and on August 8, 1974, the day Richard Nixon resigned and choppered off to San Clemente, and I was running the *Daily News* on September 11, 2001, the gleaming morning when the twin towers collapsed on the most horrific day in the history of New York City.

I'd written more than 2 million words on everything from Lana Turner's runaway daughter, Cheryl Crane, to Robert Kennedy's run for the White House, edited nearly a thousand issues of *Newsweek, New York,* and *Esquire,* and put out more than a thousand tabloid *Daily News* front pages.

One day very late in the game, I finally found the right metaphor for my career: It was a carousel ride—a media merry-go-round where one kept rising and falling and sometimes getting thrown from the horse. I was always encountering specters from the past who showed up again and again as benefactors and antagonists, comrades and rivals.

And if I was honest, and looked closely enough, I might recognize one of the ghosts as myself.

2

THE LITTLE FUGITIVE

ONCE, AT *NEWSWEEK* IN the late 1960s, I found myself at dinner with three colleagues. One was a direct descendant of John Jay. The second could trace his roots to James Madison and the family that lent its name to Blackwell's (later Welfare and, finally, Roosevelt) Island in the East River off Manhattan. The third, Lucy Anne Howard, was descended from the renowned Peale clan of early American painters, Benjamin Franklin, and a Confederate pirate captain named James Waddell, who preyed on Union ships long after the Civil War had ended. I kept my family tree to myself, partly because it was mostly a mystery to me.

True to the "don't ask, don't tell" credo of so many of my parents' generation, all I knew of my pedigree was that my mother's parents had emigrated toward the end of the nineteenth century from Bialystock, a Polish-Jewish metropolis of sorts that had been absorbed into Russia. An immigration officer in New York had looked at my grandfather's unpronounceable name and asked him what his family did in the old country. The reply sounded like "fish," and Fisher they became.

My father's people came from what my mother liked to call "the caves," Galicia in the Polish-Ukrainian neverland ruled in their time by the Austro-Hungarian Empire. This somehow emboldened many of my father's relatives to claim they were of German origin, an attempt to acquire class by association with the "Our Crowd" Jews who had come to America before the Civil War.

My paternal grandfather's name was Kosiner, but people in those days kept pronouncing it Ka-*zee*-ner, which didn't sound American enough to my father. So he dropped the *i,* hoping the name would be pronounced as if it rhymed with *close.* Instead, he spent his adult life—and I've spent mine—correcting people who invariably address us as if we all came from Oz.

The Kosiners and Fishers settled on the Lower East Side more than a century ago. In time, my mother's father ran a catering hall on East Broadway and a small hotel in the Catskills. My father's father seems to have sold umbrellas, although the details of his business life are as lost in the mists as his birthplace. By the 1920s, both families had prospered enough to move north to the brownstone blocks of lower Harlem around what was then Mount Morris Park (much later renamed for Marcus Garvey, the back-to-Africa zealot from Jamaica).

My mother was one of five sisters and my father had ten brothers and sisters. Thirteen of the sixteen married, and, remarkably, nearly all of them found spouses living on a handful of streets clustered around 120th Street and Madison Avenue. Unlike so many whose path from the Lower East Side led to Brooklyn or the Bronx and then on to the suburbs, the Fishers and the Kosiners stayed in Manhattan, eventually settling on the Upper West Side, or, in the case of my parents, farther north in leafy Washington Heights, not far from the George Washington Bridge. So I grew up in a world a shade less provincial (and much less fun) than people of my age like Ralph Lauren and Calvin Klein, whose childhoods were spent in the pulsing Jewish neighborhoods around Pelham and Mosholu parkways in the Bronx.

Washington Heights during World War II was an oddly cosmopolitan backwater. Broadway was the great divide. The Jews lived in mostly renovated six-story brown, yellow, and gray brick apartment houses that ran west to the Hudson from the huge Columbia-Presbyterian Medical Center on 168th Street to the hilly streets just north of the bridge. The Irish lived in buildings more reminiscent of tenements, running east toward the Harlem River.

The Jews were an amalgam. The somber refugees from Hitler gave the neighborhood a settled, German tone. Dressed in black, small, quiet couples shuffled along the streets or sat together in the parks talking in whispery German—never Yiddish—the women often carrying those mesh shopping bags last seen on Alexanderplatz. The other distinctive group was made up of refugees, too, but these were mostly Russian intellectuals, hard-core Stalinists, and democratic socialists, bitter political rivals often in the same family, whose book-lined apartments were filled with leftist tracts and records by the Red Army Chorus and the black American Communist culture hero Paul Robeson.

And then there were the Kosners and a handful of their ilk—American-born, second-generation, lower-middle-class assimilationists who shopped at Saks and Best & Co., loved Broadway musicals like *South Pacific* and *Guys and Dolls,* and proudly displayed their Book of the Month Club best sellers by Frank Yerby and Edna Ferber.

In the summer, the Irish rode the subway to Rockaway and Coney Island, the German refugees who could afford it melted away to bungalows in Connecticut, the Commies headed off to upstate proletarian camps, and the Kosners went to middle-class Long Beach on the Atlantic, with its boardwalk lined with frozen custard stands, pokerino parlors, miniature golf courses, and cute townie girls.

To my mother, who had a tall, docile, twentyish Negro girl from the Carolinas as a full-time maid to help her keep our tiny apartment overlooking Broadway immaculate, the sad, whispery German refugees and their children were "refs." The lefty mothers, with their makeup-free pusses, austere bowl haircuts, and ugly brown space shoes, were "the intelligentsia" with a dismissive hard *g.* My mother knew we were the real Americans.

The war was a palpable presence as I was growing up in the Heights, and not just because the sad refugees brought the reality of Hitler to every corner. To ensure more daylight hours at the end of the workday, War Time had been imposed. It pushed the clocks ahead two hours so that when the time read 7:00 AM it was actually five and pitch black. To save on gasoline, the milkman delivered from a horse-drawn cart, and often the first sounds I'd hear as I awoke for school were the clops of the Sheffield Farms dray plodding up Broadway.

My mother went shopping clutching booklets of blue and red ration stamps (and we would have had a gas rationing sticker on the windshield of our car if we'd had a car). Each morning, I'd head off to school after the war news from Edward R. Morrow in London and others on the CBS Radio Network. The reports always mentioned the Red Army attacking the Nazis or being driven back by the Nazis. I pictured masses of troops all clad in crimson or scarlet marching behind tanks the color of fire engines. I was ashamed to ask anybody what this Red Army was, and it was years before one of my Communist playmates told me about Our Heroic Soviet Comrades.

There were no new metal toys to be had so we played with clunky carved wooden soldiers wearing World War I–style pie dish helmets and stubby wooden trucks and tanks. The only excitement came every few months when word flashed around the neighborhood that this or that candy store had got hold of a stash of frozen Milky Way chocolate bars, a contraband delicacy in these deprived times. From nowhere, children looking like Depression urchins in their plaid mackinaws and corduroy knickers would line up silently outside the shop—only to learn that the precious candy had run out, if there had even been any on sale.

In war and peace, my mother was very particular about how I dressed for school, taking me downtown on Saturdays to the spiffy Lilliputian Bazaar at Best & Co. on Fifth Avenue or to the children's department at Macy's. I particularly loved going to Macy's because that meant a hot dog and an orange drink in a tall, thin glass at Nedick's, a shop wedged right into the corner of the department store at the northwest corner of Herald Square. It also meant a glimpse of a funny little man who was always posted in front of Nedick's clutching a stack of muckraking ten-cent tabloid papers that he may have written himself. He was a crusader against unhygienic food and dangerous products—a kind of Stone Age Ralph Nader. "Rat hairs found in Velveeta cheese!" he'd cry. "Coca-Cola syrup rots meat in test tube!" Hardly anyone bought his papers, but he never gave up.

My mother was most critical of the way the "refs" dressed their kids, as if they were attending some polytechnic in Hamburg rather than P.S. 173. Their shiny black shoes, so alien compared to the brown lace-ups she got me at Best's or Indian Walk, particularly annoyed her. The truth was, I was turned out like none of the other pupils at 173. The Irish kids—those whose parents couldn't afford to send them to the parochial school, the Church of the Incarnation a couple of blocks away, or who had been thrown out for hooliganism—dressed like ragamuffins. Most of the Jewish kids wore the knickers and mackinaws sold on Broadway. Little Edward had gray flannel trousers, those Best & Co. brogans, and an array of leather jackets more appropriate for our pilots bombing the brains out of the Nazis from their B-17s and Liberators over Frankfurt and Düsseldorf. My father was in the men's and boys' outerwear business, and he'd decked me out in samples from the time I could zip a zipper.

Inevitably, I hated being different. I was obsessed with getting one of those plaid mackinaws and a pair of scratchy corduroy knickers so I could look like everybody else, and I tormented my mother until she consented to take me to the boys' store a few blocks up Broadway from our apartment where all my schoolmates got their clothes. After my father got home from work that evening, I modeled my new duds.

As it happened, I was the smallest (and youngest) boy in my class—so short and bone-skinny that my mother had packed me off to Dr. Pecker for an exam to make sure I wasn't an incipient dwarf. As my parents watched, I pulled on the baggy knickers, tugging the belt so tight to keep them from falling down that the wartime ersatz fabric bunched up and my legs, in their loose dark hose, stuck out like toothpicks.

Then I donned the red-and-black plaid mackinaw, zipped the hood over my head, and stood in front of the bedroom dressing mirror. Staring back at me was a goblin from the brothers Grimm, a tiny, shrunken figure with a pinched, ashen face peering out from a massive dark cowl. Standing behind me on either side, my mother and father erupted in shrieks of derisive hilarity. My regular-boy outfit went back to the store the next day, and my parents never let me forget my pathetic folly.

In memory, the school seems a relic of the days when the New York public schools were celebrated for their rigor and earnest accomplishment. It was at the foot of 174th Street, just down the block from my apartment house on Broadway. P.S. 173 was part of the Great Depression–inspired explosion of public works. It was built of red brick with touches of white Georgian trim, six stories high, U-shaped, enclosing a paved schoolyard below street level. World War II, or some budget squeeze, had ended construction before the second leg of the U was erected, leaving an L with one leg knifing into the schoolyard like a vast ocean liner's prow. (This made for idiosyncratic ground rules in the pickup softball games played there all weekend: Balls hit off the building façade were in play and anything caught on the fly off the wall was an out, much to the disgust of the neighborhood sluggers.)

As was the case in the public schools in those days, the teachers were all women, a few of them Jewish, but mainly Roman Catholic or Protestant. The principal was a birdy old woman who looked like a daughter of the American Revolution, but was probably Irish Catholic, too. Classes in each grade were numbered one through six, with all the smart little Jewish boys and girls in the one or two classes and the other sections filled with parochial school rejects and the odd Puerto Rican or Greek or Italian immigrant's kids. Discipline was old-school, although less fearsome than in the parochial schools, where, I was told, the nuns delighted in rapping miscreants or slow learners on the knuckles with steel rulers.

In third grade, the teacher would patrol the aisles of our classroom with a thin, hard-covered maroon spelling book clutched in her hand. She'd come up behind one or another terrified child and pose a "spelling demon" like "bicycle." *"B . . . i . . . c . . . i,"* the young scholar would begin. *Thwack!* would go the spelling book on his head.

From kindergarten, I was known as a very bright child, lively and talkative, with a vocabulary far beyond my five years. But when, in first grade, Miss Kafka began teaching reading by showing flash cards to the class, something was clearly wrong. Miss Kafka would flash an *A* and little Edward would pipe up *C.* After a few days of this, my mother was summoned to school and I was dispatched to the eye doctor, who found that my vision was 20/200, so myopic that I couldn't see even the big letter at the top of the eye chart.

When I put on my first pair of glasses, it was literally a revelation: The movies, I now marveled, weren't the big black-and-white and colored swirls I'd been peering at since age two. And on the streets, you could actually recognize people by their faces. Bright as I was supposed to be, it had never occurred to me that other people saw clearly while I faked my way through a fog. I thought everything was supposed to be blurred.

The glasses, not thick but made of fragile glass, were a torment. Children were even crueler than they are now, totally unfettered by today's lip-service sensitivity to handicaps and deformities. "Four eyes" was the kindest entry in the litany of ridicule. I tried to deal with the problem by taking off my glasses at every chance, slipping them into a case that I stuck in a pants pocket. Invariably, someone would shove me down in a game, or I'd forget and sit on the glasses. It happened so often, and I was so terrified of having to report another disaster to my mother, that I surrendered and kept the glasses on despite the taunts.

The glasses were terrifying in another way: There was always the chance that an errant playground spaldeen or softball would shatter them and blind me. And there was already enough to worry about. Every child growing up at this time lived in dread from Memorial Day to Labor Day of catching polio at a swimming pool or other public spot and spending the rest of his or her life clanking around in leg braces or, worse, imprisoned in an *iron lung*!

The March of Dimes, the polio charity boosted by our crippled president,

Franklin D. Roosevelt, raised money in movie houses by showing newsreel-style appeals followed by the ushers passing clinking donation cans through the audience. The appeals always featured young polio victims being tended in their shiny pods by nurses whose kind faces radiated pity at their hopeless plight. A child's face could be seen only in reflection in the horizontal mirror rigged atop the dread canister so the unfortunate within could see around his constricted world. The fear wasn't based merely on paranoia. Every summer, the dread word would pass that Herby Rothschild from class 4-1 or Joey Vierra, who was away at camp, or someone else we all knew was the latest victim. I was never allowed to go near a public swimming pool. The one time I snuck off to the municipal pool in Long Beach, my mother hunted me down and literally dragged me out of the chlorine-reeking water.

Aside from the polio dread, my life in elementary school was as near perfection as I could imagine. The school had about a dozen boys and girls who would have been immediately identified today as gifted. We all were in the first section of each grade and moved through our school years as a class within a class. Nearly every week, teachers and teachers-in-training from the Bank Street College of Education and from Juilliard would run special programs for us or just observe us being brilliant. Often the principal, Miss Hines, would come to class leading some dazzled visitor. When she swept into the classroom, we all slid to the right from our desks and stood erect in the aisles. The boys bent one arm at the elbow across their waists, slid the other behind their backs, and bowed deeply. The girls curtsied. "Good morning, Miss Hines," we intoned in unison.

Once, four of us were chosen to represent the school at a radio quiz show presided over by Buffalo Bob Smith, the creator of Howdy Doody. The marionette Howdy, who was to become a TV star rivaling Milton Berle, had not yet been invented. In those radio days, he was just a voice. Buffalo Bob would signal his advent to the audience by whipping a red bandana out of his back pocket, and everyone would laugh uproariously. I answered the climactic brain-buster from Buffalo Bob (Q: If you had a record and the label fell off, how would you know what was on it? A: Play it.), and we were rewarded with albums of educational recordings for P.S. 173.

My school days were made even more pleasurable (or claustrophobic) by the fact that many of the teachers would take their lunches at a drugstore on Broadway at 175th Street, where my mother often joined them for a bacon-lettuce-and-tomato sandwich and an earful of little Edward's latest show of brilliance. It was at one of these lunches that a teacher passed the word to Annalee Kosner that she'd spotted Edward's IQ in his permanent record and that it was 179, as high as she'd ever seen. This was the start of the Kosner family myth that Edward was a genius, a distinction never again tested and surely never confirmed by any academic or other achievement.

The war had another profound impact on me. Convinced that America had to do everything possible to defeat the Axis, school officials decided that bright pupils should be accelerated, presumably so that they could get to M.I.T. faster and outthink the Germans. No sooner had I finished the first half of first grade than I found myself, along with some pals, drafted into second grade. The same thing happened the next year with the third and fourth grades.

The war ended on August 14, 1945 (barely three weeks after my eighth birthday), the great day hailed in Long Beach by the warbling air raid sirens and people dancing with joy and relief on the boardwalk. By now, I was improbably in the fifth grade, and I was a month shy of my tenth birthday when I finished sixth and graduated from elementary school. This worked reasonably well as long as I was in the nurturing bubble of P.S. 173. I was tiny—the shortest, or nearly shortest, boy or girl in my class. But most of my school friends were about the same age, equally bright, and not much bigger. We hung around together, played ball in the P.S. 173 schoolyard or the dirt field at Jay Hood Wright Park across Fort Washington Avenue from the school, and went to the movies at Loew's 175th Street, a mammoth mock Oriental palace on Broadway.

But the Catch-22 in my charmed life couldn't be denied forever. Even in sixth grade, many of the girls were a foot taller than I was, and a few were plainly growing breasts. When I went to Long Beach with my parents each summer, I tried to run with other kids from the city who were in the same grade—inevitably to find that they were two years older than I was and had no interest in me. Some were already shaving, and their wallets showed the telltale ring where they had stashed a Trojan just in case.

The same thing happened when my parents bundled me off for camp the summer I turned nine. I didn't really want to go because I enjoyed such freedom in Long Beach. Camp Deer Run was started by one of my mother's cousins, Bernie Alexander, and his wife in 1946. It was located outside the hamlet of Sugar Grove, Pennsylvania, just south of Jamestown, New York, and about fifty miles from Lake Erie, fully 500 miles from New York City. In its charter year, the camp had only twenty-six campers—thirteen boys and thirteen girls—clustered in six bunks not far from the man-made lake. The summer cost my parents $750, easily the equivalent of $10,000 today.

To get to camp, we took an overnight train from Pennsylvania Station. I remember putting my clothes in the little mesh hammock that stretched across the berth and starving: Inexplicably, the Alexanders neglected to provide any food but a candy bar or two for their charges on the long ride through the night past Scranton and Altoona. Once in camp, I was assigned to the intermediate bunk with three or four other fifth and sixth graders. But I simply couldn't keep up with boys two years older. After taps, my eyes would close just as they started roughhousing, and they teased me unmercifully. After about a week, I was demoted to the baby bunk with boys my own age, who were still in fourth grade.

I spent the summer taking pictures with my Kodak folding camera and making a copper ashtray in the crafts cabin. The ultimate indignity came when the camp staged its scaled-down version of color war. Because there were so few campers, the boys competed against the girls in some events. I was assigned to a rowing race against one of the girls. Her name was Bubbles and she was a dwarf with a large head, a muscular torso, and short, bandy legs. Bubbles was an accomplished rower, especially adept at the rhythmic fisherman's stroke, and she easily left me ignominiously in her wake.

At the end of the summer, we took the sleeper back to New York, again sustained only by a Clark Bar or two. At Penn Station, I inhaled the wonderful, sooty New York air and rushed into my mother's arms, clutching my summer handiwork.

"Ah, the $750 ashtray," said Annalee as she gave me a big kiss.

I never returned to the camp and never heard a word about it for twenty-five years. One day in 1975, soon after I was named editor of *Newsweek,* a large manila envelope arrived at my desk. Inside was a letter from Bernie Alexander telling me how proud he was that an alumnus of Camp Deer Run had been such a success. He enclosed a small brown felt camp pennant and a wooden plaque that all the first-year campers and counselors had signed with one of those wood-burning pens. There was my childish scrawl and, across on the girls' side, there was Bubbles' neat, round signature.

* * *

Growing up in Manhattan in the years right after World War II was a joyful adventure that I came to fully appreciate only years later when I could compare it to the crowded, perilous, expensive city of the late sixties and seventies. If safety was an issue, my friends and I were never aware of it. From the age of ten I began venturing downtown alone, first on the great green and yellow Fifth Avenue buses. Within a few years I was taking the A train (although at that point I would have thought Duke Ellington was King George VI's cousin).

There were two Fifth Avenue bus lines near my house, as well as the déclassé red and yellow buses that had replaced the rackety trolley cars running up and down Broadway beneath my fourth-floor window. The No. 4 bus was a single-decker that ran down Riverside Drive to 110th Street, where it turned east to Fifth Avenue and on down to Thirty-fourth Street, then swung west to Penn Station. But the glories of the Fifth Avenue Coach Company, as it formally styled itself, were the double-decker No. 5's, cousins to London's great red dreadnoughts. The 5's started at the Columbia Presbyterian Medical Center at 168th Street and Broadway and ran all the way down to Washington Square, traveling south for part of the way on Riverside Drive. The No. 5 stopped right outside my father's office, at 200 Fifth Avenue at Twenty-third Street, then, as now, known as the Toy Building.

All the drivers and fare collectors on the Fifth Avenue buses were Irish, many with the dramatic brogues that Mike Quill, their union chief, preserved into the 1960s. The trick of riding the No. 5 was to wait until a fresh bus rumbled up to start its run at 168th Street, board the bus first, then race up the spiral stairs to the upper deck and take possession of the first seat on the left at the front. There, perched right over the driver on the first level, one could easily imagine steering the 5 on its majestic run downtown.

My first solo journey was a ride to the Museum of Natural History on Central Park West and Seventy-seventh Street, with its giant suspended whale and Indian war canoe manned by its spooky crew of effigies. Next, I went to the Metropolitan Museum of Art, on Fifth Avenue. Going to a museum in New York on Saturday in those days was nothing like today's traumatic forays into the mobs drawn to blockbuster shows at the Met or the Museum of Modern Art. *It was free and there was nobody there.*

I can see myself wandering through the all but deserted galleries of the Met. There would be a couple of somnolent guards trying to look awake, and here and there an art student with a portable easel copying a masterwork. You could see the dust motes in the golden haze from the skylights. The only sound would be the creak of the shiny wide-planked floorboards under my Indian Walks, and the squeak of the copyist's brushstroke on the canvas.

Within a few years, my friends from the Washington Heights *intelligentsia* and I started going to the Museum of Modern Art on Fifty-third Street off Fifth Avenue. MOMA was a lark, and each visit had its undeviating course—Brancusi's phallic abstract sculpture *Bird in Flight*, Malevich's nearly blank canvas *White on White*, Pavel Tchelitchew's surreal *Hide and Seek*, with its grotesque children's heads nestled in the scary tree, Peter Blume's head of Mussolini glowering from the ruins of his *Eternal City*, and Picasso's *Guernica*. MOMA was even emptier than the Metropolitan, and I used to feel sorry for the place because nobody seemed to want to go there. But the real attraction at the museum for us wasn't the oddball art. It was the silent movies shown at 3:00 PM in the small auditorium in the basement.

Tickets cost a quarter and there was a pianist to accompany the screen action with virtuoso runs and rags. It was in the MOMA basement that I first encountered Chaplin and Keaton and Harold Lloyd, the Gish sisters and John Gilbert, *Birth of a Nation*, Carl Dreyer's *The Passion of Joan of Arc,* and Eisenstein's *Battleship Potemkin* and two *Ivans*. The movies were exotic and beautiful and sometimes boring, and the look of them was unforgettable.

In the same way that a ten-year-old could wander into a museum and have the place nearly to himself, going to a baseball or football game was a casual choice that could be made at the last minute. One Saturday morning, my father's twin brother, Ben, called our house and invited me to see the Giants play the Pittsburgh Pirates. We took the bus down to 155th Street, then walked down from Coogan's Bluff to the old green horseshoe called the Polo Grounds. Uncle Benny bought two field box seats in the bright sunshine just behind third base for three or four bucks each. There were ten or twelve thousand other fans on hand. Uncle Benny treated me to a scorecard and watery hot dogs, and watched while I collected autographs during batting practice. When the game ended we retraced our steps and took the bus home. Around the same time, my father took me to Babe Ruth Day at Yankee Stadium. I saw the cancer-doomed Bambino, shrunken in his baggy pinstripes, and I became a Yankee fan for life.

Another uncle—Sam Robbins, who was married to my mother's beautiful, demure sister Belle—took me to Ivy League track meets at the old Madison Square Garden, at the run-down Engineers' Armory near the Medical Center, with its oval track painted on the flat wooden drill floor, and outdoors at Randall's Island, the athletic wonderland under the Triborough Bridge created by Robert Moses. Hardly anybody went to these meets—even the Garden was only half full—and they had an intimate charm unimaginable today.

Sam also took me to my first college football game—Columbia versus Yale at the old Baker Field at the northern tip of Manhattan—and, on autumn Sunday afternoons, to the pro football Giants at the Polo Grounds. There, using twenty-five-cent passes provided by yet another uncle, we sat in the lower right-field stands and watched what we could see of the game from behind the end zone, about the worst seats in the house. Our fellow spectators were mostly priests and coaches from the Roman Catholic high schools and colleges in the area, kind, ruddy-faced men who were true fans. Those freezing, blustery winter afternoons watching the hapless Giants lose game after game fixed me with a lifelong addiction to the team, an almost obsessive compulsion to watch every minute of every game every year that has survived two marriages, but just barely.

Passes and buying wholesale were second nature in my family. Because my father was in the clothing business, much of what he, my mother, and I (after age ten or so) wore was procured at "wholesale houses," manufacturers' lofts in the Garment District. On Saturday mornings, my father would take me to one of these linty factories on lower Fifth Avenue, where we would meet a Larry or a Phil or a Manny who was the contact.

"Shake hands with Larry/Phil/Manny and tell him what you want," my father would command.

Desperately avoiding eye contact, I'd clutch Manny's paw and choke out that I wanted a pair of charcoal gray trousers or a tweed jacket.

Manny would disappear into the back and return with several pairs of pants or an armful of jackets. The trousers would be brown, blue, or black—anything but gray. The jackets would be corduroy. But the politesse of the situation required me to feign joy at what I was being offered. After all, Manny was doing us a huge favor by getting the goods for us wholesale.

Often I was saved because the proffered clothing was ludicrously too big for me. But more than once the verdict was, "The tailor can take in the waist" or "He'll grow into it."

I never bought any important clothing at retail until I went to college, and nothing I wore was what I wanted or really fit, except for the sample-size leather jackets that my father's company made outside Boston.

And I was picky. As my bar mitzvah approached, I had an unshakable determination about how I was going to look: like Frank Costello, the gangster and George Raft wannabe, the star witness at Senator Estes Kefauver's televised crime hearings. The forties had just turned into the fifties, and men were decked out in deeply draped double-breasted suits and hand-painted ties. I had my tie all picked out—it featured a vivid swirl of marimba sticks—and all I needed was the suit and the shiny wingtips.

Thus, the great Quest for Edward's Suit. It began paradoxically enough at retail stores—DePinna, Rogers Peet, Brooks, the finest establishments in the city. At each stop, the salesman blanched at the idea of dressing a young master in *a double-breasted suit!* The store had no such thing and he couldn't imagine where one might be found. Desperate, we headed downtown to Seventh Avenue and Seventeenth Street to Barney's, today the ultimate cool department boutique for men and women in midtown, at that time a ramshackle discount emporium famed for its radio slogan, "Calling all boys to Barney's Boys Town."

We approached a salesman and, as he began sorting among the suits in my size, my mother, who was offended by the very idea of Barney's, sat down in a rickety armchair—which promptly collapsed. "Let's go," said Annalee, and we were back on the street before the man from Boys Town could whip some prospects off the rack. Eventually, some wholesale Manny or Phil turned up a light blue double-breasted suit that actually fit, and Edward, hair glued into a pompadour, was bar mitzvahed looking like Meyer Lansky's nephew.

Like other assimilating second-generation American Jews, my parents were observant in the most idiosyncratic way. My mother lit the Sabbath candles and patronized Shulman, the cranky kosher butcher, but often served ham steak Hawaiian from Safeway. Templegoing was for greenhorns, or "mockies," as they were called, a phrase whose origin I never learned. Once a year, on Yom Kippur, my mother and Aunt Selda would sneak into *shul* for the Yizkor service for the dead. My father's idea of observing the High Holidays was to dress in his best camel's hair sports jacket and *walk past* several of the neighborhood temples, a Havana cigar in his hand. I was permitted to skip school, but not to play ball in the park.

Yiddish was neither spoken nor understood in our house—except for a full vocabulary of curse words. Their meanings were only imprecisely grasped, but their onomatopoeic eloquence was unmistakable. My favorite was *paskudnyak,* a revolting, nasty person. Observant or not, my mother was determined that I would be bar mitzvahed. No matter that we belonged to no temple and that I knew no Hebrew and had barely been inside a *shul.* I was enrolled in after-school Hebrew classes at a Conservative congregation housed in a YMHA near the George Washington Bridge.

Two or three afternoons a week I'd slouch over to the Y and take my seat in a class taught by a young rabbinical student with a giant nose and a gruff manner. Hebrew was instilled by rote: We learned the letters and accents that determined pronunciation, but never the meaning of the words we chanted. Many of my fellow scholars knew Yiddish and some Hebrew, and, as I did with my leftist and German-Jewish school friends, I felt shallow by comparison—an outsider even among these aliens. To strike a spark and break the boredom, I tried asking smarty questions.

One dreary afternoon, I piped up: "Isn't it possible that the dietary laws banning pork and shellfish came about to protect people from trichinosis and other illnesses?"

"No, came from God," replied the young rabbi-to-be, ending the discussion.

Since I was born on July 26, I should have become a man on the first Saturday after my birthday. (Never before the birthday: Jews don't take for granted that you'll survive that last week to make it to thirteen.) But my mother wanted to stage my gala at the Tavern on the Green in Central Park, and it wouldn't do to have the party in the middle of the summer, when everybody was away. So she negotiated with the rabbi to hold the rite on a September Saturday conveniently after Labor Day. This created the problem of how I was going to remember the two-and-a-half-page portion of the Torah that I would have to chant (without understanding a word) on the big day. The ingenious solution was for me to practice before dinner each night in Long Beach. Once a week, I'd take the Long Island Railroad into Penn Station and then catch the A train up to the Y, where I would perform for the rabbi. He'd correct my pronunciation and send me back to the beach for another week of nightly incantation.

It was a sign of the times that a thirteen-year-old boy who looked ten could make that round trip every week without anyone worrying that it might be his last. I actually loved the weekly commute, partly for the adventure, but essentially because it gave me a secret advantage in the cutthroat world of collecting, trading, and flipping bubble gum baseball cards, our main preoccupation at the beach. The cards were sold in packs of five with a square of pink bubble gum that tasted like sugary cardboard and was immediately tossed away.

As it happened, the latest cards were on sale in the city a week or two before their advent in the candy stores of Long Beach. So each week after chanting for the rabbi, I'd stock up on the latest Tommy Henrichs and Mel Parnells at Lesnick's candy store on Broadway and triumphantly swap them for exorbitant rewards from the Long Beach have-nots.

When the big Saturday of the bar mitzvah finally came, I sang like a little Jewish prince and my mother *kvelled* with pleasure.

The absence of any sense of Jewish culture wasn't the only gap in my upbringing. The single bookshelf in the hall was filled with best-selling novels, and my mother was addicted to soap operas that poured from the radio from ten or eleven in the morning until four in the afternoon, when *Tom Mix* and the other serials to which I was addicted began. I heard so many episodes of *Helen Trent*, *Mary Noble, Backstage Wife*, and *Young Doctor Malone* that I unconsciously absorbed all the conventions of the genre.

If a character paused for a moment, then reassured another character that he or she was all right, that meant a brain tumor was already hatching in the skull. I could sniff out the unknown evil twin who'd show up to torment the hero or heroine, the amnesia that turned a beloved husband into a stranger, the dream sequences that could propel the plot into nightmare wrinkles only to be obliterated when the character awakened to realize he hadn't robbed the kindly neighborhood druggist or run over his blind niece. Decades later, when hour-long soaps like *Dallas* and *Dynasty* ruled prime-time TV, I could unerringly predict plot turns because these glossy shows used the same shop-worn devices as my mother's beloved radio dramas.

In the midst of this lower-middle-brow mix, there was my father's inexplicable love of opera. I never learned how he'd got hooked, but I grew up to the sonorous commentary of Milton Cross, who was the announcer for the Saturday afternoon broadcasts from the Metropolitan Opera. For a time, my father went to the opera several nights a week. I would awaken for school the next morning to find the programs, and often the libretti from *Tosca* or *Carmen, The Flying Dutchman* or *Rigoletto,* on the hall table. One morning, he announced the debut of a great new tenor with the exquisite name of Ferruccio Tagliavini.

"Almost as good as Bjoerling, boy," he said, referring to the reigning tenor of the day, the Swede Jussi Bjoerling, a high compliment indeed.

Typically, my father never bought a ticket to the opera in his life. Instead, he cultivated a group of off-duty cops and firemen who would don dinner jackets and homburgs and moonlight as ticket-takers at the old Met house on Thirty-ninth Street and Broadway. His favorite was a handsome Irish cop named Frank. My father would provide Frank with bomber jackets for himself and his kids, and Frank would give Sidney entrée to the great house. Before curtain time, Sidney would queue up with the other operagoers at Frank's turnstile. Instead of a ticket, he'd palm an empty matchbook in his right hand. Sidney would hand the matchbook to Frank, who would ceremoniously tear it in half as if it were a real ticket, hand the stub to my father, and wave him in with a tip of the homburg. Once inside, Sidney relied on other pals who were ushers to steer him to an empty seat. He even had an understanding with the little old lady who ran the Opera Guild room to cigar-sit his Havana during the acts.

My father took me to the Met before I was ten years old, starting me off with *Hansel and Gretel,* in which the wicked witch disappeared in a puff of smoke, and progressing to *Carmen,* with Robert Merrill as the toreador Escamillo making his triumphant entrance on a white horse. During one of our Saturday afternoons at the Met, my father steered me to an empty box in the first ring. The box, it turned out, belonged to Edward Johnson, the Met's general manager, who generously (if unwittingly) had made it available to Sidney Kosner and his son, Edward. I squirmed in my seat through *Die Fledermaus,* burning with the embarrassment and humiliation of being a squatter without a real seat of my own.

It took me more than thirty years to realize how privileged I'd been to be taken to the opera on the cuff and given the best seat in the house—but those episodes must have nurtured the sense of entitlement that drove me through much of my life.

My father's other great treat for me as I was growing up was the Ringling Bros. and Barnum & Bailey circus in the spring. Every year Sidney would mysteriously procure three of the best seats at the old Garden, and he, my mother, and I would have dinner in one of the fancy mirrored restaurants I favored, where I would always order a shrimp cocktail and prime rib. The shrimp would come hooked over the lip of a cup of cocktail sauce within a larger goblet of cracked ice.

One year, my father decided to change the routine—always a dangerous step with a little boy so fiercely attached to familiar rituals. Instead of Dunhall's, he took me over to Second Avenue to a strange steak house. The place looked like a dive, with sawdust on the floor and big cartoons coated with shellac covering the walls. Men and women sat with drinks in booths, giggling and flirting and enjoying themselves more than any married couples I'd ever seen. There was no big tasseled menu, just a middle-aged waiter with a white apron tied around his waist who told you that you were going to have steak, roast beef, lamb chops, or lobster.

Edward didn't like the looks of the place. And when the shrimp cocktail arrived, his worst fears were confirmed. Instead of the dewy presentation bowl of cracked ice, the shrimp sat on a simple white plate with green trim. The tantrum erupted. Instead of the dinner I was sure I deserved, I'd been taken to this *dump*! Tears rained, feet kicked. The boozy couples glanced over at the man and woman with the crazy little boy and went back to their Manhattans. Years and years later, I realized that my father had taken me to the Palm, the best steak house in the city at the time and still celebrated more than half a century from that dire night.

Had today's standards been applied to me, I would have been diagnosed as intensely neurotic with a tinge of obsessive-compulsive disorder. I was gripped by all sorts of phobias and anxieties. For a time, I awoke in panic in the middle of the night convinced that I was going to be a midget with glasses and braces—a hideous outcast. I had a morbid fear of eggs and of crabs. Even as I scampered around the beach at Long Beach with a towel tied around my neck to simulate Superman's cape, I was terrified that a neighbor girl named Francine Pitt would drop a wriggling crustacean on my head.

I often hid under the card table that my mother and her chums used to play mah-jongg. Although I was raised at the shore, I refused to put my face in the water. At home, I would only eat food cooked by my mother. Once, I fled from a birthday party for my friend Bruce Frank when his mother brought to the table a roast beef she'd prepared and expected me to eat.

I was terrified that my mother or father would die. At camp, when I didn't immediately get a letter from home, I became convinced that my mother had drowned in the ocean and the news was being suppressed. When the first letter arrived after the July Fourth weekend, I scrutinized the penmanship, certain that my Aunt Selda was forging her sister's handwriting to hide the secret. The only camp food I would eat was macaroni and cheese and coleslaw. I wouldn't put my face in the lake, so I spent the daily swim periods languishing on a wooden bench at the waterfront and never learned a stroke.

In New York, even though P.S. 173 was just down the block from our apartment, I raced out of the house in the wartime predawn to be the first one at school, where I'd post myself at the entrance and open the doors for the teachers. On his way to the subway station, my father would pass me standing in the frozen darkness and shake his head in pity and wonder. Soon enough, my parents forbade me to leave my bed before a certain hour, hoping the time it would take me to get dressed would ensure that I couldn't get to school first to indulge my compulsion. At first, I outfoxed them: Without an alarm clock, I'd awake exactly at 6:00 or so and secretly dress under the covers so I could spring out the door right after 7:00 and race down 174th Street. Occasionally, my mother or father would slip into my room to make sure I wasn't up and readying my getaway. I'd feign angelic sleep with the covers pulled up around my neck to hide my telltale clothing. Devious as I was, no one could outwit my mother. One morning she caught me and I was suitably shamed. But nothing could keep me from my mission.

A child exhibiting my symptoms these days would be dosed with Xanax or Ritalin and counseled within an inch of his neurosis. No one gave me so much as an aspirin or a word of good cheer. Edward was very bright and a little peculiar and that was that.

Like the paranoiac with true enemies, I was the prisoner of insecurities that had a solid basis in reality. I must have sensed how precarious our little family's place in the world actually was. My father seemed to make a good living, but (as I later pieced together) a lot of his money was made trading black-market goods during the war. Naturally enough, he was not always scrupulous about his taxes—indeed, he simply ignored his New York State taxes until he was caught and had to pay what he owed plus penalties. He also seemed to have an aversion to paying some bills. From time to time, strange, gruff voices telephoned the apartment in the morning, prompting my father to tell my mother to tell the caller that Sidney was unavailable. Then he'd dash into our tiny bathroom and turn on the water—as if the bill collectors could spot him if he remained in the bedroom. There were also murmured conversations about trouble with the Pritzkers, the Boston family he worked for as the New York sales manager for their outerwear line.

And there were always coded mutterings that turned out to be about a relative or friend who had cancer, an unappealable death sentence in those days. Now and then, I'd be dragged to see some relative I'd known as a plump, pink presence only to encounter a shrunken, jaundiced wraith plainly not long for this world. Soon, I'd hear someone whispering about "Riverside," the funeral home favored by my family and others like them.

My relatives on my father's side were a menagerie. Based on their looks and affinities, my father and his ten siblings were divided into three subtribes. My father, his identical twin, Ben, their blond baby sister Rosalyn, and a tall brother named Larry were united by their good looks and comparatively normal personalities. Then there was Uncle Seymour and Aunts Ruthie and Helen, high-strung, pinch-faced Kosiners who never married and attached themselves to Rozzy, who was married to a very strange, permanently tanned scrap-metal dealer named Julie. Finally, there were my Aunts Sadie, Jeanne, and Tessie, and Uncle Ralph, a penny-pinching stationery salesman who sported an Oliver Hardy mustache and a Norfolk jacket. They were portly and slightly older than the rest.

Many of the Kosner/Kosiners had nicknames, some relating to past exploits or physical characteristics and some inexplicable. My father was called Steerage, usually shortened to Steer, because, so the story went, he once got drunk at a shipboard bon voyage party and disappeared, to be discovered hours later passed out belowdecks. My father celebrated his birthday on November 28, while his identical twin celebrated his a month earlier. (After my father's death, I found his birth certificate and learned that both of them had it wrong.) Uncle Larry was called "the dancing bear." Aunt Ruthie became a Christian Scientist and played the accordion while decked out in white plastic boots like a cheerleader. She had a long succession of boyfriends, all named John. Aunt Jeanne was onomatopoeically dubbed *phumphotch* because of the snorting sounds she made while trying to clear her sinuses. Her husband, a lively little man whose fabled weak heart kept him from working, was known as "twinkle eyes" because of his bulging pupils.

Ralph was so cheap he saved rubber bands and paper clips even though he was in the business. Not to be outdone, Aunt Sadie could wring nine blintzes—crepes—from a single egg, a family record never seriously challenged. Sadie had a morbid fear of dentists and disguised the holes in her teeth with tiny kneaded balls of rye bread. Called for his army physical, Seymour fasted for a week, threw a convincing nervous breakdown for the draft board, and then went back to the racetrack for the duration of the war.

Aunt Tessie was the rich one, married to Milton Davis, a successful garmento, but she couldn't bring herself to have her son Alfred's cleft palate surgically repaired, and he spent his life as a misfit who could barely be understood and entertained himself playing show tunes on the piano.

The sisters and brothers were constantly feuding with each other and their equally peculiar spouses and in-laws. Many of the fights lasted so long that the warring parties had to be reminded why they weren't speaking— usually because one had given another's child a cheaper gift than hers had gotten the year before.

The twins, Sidney and Ben, were understandably close. They delighted in tormenting the world. During the Depression, they'd go apartment shopping. They didn't need a place to live, but wanted to see what outrageous concessions they could extract from rental agents desperate to find tenants for their empty buildings. At one West Side apartment with a long entry hall, the agent agreed to their every demand and they'd run out of excuses not to rent the place.

Finally, Benny called out: "Sid, this hall would be great for the greyhounds!"

"What greyhounds?" said the agent.

"Didn't Ben tell you?" said Sid. "We race greyhounds and we could exercise them in this hall."

The agent hustled them out the door before they could say another word.

Close as they were, Sidney and Ben, who later lived in Beverly Hills and sold lingerie, once didn't speak to each other for ten years and then suddenly resumed as if nothing had happened.

They began communicating with each other by making spurious person-to-person calls using Yiddish curses for party names and jabbering back and forth while the poor *shiksa* long-distance operator tried to sort it out.

The phone would ring at our home and the operator would say, "I have a person-to-person call from California for Mr. Passcagnack."

"It's *Mr. Paskudnyak*," Uncle Benny would correct her.

"Mr. Paskundnyak is out," my father would tell her, but *Mr. Momser* just walked in. Would the party like to talk to Mr. Momser?"

"Please, sir, let me do this," the operator would say, struggling to regain control as the expensive long-distance seconds ticked by. "Would you like to speak with Mr. Mamzer?

"Is that Ike Momser or Mike Momser?" Uncle Benny would ask.

Just before the operator cut them off, my father would say that Mr. Paskudnyak would be back in fifteen minutes.

Fifteen minutes later, my father would place a person-to-person call from *Mr. Paskudnyak* to *Mr. Meesameshinna* (don't ask!) at Benny's number and the farce would resume.

Finally, the telephone company cops caught on and threatened to take away Sidney's and Ben's phone service unless they knocked it off.

My mother's four sisters had their peculiarities, but they considered themselves more refined than the Katzenjammer Kosiners, and they were, too. The firstborn, Jean, had been married to a gambler and playboy and had died of tuberculosis. Jean's death contributed to the enduring pall that hung over my mother and her sisters in all the years I knew them. It had begun when their father died young, and nothing could dissipate the sense of inevitable calamity that gripped them. The eldest survivor, my Aunt Freda, was a talented milliner who had worked to support her younger sisters. She seemed destined to be a spinster but relatively late in the game married a handsome silver-maned man named Lou Levenberg, who looked remarkably like Edward Stettinius, FDR's last secretary of state, but who more prosaically sold meat-slicing machines to butcher shops. They lived in shabby gentility in a tiny apartment at the Park Crescent, a once-grand residential hotel at

Riverside Drive and Eighty-seventh Street, where, incongruously enough, Vladimir Nabokov perched for a time in 1959 while working on *Pale Fire*.

The next sister was the beauty of the family, appropriately named Belle. She had worked for a time as a secretary and was married to Sam Robbins, the uncle who took me to track meets and the Giants football games. Sam was a dentist who had his office in his home, a four-room apartment at 820 West End Avenue at 100th Street. He had come from a German-Jewish family and had gone to the University of Pennsylvania. Sam was the only member of my mother's or father's family, including spouses, who had gone to college. Some of the others were very bright, but, in the fashion of the times, all had left school by the eighth grade.

Sam may not have been a particularly gifted dentist, but he was a cultured man. In fact, he and my Aunt Belle were more responsible than anyone for introducing me to the world of ideas beyond Washington Heights. It was at their flat that I first encountered the *New Yorker* magazine; the *Nation,* the left-wing weekly that was *really* left-wing then; and *Commentary,* the secular Jewish intellectual review begun by Elliot Cohen and carried on by Norman Podhoretz, who became my luncheon chum a half century later.

It was in the Robbins' living room that I first opened Vernon Parrington's great work, *Main Currents in American Thought,* and *The Age of Jackson* by Arthur Schlesinger, Jr. One Christmas, Belle and Sam gave me E. B. White's *Stuart Little.* I cherished the slim book with its wonderful line illustrations by Garth Williams and in later years read it to each of my three children before retiring it to the bookshelf, where it still rests. A few years later, my Christmas gift book was *The Sea Around Us* by Rachel Carson. Sam taught me to play chess and let me join him working the *Sunday Times* crossword puzzle, which I have done ever since.

My parents would often visit Aunt Belle and Uncle Sam after dinner on Saturday nights. Sam would give Sidney a J&B highball or two and they would all listen to *La Bohème* or *Madame Butterfly* on the big Capehart record player, the tears flowing as Mimi expired or Cio Cio San plunged the dagger into her kimono. Because of those long-ago evenings, I can never go to a performance of either of those operas without weeping.

Sam and Belle were the family cosmopolitans. They summered at Lake Winnipesaukee in New Hampshire, far from Long Beach and its pokerino palaces. William Langer, the distinguished Harvard historian, was one of their summer pals. Sam's sister was married to David Driscoll, who wrote the lachrymose radio soap opera *Young Doctor Malone* and had taught the young writer Irwin Shaw at Brooklyn College. Sam and Belle had all Shaw's books, and it was at their home when I was fifteen that I read two of Shaw's great short stories: *The Girls in Their Summer Dresses,* and one about a young man who writes radio serials to help finance his eccentric father's inventions and his homely sister's concert career. Taking a break one afternoon, he joins a sandlot game in Brooklyn Heights. The epiphany comes when the twenty-five-year-old narrator fields a grounder and the kid playing next to him says, "Nice play, mister." The story is called *Main Currents in American Thought.*

David often gave me *Young Doctor Malone* scripts, and my father would bring home the scripts from the intermission programs during the Saturday Met Opera broadcasts. Clutching the scripts at the tiny table in my tiny room, I'd replay the shows, acting out all the parts myself, an only child entertaining himself in lunatic privacy.

As part of his campaign to, as he put it, "keep Edward from becoming a little barbarian," Sam and Belle took me to a restaurant called Casa Johnny on Fifteenth Street between Fifth and Sixth avenues, where I had my first Italian dish, veal parmigiana with a side order of pasta pomodoro, exotic and delicious. At Saturday lunches in their small dining room curtained off from the patients' waiting room, Aunt Belle served me Genoa salami on thin Arnold bread with Gulden's sharp mustard washed down with a cup of dark, piquant Lapsang souchong tea—a tasty alternative to the kosher salami on rye with French's mustard and root beer that was my favored fare.

Sam himself had singular tastes. His breakfast every morning was a lemon Coke at a candy store around the corner on Broadway, where he'd buy the *Herald Tribune* and the Italian paper *Il Progrèsso* to help with his Italian lessons (the better to enjoy opera) and a couple of packs of Fatimas, the king-size cigarettes made of strong Turkish tobacco. When I'd ask him why he smoked Fatimas rather than Chesterfields or Lucky Strikes like everyone else, he said the poor brand would lose half its sales if he switched. The same went for the *Nation* magazine—"I'm probably half their circulation," he'd say with rueful pride.

Dr. Robbins' dental practice was never very robust, but for a time in the late 1940s it got a boost from the football Giants, whose coach, Steve Owen, lived in the Whitehall Hotel at One Hundredth Street and Broadway along with some of his players. In those days, pro football players were paid a pittance, $7,000 or $10,000 a season for a lineman, and every penny counted. Nearly all the players had lost front teeth, and keeping their dentures in shape was always a concern. Many of the second-stringers couldn't really pay, so Sam would let them barter for his services. He was proud of a built-in supply closet one of the defensive backs had built him in exchange for a bridge. During my visits, he would often take me into his cramped darkroom and workroom, where he'd develop X-rays, mold gold inlays, and let me grind up the mercury amalgam used to fill cavities, or, as I learned to call them, dental caries.

My mother's third sister was Selda (Americanized from Zelda), who was only eighteen months older than Annalee and closer even than blood. The two had grown up together, being taken out of school each spring and shipped to the Catskills, where their father ran a hotel in the warm weather. Exiled and lonely, they'd spend their days rocking together in a hammock and singing, "Moonlight in Kahlua" to Selda's strumming ukulele. After their young father died, Selda became Annalee's fierce guardian, once famously beating a rough girl who'd snatched the artificial cherries from Annalee's holiday hat.

Selda let Annalee boss her around, and she often needed direction. Selda had a good heart, but she'd do inexplicably dopey things. Once, without consulting anyone, she dyed her hair bright red. A few weeks later, she showed up at our house on a Sunday afternoon that happened to be St. Patrick's Day in a kelly green suit, a hysterical faux pas on the West (and Jewish) side of Broadway. My mother sent her home to change and, on Monday, to the beauty parlor, as they called it, to get the red out.

During my childhood, Selda worked in a succession of Fifth Avenue women's shoe shops. She was a good saleswoman and an even better thief: She would regale us with the ingenious schemes she and her colleagues dreamed up to skim money from their sales into their pockets rather than into I. Miller's cash register. She was married to a tall, quiet Internal Revenue Service agent named Walter Cohen, who was the most boring man I've ever met. There was a popular horror movie of the time called *I Walked with a Zombie,* and Selda liked to say it was the story of her marriage. Selda and Walter lived in a sunny apartment on the Hudson River a few blocks from our place. Their windows offered a panoramic view of the Palisades in New Jersey and of the silvery, elegant George Washington Bridge. But the magnificent river was so much a part of my childhood that I never marveled at the views, and it wasn't until decades later that I realized how cavalier I'd been about these amazing vistas.

When I was six or seven there was a sudden spasm of whispered conversations and cryptic phone calls, and finally my mother told me that Aunt Selda and Uncle Walter were getting divorced. Selda would be marrying Nat Levin, a man whose parents lived in our building. In fact, Selda would be living for a time at 635 West 174th Street, just one floor below our apartment!

I was traumatized by the news. The idea that one of my aunts and uncles could get *divorced* was devastating to a child with my near-clinical case of insecurity. I stopped speaking to Selda, fled from the sight of her, and skulked down the back stairs of our building to make sure that I never found myself in the elevator with her. Selda was deeply wounded by my behavior, but she loved me so much that she made allowances and eventually I got over it.

In later years, I puzzled over the extremity of my reaction. Divorce was rare in the 1940s, but it did happen and my aunt's certainly shouldn't have turned me into a wild child. I never could manage an explanation of my uncontrollable feelings of fear and rage. Then, one day in the late 1980s when I was visiting Selda in the little senior citizens' apartment she shared with Freda in—where else?—Long Beach, Selda casually said, "You know, I raised you for the first nine months of your life."

And then, as I sat transfixed with horror and relief, the story came out. My mother's mother, to whom Annalee had been devoted, died the month before I was born. This had devastated Annalee, and after I arrived in the midst of a raging thunderstorm on July 26, 1937, her postpartum depression had turned into a breakdown so severe that she neither could nor would care for me. So Selda had moved in and, for all practical purposes, had been my mother for the first year of my life.

Now I had the explanation that no psychotherapy could have teased forth for my unhinged reaction to Selda's breakup with Walter. It wasn't my aunt's divorce, it was my surrogate mother's—there had been a secret, invisible bond between us.

"Do you think you might have mentioned this to me earlier so I might have understood myself a little better?" I suggested to Selda as gently as I could.

"Oh, Edward darling, we never wanted to upset you," she replied.

Nat Levin was as different from Selda's first husband as a second husband could be. A warm, noisy, energetic man with a prizefighter's mug and a cop's manner, he'd never joined the force, perhaps because Jews weren't especially welcome. Instead, Nat became a private detective. But his real life was as a cop and fire buff, hanging around the precincts and firehouses. He knew hundreds of firemen and the numbers of fire boxes all around Manhattan. If you were walking on Broadway with Nat when a fire engine raced by, he'd know with a glance its unit number, the location of the fire house, and the name of the captain. He'd even know the name of the Dalmatian riding along on the hook and ladder.

At family parties, Nat would sometimes let me hold his police special, which he'd never fired on the job. He'd entertain with stories from the Harlem station house where he'd hung out years before. He'd tell how the detectives would dangle a suspect by the ankles from the third-story window of the squad room over the air shaft in the back of the precinct. If the poor wretch wouldn't confess, they'd let go one of his ankles. As Natey told it, they never had to release the other one.

Another favorite stunt was to grill a witness or suspect in one room. Through the thin wall in the next room, another detective would slam a thick phone book against a desk while a third cop moaned and howled in pain until he'd finally scream, "Okay, I'll tell you—just don't hit me again." This presumably would induce the real suspect to talk. Of course, when the stunts didn't work, the cops would simply beat the crap out of the guy and then write his confession for him.

After their marriage, Selda and Nat moved to Long Beach, where Nat reconfigured his private detective agency into what we now think of as a security service. He provided armed and unarmed guards for various businesses and city agencies in Long Beach, where his path was smoothed by his friendships with many of the local Democratic hacks.

I had been going to Long Beach with my parents each year beginning with my first birthday, when we had a small place in an apartment hotel called, with Freudian irony, the Prince Edward. The next year, we moved to the Commander, across Broadway from the boardwalk and the beach, where three of my father's brothers and sisters also roosted. The Commander was

owned by two Slavic brothers whose year-round tenants included an impe-
cunious piano teacher and the parents of the town's all-powerful Democratic
party boss.

Just seven miles from end to end despite its name, Long Beach is the third
in the string of barrier beaches on the Atlantic stretching from Coney Island
to Amagansett, more than a hundred miles to the east. It was originally developed as a resort for the rich. At the turn of the twentieth century, Long Beach
boasted the largest hotel in the world, a 1,100-foot-long behemoth that
promptly burned down. Then the promoters' dream shifted. They wanted to
make Long Beach the French Riviera or, depending on who's telling the story,
the Venice of the American East. Every home had to be built in pastel stucco
in the same Mediterranean style with a red, blue, or parti-colored tile roof.
The main streets were paved in red brick to simulate canals. At the east end
of town, real canals were dug—and incongruously named for Gene Sarazen
and other golfers of the time—and a coral confection called the Lido Beach
Hotel rose near the ocean, there being no handy lagoon.

But all the development schemes flopped for one reason or another. Many
of the oceanfront hotels were Art Deco gems, like their counterparts in
Miami Beach, but nobody in Long Beach seemed to notice or care. One of
the few Democratic towns on Long Island, Long Beach had earned its reputation for corruption during Prohibition when it was a bootleggers' Eden.
The first mayor had been indicted for stealing, and one of his crooked successors was shot to death near the boardwalk by his own police bodyguard.
The respectful citizenry named a street in his memory—Edwards Boulevard.

By my era, Long Beach had become a middle-class Jewish bastion with a
solid year-round population, a loyal band of summer renters, and a daily influx
of beachgoers from the city, just forty-five minutes away on the Long Island
Railroad. For me, it was a paradise. Each summer I'd form a band of fellow
émigrés, and we'd spend the long, lazy days at the beach, playing ball in the
vacant lots or miniature golf or biking the length of the boardwalk. After
supper, we'd hit the boardwalk again, feeding nickels into the arcade games,
downing tutti-frutti frozen custards or lime rickeys, and watching the Amazing
Valdo con the marks with his mentalist act. When it rained, the movie theaters
opened in the afternoon. It was in the tiny, stuffy Lido Theater that I first saw
Great Expectations, Hell's Angels, and *Scarface.*

As much as I loved my time in Long Beach, it fed my sense that I didn't really belong anywhere. I'd show up with the other summer insects on Memorial Day—my mother called it Decoration Day—and disappear after Labor Day just as the locals were resuming their real lives. Back in the city, I'd miss Long Beach so desperately that I'd fantasize what it would be like to be a townie.

Like my father, Nat Levin had stealth connections all over the place that resulted in passes to sports events and, once, a baseball autographed by the entire 1948 New York Yankees—a treasure so archaeological that Yogi Berra signed himself Larry Berra. It's a souvenir I still have in my office.

Nat generously once got us the tickets for my annual circus ritual—a good deed that turned into a disaster. When we got inside Madison Square, I discovered that the seats weren't like my father's—near the center in full view of all three rings and the aerialists—but under an overhang at the end of the arena next to the blaring circus band. Another tantrum.

Nat was organized to within an inch of his life. He was obsessive about the Ronson and Zippo lighters that were the talismans of that age of smokers. Indeed, he regularly bought packs of lighter flints and cans of lighter fluid by the dozen so that one cabinet in his home looked like a tobacconist's supply closet.

As the security czar of Long Beach, Uncle Nat also supplied minimum-wage snoops to check, for example, whether drivers of the municipal buses pocketed any of the fares on their runs. During my adolescent summers, Nat often got me work. I would climb aboard one of the blue-and-white Long Beach buses at the start of its run, record its number and time of departure, and then count the passengers on the ride to the end of the line. Then I'd hop off and do the same thing on the next bus back to the starting point.

This wasn't as easy as it sounds because nearly all the riders on the Long Beach buses were black maids, rendering thirteen-year-old secret agent Kosner painfully conspicuous on the long rides to West End and Lido Beach. I lived in dread of being challenged by one of the sharp-eyed drivers, but I never was, and I never found out if my undercover work caught any miscreants.

When I was fifteen, Nat arranged for me to get a summer job with the Long Beach highway department, a patronage plum that paid $1.65 an hour (the equivalent today of about ten times as much) for very little work. But first I had to perform the ceremonial ring-kissing at the knuckle of the Democratic kingpin of Long Beach, a tall, sporty man named Phil Kohut. An appointment was set up at Kohut's office at the Long Beach Democratic Club, and after dinner one night I showed up for my command performance. Nat coached me on what Phil would ask and what I should reply and the meeting went off precisely by the script. At the end, Kohut looked at me as if he were weighing an important personnel decision, then nodded and said, "I think you'll do."

The next morning at 7:30, I reported in dungarees (as jeans were then called) and white T-shirt to the highway department garage and was assigned to a truck with a crew of two municipal lifers and a couple of guys in their twenties who also had well-placed Democratic uncles. Then we drove out onto the streets, picked up our shovels and brooms, and began sweeping. After no more than ten minutes of work, we retired behind the truck while a lookout kept watch for the highway commissioner, a funny little man named Hershkowitz who used to drive around town checking up on his crack staff. If he found someone sweeping languidly, he'd shout, "Two hands on the broom!" Hershkowitz was also a deputy fire chief, and, thoughtfully enough, he made his rounds in his fire chief's car, visible for ten blocks in any direction. At the sight of a bright-red car approaching, the sentinel would whistle. We'd spring from the shadow of the truck and begin demonically sweeping and shoveling, two hands securely on every broom.

Working or hiding, promptly at 9:30 we'd down tools, hop back in the truck, and head for the half-hour coffee break, which required a ride crosstown to the diner and, of course, a postbreak ride back across town to the work site. At 11:45, it was time to go to lunch, and all labor ceased at 2:45 for the ride to the dump before the return to the garage, where we dispersed after another hard day's toil.

On many of our daily rides around town, my twentysomething fellow sweepers would spot an attractive or not-really-so-attractive young woman pushing her child in a stroller along the sunny sidewalks. They'd spring to attention, port their brooms military style, snap off a salute, and cry, "Young Mother!" at the startled girl. I'd cackle along with the other macho men although I wasn't really sure why.

After a couple of weeks, I was transferred to the beach patrol, assigned to rake the sand and pick up trash with another crew. The street sweepers were white and the beachcombers were nearly all black, but their work routine was remarkably similar—except that instead of hiding behind the truck, the beach crew camped under the boardwalk for most of the day, playing whist for small stakes.

Long Beach's Democratic machine may have been crooked in the style of the times, but it had heart. Every year, the city fathers and merchants would stage Orphan's Day, when thousands of parentless children and other unfortunates would be bused into town for a round of splashing in the Atlantic, free spins on the boardwalk rides, and handfuls of nickels to play Ski-Ball and the other games, along with free hot dogs and frozen custards. They came from all around the area and brought with them a distinctive metallic smell that I later recognized as the tang of poverty. Many of the children were black, the only African-Americans ever seen in town except for a small group clustered in a tiny ghetto behind the railroad station.

Black or white, the orphans were pathetically grateful for the outing, although that didn't stop them from trying to cadge extra coins for the penny arcade or a fifth or sixth grilled dog. One Orphan's Day, I volunteered at the arcade, doling out precisely five nickels to each child. An orphan would grab his nickels and an instant later reappear on the line with his hand out.

"I just gave you five nickels," I'd rebuff the supplicant.

"That was my brother. Honest," the urchin would reply, all innocence, and dash off with five more of Mr. Faber's coins.

The climax of Orphan's Day was a performance on the boardwalk by Cab Calloway, the jive master whose signature song was "Minnie the Moocher." Decked out in one of his exuberant white satin tail suits, Calloway put on a spectacular show for the orphans, who would join him in chorusing "Hi De Hi! Ho De Ho!" Around 4:00, their faces sandy and seared by the sun, their shoulders slumped with fatigue, and no doubt with fierce bellyaches, the children were herded back on their buses and their sad caravan rolled out of town, leaving us to count our blessings.

From his first marriage, Uncle Nat had a son named Donald, who was only a month older than I was. Donald lived with his mother and stepfather, Sol, who ran the hotel at the Miami airport, on an island off one of the causeways that connect Miami Beach to the mainland. He would spend the summers with Selda and Nat, and he became my companion and, for a time, the closest thing to a brother I ever had.

Actually, Donald and I had hardly anything in common. He liked movies and popular music, but had no interest in sports and couldn't play any. In fact, Donald threw and caught a baseball like a girl—which created embarrassing moments when his father brought out the catcher's mitt and scuffed baseballs he'd gotten from a chum who worked for the Brooklyn Dodgers. Nat and I would pitch to each other while his son sat off to the side, chewing on his cuticles and making nervous jokes. Nat tried to take Donald's girlish manner in stride, but you could see that it broke his heart.

Donald's other interest was clothes. When he first came to Long Beach, he dressed like a young Miami Beach dude of the fifties, all pink and black, with Cuban Guayabera shirts and suede shoes. I had already started wearing my version of Ivy League garb, chino slacks and dirty white bucks, which Donald ridiculed. One day, Donald suddenly converted—he announced he was discarding all the flashy outfits he'd accumulated from Male Wear by Block on Park Street—and soon emerged in crisply pressed army pants, penny loafers, and crew-necked Shetland sweaters.

Eventually, Donald went to the University of Florida in Gainesville and to Cornell's school of hotel management. When he was barely twenty-one, he married a busty redhead named Brenda, the daughter of a Pennsylvania butcher, in an elaborate pink-and-black ceremony at the Fontainebleau in Miami Beach. The marriage lasted barely nine months. For the rest of his life, Donald was a bachelor, booking conventions and weddings for the Sheraton hotel chain in Akron, St. Louis, and, finally, Boston. He would come to New York two or three times a year, where he would go to a show every night and every matinee and obsessively collect Broadway posters. Periodically, Selda would show us pictures of Donald with a woman he'd met while working in St. Louis, a plain divorcée or a widow with a couple of kids. After he left St. Louis, Donald would visit her but it never seemed to go beyond that.

Over the years, Donald and I drifted farther apart. Then, early in the 1990s, I got a call from a cousin on his mother's side who reported that Donald had fallen to his death from the roof of his apartment house in Boston the night before. He had uncommonly failed to show up at work earlier in the day and didn't answer his phone. A colleague had gone to his flat, but had been turned away at the door by a disheveled and woozy Donald. On the roof from which he'd fallen after midnight police found a plastic basket containing some of his laundry. The cousin said he believed Donald had become disoriented and had gone to the roof to hang up his clothes, gotten dizzy, and fallen over the parapet.

The Boston authorities listed the death as an accident, although they found Donald's financial records neatly arranged on his desk. I called the gruff Boston detective who'd handled the case. He said Donald's refrigerator had little in it but a half-empty bottle of wine. There were no notes or narcotics found in the apartment and no AIDS drugs or anything suspicious in the medicine cabinet. At Donald's funeral, his theatrical posters were propped against his coffin, and show tunes accompanied his tearful coworkers as they talked about how much he adored Broadway.

Donald's pathetic death was actually in keeping with the sad ends of so many of the Fishers and their spouses, for the sure sense of impending tragedy that clung to the Fisher sisters turned out to be prophesy.

Freda's husband, whose deliberate manner was the only sign of his heart condition, died one day as quietly as he'd lived. Not long after that, a massive coronary killed noisy, nonstop Nat Levin while he was vacationing in Florida. At Thanksgiving in 1953, just as I was starting college, Sam Robbins came back from walking his tawny cocker spaniel Sandy on West End Avenue complaining that he was short of breath. After the holiday, he went to the doctor and was almost immediately diagnosed with hopeless lung cancer and sent home to die. All those Fatimas had doomed him.

Without telling me that Sam had only a few weeks to live, my mother sent me to visit him one Saturday. I knew that my uncle was seriously ill, but I had no notion of how ravaged he was. I walked into the living room on West End Avenue to find Sam dressed as usual in a white J. Press buttondown shirt and regimental tie. Wan and noticeably thinner than the last time I'd seen him, he was secured in his chair by a bedsheet bound around his waist. In front of him was another dining chair, its back facing him with a pillow across the top of the chair back. He greeted me and tried to carry on a conversation, but in the middle of a sentence he'd lose consciousness and his forehead would crash into the pillow. In a few seconds, he'd revive and try to go on, but soon he'd black out again. During his lucid moments, Sam would ask for a cigarette and Belle would light one for him; the doctor had told her he was far past any Fatima doing more harm.

In the midst of this horrific tableau, my aunt sat at his side, trying to act as if nothing extraordinary was going on, just another Saturday visit from Edward to his beloved uncle. For the first time in my life (but certainly not the last), I felt I couldn't bear to witness what I must witness. The urge to bolt from the room was overwhelming, but I knew that I had to play out my role until I was told I could go. So I did. The scene etched itself so deeply into my mind that a half century later I can recall every detail, and, above all, the feeling of dread that gripped me.

Sam died early in the new year. Belle had hardly begun to adjust to widowhood when she began to feel the first twinges of what turned out to be colon cancer. She was dead within eighteen months.

So in the numbing span of a few years, my mother's family was reduced to Annalee and her two widowed sisters. We paid so many visits to Riverside that I was embarrassed when the solemn men who worked the lobby of the funeral home greeted us. I could imagine them nodding at each other, thinking, "Here they come again."

Loving and attentive as all my doomed aunts and uncles were while I was growing up, my parents were the center of my only-child world. Although they fought and bickered all the time, they were hopelessly devoted to each other and they adored me in their own fierce fashion.

My mother was the disciplinarian, relentless in her determination that I toe the mark. I could do no wrong as far as my father was concerned. When Annalee would catch me in some impish mischief, I'd race through our tiny apartment and dive under the fold-up cot that was my childhood bed. A moment later, my mother would explode into the room with a broomstick and poke me out of my refuge.

Once, when I was five or six, my father returned to Long Beach early one Friday afternoon to find me in tears, the imprint of my mother's hand still visible on my damp cheek, a swat that I doubtless deserved. While Annalee fumed, Sidney swept me off to the five-and-dime on Park Street, where he bought me a set of tiddlywinks—a game in which you pressed on one small plastic disc with another and tried to propel it into a tiny plastic cup. This episode was forever enshrined in the family oral tradition as a peerless example of how my father shamelessly subverted my mother's best efforts to keep me from being a spoiled brat.

Despite the early death of her father, my mother had been sheltered as a girl and she was sheltered as a wife and mother. She may have worked as a secretary very early on, but for virtually all her adult life, Annalee was the platonic ideal of the housewife.

She was a superb cook, a housekeeper so meticulous that Eva, our maid through all my years at home, spent most of her time cleaning an apartment that was already spotless. No one would mistake Annalee Kosner for Sister Parrish, but apartment 4C—a smallish living room and bedroom, a galley-style kitchen off a short hall where we had dinner, and my room, all of 6 by 9 feet—was stylish in its way. My mother had found some little old Italian furniture maker somewhere way downtown and commissioned him to make a bedroom set she called French Provincial and a wall-sized breakfront with snug-fitting felt-lined silverware drawers that smelled expensive. Some of my friends from the *intelligentsia* liked to challenge her: They'd ask her to leave the living room and then they'd nudge one of her curios—say, a carved wooden figurine of an old Chinese man leaning on a stave—a millimeter or two from its accustomed perch. Summoned back, Annalee would instantly spot the move and put the object back precisely where it belonged.

My mother had learned to cook from her mother when they were at home together while Selda, Belle, and Freda were out working. All the food was simple and it was all perfect: Friday night roast chicken or duck with crackling skin and moist, fragrant breast meat, beef stews filled with carrots, potatoes, and onions, and pot roasts with tangy gravy. There would be beef and barley or chicken soup to start and, on the side, scrumptious noodle puddings—*kugels*—studded with raisins. Dessert was often raspberry Jell-O with Del Monte fruit cocktail suspended within.

When I would come home for lunch from P.S. 173, waiting for me would be savory grilled hamburger or an exquisite American cheese sandwich, toasted to golden perfection, and a glass of frosty chocolate milk—Hershey's chocolate syrup only—to wash it down.

In the old-school way, my mother would do her marketing in a grand promenade along Broadway each morning with stops at Gus, the Italian vegetable man, Shulman, the grumpy red-haired kosher butcher with the blood-stained apron, and the Daitch dairy shop, where the clerk would expertly carve a quarter pound from the huge block of sweet butter and wrap it in waxy paper. Safeway had just begun competing with the *ur* supermarket, A&P, where Annalee stocked up on Rice Krispies, Campbell's Tomato Soup, My-T-Fine chocolate pudding, and Red Circle coffee in the yellow packages.

On one of these A&P visits, I followed my mother to the coffee section, where the beans to be ground into the store's Bokar, Eight O'Clock, and Red Circle blends sat on the floor in big open jute bags. I stuck my face close to one bag to inhale the aroma. For an instant, I had the sensation that *one of the beans had gone up my nose,* but I knew that was ridiculous and said nothing about it. I went to sleep that night but snapped awake after an hour. That bean was up there after all. My hysterical screams brought my mother and father on the run. Any normal child would have simply blown his nose a couple of times and freed the kernel, but nose-blowing was a skill that young Edward refused to master. So trusty Dr. Pecker was summoned. (In those days, the family doctor would come to the house at all hours of the day or night.) He rummaged in his black bag for a pair of long-nosed tweezers and, after a few exploratory probes, performed the beanectomy with a flourish, ensuring his place in the fast-growing Legend of Edward.

On her Friday rounds, Annalee would visit the Harlem Savings Bank at 181st Street, just across from the RKO Coliseum theater, where the new movies that didn't run at the Loew's 175th Street were shown. Each week, my mother would deposit a dollar in her Christmas Club account and would collect $50 in early December to spend on small gifts.

Unlike her sisters, who tended to be a little fleshy, my mother was sleek, about five feet six inches, with gorgeous legs and a flat tummy. She had rich dark hair and shiny white teeth that flashed when she smiled. Her one flaw was the Fisher nose, which Freda and Belle had somehow avoided, but which could be appreciated in full glory in pictures of her mother and departed sister Jean and in Selda's glorious schnoz. Annalee's solution was to have a nose job—quite a brave step in those days. She was never really satisfied with the results, but after the surgery, and with a Long Beach tan, she turned heads. She looked good in her clothes, even the frumpish outfits women wore during the war and right after.

Annalee had a quick mind and sure common sense, but she was no intellectual. She favored the *Daily News* and would read Winchell in the *Mirror,* loved radio soap operas, Broadway musicals, and *Your Hit Parade,* and was a proud member of the Book-of-the-Month Club. And she adored the movies. She and Selda would see everything. They approved of elegant stars like Joan Crawford and Barbara Stanwyck, but loathed snooty Katharine Hepburn and B-movie molls like Lizabeth Scott. They often took me along with a jar of chocolate milk to keep me quiet. They even dragged me to *Spellbound* when I was seven, and the creepy Dali dream sequence gave me nightmares.

In those days, movie studios could own theaters. MGM had the Loew's chain, so all the great MGM swashbucklers and musical extravaganzas were available just across the street. Loew's 175th Street eventually became the tabernacle of a black evangelist named the Reverend Ike, but in its heyday it was a prime example of movie palace magnificence. The theater opened in 1930 and would hold nearly 3,500 moviegoers in unsurpassed splendor. Once past the box office, you entered a huge lobby with luxurious patterned red carpeting and a vast candy counter to your right. The decor looked vaguely Asian—it was supposed to be Indo-Chinese—but it could just as well have been Moorish or cockamamie. The entrances to the orchestra seats were on the left, but the real thrill was the grand staircase that led up to the loges—the extra-comfy seats in the first rows of the upper tier—and the balcony seats beyond.

The loges required special tickets that cost a quarter or fifty cents more than general admission. You had to show your tickets to the uniformed loge ushers, who would check them with pocket flashlights and then beam you to your seats. My father solved the loge problem by buying regular tickets and duking the loge usher with a buck. With the money in *his* pocket rather than MGM's, the usher was happy to oblige.

For a time, I thought every movie took place on an ocean liner with Xavier Cugat in a white dinner jacket leading the band and clutching a Chihuahua while lecherous George Brent pursued virginal Jane Powell, who sought counsel from kindly Laurence Melchior or C. Z. "Cuddles" Sakall. Or in a swimming pool with Van Johnson gurgling underwater as he tried to match Esther Williams' backstroke. Or during the Golden Age of Spain (and Samuel Shellabarger), with Tyrone Power gritting his teeth as they cauterized the sword wound on his forehead with a red-hot poker.

Although nothing explicit was ever said and she always looked resplendently healthy, there was always an air of fragility about my mother. I didn't learn about her nervous breakdown until fifty years after it happened, but there also seemed to have been a miscarriage before I was born, almost a decade after my parents married, and there were cryptic allusions to what must have been a hysterectomy when I was five or so.

Part of the Legend of Edward was how hard it was for Annalee and Sidney to produce him and the certainty that I could never have a brother or sister. Even the story of my birth was fraught. It appears that Macy's, rather than the stork, had delivered me. As my father loved to tell the tale, they had ordered a set of dishes from Macy's. The box arrived battered and torn, and when they opened it, they found, not service for six, but little Edward. They debated returning the box for the ordered dishes, but finally decided to keep the kid because he was so adorable.

I was named for the hapless Edward VIII, who had abdicated the throne the year before, and one of my mother's early enthusiasms was to dress me as an English schoolboy, or what Washington Heights thought young lords wore. So there are pictures of me in elegant Jersey shorts outfits and camel's hair winter coats with leather leggings.

Looking back, it's clear to me now that the fancy outfits and the innocent pretensions behind them contributed to the feeling that gripped me as a child that my life was a brave show masking a precarious core. My mother always seemed to be expecting *something terrible to happen* and I came to share the anxiety. That probably explains why I became such a collector—of stamps and coins, miniature soldiers, model cars, comic books, out-of-town newspapers. Helpless in the world, I could at least control my collections— adding and subtracting items, endlessly fiddling with the order of display, struggling for order, yearning for permanence.

One of my fixations was trading cards. I collected not only bubble gum baseball cards, but cards showing professional football and basketball players, American Indian tribes (the Flathead were the rarest, the Pottawatomie the most common), and even an elegantly painted set of scenes from World War II, including the infamous Bataan Death March. I also had sets of larger cards that sold for a penny or a nickel at the penny arcades on the boardwalk at Long Beach. One set had glamorous head shots of Hollywood stars like Deanna Durbin and Dan Duryea. Another, in greenish duotone, had all the great boxers of the thirties and forties like Fritzie Zivic and

Kid Chocolate. And there were baseball cards, too, sepia action shots of prewar stars like Taffy Wright, Pete Reiser, and Emil "the Antelope" Verban. I'd actually filched most of the arcade cards by jiggering the coin slide to tease them out of the vending machine.

A prize of my collection was a complete set of baseball cards published in 1950 by the Bowman Gum Company of Philadelphia. These cards were handpainted over photographs and are revered today as among the most beautiful ever produced. By that bar mitzvah summer, I had managed to get all but two of the 252 cards in the set—number thirteen, a first baseman for the Philadelphia Athletics named Ferris Fain, and number fourteen, Alex Kellner, an A's pitcher. No matter how many packs of gum I bought in New York or Long Beach, these two eluded me. Finally, in desperation, I wrote to the gum company offering to pay whatever it cost to complete the set. By return mail, without even the courtesy of a covering letter, came Fain and Kellner.

I preserved my painstakingly acquired collection in a couple of shoe boxes through my late adolescence right up the week of my first marriage when, not quite twenty-two, I was about to move out of my parents' home.

"Now, Edward," said my mother, "you're going to be a married man, so you're not going to take those childish baseball cards with you, are you?"

"Of course not," I replied and dumped the shoe boxes down the garbage chute—a decision I've regretted nearly every day in the past forty-five years.

I was in love with my mother as only an only son can be. And neurotic as I may have been, I knew instinctively even before puberty that I had to separate from her emotionally and get out from under my parents' roof as quickly as I could. The emotional break can be tracked in the big photo album my mother carefully assembled (and that I still have), its black craft-paper pages filled with those scallop-edged snapshots from Brownie box cameras. In all the pictures through my tenth summer, the little boy has an open, smiling face as he poses with his parents or his new Colson bicycle (wholesale, of course). Then the expression on the boy's face changes. He looks bored or pained and he leans away from the family embrace at the shutter snap. This marked the start of my long, sullen withdrawal from my parents, my mother especially. I never could explain to her why I acted the way I did, nor could I explain it to myself. I just knew I had to do it.

The paradox was that I admired so many qualities in my mother: She thought clearly and never dithered over decisions; she was brave about sickness, always went to the doctor and dentist, and never flinched from whatever treatment was prescribed; she chose her clothes with easy taste and assurance and always looked wonderful. Although I was the only child she'd ever have, she never hovered over me or restricted what I did as so many nervous mothers did in those days.

I had the freedom of the neighborhood as far back as I can remember. I was riding the buses by myself from the age of ten and began taking the subways with my friends a few years later. I had a three-speed bicycle, an imported Rudge, from the time of my bar mitzvah, and soon was taking ten- and fifteen-mile bike trips across the George Washington Bridge and up the Palisades Parkway in New Jersey. During the summers, I rode all over Nassau County, pedaling along the shoulders of busy roads as cars, buses, and huge trucks raced by. Never once did Annalee forbid me to go anywhere, give me a curfew, or demand that I check in to let her know that I'd survived.

During the great Christmas week snowstorm of 1947, when I was ten, my mother allowed me to go with my friends to the movies at the Coliseum on 181st Street and Broadway. We dawdled on the way home, tossing snowballs and marveling at the snowbanks drifting against the cars. Late in the afternoon, my Aunt Belle called to make sure I was all right. When my mother told her I hadn't got home yet, Belle urged her to rush out onto Broadway and look for me under the giant mounds, where I certainly was buried. Annalee laughed at her and told me the story with great glee when I finally made it home after dark.

My father was equally relaxed about my adventures. Indeed, aside from making sure I kept my doctors' and dentists' appointments, my parents never supervised my activities or directed me to do anything, except to look people in the eye when introduced and shake hands firmly. Because neither had gone past the eighth grade, they never meddled in my education or even gave me advice about it. They never complained if I spent hours reading comic books or listening to *Mr. Keen, Tracer of Lost Persons,* and *Inner Sanctum* on the radio, nor did they encourage or discourage my friendships.

Perhaps they knew they were dealing with a very smart little boy who would inevitably find his way, or perhaps they were intimidated by me, unlikely as that might be. Whatever the reason for their laissez-faire approaches, the result was a priceless gift of self-reliance.

Throughout my life, I have always had the conviction that my accomplishments and my failures are my own. No one greased the way for me or led me astray. And whatever advice or direction I might have gotten the decisions were mine, as was the ultimate responsibility.

This was no small endowment for someone whose career would essentially consist of forty-five years of making decisions, sometimes hundreds a day, some as trivial as the placement of a comma, some as resonant as putting the headline **IT'S WAR** on page one of the *Daily News* edition that reported the 9/11 attack.

Beyond self-reliance, I have been haunted by the conviction that I ought to be able to anticipate when someone would prove to be untrustworthy, even if that person had no inkling of his own mendacity. It was the job of the man or woman responsible to know people's weaknesses and how they would respond in a tight corner. Indeed, the success of an enterprise might depend on keeping people out of circumstances where their flaws would be exposed. I once confounded a therapist by arguing that a man was responsible for the harmony and well-being of his family even if he couldn't regulate the behavior of his wife and children. I agreed that such a conviction was narcissistic and neurotic and counter to common sense. But I knew I'd end my days believing it no matter the rational arguments to the contrary.

If my mother was a set of paradoxes, my father was one big contradiction. The world knew him as a genial, gregarious salesman, a man who seemed to know everybody and to be genuinely pleased every time he encountered one of his countless acquaintances or business pals. In fact, if Sidney didn't hate the world beyond my mother and me he certainly held it in low regard. This one was a phony, that one a "shit heel," his favorite term of contempt. Bosses and customers would screw you if you let them. Perhaps to show the world, perhaps because it gave him a feeling of superiority, Sidney was a sport. No one else picked up a check or bought a drink if he was at the table or bar, as he so often was.

Sidney had a natural flair for clothes. As I write this, he is gazing down from a wall in my office at home. The picture was taken when my father was in his late twenties or early thirties, just before or after he married my mother. Young and handsome, with friendly eyes and a high forehead, he is perched on a white wooden fence, dressed in a camel's hair cardigan over a white shirt and wide tie, plus fours, gaudy argyle socks, and shiny brown wingtips He looks like a character out of Fitzgerald, or the manager of the Yale baseball team, although the closest he got to the Ivy League was a rainy football weekend during the Depression when he and Ben bought a trunkful of umbrellas and peddled them outside the Yale Bowl.

For all his seeming gregariousness, my father liked to be alone. On weekends at Long Beach, he would be up before seven, and by eight he'd be on the beach with his chair and giant Philco portable radio. He'd set himself up with the seagulls, far from any other early beachgoers. By 11:30, as the beach was beginning to fill, he'd pack up and head back to our apartment across the street. In New York, he'd take long walks by himself, humming *E Lucevan le stelle* from *Tosca*.

Selling goods all his life gave my father an unerring sense of true value and an unforgiving eye for people who didn't know how to do their jobs or were too lazy to try. Perhaps as a way to ventilate the aggression he hid under his open smile, Sidney loved to torment other salesmen. If he had nothing else to do, he'd drop into a clothing or appliance store and put one through his paces, trying on outfits he had no intention of buying or comparison shopping Dumont and Magnavox TVs. One Friday night, he showed up in Long Beach with his pockets full of jewelry. On the way to the train, he'd stopped off at Tiffany and talked a salesman into letting him take a selection home for the weekend for my mother to try on. Another hobby was returning used items to department stores. When my mother changed the color scheme of her tiny kitchen, my father marched off to Macy's with her three-year-old Can-o-Mat can opener and returned with a brand-new one in a color that matched the new walls.

One of my great joys was to spend Saturday afternoons downtown with my father. It seems very nineteenth-century, but in those days many men went to their offices for a half day on Saturdays. Beforehand, my mother would take me shopping on 181st Street, which had an array of small department stores like Werthheimer's, and sometimes to lunch at the double-decker Automat up the block.

The Automat was the McDonald's of its day, with dozens of branches around town. All of them were identical, with cashiers in the front who would change your paper money into handfuls of nickels and quarters. Like casino croupiers, they could count by feel, faultlessly dealing out twenty nickels or eight quarters without a glance. The coins were fed into slots in the long wall of tiny windowed compartments, each with its portion of baked beans in a brown crock, ham and other sandwiches, rice pudding, and slices of apple and cherry pie and slabs of chocolate and angel's food cake. Coffee, cocoa, milk, and chocolate milk could be procured in china mugs or sparkling glasses from coin-fed spigots in the shape of open-mouthed fish. There was also a long steam-table array of meat loaf, salmon croquettes, mashed potatoes, and other hot cafeteria fare. You carried your tray and silverware around and sat at any table, often sharing one with strangers. A creature of habit, I always had the same thing: a portion of baked beans, a ham sandwich on white bread, and a glass of chocolate milk. The baked beans were a particular marvel, with a slightly crusty surface that always included a crisp rasher of bacon. I can still taste that first bite.

Once I was able to travel by myself, my father would take me to lunch at a Garment Center delicatessen called Gertner's on Fifth Avenue, a block or so from his office at Twenty-third Street, where I'd have a corned beef sandwich with a cream soda. The real treat was visiting his office and the adventures we'd have afterward. The office was decorated with faux antiques and sporting prints to mimic an English country house and it was filled with the gamy aroma of the sample leather jackets hanging on racks in the showroom.

There would rarely be customers on Saturday, but sometimes men who worked in the toy showrooms that filled the rest of the building would stop by to schmooze. The biggest toymaker of the day, Marx, had its headquarters in 200 Fifth. Marx made wind-up toys fashioned from tinplate, and during the early 1940s, when all available tin was consigned to the war effort, they were impossible to buy. Memorably, one Christmas in the depths of the war, my father came home on Saturday afternoon with a huge carton. It turned out to be a cornucopia of unattainable Marx treasures, including a wind-up tank that could climb a 40 percent grade while sparks flew from its revolving turret. Once again, those bartered bomber jackets had been more than worth their weight in tinplate, in this case.

Another toy palace was usually the starting point for my Saturday excursions with my father, the Gilbert Hall of Science, a storefront at the north end of the X made by Broadway and Fifth Avenue where they cross at Twenty-third Street. Inside were Erector sets and chemistry kits, but the real attraction was the model trains chugging with blinking lights around the store on tracks that passed through tiny townscapes, over trestles and through tunnels. The Gilbert trains were called American Flyer, and they were made in H.O. gauge, smaller and more refined than the Lionel set I had at home. As the trains racketed along, the locomotives would sound a mournful toot and occasionally emit a white puff from the smokestack, triggering an exquisite yearning in my young collector's heart.

After the Gilbert Hall of Science, it was off to the first floor of Gimbel's, near Macy's, in Herald Square, where an émigré named Jacques Minkus ran the famous stamp department. My father would give me a dollar or two, and I would cruise the counters until I settled on my choice—a plate block of four commemoratives or an engraved decorative envelope bearing the first-day-of-issue cancellation of a new stamp.

I can't remember how I first got interested in stamps, but collecting them, arraying them in albums, and tweezing them into little glassine envelopes or clear plastic mounts fed my need to control parts of my small, fragile world. I quickly accumulated quite a stash, supplementing my Minkus acquisitions with items from a dingy hobby shop not far from my home presided over by a gray man named Marty, who looked as if he spent most of the store's meager proceeds in the gin mill around the corner.

From Marty, I bought all my British and French colonial stamps. The Brits especially catered to collectors by issuing exquisitely picturesque stamps for all their far-flung dominions and colonies, from Aden with its camels to Zanzibar with its exotic clove trees. Even tiny Pitcairn's Island, where the *Bounty* mutineers wound up after consigning Captain Bligh to an open boat in mid Pacific, had its colorful postage available at Marty's. I loved some of the stamps so much that I'd slip them into an eyeglass case and snatch glances at my beauties during school.

After Gimbel's we'd explore New York. Over the months, my father took me to the top of the Empire State Building and to the observation deck of Rockefeller Center, where you could see the Empire State Building just to the south and the George Washington and Triborough bridges to the north. We'd take the boat to the Statue of Liberty (where, in those days, you could climb all the way up the inner staircase and look out at the skyline through the statue's crown) and a Circle Liner all around Manhattan Island. We took the ferry to Staten Island and back, and all the ferries that crossed the Hudson to Hoboken and Jersey City. Once, my father took me by bus to Secaucus, now the site of the football Giants' sleek stadium, then the home to smelly pig farms. Another time, we went to Hubert's Flea Circus in a Forty-second Street basement, where we watched through a magnifying glass while the tiny creatures did their routines, one of them propelling a wee carousel. On a platform to the side an armless man wove raffia rings with his toes, and my father bought me one for a quarter.

Years later, first as a boy rewrite man for Dorothy Schiff's *New York Post* and then for thirteen years as editor of *New York* magazine and later at the *Daily News,* I felt I had an unerring understanding of the city, born of those Saturday expeditions with my father. I could instinctively distinguish the authentic from the posturings and fantasies of the parvenus who thought they'd mastered New York in the eighties and nineties.

3

NEWS BOY

IN MY LAST YEAR at P.S. 173, I edited the mimeographed school newspaper. I also played the editor, along with my friend Herbie Graff, who was even smaller than I was, in the school play we wrote as a project with some of the innovative Bank Street teachers brought in to work with us. The play was about freedom of the press, and flashed back from the boy editors on the stage to John Peter Zenger, the crusading colonial printer who was arrested by the British and defended by Andrew Hamilton in a landmark case. Our play used innovative coups de théâtre, including one of the girls playing a reporter who made a dramatic entrance running down the center aisle of the auditorium.

In a sense, I'd been a journalist all my young life. When I was five or so, I dictated a letter to my mother during one of her hush-hush medical episodes, with my Uncle Sam serving as transcriptionist. While Sam typed, I brought Annalee abreast of all the news, including the latest war developments, concluding one update with a breezy "So much for Churchill!" A few years later, I turned out a newsletter for our residential hotel in Long Beach.

The school play was the triumphant exclamation point of my charmed elementary school life. In September 1947, barely two months after my tenth birthday, my class 6-1 chums and I were cast out of Eden and began seventh grade at Junior High School 115. A gray Lubianka, 115 (or Humboldt Junior High School, as it was known to the Board of Education) was several blocks to the east of Broadway and a world away from P.S. 173. It looked as if it dated from the Civil War and smelled worse. The corridors were jammed with a noisy horde of seventh, eighth, and ninth graders from the neighborhood, all of them older and burlier than our precious little band of grade skippers and a fair number of them enrolled in classes designated

CRMD (which I soon was told stood for Children with Retarded Mental Development).

The refugees from P.S. 173 were mostly segregated in two sections labeled SP. This stood for Special Progress, but was caustically derided as "sweet potatoes" by Mr. Press, the macho phys ed teacher who sported a whistle on a lanyard around his neck. The rest of the classes were numbered one to nine in an undisguised pecking order of brains. Sections one through seven were coed, but the eighth section had only girls and the ninth was stag, presumably out of concern over what would result if the sexes were allowed to share a classroom. The girls of 7-8, 8-8, and 9-8, with their bulging breasts and acned brows, bore little resemblance to Paula Laden and Hanna Lou Fleisher of 7 SP1. Their male counterparts had mustaches and thick muscles under their white T-shirts, some with packs of Camels twisted into the sleeves.

The 9-9 boys' section was tended by a funny, gentle man named Murray Stoopack, who kept his charges nonviolent by letting them listen to the radio and read comic books during classes. This worked even though 9-9 included at least one and possibly both of the Henshey brothers, dough-faced youths with beer bellies who were notorious even among their fellow Blackboard Jungle delinquents. The principal of JHS 115, Oscar Dombrow, tried to raise the general tone by rather grandly renaming the school The City of Humboldt and choosing a student as its "mayor." Dombrow's dreams were dashed when the mayor of Humboldt stabbed a constituent in the behind and had to be expelled.

If the corridors of 115 were a gantlet of torment, just getting to school was a trial in itself. In those days, little Jewish boys who ventured east of Broadway were fair game for the Amsterdams and other Irish gangs who delighted in chasing them down the street flailing old stockings filled with lumps of colored chalk—a primitive version of paintball. Halloween, especially, stimulated them to particular frenzy. So we would walk in convoy up Broadway to 177th Street and then east toward St. Nicholas Avenue. About a half-block from the school, we'd pass the open kitchen door of a Dickensian sausage factory with its pale inmates stirring steaming vats of offal. The place gave off an odor I can still summon up at will, a kind of madeleine that evokes my three dismal junior high school years.

Thinking back, it seems that I was jangled and distracted the whole time. One of the reasons was that television arrived in the Kosner home just as I started at 115. Typically, my father got it wholesale—he knew somebody at Bruno, the RCA distributor in New York—and it was the first 16-inch set manufactured. The other sets available at the time had even tinier 10-, 12-, or 14-inch screens. There were even sets, made by Dr. Allen B. Dumont, who perfected the cathode ray TV tube, that had a round screen—a dead end on the evolutionary path of TV, but popular for a while. Our 16-inch RCA black-and-white beauty came in a shiny walnut cabinet perched on its own four-legged walnut stand with a little drop-down panel that opened to reveal the controls.

I had seen television in Aunt Rozzy's apartment on 176th Street and in the windows of appliance stores on Broadway and downtown, but to have one's own set was a luxury, even if there wasn't much on it. People in New York could watch programs, such as they were, on seven channels: CBS had channel two, although the iconic eye had not yet blinked open; NBC, which was owned by RCA, had channel four; Dr. Dumont of the round TV screens had his own Dumont Television Network on channel five; ABC owned channel seven; WOR, the Mutual Radio Network, had channel nine, with its huge transmission tower on the New Jersey Palisades; and the *Daily News,* "New York's Picture Newspaper," owned channel eleven, which it named WPIX after a contest. Even in those primitive days, there was government concern, so channel thirteen was, nominally at least, a New Jersey station.

The people from Bruno delivered the set and a technician went up on the roof of our six-story building to install the antenna, an H-shaped metal rig that picked up the signals broadcast from Rockefeller Center (for channel four) and the Empire State Building for the rest, except for channels nine and thirteen, which beamed from the Jersey tower. He ran the antenna cable down from the roof, connected it to the back of the set, and flicked the switch. The screen filled with a test pattern blurrier than the world looked to me before I got my glasses. As he switched from channel to channel, my heart sank. The picture was either blurry or a blizzard of what I learned was called "snow," the visual equivalent of static caused by a weak signal.

The problem was simple enough. Our rooftop was at the point of a triangle formed by the towers of the medical center six blocks to the south, and the George Washington Bridge six blocks to the northwest. And right across 174th Street were two thirteen-story buildings called the Broadway Temple that were all that survived of an ambitious plan to build the worldwide headquarters of the Methodist Church in Washington Heights, a scheme scuttled by the Depression and World War II. The TV signals from midtown and that Jersey tower ricocheted off the hospital and bridge and Broadway Temple to produce the blurry, jumpy pictures.

The only solution was to disconnect the roof antenna and replace it with a pair of chrome rabbit ears atop the set that could be waggled for each station to bring in a barely visible picture. And so, for years to come, TV watching for us was an orgy of caressing the poles of the indoor antenna, a Sisyphean ordeal. Still, the lure of TV was so powerful that the endless fiddling was a small price to pay for *Milton Berle; Kukla, Fran and Ollie;* and the now corporeal *Howdy Doody.*

Nominally a kids' program, *Kukla, Fran and Ollie* was actually the first hip show on TV long before the concept of hip was understood by anyone but jazz musicians and what would now be called their groupies. Kukla, who looked and sounded a bit like Adlai Stevenson, and Ollie, a droll alligator, were hand puppets created and operated by Burr Tillstrom. They lived in a little proscenium and chatted and flirted with Fran Allison, a WASPy postwar babe with a pert manner and an Ipana smile. There was also the subversive *Lucky Pup,* which starred a magician hand puppet named Foodini and his assistant, Pinhead, and opened with a ragtime piano-playing marionette who puffed smoke from the cigarette hanging from his lip. And there was Howdy, whose repertory company for TV had been expanded to include Clarabelle, the mute clown with the honking bicycle horn, Mr. Bluster, and Princess Summerfallwinterspring, the Indian honey.

The early advent of TV in our house meant that I was to live the full arc of American television, from the scratchy old Felix the Cat cartoons that seemed to be the entire repertoire of channel thirteen to today's vast wasteland of digital hi-def with its hundreds of niche cable channels and not much worth watching. Sitting on my mother's green wall-to-wall carpeting in front of the jittery screen, I saw it all: Berle's *Texaco Star Theater,* Caesar and Coca—first on *The Admiral Broadway Review* and then on *Your Show of Shows*—the Golden Age of TV live dramas on *Studio One, Philco Playhouse,* and the *Kraft Television Theatre,* Ernie Kovacs, *The Continental,* the Friday night fights from Madison Square Garden with Sugar Ray Robinson, Kid Gavilan, and Jake La Motta, Leonard Bernstein's children's concerts, and Orson Welles' modern-dress *Julius Caesar* on *Omnibus,* with Mark Anthony delivering his eulogy in the rain to a crowd of trench-coated men under black umbrellas.

As it happened, *Kukla, Fran and Ollie* was responsible for my first (but by no means last) academic crisis. I had got in the habit of settling down to watch the show while doing my homework for hygiene, a nuisance class taught by a gym teacher. In fact, I rarely took my eyes from the tiny screen as I scribbled the assignments in my notebook with its marbleized black-and-white cardboard covers. Near the end of the term, Mr. Prezioso offhandedly announced that he would be collecting our hygiene notebooks at the end of the week, and that our grades would be determined in large part by what he found in them. Had he done so that day, I would have gotten an A in *Kukla, Fran and Ollie* and an F in his class. A grade-grubber like everyone else, I was in a panic—so desperate that for once I consulted my mother about a problem.

"It's simple," said Annalee. "You'll have to redo the notebook the right way."

I knew that was ridiculous but, as usual, she was right. I reconstructed the entire term's work in reasonably neat penmanship and escaped Mr. Prezioso with a respectable B+. Few of the other teachers made much impression on me. There was a social studies teacher who used to wing erasers at back-row talkers and a sad man named Skidelsky, who wore the same shiny blue suit every day and arrived in biology class one morning holding up a glass microscope slide.

"This is a sample of human sperm cells," he announced. "Homemade."

He got his laugh, but only from the quicker-witted scholars.

As at P.S. 173, I was the editor of the school newspaper, a modest offering that the typing teacher entered on blue stencil sheets for us and ran off on the primitive mimeograph machine. In eighth grade, I found myself summoned to the principal's office. Not content simply to edit the Humboldt *Hilites*, I had named myself drama critic and panned Miss Mullaney's class play—an unheard-of act of lèse-majesté. Mr. Dombrow seemed most concerned with the fact that I had hurt kindly Miss Mullaney's feelings. I told him that I was simply exercising my journalistic prerogative—the play was really poor—but that I could understand if she were upset. Harmless in itself, the episode foreshadowed greater dramas to come.

The central task of junior high school was escaping to high school, and for me the stakes were particularly high. New York had a vast array of neighborhood high schools and an assortment of vocational schools where students with scant academic interest or ability learned how to repair cars or airplane engines or how to bake pastries. The Ivy League of the public highs comprised four specialized schools: the fabled Bronx High School of Science; Stuyvesant, on the Lower East Side; Brooklyn Tech; and the High School of Music and Art, near the City College campus just a few miles south of my home.

Science, Stuyvesant, and Brooklyn Tech were for students with aptitudes in math, science, and engineering. Music and Art's name defined its specialty. To get into any of these schools, one had to score above a certain grade in rigorous citywide exams. Those who didn't make the cut were consigned to their neighborhood schools. Some, like Erasmus Hall in Brooklyn and DeWitt Clinton in the Bronx, once had stellar academic reputations and were still considered respectable. The neighborhood high school for Washington Heights was George Washington, atop a hill on 193rd Street. As a refugee in wartime, Henry Kissinger had gone there, but by 1950 more of the GW students excelled in shop than Realpolitik.

Tiny and brainy, with glasses and braces, I lived in horror of doing poorly on the big test and being sentenced to George Washington while my friends went on to Science or Music and Art. The only thing worse than not getting into Science would be admission to the place, since I had no real gift for physics or chemistry and was at best a mediocre math student. Thus, either way, I could look forward to three years of humiliation.

I was always good at standardized tests, and I got into Science readily enough. But the reality of life for me there was exactly as miserable as I had feared. Although most of my Washington Heights pals had been skipped with me, almost all our new schoolmates were of normal age for the grade—fully two years older than we were. What's more, many had started at the school as freshmen, not tenth graders as we were, and so had already made friends and knew the Science routine. On top of that, they loved physics and advanced chemistry and precalculus and were scarily good at it.

So there I was, still getting 90s and 95s in English and social studies—my solid geometry—and barely surviving the hard sciences and math. For someone who had been told nearly from first breath how brilliant he was, it was nightmarish to cower at my desk surrounded by beady-eyed junior Einsteins, their hands desperately shooting in the air to get called on. Time and again, I'd be silently thanking *Yahweh* for allowing me to grasp the teacher's basic proof of a math problem, only to have one of them leap up and exclaim: "Mr. Goldblatt, Mr. Goldblatt, you can reverse the X axis and invert the third integer and get the same result by doing it backwards!" "Very good, Leonard," Mr. Goldblatt would say with a benign smile as the sweat broke out on the back of my neck.

My nadir came in my final term at Science. Each student was required to take at least one advanced science course, and for some reason I'd chosen a chemistry course called qualitative analysis. It was taught by a bearded little fellow in a lab coat named Dr. Harwell, one of the many no doubt brilliant men who had become New York schoolteachers for want of any other job in the Depression and never left. The course consisted of theoretical work based on a fat, incomprehensible textbook and lab work. Dr. Harwell had dozens of little numbered test tubes containing mysterious mixtures. Using the appropriate procedures, it was our task to test the contents of the tubes and identify the metals or compounds they contained. Each tube had at least one and perhaps as many as five ingredients, the correct answers recorded in a little black notebook the good doctor kept in the pocket of his lab coat.

The lab was a smelly hive of activity as the students pipetted sulfuric acid into their samples, heated the tubes over Bunsen burners, or spun them in centrifuges to precipitate little white globs of God-knows-what. Then they would write their results on slips of paper and hand them to Dr. Harwell. He'd check his little black book, congratulate them on the correct answer, and give them a fresh tube from the next test grouping.

On Friday mornings, there would be a ten-question quiz based on the week's textbook chapter. On Thursday nights, I'd toss sleepless in my bed contemplating certain shame next morning—and every Friday morning I would indeed be shamed. Harwell would hand out the little blue test pamphlets with a page of questions. I'd write my name on the cover then scan the questions—and realize that I couldn't answer a single one. Meanwhile, the room was filled with the odd clicks and whooshes of slide rules being operated at warp speed by my classmates, the precursors of today's computer nerds and brainiac dorks. I simply folded my hands and stared out the window, my stomach a knot of sick fear. For the first and only time in my life, I found myself unable to perform an intellectual task—indeed, helpless even to know where to start.

The lab work was a fiasco, too. While the other students progressed through the five test groups of samples, I couldn't get beyond the very first group, which contained some combination of the elements lead, tin, and antimony. Even I knew that there were only seven possible combinations, but shrewd Doc Harwell would let you submit only one answer per period and made you show your lab work, so guessing was out. February turned to March and on to late April. The rest of the class had finished the five groups and was doing extra credit work. I was still stuck on group I. Now I knew that I was going to fail the course and fail to graduate with my class and have to find a summer school that taught advanced chemistry or I wouldn't be able to go on to college. Bathed in flop sweat, I lay sleepless every night, not just on Thursdays before the quizzes.

Then a miracle happened. To this day, I don't know whether I finally got the idea or, more likely, Dr. Harwell took pity on a tormented wretch. When I handed him my latest *Pb, Sn, Sb* slip, instead of solemnly shaking his head from side to side, he nodded with enthusiasm, patted me on the back, and handed me a test tube from group II. Somehow, I completed all the lab work in the semester's last two periods. When I got my grades, I discovered that Doc Harwell, the good old soul, had awarded me a compassionate 65 that permitted me to graduate after all.

I wasn't a lost soul only in the chemistry lab. There were plenty of what we think of today as nerds at Science, but there were also some cool kids, including Robert Casotto, who wore jeans and T-shirts, styled his hair in a shiny ducktail, and grew up to be Bobby Darin, the true son Sinatra never had. After school, they hung out in the basement lounge, where they played records and danced the lindy. Some of the girls were cute, and a few were reputed to be fast. I couldn't dance the lindy or even the box step, and I never set foot in the lounge. Although I went on movie dates in Long Beach with girls my own age, and even got to second base with one, I was too stricken to approach any of the Science girls.

I was never invited to any school parties and never went to any of the dances. I joined a group of other social flops at the senior show and sat in wallflower gloom while one of the popular girls in a cowboy hat sang "You Can't Get a Man with a Gun" from *Annie Get Your Gun* while brandishing a Daisy air rifle. (In the early 1980s, I went to a class reunion and found myself sitting with one of my old companions when the same girl, a bit heftier now, popped up with the heirloom cowboy hat and BB gun and sang the same song. In an instant, thirty years melted away and the clammy misery was back.)

I never really participated in any school activities. In the *Observatory* year-book, my club affiliations are listed as Science Sq., Lunchroom Sq., and Fire Drill Sq., the lowest of the low. Through a quirk of timing—and my own weird pride—I didn't even work on the school paper, the one thing I could do well. The year before my friends and I showed up at Science, New York City's teachers had got into an ugly pay dispute with the Board of Education. Forbidden by law to strike, they boycotted all extracurricular activities, so there had been no drama club or debating club or newspaper. An agreement was reached as the new school year began, and the school authorities resurrected the *Science Survey* by drafting one of the English classes as the staff of the reborn paper. My friend Tom Baer was in the class, but I was in another section. By the next term, Baer and others had become editors, and I simply wasn't going to join the paper as an underling. So I killed time at the Science Club, where our principal activity was fiddling with little metal gizmos called alligator clips.

Now it was time to think about college, and all the problems and complexities of my peculiar situation suddenly came into play. Most obviously, I would be starting college at sixteen, too young to think about going out of town. For another, my parents' shaky finances made it unlikely that they'd be able to pay expensive tuition. What's more, my academic record at Science was mediocre. In its relentless competitive way, the school calculated each student's average to three decimal places. Mine was an unimpressive 82.414, and my score on the equivalent of the SATs was comparably lame.

Still, I wrote away for catalogs and applications to many top schools. When the Dartmouth catalog came, I was smitten by the austere black-and-white picture on the cover of a classic New England steeple. I longed for college life so keenly that I ached, picturing myself strolling across some autumn-leaf-strewn quadrangle, the tail of my striped muffler thrown over a tweedy shoulder as I headed to Lit class taught by an even tweedier old prof. In fact, the closest I got to the Ivy League was a brief interview at Columbia.

I prepped for the meeting as shrewdly as I could, choosing my outfit with painstaking care: my one and only tweed jacket—an oatmeal number with leather buttons—a white shirt and simple tie (I hadn't yet acquired the

iconic Brooks Brothers oxford button-down and silk rep tie), gray flannel
trousers, and penny loafers. After long deliberation, I chose to carry a thirty-
five-cent Mentor paperback of a book called *The Universe and Dr. Einstein*
by Lincoln Barnett. Clutching *Einstein* like an amulet, I found my way
across the campus to the interview room in Schermerhorn Hall.

What the Columbia prof thought of the gaunt, nervous fifteen-year-old
seated across the desk from him that afternoon I'll never know, but he was
kind despite the preposterousness of the boy's quest. He explained that
Columbia and other universities had had a dismal experience with fourteen-
and fifteen-year-old freshmen who had been enrolled after the war through
a Ford Foundation program, and they had decided to admit no more
underage applicants. So, as it happened, the skipping mania that had so distorted my life since P.S. 173 delivered a final blow.

NYU, which had a pedestrian academic reputation at the time, wasn't as
fastidious as Columbia and accepted me without a blink. But it made little
sense to pay tuition for a third-rate education on University Avenue in the
Bronx when I could get a second-rate one for nothing at tuition-free City
College, hardly fifteen minutes by bus down Broadway from my home.
What's more, my knack for most standardized tests had won me a New York
State Regents Scholarship, which paid for my books and fees each year and
left plenty over for button-down shirts and rep ties, which cost about $3.95
in the University Shop at Brooks. Despite my showing on the College Board
exam, I aced CCNY's own admissions test, which was dominated by visual
and verbal analogy questions, finishing in the 99.5 percentile.

4

APRIL FOOL

NO ONE WOULD MISTAKE City College, with its concrete campus of gray stone Academic Gothic buildings, for Dartmouth. The academic rigor of its faculty and curriculum and the brilliance of its mostly Jewish working-class students had won CCNY its reputation as the poor man's Harvard in the first half of the century, but by the 1950s much of that luster had worn off. There were still plenty of kids from poor families, especially among the night-school students, most of whom had to hold day jobs. But an increasing share of the student body was made up of lower-middle and middle-class youngsters.

Today, many of them would qualify for the top tier of private colleges, but in the fifties all those schools had admission quotas that excluded all but a handful of brainy Jewish students. So rather than venture to Wisconsin or North Carolina, state universities that seemed more disposed to smart Jewish kids from New York, or pay NYU tuition, many students got on the subway or bus for CCNY.

After the academic trials of Bronx Science, City College wasn't all that daunting. In my first semester as a sixteen-year-old freshman, I scored A's in Western cvilization, English, and, improbably, calculus. I was meticulous, and quickly discovered that my facileness at the portable typewriter meant that I could turn out essays and longer papers that routinely came back with top grades and flattering comments from the instructors. But outside the classrooms, I was a lost soul. Few of my Bronx Science friends had followed me to City College, and those who had were quickly swallowed up in the huge school. I found that I had little in common with the students I met in class and, of course, I had no social life.

Still tormented by my Ivy League fantasies, I found CCNY depressing beyond words. All the students would scoot for the subway station or bus stop as soon as the bell sounded ending the last class of the day. The college buildings, for all their architectural distinction, were dingy and run-down, the cafeteria jammed and squalid. My speech class was taught in what was called Army Hall—the Union Army from the looks of it—a nineteenth-century pile off Amsterdam Avenue so decrepit that the laths showed in the crumbling walls, and neighborhood children often capered in the corridors. The jewel of the campus was Lewisohn Stadium, a pillared concrete amphitheater celebrated for its summer concerts. During the school year, the stadium's dirt field was used by the soccer and lacrosse teams and for phys ed classes, even though it was studded with broken glass from discarded Coke bottles.

There were a few fraternities at CCNY, with their own ramshackle brownstones, but the social burden was carried by a peculiar institution called House Plan. All freshmen were assigned by lot to one or another group of about two dozen students. Male and female "houses" were then paired up for mixers and such. My unit was named Steers '57 (for our scheduled graduation year). Within the first few weeks of the semester we were assigned a party in a room at the Ninety-second Street Y with a girls' "house." I showed up at the appointed time and place and stood around with my nervous comrades until a comparably funny-looking clutch of girls showed up, giggling behind their hands at their unpromising swains. There were ginger ale and pretzels and a phonograph, and the party was even more ghastly than I had feared. It was my first and last House Plan mixer.

Somehow, I made it through that first year at City College. I earned good grades and found a few kindred spirits, but spent most Friday and Saturday nights staring morosely out my window on Broadway or watching the still-blurry TV set in the living room. I felt myself out of place in my neighborhood, at school, at home, among people my own age, and among the eighteen-year-olds in my classes at CCNY. I was a wretch.

If advanced chemistry was my nadir at Bronx Science, the depths of despond for me at City College came in the spring semester of my freshman year, when we had to submit our "elective concentration" choices for the rest of our college careers—in other words, to choose our majors. I thought and thought and came up with nothing. The obvious choices, English or history, somehow weren't appealing, especially when I read the specifics of most of the small-bore electives I'd have to take in either subject to fulfill the requirements.

In desperation I scoured the encyclopedic course catalog for an alternative—and found it. Eureka! I would major in meteorology and be a weatherman! When I awoke the next morning and suddenly remembered my choice, I felt so depressed I could hardly get out of bed. I was truly lost, a nondescript failure not yet seventeen.

Classes ended soon after Memorial Day, and once again I moved to Long Beach with my parents, but, miraculously enough, my *Vitelloni* days horning around with the guys came to an end. My best friend and I managed somehow to attract the interest of two townies, sweet and even slightly flirtatious high school girls who found two college men from the city more appealing than the boys they spent the rest of the year fending off. My pal and I would spend the mornings shooting hoops at the high school. Then we'd meet the girls at a beach away from the center of town for long afternoons on their blankets serenaded by Doris Day singing, "Secret Love," or the Crewcuts doing "Sh-Boom" on the portable radio. A couple of nights a week, we'd neck under the blue lights in the balcony of the Laurel Theater, oblivious to *The Creature from the Black Lagoon* slithering out of the muck onscreen. By midsummer I'd succeeded in getting my girl's brassiere unhooked, but I never got much farther.

Still, I could hardly believe that I actually had a girlfriend and was finally doing the teenage things that I'd longed for on those solitary weekend nights in Washington Heights. There were the fraught conversations, the near-breakups and reconciliations, the jealousies and intrigues—the whole Archie Andrews repertoire of adolescent angst and ardor. But my joy was shadowed by the melancholy realization that while my summer love was age appropriate, she was unsuitable for the college sophomore I was about to become. I tried to picture her parsing Schopenhauer or Spinoza in my philosophy class at CCNY or comparing and contrasting the Sumerians and the Akkadians. So even my brief fling with pubescent normality felt awkward and skewed. It seemed so easy for everybody else to be themselves and so hard for me.

I brought some of the warm glow of the summer back to New York with me, but the reality of my dreary college life soon chilled that. Back at City College, I had no idea what I wanted to do, and had no one to not do it with. As I got off the Broadway bus the first morning of my second year of college, I felt the twist of anxiety in my gut. Even lighting up an Old Gold—smoking was another summer advance—couldn't soothe me.

A week or two later, I found myself on a stone bench under the flagpole that anchored what passed for a quadrangle at City College. It was noon on Thursday, the start of a weekly two-hour club period when student-activities groups met in classrooms or offices scattered around the campus. I had joined none of them as a CCNY freshman and had no intention of doing so in my second year. So I was just idling there when Charles Meyers, another lonely Washington Heights ironist who had become my only CCNY friend, happened by.

"*The Campus* is having a meeting for people who want to join the paper, and I'm going over there," said Chuck.

With nothing better to do—in fact, with nothing at all to do—I picked up my books and said, "I'll walk you over."

And then my life truly began.

Ever since then, I have puzzled over this first wave of the wand of chance that has ruled my life. For a man helplessly addicted to habit and ritual, an organizer and a list-maker, it is incongruous to admit that nothing important to me has ever happened by plan. Indeed, every major turning in my life and career has been the result of inadvertence.

What if Chuck hadn't happened by, or what if it had been raining and I'd gone to the cafeteria instead of the flagpole bench? Or what if I'd shrugged him off and turned back to the *Times* crossword puzzle? I might have eventually found my way to *The Campus* on my own, but not likely—and then what would my life have been? The answer to that question is too alarming to dwell on.

So we crossed Convent Avenue and walked along the long ground-floor corridor of Shepard Hall, the main building, until we found a scarred wooden door with the logo of *The Campus* Scotch-taped to it. The door was half open and inside we could see a small room with scruffy, paper-strewn desks and a few scarred office typewriters. Piles of old copies of the four- or eight-page tabloid were stacked on the floor. There were a couple of nasty ashtrays and a single telephone. Students who were obviously editors or staffers were draped over the metal chairs, some with their feet parked on the long table in the center of the room. Others stood uncertainly around the walls—the "candidates," as they were called, suggesting that not every novice who showed up would be accepted on the paper.

Before anyone could say a word, a warm glow began to seep through me that relaxed the tense clutch of my neck muscles and brought the tinge of a smile to my face. For the first time since those sunny days at P.S. 173 a decade before, I knew I'd found where I belonged.

Over the next four years—I spent an extra year at school because of my involvement with the paper—I logged more time working on *The Campus* than in any classroom or library. I survived on three hours' sleep a night and a diet of corned beef sandwiches and greasy french fries gobbled at the print shop. I got thrown out of school for a semester for publishing a scurrilous April Fool's issue of the paper, finally got to make love to a girl, fell in love (with a different girl), found a wife and lifelong friends, got myself enmeshed in a secret struggle against Communist students who tried to take over the paper, and learned the rudiments of nearly everything I know about journalism and managing people.

Through the paper I found the inner world of the college invisible to me as a freshman—the ambitious young pols of the student council, the pretentious scribblers of the literary magazine, the coaches and athletes, the future warriors of the ROTC, the president of CCNY and his deans, even the college PR guy angling for a favorable feature in the Sunday *New York Times*.

I found that I had an instinctive understanding of how to do everything on the paper. I could write more stories faster than anyone else, do better headlines, catch mistakes, lay out the pages, even take pictures if no photographers were around. I had pitch-perfect news judgment and, best of all, when there was no news I could come up with fresh angles to refurbish old stories or dream up offbeat features. I could make decisions without dithering. If the flu flattened the staff, I literally could put out the paper myself, even hand-setting the headlines at the printer. The work was endless, but for me it was effortless. I simply could do it all better than anyone else.

Parochial as they may have been, City College and *The Campus* had an authentic journalistic tradition. Over the years, the paper had produced a pantheon of important journalists, among them Bernard Schorr; the Kalb brothers, Marvin and Bernard; and A. M. Rosenthal, a former *Campus* editor in chief, a winner of Pulitzers as a *New York Times* foreign correspondent, and later the man who remade and ruled the paper in one of its golden ages. There were other undergraduate newspapers, one each for the night-school students and for the business school down on Twenty-third Street, and a competitor for *The Campus* called *Observation Post,* which evolved from a paper started by returning veterans after World War II. There were just two journalism courses in the English Department, but they were taught by a legendary figure named Irving Rosenthal, who had started them so long ago nobody could remember the date. Each semester, Irv would gesture toward the lecture chairs in his classroom and tell the class: "Sitting in those seats just a few years ago were Bernie Kalb and Abe Rosenthal, and someday I may be able to mention your names along with theirs."

At colleges like Columbia, Yale, and the University of Virginia the student paper came out five days a week and the editors had at least a sense of what it's like to work on a daily with urgent deadlines and last-minute improvisation. But City College had something better: competition. *The Campus* and *OP* each came out only twice a week, but they alternated, publishing Tuesday and Thursday one week, Wednesday and Friday the next. So for the staffs, each edition was like a daily, with the pressure to top the paper the opposition had put out the day before and the fear of being scooped the next day.

On my first day as a *Campus* candidate, I wrote a paragraph about some upcoming club activities, and I was thrilled the next day to find my squib on page three just as I had typed it. The next story was five or six paragraphs long, and from then on I had at least one piece, and often more, in each edition of the paper. I was assigned my first "copy night" at the office, during which stories were edited, layouts drawn, and headlines and captions written, and my first night "on stone" at the printer's down near my father's old office on Twenty-third Street, where we read proofs and made adjustments for late stories and mishaps. And I drew my first assignment to distribute the papers, finding the delivered bundles at 8:00 AM and stacking the copies at the entrances to the various classroom buildings. After the last bundle was untied, I lounged against a wall watching early students pick up my paper and a few actually start reading it.

Now *The Campus* became the center of my life. Semester after semester, I moved relentlessly up the masthead, and as the senior editors graduated and moved on, my new friends and I began to shape the paper and its distinct little society. We were quick, funny, cynical as only postadolescents can be, scathing in our contempt for the campus politicians, the arty set, the ROTC commandos, the faculty geezers, and practically everyone but a poor soul named Raymond who sold bagels and pretzels on Convent Avenue.

Even before I became the editor in chief in 1957, when I was twenty, I ruled the paper with an iron hand and a withering tongue. I drafted an intricate stylebook patterned after the one in force at the *New York Times* that prescribed with rigid authority usage rules and even headline-font sizes. Each Friday afternoon, I would preside over a critique of the week's papers, finding ineptitude practically everywhere I looked. The poor editors and writers had to endure humiliating dissections of their solecisms and lame leads in hopes of a rare nod of praise from the perfectionist chief. Then we'd adjourn to the Emerald, a throwback Irish bar marooned in Harlem, where we all drank bad Scotch and made fun of everybody who wasn't fortunate enough to be in the magic circle of *The Campus*.

Among the objects of our smart-ass scorn were the leaders of the student government, among them Henry Stern, who survived our ridicule to enjoy a distinguished career as a politician and longtime parks commissioner of New York, and Meyer Baden, who as Michael Baden became the city's medical examiner and ubiquitous kibitzer on cable TV coverage of crimes like the O. J. Simpson case. Another target was a tall, preternaturally dignified young man who marched around the campus every day in his ROTC uniform with the special braid signifying his leadership of the Pershing Rifles, the military honor society. We had a one-column head shot of him that frequently ran with stories about ROTC over the caption **Cadet Col. Colin Powell '58**.

In every visible respect except heft, Powell was the same man familiar to millions of Americans decades later as George H. W. Bush's military overseer of the Gulf War and as George W. Bush's secretary of state. He had the same steady gaze and air of authority and he spoke in the same deliberate cadences of command. When he was interviewed by *The Campus* or *OP,* his quotes were always exemplary. The fact that he was drilling a ragtag unit of wannabe soldiers hut-hutting around dusty Lewisohn Stadium in the middle of the Age of Eisenhower made no difference. Powell had no more sense of what the future would bring for him than I did for my own career in journalism, but somehow the man was manifest in the boy.

Our compulsion to ridicule and satirize the people we covered in *The Campus* had gradually built over the years, and it finally produced the inevitable disaster. In the spring of 1956, we conceived an April Fool's issue that made us briefly notorious and ultimately became part of the folklore of City College—a paper that picked at the scab of the college's most painful wound and managed to offend nearly everybody.

In the late 1940s and early 1950s, proletarian, pavement-bound CCNY fielded some of the best college basketball teams in the country. This was in the days before recruiting scholarships, sleek field houses, and multimillion-aire coaches had turned college ball into the minor-league professional game that now dominates TV each March. City College had an extraordinary coach named Nat Holman, an original Celtic, and drew its talented players from the schoolyard courts and high school gyms where the heady New York style of basketball was invented and perfected. In 1950, CCNY had won both national championship tournaments, the NCAA and the NIT, in a Madison Square Garden jammed with delirious fans.

Then came the thunderclap of doom and disgrace: it turned out that gamblers had connived with some of the CCNY Beavers and with players from other local colleges like NYU and Long Island University to fix the outcome of games by shaving points. The teams would generally win the fixed games, but the players made sure their margin was within the point spread set by the bookmakers so that bettors would lose their money despite the victory. Coach Holman knew nothing about the schemes, but his career and reputation were ruined. CCNY forfeited its titles and left the Garden forever, playing its games against humble opponents like Hunter and Brooklyn College in the tiny campus gym under an earnest new coach named Dave Polansky.

The postscandal president of City College, a white Protestant minister named Buell G. Gallagher, who had headed a black college in the South and bore an unnerving resemblance to Abraham Lincoln, was the jut-jawed shepherd of the new basketball morality.

GARDEN BASKETBALL BACK!

shrieked the headline on the issue of *The Campus* students found on their return to school after the Easter break, and the story went on to quote President Gallagher burbling about how wonderful it was that CCNY had shaken off the scandal and was again embracing big-time basketball. Just to make sure nobody would catch on immediately, we also published a rogue edition of *Observation Post,* which contained legitimate news, but also reported the return of CCNY basketball to the Garden.

I was the news editor of *The Campus* at this time, and played a big hand in putting out both papers, making sure the counterfeit *OP* looked slovenly and illiterate to embarrass our competitors. Most of the work had been done one night in the scruffy print shop on the Lower East Side where *The Campus, OP,* and the Hunter student newspaper now were published. As it got later, any sense of reality we had left was engulfed in a manic tide. People would chip in the maddest story idea they could imagine, only to be topped by something even more scatological or demented. Finally, somebody noticed that there was a hole in the bottom of page one and suggested a caption story: a picture of a little old lady with the headline

College Prostitute
Retires After 50 Years.

All we needed was the picture of the little old lady. Photos in the paper were printed from metal halftone engravings, or cuts, mounted on wooden blocks and stored in long, flat drawers in the print shop, one or two drawers for each school paper. *The Campus* and *OP* files yielded nothing. Then someone stuck his thumb in the Hunter *Arrow*'s drawer and pulled out a plum: A shot of a prototypical biddy in a demure hat. **Millicent Church,** read the identification scrawled on the back—and the retiring college prostitute was instantly christened "Milly Crotch." Hilarity—hysteria, actually —reigned in the funky little print shop.

Next morning, the April Fool's *Campus* and the bogus *OP* were snapped up around school by students who were mildly amused but generally puzzled by the papers. Most of us were sitting around the office congratulating ourselves on our comic coup when a call came summoning the editors to the office of the dean of students upstairs.

We assembled before the stone-faced dean—a man named Daniel Brophy, who would easily be pegged as a monsignor had he been wearing a clerical collar—expecting a mild tongue-lashing for making fun of the college basketball scandal or perhaps for counterfeiting *Observation Post.* But, as it quickly became clear, Dean Brophy didn't care about any of that. What he

did care about was that the little old lady we'd pictured as the college prostitute was actually the oldest living alumna of Hunter College.

"You're out and your paper is out," barked the dean.

It took a bit to sort out the true culprits from the more or less innocent
bystanders, but by the end of the day five of us had been suspended from
school for the rest of the semester at least. The paper could resume publication in time under a new editorial board untainted by our folly.

Back in the office, giddy with all the drama, I picked up the ringing telephone. The man on the other end identified himself as the son of Mrs.
Church, and he administered the rebuke we'd expected from Brophy. I can
still hear his parting words.

"I can only thank God that my mother is blind," said her infuriated son,
"so that she'll never be able to see how you boys shamed her."

Now that the adrenaline rush had spent itself, I realized that I had to go
home and tell my mother and father that their brilliant son had been booted
out of college for a lame stunt that sounded even lamer in the retelling. My
mother, bless her, took the news in stride and spared me the lecture that I'd
so richly earned. Next day, the New York newspapers carried stories about
the episode. And, true to their nature, most of the papers managed to
mangle my name as Kasner or Korner, so when cousins and friends started
calling my mother, they all said the same thing: "I thought for a minute that
was Edward in the papers, but Edward would never do anything like that
and, anyway, the name is spelled differently." Annalee quickly set them right.

I put on an insouciant front, but I was actually crushed by my banish-
ment from school. It would make a great anecdote later, but in the moment
I was humiliated. Some of the incipient radicals on the student council tried
to turn us into civil-liberties martyrs. In a tone-deaf homage to the Scotts-
boro Boys and other victims championed by the left, we were proclaimed the
"St. Nick Five" and rallies were staged on campus clamoring for our rein-
statement. I shunned all of it. I wanted to get back in school and resume my
life, not shine as a symbol of oppression.

But destiny's wand had waved again and my life had irrevocably changed. As
it turned out, the next four months were a one-and-only chance to live
another life—or, at least, be a tourist in another life—unlike anything I'd
ever known before or would ever know again. I had to get a job and I had

to be clever about it, so I concocted a tale about leaving college to help support my parents to explain why an obviously bright young man was interested in being a flunky in the advertising department of Exquisite Form Brassieres.

I'd been sent to Exquisite Form by an employment agency on Forty-second Street that specialized in jobs in what's now called media. The nice brassiere folks bought my story for their own reasons and I took the job, which paid $40 a week, the equivalent today of about $350. My tasks were mostly to fill wrought iron rotating display racks with compact packages of the made-in-Japan $2.50 brassieres the company imported so the racks could be photographed for ads and little brochures. The offices were on Madison Avenue in Murray Hill just south of the Morgan Library.

Menial as my work was, I couldn't help learning about what today is known as the "corporate culture" of Exquisite Form. The brassieres were designed by a woman who looked like Ida Lupino, and featured what the ads called the "cantilever effect," a lift, as it were, from an architectural concept. Exquisite Form's best seller had the inspired name "Hi-Low Witchery," but around the shop the bras were called "bubby sox" and "meat-packers." The CEO of Exquisite Form was one Garson Reiner, whose main claim to fame was that he was never to be photographed, which prompted all sorts of delicious speculation about what I'd later learn to call "Mob links."

One of the fringe benefits of the job was that I could swipe as many bras as I wanted while at the warehouse getting stock to fill the sales racks. So in Manhattan and Long Beach I could suavely ask girls, "What's your size?" and produce free "bubby sox" next time I saw them, a reincarnation of my father and his samples. Still, after two months I was ready to improve my lot. Someone mentioned that a press agent named Larry Gore had a job for an apprentice that would pay $45 a week, fully five dollars more than I was making. So I went over to Gore's office in a high-rise on Forty-second Street and Fifth Avenue and got the job. Bright and early on the last Monday in June, I reported to begin my new life as a flack.

In the midfifties media, newspapers were the main game, and each of the New York dailies had at least one star gossip columnist. The *Mirror* had the king of the jungle, Walter Winchell, but it also boasted a man named Lee Mortimer. The *Daily News* had columns by Danton Walker and Ed Sullivan, whose Sunday night TV show was a colossus. The *Post* had Earl

Wilson and Leonard Lyons, and the other papers had pale imitators whose names are lost to time.

Within a few minutes, I learned that my job at Larry Gore's shop was to invent items about Larry's clients that would be sent to Winchell, Walker, Sullivan, and on down the list in a pecking order of juice. These client items would be spiced with some possibly true nonclient items so the columnist would be rewarded for plugging Larry's guys with some less self-interested stuff. I can't remember the names of most of Larry's clients, but when I thought about it later they reminded me of Woody Allen's forlorn vaudevillians in *Broadway Danny Rose.* I do recall that one of Larry's guys was the actor Darren McGavin, who had starred in a TV newspaper drama called *Casey, Crime Photographer,* and appeared with Sinatra in *The Man with the Golden Arm.* Another was an old-timer named Arthur Tracy, who billed himself as "the Street Singer."

Ever enterprising, I strained my brain to come up with column-worthy items about these folks and turned my output over to Larry's crew, even fashioning one for Darren McGavin about, improbably, Shinnecock Indian burial relics.

One problem with the job was that Gore insisted that everybody be at work at 9:00 AM and stay until after six, when the envelopes of items were sent by messenger to the gossip columnists. You had to stay in at lunch, too, ordering from a nearby takeout place that specialized in greasy fried shrimp "baskets." This was a hardship for me because I was commuting most days from my parents' place in Long Beach, waking up by 6:30 to catch a train that would have me in the office by nine and not getting back until close to 8:00 PM. My commutation ticket and those fried shrimp were costing me most of my meager after-tax salary, but I was determined to stick it out. My first three-day week ended with the July Fourth holiday, and I took off with friends to the Newport Jazz Festival, where out of ignorance we drank motel-made Margaritas with sugar on the rim of the glass instead of salt. When I returned after the long weekend, Larry Gore fired me.

"Kid," he said, "it's just not working out."

That was the first, but by no means the last time, I'd hear those words.

This time, one of my *Campus* pals, who would become a friend for life, came to the rescue. A talented writer from Pelham Parkway in the Bronx, whose father managed the fruit stand at a big West Side supermarket, Jack

Schwartz had a summer job at Lord & Taylor, the WASPy department store on Fifth Avenue and Thirty-eighth Street. L&T was hiring stock boys and I was quickly signed on to help out in the linen department during the August white sales. The pay was just $36 a week—a useful lesson in the price one could pay by giving up a secure job (the brassieres) for a risky one that paid better (press agenting).

I was certainly the best-dressed stock boy Lord & Taylor ever had. Each day, I'd ride the Long Island Railroad to the city decked out in my chinos, blue button-down and seersucker jacket, clutching the *New York Times*. Once in the store, I'd trade the seersucker for a stock boy's green jacket and go about my rounds. These essentially consisted of patrolling the sales counters and neatly refolding the bath and hand towels the customers kept messing up as they hunted for bargains. The towels were mostly made by Martex and Fieldcrest and came in a rainbow of colors with exquisite names like Aztec Gold.

There was a Salinger touch to my L&T days: a blonde named Jane Thompson. Her job was handling special merchandise orders—say, finding a Fieldcrest towel set in Ancient Artichoke or Delft Dreams in stock only at the L&T in Bala Cynwyd on the Philadelphia Main Line. Jane was probably twenty-five and reminded me of the Chief's girlfriend in *The Laughing Man*. We were in the midst of the second Eisenhower presidential campaign and Jane, it turned out, was miraculously and madly for Adlai Stevenson. So we would talk politics as I pushed my stock cart stacked with towels past her little office off the sales floor. To complete my infatuation, Jane confided in me that she'd once seen a flying saucer.

Trapped in my skinny nineteen-year-old's body and my serf's smock, I gazed at Jane Thompson the way Cyrano or Quasimodo must have beheld their impossible loves. I could talk the talk with her, but I'd never walk the walk. I just knew that when I hopped the LIRR back to Long Beach, she headed for weekends with Mummy and Dads in Greenwich and sailing parties on the Sound or tennis on the lawn or dances at the club or whatever *shiksa* goddesses did in their own realm. My situation was actually more early Woody Allen (before he started getting the girls) than Salinger, but it hurt no less.

In a different way, I fell in love with other women at L&T, too: the matronly sales ladies who'd worked at the store forever and treated the customers with the kindly attention one would wish from a bedside nurse. These women were on their feet all day and made very little money, but they taught me a lot about keeping one's spirit and dignity when dealing with the public in an essentially menial role. By contrast, I found myself resenting the customers who kept sticking their mitts in my meticulous towel arrays. Finally, just before Labor Day, I told the assistant buyer, a tall, fastidiously dressed young man named Arnow, that I would be leaving to return to school. He told me I was a superior stock boy and could have my job back anytime.

With a couple of weeks to go before college resumed, Jack found me another pinhead job, this time as an unarmed Pinkerton guard—essentially an usher—at a jewelry trade show in Manhattan and at what was then called the U.S. National Tennis Championships (now the U.S. Open) at the West Side Tennis Club in Forest Hills. We Pinkertons were outfitted in gray whipcord uniforms with peaked caps and Sam Browne belts. The uniform pants had no pockets so we couldn't filch anything or hide our hands. The pay was $1 an hour for the first 40 hours and $1.50 for overtime. We worked twelve hours at a stretch at the trade show with two half-hour breaks for meals.

The great virtue of the job—besides leaving no time to get into mischief—was that it literally taught the value of a dollar. I'd take my dinner break at a hamburger joint on Lexington or Third Avenue called Prexy's, where I'd have a bowl of soup, a burger, and a cup of coffee. The check would be $1.25 and I'd leave a quarter tip. It didn't take long for me to realize that I'd had to stand on my feet for ninety minutes, or an hour of overtime, to earn my supper.

After three or four days, I found myself out at Forest Hills with a towel in my hand to wipe off the seats for the swells in my section. On the first big day of the matches, I made $8.50 in tips and I figured the job was a bonanza. It wasn't: people had the same seats for all the sessions and the custom was to tip the usher only on the first day. Some didn't think they had to tip at all, but we had a technique for dealing with the deadbeats, especially those with a wife or girlfriend in tow. The stiff would hand the usher the tickets, the usher would find the seats, towel them off, and start handing the stubs back. The trick was to hold them tight between thumb and index finger—releasing the stubs only when the tip hit your palm. No tip, no release—and the guy would find himself in an embarrassing tug-of-war in front of his date. It nearly always worked.

When almost everyone was seated in my section on the first day, I looked up and there was Larry Gore, the short, goggle-eyed press agent who'd fired me after July Fourth, tickets in hand. I pulled the brim of my cap down practically to my nose and angled my face away as I swabbed off the seats. Gore didn't recognize me—hell, he'd barely recognized me when I worked for him—and my Pinkerton career ended without further humiliation.

That summer, six years after my bar mitzvah, I really became a man. The woman—really a girl—was an arty blonde from City College who worked on *Observation Post*. Like me, she was a Manhattan kid. She lived on the Upper West Side with her parents and younger sister, and she was a cultivated girl who introduced me to Bach's *Goldberg Variations*, Mahler's *Kindertotenlieder*, and sexual intercourse.

She was ahead of her time, at least in taking the lead in sex. It may be that my April Fool's suspension gave me just enough "bad boy" luster to catch her eye; I certainly would never have gotten her into bed solely on my own dubious seduction skills. But one night that summer after my parents had gone to Long Beach, I managed to get her up to Washington Heights along with a pint of Black & White Scotch. After a couple of slugs, we undressed each other and hopped into the twin bed my father slept in—my mother's, of course, was sacrosanct. Inevitably, I went limp, but only temporarily.

On another Friday night a few weeks later, we took the last train from Pennsylvania Station to the Jersey shore, where her family had a bungalow in a hamlet called Bradley Beach, not far from Asbury Park. By now, I'd rather gotten the idea, and there was no sleep that night, especially because I dreaded dozing off and being found in bed with their daughter when Mom and Dad arrived early next morning. So I snuck off at dawn, hopped the train to Penn Station, and continued on the LIRR to Long Beach, where I played basketball for three hours and then went to the beach, drained and as happy as I had ever been or ever would be.

So the April Fool's fiasco turned out to be a gift. For a few months, I drifted in a carefree cocoon shielded from the force of ambition that would drive me through life. The future could wait—there was nothing to do but arrange the bras in those sales racks or straighten the bath towels or wipe off those Forest Hills seats. I can still remember the voluptuous feeling of leaving the Exquisite Form offices at 5:00 or 5:30 on a beautiful spring evening to meet up with my friends and see what adventures the night might hold.

One night, we pitched up on stools at a bar in Murray Hill called the Navigator, where I ordered my first martini. In a moment, the bartender set before me a giant beaker holding about a gallon of silvery liquid and a single green olive. I raised the glass with two hands and took my first sip . . . and almost choked on what tasted like kerosene. But I couldn't very well flunk my virgin martini and so I nursed it for about forty minutes until I'd drained the glass.

"Another?" chirped the bartender, who had my number.

I waved him off affably, eased off the stool, and padded to the door as nonchalantly as Fred Astaire, trying to decide whether I could make it to the gutter or have to puke on the barroom floor.

At the same time, I had a different taste of the suave, collegiate life that still haunted my dreams. Rich Kobakoff, a crisp, pin-neat fellow from Jackson Heights in Queens, had begun hanging around *The Campus* office. Just where Richie stood academically was never really clear. Plainly, he had been a student at some stage, but for now he never seemed to go to class. Rich was attentive and funny, but what made him unique at CCNY could often be glimpsed cruising along Convent Avenue: a cream-colored Morgan roadster, a rare, practically handmade British car that to this day is the choice of connoisseurs and the envy of everyone driving a Miata or a Boxter.

The Morgan was—and still is—painstakingly assembled on a frame fashioned from steel-hard ash wood at a single factory in Malvern in Worcestershire. A husky leather strap secures the hood, and the top has to be erected with plastic windshields when it rains. The engine practically sits in the laps of the passengers and exudes a throaty, infinitely satisfying thrum when the car accelerates. The waiting list is years long.

How Rich acquired his Morgan was unclear and how he supported it even murkier. He certainly wasn't Richie Rich. But he was incredibly—recklessly —generous with the car. Although I lacked even a learner's permit and he had violation points on his license, he regularly let me drive it on the highways around New York, and even in the city. I never quite mastered getting the car into first gear, so when we had to stop at toll gates and red lights, he would slip his hand under mine on the shifter, hiss "clutch," and "gas," and put the car in gear while I pushed the pedals on cue. When he was at the wheel, one of Rich's favorite stunts was to pull up next to a couple of wannabe hot-rodders in a Chevy or Ford. They'd mistake Richie's Morgan for a more prosaic MG, which it resembled to the untutored eye. "Hey, MG, wanna race?" the driver would challenge. Richie would look uncertain, but reluctantly agree. When the light changed, Richie's Morgan—which had a powerful Triumph engine secured under that hood strap—peeled away as he gave the bird to the Chevy proles. The exhilaration I felt as we raced through the night was so intense I can still feel it. The concept of *cool* had, of course, not yet been imagined, but we were as cool as you could be in 1956.

Besides the sex and the sports car, another gift of my suspension was the once-in-a-career chance to work with people outside the circle of journalism —a circle where I would spend the rest of my life—and to work for minimum or meager wages so that the amount of drone labor or boredom it cost to drink that martini or buy that rep tie could be precisely measured. When I became a father, I pressured my two sons, and later my daughter, while in school to take jobs serving the public in a shop or school dining hall to see life from the other side of the counter, and each of them did.

But the most profound lesson I learned from *L'Affaire Crotch* was to respect journalism. It wasn't a job or a profession or a mind game, it was a craft that demanded full concentration, and it was a calling with no place for jokers.

I returned to college in the fall of 1956 to take over as managing editor of *The Campus* with a fierce determination that the paper and I would be redeemed through good work. It wasn't long before our new commitment would be tested in an extraordinary way. What passed for popular culture that fall was dominated by a turbo-powered TV reincarnation of the quiz shows that had been a staple of radio and early television. Those programs, like *Information Please* and *Twenty Questions,* featured panels of regulars— brainy folk showing off their wit and erudition. The *schtick* of the new shows, *The $64,000 Question* and *Twenty-One,* was big money to be won by incongruous contestants of one sort or another. There was a humble cobbler named Gino Prato, who turned out to be an opera expert; Dr. Joyce Brothers, the pop psychologist who knew all sorts of boxing trivia; and a 10-year-old boy named Robert Strom, who was a science prodigy. *Twenty-One* also turned oddball "geniuses" into instant pop stars.

One of the first was a City College student named Herb Stempel, who had actually been my classmate in freshman history with Professor Bailey Diffie. When Stempel showed up on *Twenty-One,* I remembered him flirting with girls—actually, *trying* to flirt with girls—in the moments before Professor Diffie shuffled in and turned our attention to the Code of Hammurabi.

Stempel was a chubby fellow with thick glasses who was older than most of the other students. On TV each week, Herb wore the same shiny blue double-breasted suit. The host, an old TV pro named Jack Barry, who produced the show with his partner, Dan Enright, told viewers that Herb was a poor but brilliant CCNY student and implied that Stempel wore the same suit because he couldn't afford another.

As Stempel won week after week, he became an obvious subject for a story in *The Campus*. A feature writer tracked down Herb to a house in Queens where he lived with his wife, and it turned out Mrs. Stempel had a lot to say. She insisted that Stempel wasn't the impoverished wretch Barry made him out to be; they were actually a regular middle-class couple. Worse, Herb had lots of nice clothes—the producers made him wear that schlumpy blue suit as part of the act!

A few days later, a modest story by my friend Jack Schwartz appeared under a two-column headline on page three of the paper with a small picture of Stempel in his blue suit pondering a toughie in *Twenty-One*'s "isolation booth." The story was a bland local-boy-makes-good piece in which Mrs. Stempel complained mildly about that suit. Paraphrasing her, Jack wrote, "Herb's double-breasted blue suit, which has become his 'trademark,' is really a publicity stunt rigged by the television program's brass to gain sympathy for him." Under the picture, the caption read, **Herb Stempel's wrinkled blue suit is really a publicity stunt, his wife revealed yesterday**.

Not long after lunch that day, *The Campus* editors were called on the carpet again, summoned this time to the college public relations office where we were informed that the producers of *Twenty-One* were suing *The Campus* and the college for libel over that paragraph and caption. They demanded an immediate retraction and a groveling apology from the smart-ass *Campus* editors.

Still rattled by the April Fool's debacle, we couldn't think clearly. Why would big-time NBC producers go nuts over a paragraph and caption on page three of an obscure college paper that not even most of the students read? And besides, the paragraph and the caption were based on a quotation from Stempel's own wife!

We had another problem: none of us really understood the libel laws. We didn't know about the concepts of "malice" and "reckless disregard" or that truth is an absolute defense. Nor did we know that in this context, Stempel and Barry-Enright Productions were "public figures," harder to libel than a common citizen. Indeed, that whole notion wouldn't become law until eight years later in the Supreme Court's historic *New York Times vs. Sullivan* decision. Mrs. Stempel was denying the quotes she'd given our reporter, and the producers were claiming we couldn't prove we'd even spoken with her.

Although we knew in our guts that we'd done nothing wrong, we caved. Now a model of journalistic rectitude, I led the argument for capitulation. We issued a statement repudiating our own story, and a retraction and apology appeared in the next issue.

If you saw the movie *Quiz Show,* you know the denouement. With 50 million people watching, Stempel was dethroned by a Columbia English professor named Charles Van Doren—the son of the revered Mark Van Doren—who became so famous that he made the cover of *Time* magazine and got his own egghead slot on the *Today* show. The whole business blew up eighteen months later when a contestant on an obscure quiz show, and then Stempel himself, came forward to document how the shows were rigged with coached contestants, prearranged winners and losers, and show-biz props like that shiny blue suit. The scandal ruined careers, sent people to prison, and banished quiz shows from the air for a generation.

The intrepid staff of the CCNY *Campus* had the first whiff of the big story—had we the savvy to know what we were smelling. Who knows what kind of a furor we might have touched off if we'd had the nerve to stand by our caption scoop? I never forgot the lesson of the episode: when the reaction to a seemingly insignificant story is dramatically out of scale it is *always* the tip-off that a really big story is hidden there somewhere. It would take nearly twenty years before I could act on the rule the next time, but the payoff was a *Newsweek* blockbuster in the midst of Watergate.

5

WINNER AND SINNER

WITH THE NEW YEAR, I suddenly had two major responsibilities: I had been elected editor in chief of the paper, and I'd landed the plum job in journalism CCNY had to offer—campus correspondent for the *New York Times*.

In those days, the *Times* maintained undergraduate stringers at Columbia, NYU, and City College. They were paid $20 a week and were expected to chip in news items and feature stories about the schools, most of which ran in the second part of the Sunday main news section, which was filled with department store ads and was called "the caboose." There was keen competition for these jobs because they sometimes led to a staff job on the *Times* after a long apprenticeship as copy boy or news clerk. The great A. M. Rosenthal had been the *Times* CCNY stringer, and look where it had got him.

The campus stringers had no permanent desks in the *Times's* huge third-floor city room, a bustling chamber so vast that reporters were summoned to the city desk by a public address system. But there were usually some empty spots far in the back of the room near the row of typewriters used by the radio-TV reporters or across the aisle in the sports department. There I'd perch when I visited the paper a couple of times a week, warily eyeing the Columbia stringer, obviously my main competitor for a postgraduation job at the *Times*.

No matter how often I went there, venturing into the *Times* made my heart beat and my knees knock. I'd take the subway down to Times Square from CCNY, walk west to 229 West 43rd Street, and push through the brass-colored revolving door into the pungent, unforgettable tang of ink and newsprint. If it was later in the evening, the lobby throbbed with the vibration of the mammoth presses running in the basement. Once in the city room, I'd walk as casually as I could down the long aisles to the rear, past the incarnate bylines I could recite by heart: Meyer Berger and Peter Kihss, the great Metro reporters; Milton Bracker, a CCNY man; Hanson Baldwin, the military expert; Pat Spiegel, a jester sporting suspenders and a cigar butt; McCandlish Phillips, the stylish feature writer. Once, Brooks Atkinson, the *Times*'s famed drama critic, stepped back on the food line in the *Times* cafeteria and stomped on my toe just as he was ordering a Swiss cheese sandwich on white with the crusts cut off.

The most daunting moments were when I had to report what I proposed to write for the paper to the city editor, a rotund, red-faced man with bushy white eyebrows and arctic blue eyes named Frank S. Adams. I'd make my presence known to one of his clerks, then retreat to the end of the room to await my summons. "Mr. *Kozner,* city desk," would sound over the PA, and I'd head to the desk, my heart pounding so violently in my chest that I was sure everyone could hear it. Once in his presence, I'd choke out my summary —the college had just announced a joint study program with the Bronx Zoo or something of the sort.

"Give me a D-head, please," Adams would reply, and I'd stumble back to my squatter's typewriter, another ordeal survived.

I knew from my *Times* Manual of Style, which I'd memorized better than my bar mitzvah chant and cribbed for my *Campus* style book, that a D-head was a two- or three-paragraph story that took a two-deck upper- and lower-case headline. A K-head was a single paragraph with a one-deck head, an M-head could be four or five paragraphs with a slick two-deck italic head. After that came real stories a half- or full-column long with real headlines. Most of my CCNY stories were shorts, but I soon got the hang of feature stories for the Sunday paper. My enabler was a sweet-natured little man named Izzy Levine, who handled PR for City College and, with Irv Rosenthal, had recommended me for the *Times* job. Nearly every week, Izzy or I would come up with some cute feature—a prof who collected bugs, a Holocaust survivor who taught himself to play the fiddle left-handed after the Nazis maimed his right, and so on. These stories would turn up in the caboose the next Sunday with rarely a word changed.

Not all my *Times* stories were soft features. Several times, I hit the split page—the first page of the second section of the daily paper, where big local news that didn't make page one was played. One story was about a CCNY professor who was ousted for supposed Communist affiliations. Another, as it happened, was about the college's literary magazine being suspended for printing some dirty words. I called them "earthy colloquialisms," and was thrilled when my phrase survived the copy desk and made it into the *Times*.

Soon, I was the most prolific CCNY correspondent the *Times* had ever had, and I filled a fancy scrapbook with my clips. Still, there were those moments. Once, I reported to the city desk to turn in a three-paragraph caption story and its accompanying photograph. Sitting in Adams's chair was an old boy in shirtsleeves and a vest, a deputy city editor.

I handed him the story faultlessly typed on a "copy book" made up of three or four pages of flimsy paper interleaved with carbon sheets and the picture. He turned over the photo and stared at its blank back.

"Who's this?" he gruffed.

"The person in the story," I replied and hoped my heartbeat didn't drown out my answer.

"How do we know that if you don't write it on the back?" he said with a dismissive wave. "That's simple logic, boy!"

I carefully printed the ID on the photo and crept away, a lesson learned that has endured ever since.

Every last thing that happened to me at the *Times* was fraught with angst. I don't think I ever wanted anything more in my life than to be taken on by the paper in whatever lowly job when I finished college. I read the *Times* with the kind of attention I should have lavished on my schoolwork. I knew where all the foreign correspondents were posted. I lived for each edition of *Winners and Sinners,* the in-house critique of the paper published by its great usage expert, Ted Bernstein. I did—or tried to do—Margaret Farrar's crossword puzzle every day. To me, every M-head and D-head was another tiny step toward my goal. The hint of a smile from Frank Adams was my fix for the week, a blank stare a crushing omen.

Making everything even more dramatic, I had fallen in love. I spotted Alice Nadel one Thursday noon in the fall of 1956 in *The Campus* candidates class—the very same setting I'd wandered into with Chuck Meyers two years before. Now, as managing editor, one of my tasks was to teach the prep class for applicants, and judge which of them should make the staff.

Unlike the other applicants, Alice dressed like Betty Coed, with saddle shoes and a blue camel's-hair coat. She wore her hair in a pixie cut favored by Audrey Hepburn and her eyes were bright with intelligence. Alice, it turned out, had just transferred from Queens College, which she found bland and unchallenging. City College being so big, I'm sure we never would have met had she not decided to join the paper.

We were soon a couple, although given the era, the expression of our love went no farther than what was called heavy petting on the living room sofa of her apartment in Parkchester in the far Bronx while her father, a lawyer, snored away contrapuntally next door. Afterward, I'd slump into a cold plastic bus seat for the forty-five-minute trip back to Washington Heights.

When the spring semester began, I told Alice solemnly that for the next six months I would be totally committed to editing the paper and stringing for the *Times*. Nothing else in my life—even true love—could take precedence. I had already decided that, having lost that April Fool's semester, I'd spend five years at CCNY, pushing my graduation back to June 1958, still shy of my twenty-first birthday. I cut my spring course load to three classes—nine credits—so as not to interfere with my real education. I felt like a journalistic warrior.

The plan worked even better than I'd hoped. *The Campus* pulsed with energy, and I rode the *Times* caboose to a rich haul of clips. Then, in mid-spring, the competing student paper, *Observation Post*, collapsed in staff infighting and exhaustion. Now *The Campus* ruled, and I ruled *The Campus*. I wrote a pompous editorial assuring students and faculty that the paper would use its new power judiciously, and invited the top editors of *OP* to join *Campus* with important titles and roles.

When I returned to school the next fall for my real senior year, I had only emeritus responsibilities at the paper—kibitzer in chief—and I could devote myself to the *Times*, English literature, and writing courses, which I loved, and to my romance with Alice. Although I was just twenty and Alice only eighteen, we were already planning to marry, so eager were we to get away from our parents and make our own life. Then, as the spring term began, *The Campus* was engulfed in a Cold War nightmare that shattered friendships and bred lifelong enmities—and gave me a taste of the radical politics that would roil the next decade.

The paper had been very political in the 1930s, when CCNY was full of brilliant radicals, but by my time little of that fervor survived on campus or in the student papers. Indeed, *The Campus* restricted itself to coverage of the college—the only time larger political issues were dealt with was when visiting speakers brought them up. There were a couple of lefties on the paper. One was a smart, handsome junior named Fred Jerome, a fine writer and tireless editor whose boyish looks and easy manner made him a favorite of many of the women on staff. Jerome, we later learned, was the son of V. J. Jerome, the cultural commissar of the Stalinist wing of the American Communist Party. Another was a husky youth named Jake Rosen, one of the red-diaper babies who lived across the street from me in Washington Heights. Rosen devoted himself to the student council, but turned up at the paper once in a while and was listed on the masthead.

Early in the spring term, small stories began to appear in *The Campus* and the now resurrected *OP* about a world youth festival scheduled for the summer in Moscow. Jerome had gotten the stories into our paper because, among other things, the student council was debating whether CCNY students should join the American delegation to the festival, which was being organized by Communist and Communist-front organizations here and abroad. Years later, the feminist Gloria Steinem would write about how the CIA had covertly recruited her and others to balance the American delegation at such a festival earlier in the decade, but in 1958 we knew nothing of that.

One day midway through the semester, Jerome masterminded a lead story in *The Campus* about the Moscow gathering that mentioned in the third or fourth paragraph a post office box to which interested students could write for more information. Some of us thought the inclusion of the P.O. box in the story was odd, but nothing much was made of it. Then I began getting telephone calls from a mysterious fellow named Walter K. Kirschenbaum, who told me that two CCNY students named Jerome and Rosen had rented the P.O. box and were actually the chief local recruiters for the Communist festival.

All this was taking place in probably the most apolitical moment in twentieth-century American history—that long lull known as the Age of Eisenhower. The McCarthy hysteria had ended and the Communist Party was a joke, shattered by defections after the Soviet invasion of Hungary two years before. The idea that covert Commies were at work at CCNY and using *The*

Campus in their schemes seemed ludicrous. We immediately labeled Kirschenbaum "Walter K. Counterspy." But Kirshenbaum, who was working with some anticommunist socialists and perhaps with the FBI or CIA, was right: Jerome and Rosen were doing just what he said.

Some of us banded together to defend the paper against what plainly was a covert political takeover by Jerome, Rosen, and their comrades. We ran into obstacles right out of the 1930s playbook used by Communists trying to take over American labor unions. Suddenly there was a demand to see a copy of the constitution of the paper, a document nobody knew existed but one that turned up in a filing cabinet somewhere. Then, in a group where all decisions were made by schmoozing, came insistence on all sorts of procedural votes. And when the votes were cast, people like Jacob Rosen, and others who were listed on the masthead but never seen, materialized on cue and voted to support Jerome.

In the end, the affair was settled at a meeting of the editorial board at my apartment. Jerome was represented by one of the former *OP* editors I'd invited to join *The Campus,* who made an eloquent civil-liberties case. When the decisive vote came, friends and lovers (in the fifties sense of the word) found themselves on opposite sides. We narrowly prevailed, but the atmosphere was never the same at the paper and the bitterness lasted for years.

Soon afterward, Rosen led the American contingent to the Moscow festival, where he carried the flag and dipped it to his Soviet hosts as the delegations marched into the stadium. Then he took the group to Peking, where they put on another show.

Although we didn't grasp it at the time—how could we?—we were present at the creation of what later would be called the New Left. Rosen, Jerome, and the other Stalinist offspring were the nucleus of the Progressive Labor Party, a cadre of young Communists who identified with Mao and his permanent revolution rather than with the backsliding Soviets. Progressive Labor was a harbinger of the radical politics of the next decade—the Students for a Democratic Society and, although the Maoists despised them as romantic nihilists, the bomb-happy Weathermen. So *The Campus* provided me not only with a priceless journalistic education, but an insider's introduction to the radical politics that would so preoccupy the media in the sixties and beyond.

Now graduation was approaching, and I had to decide what to do next.

Irv Rosenthal gave me an avuncular pat on the back and assured me that
going to journalism graduate school would be a waste of time. "You're good
enough to get a job right now," he said. The problem was where. The classic
career track in those days was to get a first job at a quality small-town
paper—say, the Quincy *Patriot Ledger* in Massachusetts—and work one's
way back to New York with stops in places like Baltimore or Cleveland.
Somehow, I couldn't picture Ed and Alice up in Quincy, or, in truth, anywhere but New York.

New York was the greatest newspaper town in America. There were four
morning papers, the broadsheet *Times* and its liberal Republican counterpart,
the *Herald Tribune*; two morning tabloids, the *Daily News* and the *Daily
Mirror*, where my friend Jack Schwartz worked as a copyboy; two afternoon
broadsheets, the *Journal-American* and the *World-Telegram & Sun*; and the
tabloid *Post*. There were also four provincial sheets in the metropolitan area—
the *Long Island Press* and *Newsday* in Long Island, the *Brooklyn Eagle*, and the
Bronx Home News, an edition of the *Post*. The papers not only had political
allegiances, they divided the market along ethnic and religious lines. Hearst
owned the *Mirror* and the *Journal-American*, whose readers were mostly Irish
and Roman Catholic. The WASPs read the *Herald Tribune* and the *Telegram;*
the Jews were devoted to the *Times* and the *Post*, which was the most liberal
paper in America. The *News*, with more than 2 million daily circulation and 3
million on Sundays, was the biggest paper in the country, the bible of New
York's cops and firemen, but with many black and some immigrant Hispanic
readers. Both the *News* and the *Mirror* had made inroads in working-class
Jewish neighborhoods, although many Jews shunned the *News* as anti-Semitic.

The only paper I had any contact with was the *Times*, and I spent weeks
agonizing over how to make my approach. I finally decided to tiptoe in. I
wrote a modest note to Frank Adams, the city editor, in which I asked about
"the possibility of employment" at the paper—careful not to mention a
reporter's job so as not to rule out being a news clerk. Each afternoon, I'd call
my mother to see if a letter from the *Times* had come for me. Finally, I came
home to find a small envelope with Adams/City Desk above the *Times* logo
on the back flap. With my heart throbbing and my hands fluttering, I
opened the envelope to find a half sheet of *Times* stationery and read:

Dear Mr. Kosner,
I regret to inform you that there is no possibility of employment
for you at *The New York Times*, and I suggest that you look else-
where.

Yours truly,
Frank S. Adams

Crushed, I read the sentence over and over, hoping that I'd somehow missed an encouraging nuance, but of course there was none. My *Times* dreams had been a pathetic fantasy, and now I had no prospects at all. (I also knew I'd savor the letter decades later if I was a success, and I decided to make it the first item in my correspondence file, where it rests today to be quoted from verbatim.)

6

"I Salute You on the Beginning of a Great Career"

MY NEXT FORAY WAS many steps down from the *Times,* but in a way the outcome was even more disheartening. The *Bergen Evening Record* was published across the river in Hackensack, New Jersey. The *Record* covered every burg and hamlet in Bergen County, assigning reporters to three-town beats where they were expected to write up every brush fire, lost dog, bake sale, and borough council meeting. At the end of each week, they had to clip all their stories, paste them into strips, and measure the number of column-inches they'd managed to fill. The reporters were paid something less than $100 a week, but their checks amounted to about $40 a week before taxes. The rest was kept by the paper and paid out twice a year in the form of a "bonus," determined in part by the volume of advertising the paper carried. Since the ad revenue would vary by no more than 5 percent, this was simply a scam by the Borgs, the family who owned the paper, to keep more than half their staff's wages as a float for sixth months at a time. Quite obviously, there was no union at the *Record,* and that's the way the Borgs wanted to keep it.

Most of the reporters at the *Record* were locals, but in the last several years a couple of CCNY boys had managed to snag jobs there. One of them was a friend, Jack Monet, who covered the metropoli of Little Ferry, Moonachie, and South Hacksensack, working from 3:00 or 4:00 PM to midnight five days a week. Jack was moving on to an even more important beat and suggested that I could replace him. One day, he graciously drove me around his turf so that I could get the feel of it. I accompanied Jack as he chatted up the Moonachie fire chief to get the details of the day's brush fires and copied down the police blotter in Little Ferry. By the time we got to South Hackensack, I was more depressed than I'd ever been, but what alternative did I have?

A few days later, I put on my new Brooks Brothers suit (it looked gray in the store but in daylight it had a distinctly green tinge), put my *Times* scrapbook under my arm, and boarded the Black and Tan bus at the Port Authority Terminal for my interview with the *Record*'s boss, one James Sutphen, in his Hackensack office.

Sutphen greeted me pleasantly enough and listened patiently as I recited my accomplishments as editor of *The Campus* and at the *Times*.

Then, he leaned forward in his chair, fixed me with a piercing look, and said, "But have you ever covered anything where people do things that count?"

I was tempted to say, "You mean like the borough council of Little Ferry?" But I squelched the imp and replied earnestly, "Well, I did cover the ouster of a City College professor for Communist ties for the *Times*."

If this impressed Sutphen, he didn't show it and the interview quickly petered out. "Call me next week," he said as I headed back to the Black and Tan bus station for the long ride home.

When I called the following Tuesday, his voice was flat. "I'm afraid you don't have the experience we're looking for," said Sutphen.

So I'd not only struck out at the *New York Times,* I wasn't even *Bergen Evening Record* material. I'd taken the first two steps toward becoming a professional journalist—and hit a dead end, washed up at twenty.

Just before graduation, *The Campus* held its annual dinner, at which a successful alumnus gave a pep talk to the current staff. At the last minute, Milton Bracker of the *Times* begged off. His replacement was an odd man named Alvin Davis, whose title was night managing editor of the *Post*. Al was a high-strung, baldish, fast-talking guy whose speech was all about the fresh things he was doing on the *Post*'s night side, the midnight to 8:00 AM lobster shift during which a small staff put together the first edition of the tabloid, which came out about 9:00 each morning.

Davis said the paper wasn't interested in the run-of-the-street reporters the other papers had on staff. He wanted offbeat types—the more offbeat the better—people who could dig up stuff by phone in the middle of the night and turn it into lively copy. I listened to Davis's pitch and concluded there was nothing for me in it—he was just trying to make the poor *Campus* kids happy by suggesting there might be some new kind of future for them.

"You should write to him tomorrow and apply," said Alice after the dinner.

"It's all bullshit," I said.

"What do you have to lose?" she replied with unanswerable logic.

Certain I was wasting my time, I wrote the letter to Davis.

I'd forgotten all about it a couple of weeks later when the telephone woke me up at 8:30 on Tuesday morning. When I picked up the receiver, I could hear the unmistakable teletype and typewriter clatter that could only come from a newsroom.

"This is Al Davis at the *Post*," he said over the din, and invited me to come to the paper at 1:00 AM for a one-night tryout on night rewrite.

Now even I recognized that a one-night tryout at the *New York Post* was about as long a shot as journalism could offer, but I decided to treat it as a serious opportunity. *What did I have to lose?* Although I'd never been inside an evening paper, I had some idea of how one operated: a lot of the back-of-the-paper filler—and some of the front—was rewritten from stories in the morning papers, with a fresh, or second-day, lead tacked on. So if the *News* and the *Mirror* had stories about a grocery store owner shot in a holdup, the *Post* story next day would begin, "Police were scouring the Lower East Side today for the hungry woman bandit who shot an Avenue A bodega owner and stole $250 and two cantaloupes." The headline would read:

COPS HUNT
MELON MOLL

I calculated that I'd get a lot of shorts to rewrite. So I went out and bought the *Times, Trib, News,* and *Mirror,* scissored out each paper's version of a dozen minor stories, clipped together little packets of the stories, and put them in one of my mother's mixing bowls. Then I put the bowl on the table in my room, opened my portable typewriter, and placed my alarm clock next to it. I'd set the clock on the hour, reach in the bowl, and grab a packet at random—and give myself ten minutes to rewrite the clips into a two- or three-paragraph *Post* short. I kept at it until I'd emptied the bowl.

Before reporting to the *Post,* I had a burger with Chuck Meyers and then we had a couple of Scotches. Chuck walked me to the 181st Street subway station. As I descended the fetid stairs just at midnight, he waved and announced, "I salute you on the beginning of a great career," which we both knew were the words Emerson wrote to Whitman after the poet, soliciting the first blurb in American literary history, had sent him the first edition of *Leaves of Grass*.

7

DEVIL'S ISLAND

I FOUND MY WAY down to the *Post*'s neighborhood just north of the Battery and walked the empty streets, passing the grave of Alexander Hamilton in Trinity churchyard. I walked into the silent, dingy *Post* lobby, so different from the throbbing *Times,* and slipped into the city room, a big, dreary place with rows of empty desks and three or four people slouched at typewriters clustered around two large metal desks pushed together. The filthy windows were open to the banana boat piers on the Hudson across West Street, and big standing fans pushed around the hot, moist late spring air.

I introduced myself and settled at one of the typewriters ringing what turned out to be the city desk, a Viceroy dangling from my lips, the rest of the pack poised at my elbow. In a few minutes, the night city editor handed me a little packet of clips that looked remarkably like the ones I'd tossed in my mother's mixing bowl.

"Gimme two graphs on this," he commanded.

Unfurling the clips, I found the *News* and *Mirror* versions of a story about a woman who died when her car flipped over on a ramp in the parking garage of the Bergen Mall—probably one of Sutphen's *Bergen Record* readers I'd never write for.

Now a practiced hand at this kind of thing, I whipped off two paragraphs in five minutes and handed over the cleanly typed copy. The city editor looked a little startled, but he put paragraph hooks on my piece and sent it over to the copy desk. Then he handed me another pack of clippings.

"A book and a paragraph," he said, meaning four or five paragraphs.

And so it went through the night. About 2:30 a copy boy came around taking orders from "the Greek," an all-night hole-in-the-wall a few blocks away. Soon he set next to me a fried-egg sandwich on a roll, the grease turning the brown bag translucent, and a container of coffee. I gagged down the sandwich and lit another Viceroy.

Around 5:00 AM the sky outside the open windows began to lighten, and then it was 7:30. Barely seven hours had passed since I'd first walked into the *Post,* but it felt like seven years.

"Good job, kid. Come back tomorrow night," said Al Davis as he dismissed me with a breezy wave.

The *Post* in those days was unlike any other American newspaper, a distinction it still holds nearly a half century later under Rupert Murdoch. The paper had been founded in 1801 by Alexander Hamilton, who now reposed just a few blocks away, doubtlessly in full rotation considering the liberal slant his spawn had taken. Through most of its life, the *Post* had been a dull, conservative broadsheet. That all changed when Dorothy Schiff, an Our Crowd banking heiress, bought the paper in 1939 and later turned it into a crusading left-wing tabloid. Over the years, she had been married several times, and successive husbands had been installed as her paper's editor or publisher or both, with predictable results.

By the time I showed up, Dolly's amours were mostly exhausted, and Jimmie Wechsler was the editor. A short, energetic man with tousled salt-and-pepper hair and a trademark bow tie, Wechsler was a liberal icon—a courageous crusader against Joe McCarthy and J. Edgar Hoover and an inspired polemicist. Wechsler mostly concerned himself with the political stories, the editorials, and the *Post*'s stellar array of columnists, among them Max Lerner and Murray Kempton. The rest of the paper was under the red ballpoint pen of Paul Sann, the Sancho Panza to Wechsler's Quixote. Sann affected a crew cut, all-black outfits, and cowboy boots, and talked like a character out of a road company of *The Front Page.* He was a tabloid wizard whose page-one headlines like

**AVA
KICKS
FRANKIE
OUT**

were famous long before the Murdoch era's.

HEADLESS BODY
IN TOPLESS BAR

Sann's pages mixed mob, murder, and celebrity tales with sob stories about homeless Puerto Ricans, gouging slumlords, and police brutality. There were heavily researched, skillfully written week-long series on life in Westport or Scarsdale that were masterworks of pop sociology. And there were the *Post*'s justifiably celebrated sports pages, with marquee columnists like Jimmy Cannon and Milton Gross and the best beat writers in the business covering the New York teams.

And then there was Davis's night side, a semiautonomous enterprise that was even more peculiar than the rest of the paper. The *Post* night side was a kind of Devil's Island of journalism, with each inmate more exotic than the next. When I arrived, the night city editor was a little man with a crew cut whose name was William H. A. Carr, a cat fancier (he also wrote the Saturday pet column) with radical roots in the Midwest. His deputy was a cadaverous man named Paul Capron, who looked like Boris Karloff, chain-smoked Navy Cut British cigarettes, and, so the legend went, had been banished from West Point for romancing the superintendent's daughter. On Friday nights, the desk was run by a tall, laconic man with a *N'Orleans* accent named Stan Opotowsky, who had dropped out of school at fifteen to join the *New Orleans States-Item*. He was the fastest and best rewrite man anyone had ever seen and a superb reporter regularly dispatched by the *Post* to cover civil-rights atrocities like the Mississippi murders of Goodman, Schwerner, and Chaney.

But the real stars of the night side were the rewrite men, who worked stories on the phone, took feeds from street reporters and stringers, and routinely churned out five or six substantial stories each shift. One was Gene Smith, a pompous young guy addicted to tear-jerking narratives—dubbed Smithereens by Smith's unimpressed colleagues—in which the protagonist died in the last sentence. Another was a chubby, uneasy man named Alfred G. Aronowitz, who drove in from suburban Jersey each night in his Triumph roadster and wrote nonstop until the 7:45 AM final deadline. Aronowitz knew all about everything and was a magician on the headset, charming information out of provincial cops and hotel clerks, then writing his tales with verve.

The *Post* night side also boasted the only female night rewrite man in the city and likely the country—Betsy Luce, a tall, spinsterish woman who wrote most of the straight news while Smith and Aronowitz spun the feature stuff. All night long Betsy sipped from a white mug labeled with her name in nail polish. "Betsy sure drinks a lot of coffee," I remarked to someone early on, only to be greeted with an odd look. It turned out that Betsy's coffee was mostly Old Taylor bourbon. After work, she drove back to Hastings-on-Hudson in a white Cadillac El Dorado convertible.

I was just another curiosity in Davis's sideshow, a skinny, nervous twenty-year-old who puffed away on those Viceroys and who could write tabloid stories as if he were born in the city room. My two nights stretched into a week, then a second, and finally I was signed on for a full three-month trial, the maximum the union contract would allow.

"You're a freak," Davis told me one night with a congratulatory pat on the back.

Soon I was trusted to write major stories—page leads—that would have carried bylines if the *Post* awarded bylines to tryout writers. I did get my name in the paper by contributing a full-page profile to the Saturday magazine section. It was about a character named Harry Golden, a matzo-barrel philosopher who published an idiosyncratic newspaper called *The Carolina Israelite* in which he crusaded in a *haimish* way for racial integration. Trying to show my stuff, I overwrote the piece so much that one of the mocking old boys on the copy desk labeled me "young Thomas Wolfe."

The *Post* staffed police headquarters in Manhattan and Brooklyn from 6:00 AM until 3:00 AM and the other boroughs throughout the day. So from 3:00 AM until the Manhattan and Brooklyn shacks opened at six, the paper had no police coverage at all except for the City News Service, which was run by the Associated Press. During that three-hour period, the only word the city desk had of crimes or fires anywhere in the city came in one-sentence AP alerts that clattered off the teletypes in the wire room.

POLICE HEADQUARTERS REPORTS A HOMICIDE AT AVENUE R IN SHEEPSHEAD BAY, BROOKLYN. THIS OFFICE NOT COVERING,

one of them would read. One of the rewrite men would call the precinct to get some detail. Often the killing turned out to be a "social note" or "cheap"—code for black-on-black crime deemed unworthy of space even in the bleeding-heart *Post*. But if the crime happened to be a decent story, the city editor would turn to me and say, "Get out there."

I dreaded those moments. For one thing, I had never set foot in a police station until I came to the paper. I knew nothing of the elaborate protocol involved in addressing desk sergeants and the almighty "loots"—the lieutenants who ran precincts at night. I didn't know, for example, that "the 124 man" was the record-keeping cop who had the basic facts of an arrest on a card. I didn't know that the detective squad was usually on the second floor of the station house and that the lock on the wooden gate at the front of the room opened by pressing up on the inner edge. So I fumbled and bumbled when invited in, touching off derisive hilarity. I didn't know that when detectives were said to be "out hunting down leads" in the middle of the night, they were actually on "pillow patrol',' sacked out on cots upstairs. What I did know was that most cops hated the *Post*, which was always nattering about police brutality.

On top of that, the *Post*, unlike many of the other papers, had no radio-equipped staff cars for photographers and reporters. There were few cabs to be found at 4:00 AM around the paper. And, unlike today, there were hardly any street-corner telephones. The only cell phone was Dick Tracy's two-way wrist radio in the funny papers.

I often found myself dashing madly out of the *Post* building and desperately hunting a cab in the middle of the night, knowing that once I got to the precinct or crime scene in far-off Brooklyn or Queens, I'd have to get the story and then find a way to call it in from some all-night beanery.

Once, covering a teenage gang killing in Brooklyn, I got the mother of one of the suspects to open her door by waving my press card, which was conveniently shaped like a police badge, and letting her think I was a cop. We stood in the kitchen while giant cockroaches crawled on the peeling yellow walls.

"Ramon is a good boy," she told me. "He's going to continuation school."

Thrilled that I'd actually got a quote, I found a telephone in a luncheon-ette and called the city desk.

"Whatcha got, kid?" said Bill Carr.

"I talked to the mother of one of the suspects and she said, "Ramon . . .""

". . . is a good boy and he's going to continuation school," Carr finished my sentence for me.

"Go back, and ask her if Ramon's continuation school was in a place upstate called Dannemora."

"What do you mean, Bill?"

"He was in reform school, kid. The mothers always call it continuation school."

I trotted back to Ramon's mother, who patiently opened the door again and confirmed that her boy had indeed matriculated at the state facility in Dannemora.

"You were right, Bill," I said when I called Carr back.

"You'll learn, kid," he sighed.

Another time, I called Carr breathlessly from a fire to report that the family pooch was the only survivor of a tenement blaze.

"You got a quote from the dog, didn't you?" Carr deadpanned.

I was halfway through my explanation of why I missed the quote before I caught on.

My first crisis came about a month after I arrived at the paper. Carr handed me a slip about a double homicide in Staten Island. "This could be big," he said.

I ran out of the city room and down the empty, echoing streets looking for a cab. None had turned up by the time I got to the ferry terminal so I waited for the next boat, enveloped in despair. A half hour later, I found a cab at the Staten Island end and had him take me to the precinct, where I paid him off and tore inside like a madman.

"They're all at the scene," said the desk sergeant, practically giggling at the notion that a police reporter could be dumb enough not to know that the detectives would be working a double murder at the crime scene, not the station house.

That had been my first mistake. My second was to dismiss the cab before I knew where I was going. So I made another crazed dash back toward the ferry, where I managed to snag another taxi for the long ride to the scene, the U.S. Public Health Service hospital.

When I got there, I found my competition: two old hands from the *Journal-American* and the *Telegram,* who lived on Staten Island and were bosom buddies of the cops investigating the crime. And it was a sensational story: A young doctor at the hospital and his wife had been found stabbed to death in their beds. There was no sign of forced entry in their cottage next to the hospital and the only suspect was . . . their eight-year-old son Melvin!

By now it was after 5:00 AM, and that's all I knew. No descriptions, no detail about the wounds, about the victims, about the improbable suspect, about anything. Every time I tried to talk to a cop, he'd scuttle away and start gabbing with my nemeses from the *Journal* and the *Telegram*. It soon dawned on me what was going on: The convention at the time was for police reporters to pool information so that nobody would be embarrassed. The kernels you shared today would be redeemed next day or next week when your buddies helped you out in a pinch. But I wasn't part of the circle and was being frozen out—and the cops were playing along for the sheer pleasure of screwing the *Post*.

My life didn't pass before my eyes over the next hour, but my future did: I'd blow my first big story, the paper would be badly beaten because of my failure, my tryout would be terminated, and I'd be left without hope of getting a shot elsewhere. I could imagine the conversation in other city rooms:

Kosner. Wasn't he the kid who blew the Nimer murder at the Post? *What do we need him for?*

And without a job, I wouldn't be able to marry Alice and start our brave new life.

By 6:00 AM I was so panic-stricken I could hardly stand. And then the two old reporters decided I'd been tortured enough. They gave me enough of a fill so that I could call the desk in time for the first edition. Afterward, I stood outside the hospital waiting for the reporter who would relieve me, more exhausted than I could ever remember being.

Precisely at eight, a day side reporter named Tony Scaduto arrived to take over. Tony was clean-shaven and bright-eyed with a spring in his step as he gazed at the drained creature before him. "Helluva story, huh?" said Tony. *If he only knew,* I thought to myself.

As I started to head for the ferry, another old boy pulled up in a gray Checker sedan with the familiar *Daily News* camera logo on the door. "Want a lift to the ferry, kid?" asked the driver. He turned out to be one of a legendary pair of Doyle brothers who covered police for the *News,* the cops' favorite New York paper.

"Been on the street long, kid?" Doyle asked pleasantly, as if he couldn't tell the answer with one glance at his spent passenger.

"This is my third week," I confessed.

"Got two dead?"

I assured him that I did.

"You'll be all right, kid," said Doyle as we pulled up at the ferry terminal.

I made it through the summer with no further close calls, although I tensed up at 3:00 AM each night and couldn't breathe normally until six, when the switchboard operator announced that the Manhattan and Brooklyn police shacks had checked in. Now all I had to worry about was having to write a big story on deadline. One morning I did—a massive subway delay just as the rush hour was beginning—and was amazed to find it the page-one lead, called "the wood" because the three- or four-inch headline letters were actually made of wood.

With that I relaxed a bit, although I kept having a nightmare in which I was trying to write the wood story as the clock moved inexorably toward the deadline. I'd write the lead and second paragraph and be starting on the third when I'd suddenly realize that the first paragraph wasn't right. I'd fix the lead only to find that the second paragraph now was screwed up. Every time I fixed one thing, another wouldn't work—until I woke up sweat-soaked and nearly quivering.

Still, I knew that I'd done so well on my three-month tryout that I'd likely be hired when it ended in mid-September. But when the big day came, Al Davis had bad news: the paper had reclassified my trial as a summer replacement and now I'd have to go through another three-month tryout. With Frank Adams's snub, Jim Sutphen's rejection, and the *Post*'s shenanigans, I was beginning to feel fated to fail. But I had no choice except to press on. Within a month, another big test arose without warning.

On October 23, 1958, in Spring Hill, Nova Scotia, a mine shaft collapsed, trapping 174 miners miles underground. Seventy-five died and eighty were rescued in the first effort. Twelve more were rescued six days later and all hope was given up for the last seven.

In those days, my workweek ran from Monday night through Saturday morning. I loved the Friday night shift because the Saturday paper was small, the first edition deadline was early, and the pressure was off. In fact, the hours right after deadline Saturday morning were the most relaxed in the six-day publishing cycle of the paper. On Saturday morning, July 28, 1945, the *Post*'s news editor became a legend when he stood up and announced that he was going for a quick haircut. "Don't call me unless a plane hits the Empire State Building," he called over his shoulder as he strolled out of the city room. At 9:49 AM, an army twin-engine B-25 bomber bound for Newark Airport in the fog crashed into the seventieth floor of the skyscraper. At the *Post,* they couldn't figure out how to call him at the barber's without the news editor thinking it was their sick idea of a joke.

This Saturday morning in early November 1958 the skeleton rewrite staff was waiting around for the first editions to come up from the press room before heading home or out for a morning drink. Stan Opotowsky, the Friday night city editor, was leafing through the late edition of one of the morning tabs, smoking a king-size Chesterfield with his long legs up on the city desk when a copy boy came dashing over with a piece of wire copy: With all hope lost, seven more miners had miraculously been found alive at Spring Hill twelve days after the collapse.

I was riveted by the news—and by my own fear. Opotowsky, the ultimate pro, was going to handle this, but was I? The mine disaster story was supposed to be over and there were no more reporters in Spring Hill, not even stringers. There was, of course, no all-news radio or CNN to crib from. All Stan had was the AP and three rewrite men, one of them a scared-stiff twenty-one-year-old. How was I going to write a big dramatic story under such pressure? What if I choked?

I've never forgotten the next couple of hours and the lesson they taught me. Opotowsky sprang into action, which meant that he took his feet down from the city desk, lit another Chesterfield, asked when the next deadline was, and started scribbling a story list on a little yellow pad. He instructed Ben Green, the switchboard operator, to get from the long-distance operator any phone numbers in Spring Hill, ring them, and switch the call over to Stan if he reached anyone. Sure enough, Green got a couple of locals to answer their phones and Stan in his soft *N'orleans* way asked them to run over to the minehead, get any information they could, try to talk to the survivors or to relatives, and then call him back collect. All the while, he was sorting the wire copy into little piles that matched the stories and sidebars on his list. Then he stood up and went from typewriter to typewriter on the rewrite bank. At each, he wrote the lead paragraph of a story, then handed a wad of wire copy to the rewrite man whose seat he'd borrowed. At my desk, he wrote a lead about the cascade of dramatic vignettes triggered by the amazing rescue. He handed me some wire copy.

"Just keep it coming. Don't worry about the sequence or numbering the pages or anything," he said. "I'll take care of it."

Then he went back to his place at the desk, put his feet up, and lit yet another Chesterfield, the calmest man in the city at that moment.

And, of course, I wrote longer, faster, and better than I ever had before and probably since. I'd toss each take over to Stan and he'd toss back some more wire copy. So did the other rewrite men. The instant stringers from Spring Hill started calling in and we began inserting their quotes and color into our pieces. Before I realized what was happening, all the stories were written and edited and Stan was working on an amplified story list for the replate.

Watching Opotowsky, I understood the root of his confidence: Stan knew that if we all passed out at our typewriters, he could write all the stories himself—and he could lay out all the pages and write all the headlines, too, if he had to. He could do all the jobs himself, so of course he was calm. What was there to worry about? He had Stan. I had felt that way on *The Campus,* but not since. I resolved that I would be like Stan and master that same poise under pressure. The memory of what he did that day so long ago would come back to me at every big news moment of my career—the space flights, the Kennedy and King assassinations, Watergate, the Jonestown suicides, the "tied" 2000 presidential election, 9/11, and the war in Iraq, and I'd smile to myself and be Stan the man.

Just as my second three-month tryout was ending, the *Post* was hit by a wildcat strike of the drivers who delivered the papers. The deliverers' union was notoriously corrupt, and Dolly Schiff was famously parsimonious— always pleading for favorable contract terms from the unions because her poor, liberal, underdog paper was so needy, so the ingredients for calamity were always present. The *Post* tried to publish by selling copies right out of the lobby of the building, but that scheme soon collapsed and the paper shut down while its competitors kept publishing. The strike ended in a couple of days, but to hear Dolly tell it, the damage was profound, so serious that she announced a freeze on any new staff hiring. The only person about to be hired was me, and now I knew that I was destined never to get a break in journalism. But at the last moment, Davis wangled an exception and I officially joined the night rewrite bank of the paper.

Carr was replaced on the desk by a small, kind man named Bob Friedman, whose last job in journalism was as managing editor of the *Daily Worker*. Friedman had quit the *Worker* and the American Communist Party in the great 1956 defection after the brutal Soviet suppression of the Hungarian rebellion. About 3:30 or four each morning, Friedman would awake from a reverie to find himself sitting at the night city desk of the *New York Post* and a poignant Talmudic sigh would escape his chest. I'd answer with a one of my own and our brief sighing serenade would momentarily break the monotony.

One night, a copy editor and rewrite man named Ernie Tidyman was assigned an obituary of Joel Chandler Harris, the author of the *Uncle Remus* stories, written in black dialect about Br'er Rabbit, Br'er Fox, and the Tar Baby. Tidyman wrote a straight version and then one narrated in dialect by Uncle Remus himself. The straight version was sent to the composing room, but no carbon copy was left in Al Davis's in-box, which he scrutinized when he showed up at 2:00 or 3:00 AM Instead, a carbon of the Uncle Remus version was placed at the bottom of Davis's dupes.

In the hours leading up to deadline, the inside pages of the paper, where relatively minor stories filled out the spaces around the Alexanders' ads, were made up and sent to the press room. Davis showed up and began working his way slowly though the carbons. Suddenly, about 5:30 AM, he leaped from his chair clutching a couple of sheets of paper and dashed like a crazed water buffalo through the swinging doors to the clattering composing room.

He'd fallen for Tidyman's stunt: He'd suddenly realized his night side madmen were about to run a story in Negro dialect in America's most liberal newspaper and that a nuclear bomb was now being locked onto the presses! When one of the composing room dummies—as the deaf-mutes who worked there were affectionately called—showed him the straight obit that was running, Davis realized he'd been had and plodded back to his desk in the newsroom with a sheepish grin on his still-red face. Tidyman survived the night, and went on to riches and some fame writing the *Shaft* novels about the black detective and the screenplays for *The French Connection* and *High Plains Drifter*.

Killing time on other long lobster shifts, the rewrite men amused each
other with mordant mind games. A favorite was devising the best shortest
wood. The winner was

POPE
ELOPES

Amid all these characters, by any measure the oddest figure was a tiny
man named Dexter Teed. In his tweed jacket with leather elbow patches and
with his neatly trimmed brush mustache, Dexter could have passed for a
1950s version of Melville's Bartleby the Scrivener. Each night, he silently
turned out the Press Digest, a compilation of excerpts from the editorial
pages of the other papers that ran right under the Herblock cartoon on
Wechsler's page. After he handed in his copy, he toddled off into the night
to Julius's, a Village bar, where he tanked up until closing, then came back
to the paper to write make-work obituaries that never ran.

Just before dawn one morning, somebody glanced over at Dexter's desk
in the corner and saw him slumped over his Royal. While nobody was
looking, and without a sound, Teed had fulfilled the newspaper man's ultimate destiny—he'd died at his typewriter. Dexter was reverently laid out
across a couple of desks and covered with sheets of the morning papers to
await the police and his son, who showed up dazed a couple of hours later
to formally identify his old man. "Get me the clips on Dexter Teed," somebody on the desk commanded, and a rewrite man went to work on his brief
obituary. In it, we learned that Teed, among many accomplishments, had
given the sports teams at his beloved upstate Colgate the name Red Raiders
of the Chenango.

Over the next four and a half years I learned everything there was to know
about raffish, inventive tabloid journalism. The work was nothing like the
earnest, scrupulous reporting and writing I'd ached to do at the *Times,* but I
found it seductively engaging. A lot of it was trivial and nearly all of it was
low-rent, but it was almost always fun.

I learned how much information could be scrounged up in the middle of
the night with a telephone—finding politicians, sheriffs' deputies, celebrities,

eyewitnesses to disasters, victims, and survivors. I quickly grasped that people were unreasonably willing to start blabbing to a stranger who wakes them up at 3:30 in the morning. And that they sometimes revealed themselves in especially illuminating ways. One night, I woke up the Reverend Dr. Martin Luther King, in Atlanta to get a comment about some civil rights development. King answered the phone sleepily, but immediately snapped into form.

"I would say, comma," he dictated, and rattled off a useful quote that I was careful to capture verbatim.

Years later at *Newsweek,* I could never think of King without remembering the calculated professionalism he showed in the middle of the night years before. Preacher and moral icon, Martin Luther King was a politician so skilled that he made the pols look like amateurs.

I learned that with a few clips, and perhaps a phone call or two, I could write in a half hour a confident obituary of Sergeant York, Marion Davies, or some other luminary from another age I'd barely heard of. I learned to write dateline stories full of local color and sparkly quotes while chained to my typewriter on West Street. I wrote up a backstage robbery at *The Sound of Music* as a Rodgers and Hammerstein musical with parody lyrics from *Carousel* and *South Pacific.* When the *New Yorker*'s theater critic, Kenneth Tynan, got into a silly spat with producer David Merrick, I wrote it as a parody of The Talk of the Town.

Once, I was assigned the holiday roundup and did it as an acrostic. The first paragraph read "T is for the turkey that little Tommy Jones feasted on at a Lower East Side settlement house" and the first letters of the twelve paragraphs spelled out T H A N K S G I V I N G. After deadline, I sat at my typewriter, dazzled by my own ingenuity. Out of the corner of my eye, I saw Paul Sann, the executive editor, scribble something on a galley proof with his signature red ballpoint and hand it to a copy boy, who headed in my direction. A compliment from Sann was rare, but I knew my acrostic was worthy of one. Savoring the moment, I opened the folded proof.

Sann had circled one letter in

T H A N K S G I V I N G

and written in his precise hand, *And S is for shit!*

That kind of tough love—or sadism—was the style at the *Post* and other papers. Rookie or veteran, no one was coddled—indeed, to be talked to gently was a sign of *dis*respect. It meant you were so lame you couldn't be treated like a regular reporter. Sann was right, in his way. Inventive as it was, my acrostic was precious, a clever evasion of the fundamental tabloid task of stringing the holiday giblets together without showing off.

I was quick enough to pick up the management style. After toiling at night for a couple of years, I was elevated to be day side assistant city editor. This meant that, starting at six each morning, I'd sit across from the city editor, Johnny Bott, handling reporters on the phone, editing the stories Johnny didn't, and generally being helpful. Taking my cues from my elders, I was the hardest-bitten kid assistant day side city editor journalism had ever seen.

On the city desk one morning at nine, I looked up from my English muffin and was startled to see a dark-haired, self-possessed young woman of about my age sitting opposite me. Bott and the other top editors had gone over to Sann's side of the city room for the morning conference. The young woman had walked in, surveyed the scene, and plunked herself into the only big executive chair in sight.

"I'm Nora Ephron," she said. "And what should I do?"

"The first thing you should do," I replied, "is get your ass out of the city editor's chair and go sit over there."

Nora's parents were friendly with Dolly, who had arranged a day side tryout for their daughter, who turned out to be one of the most talented comic writers and movie directors of our time, the creator of *Sleepless in Seattle* and other hits. Nora, who had been a fact checker at *Newsweek,* did indeed have a short but productive run at the *Post* before going on to better things and has been a friend ever since our first grim encounter.

Not long after that, another young tryout showed up. Her name was Charlotte Curtis. She came from Columbus, Ohio, and was at the paper because she was a friend of a tall, amiable drunk named Gene Grove, who had wangled a night rewrite job at the *Post.* Charlotte was given a desk just behind me. One morning we got word of a possible kidnapping at Columbus Hospital, which in those days was on Eighteenth Street. I whirled around, saw that Curtis was the only reporter in sight, and ordered her to get to the hospital.

"Can you tell me where it is?" she said reasonably enough.

How was Charlotte to know that at the macho *Post,* a reporter—even an out-of-towner—was never supposed to ask how to get to an assignment. You were to dash out of the city room—and if you didn't know where you were going, you'd surreptitiously call the switchboard from the pay phone in the lobby and get the directions.

"That's for you to find out," I snapped and turned my back.

Charlotte's tryout at the *Post* was a sham. She'd already been hired by the *Times,* and Grove was just scoring her a couple of weeks' pay until she started on Forty-third Street. She became the nonpareil social reporter of her time, a chronicler of the '60s and '70s in New York whose work is still admired. Years later, when we'd run into each other at parties around New York, Charlotte would be kind about my bad manners that morning.

One midnight in 1960, when I was still working on the night city desk, yet another young tryout wandered in. He was in his early twenties, handsome in an Irish pug way. He was dressed in a short-sleeved shirt open at the collar and carried a copy of Malcolm Lowry's *Under the Volcano.* He introduced himself as Pete Hamill and said Jimmy Wechsler had arranged a night side tryout for him.

We all snickered at the name. It had been attached to a long letter to the editor Wechsler had published a few weeks earlier on the editorial page, one of those "we-are-the-youth-of-America-and-we-are-disgusted-by-the-conformity-of-the-Eisenhower-Age" plaints. Hamill had been in the navy and spent a year at Mexico City College on the G.I. Bill, but his only brush with journalism had been as art director of a Greek-American magazine. Still, Wechsler was impressed enough by his letter to give him a shot.

Pete had never been in a city room before, and even hard-nosed young Kosner felt for him. I gave him a batch of the copy "books" we used—three sheets of copy paper interleaved with two carbon sheets, the whole folded in half diagonally by the copy boys. I showed him how to type his name in the upper left-hand corner of the first page with a slash and then the "slug," the word or phrase identifying the story: *rob, rape, transit, storm,* or some such. "If it's a murder," I cautioned, "don't slug it *kill*—that means kill the story. Slug it *slay.* And don't write *-30-* at the end. They only do that in the movies. Just write or type a #."

Hamill rewrote a few shorts and, toward the end of the shift, he was given a story about a workingman who had lost a leg in an accident. Pete made some phone calls and then laboriously began writing the piece. When he was finished, he'd turned out two books and a paragraph—250 or 300 words—that were so good his maiden story ran at the bottom of page three or five in the first edition that day.

Thus began one of the stellar writing careers of our time, and for me a life-long friendship and collaboration in which we worked together not only at the *Post* but also at *New York* magazine, *Esquire,* and the *Daily News.* Over nearly half a century, Pete has distinguished himself as a reporter, foreign correspondent, columnist, best-selling novelist (*Snow in August, Loving Women, Forever*), screenwriter, and memoirist (*A Drinking Life*). He's the only man to serve, if briefly, as editor in chief of both the *Daily News* and the *Post* and is revered not just for his talent, but for his generosity to other writers.

Pete soon wrote his way onto the staff and hooked up with Al Aronowitz on a run of amazing celebrity series crashed on (actually, often *after*) deadline. One was prompted by Ernest Hemingway's suicide in 1961, another by the death of Marilyn Monroe the following year, a third by the arrival of the Beatles. These series were full of facts and quotes and written in a fluid magazine style unknown in the newspapers of the day.

The Dolly Schiff *Post* is mostly remembered today for its bleeding-heart liberal politics. Opotowsky used to joke that Wechsler's editorial the day after the Soviets nuked New York would begin: "What did we do to provoke Moscow?" But the real hallmark of the paper was the ambitious series it published. Weeks, sometimes months, were lavished on these efforts, with teams of reporters and researchers contributing material to writers who managed to synthesize it all in six or twelve installments. The subjects ranged from dance studios to life in Levittown to teenagers and sex. For that one, I had to slink into high schools and ask sophomores how often they masturbated.

After a famous multiweek exposé of Walter Winchell, still the most widely read—and most vindictive—gossip columnist in the land, the *Post* decided to take on the holy of holies: J. Edgar Hoover and the F.B.I. Hoover had practically invented publicity spin, and he and his G-men were near-universal paragons of patriotism and rectitude. Exposing Hoover's mythmaking, the bureau's hushed-up misadventures, and the peculiar friendship between Hoover and his deputy, tall, handsome Clyde Tolson, was courageous—reckless, actually. The country had barely emerged from the McCarthy era, and an accusation of being soft on communism could still end careers—or publications. After months of work, the FBI series was hopelessly bogged down, but the *Post* was indelibly identified with it, and the project had to be rescued. Al Davis was put in charge of the salvage operation, and he drafted me to help.

I was stashed in an upstairs office that was shared by two remarkable men: Murray Kempton, then the *Post*'s labor columnist, later to be recognized as the successor to H. L. Mencken, another son of Baltimore, as the most elegant, erudite, and original essayist in American journalism. The other was an odd duck named Bill Dufty, who helped Wechsler put out the *Post*'s editorial page and in his spare time ghostwrote Billie Holiday's autobiography, *Lady Sings the Blues,* which began with these famous and apocryphal lines: "Mom and Pop were just a couple of kids when they got married. He was 18, she was 16 and I was 3." Dufty and Al Davis were hippies in the original sense of the word: whites who tried to hang out with black jazz musicians. Indeed, Dufty was cool before the concept was invented. Years later he became a crusader against refined sugar and married Gloria Swanson, even then long past her *Sunset Boulevard* afterlife.

Now twenty-two, I sat dazzled hour after hour in that office listening to what was actually a single, endless, oblique, elliptical conversation between Kempton and Dufty. From one day to the next the ostensible topic might be politics or jazz, painters of *Quattrocento* Florence, or Willie Mays, but the real subject was the joy of *knowing.* Sometimes there would simply be an exchange of opinions on, say, whether Thelonious Monk or Charlie Parker was the greater artist. But without even a hip fake, Dufty or Kempton would suddenly turn ironic and argue the exact opposite of what he believed. The other would take the cue and invert his own case, then the talk would dart off in a fresh, boggling tangent. I had simply never heard anything like it. In a sense, I felt as out of my depth as I had in Dr. Harwell's advanced chemistry class at Bronx Science. But while I never envied the tyro chemists, I knew that I could never think of myself as sophisticated—Al Davis's favorite term of approval—until I could attain the fluency Dufty and Kempton flaunted so offhandedly.

Despite the siren song of Dufty and Kempton, I did a lot of work on the FBI series. I read years of references to the bureau in the columns of Winchell, Westbrook Pegler, and George Sokolsky, Hoover fans all. I became an instant expert on the Rosenberg espionage case, tracking how evidence gathered by the FBI led to their executions and how it was challenged by leftist lawyers in their endless and ultimately unsuccessful appeals.

Remarkably, the *Post* sent me to Los Angeles for ten days to do a single piece for the series on the making of a hagiographic movie called *The FBI Story*, which starred Jimmy Stewart as a heroic agent and was directed by Mervyn LeRoy, who, appropriately enough, had produced *The Wizard of Oz*. My mission was to uncover evidence of FBI pressure to make the movie even more idolatrous. LeRoy and Stewart refused to talk to me, but I did manage some surreptitious meetings with a couple of New York performers who played supporting roles, including Murray Hamilton, a wonderful character actor who had a thirty-five-year career in movies and TV. Hamilton, or another of them, slipped me a script, but all I could come up with was a mildly entertaining feature piece without a hint of FBI tampering.

I basically struck out again on my other FBI reporting adventure, this one to Washington, where people were even more reluctant to dish dirt on Hoover than they were in Hollywood. As it happened, the trip to the capital almost ruined my life and career just as it was starting, but I didn't learn that chilling story until twenty years later.

Davis put me up at the Raleigh Hotel, a few steps from FBI headquarters at the Department of Justice. It would be nice to think that he chose the hotel to inspire me with a glimpse of my prey, but the truth was that the *Post* held a due bill from the Raleigh for some bartered advertising, so my trip was essentially on the cuff. In Washington, hardly anyone would talk to me except Joe Rauh, the head of the very liberal Americans for Democratic Action and an old chum of Wechsler's, and a nice elderly gent named John Carroll, a Democratic senator from Colorado who wanted to help but didn't have much to offer. I hardly knew anyone in Washington, so at the end of each fruitless day I'd have a couple of drinks and dinner alone at a depressing little German restaurant near the hotel, then return to my lonely room and read the *Congressional Record*. Finally, I exhausted my few contacts, and went back to New York.

Nearly twenty years later, now the editor of *Newsweek*, I got a phone call from a *New York Times* reporter named John Crewdson, who was investigating dirty tricks by the FBI and CIA during the Cold War.

"Are you the Ed Kosner who worked for the *New York Post* and stayed at the Raleigh Hotel in Washington in 1959?" asked Crewdson.

"Yes, I was working on a series on the FBI for the paper, "I replied. "How do you know about it?

"Do you know the FBI had a plan to plant drugs in your room, tip off the D.C. cops, and have you arrested?"

I got chills as I listened to Crewdson describe the stunt. It was perfect: The pinko *Post* sends a doped-up kid down to Washington to do a hatchet job on J. Edgar Hoover. Who would have believed my claims of innocence? *Wasn't that the same kid who got thrown out of college a couple of years ago for publishing a dirty paper?*

At the last minute, Crewdson told me, a deputy director of the FBI got wind of the plot and squelched it. And what if he hadn't? Even if the charges were later dropped, I'd be damaged goods. After passage of the Freedom of Information Act I tried hard to get more detail on this bizarre episode, but the FBI insisted there was nothing about it in the files—indeed, that the bureau didn't even have a file on me.

Strange as it turned out to be, working on the FBI series was a welcome break in my lobster-shift routine at the *Post,* hardly an ideal life for two newlyweds barely out of their teens. Alice and I had married at the end of January, a couple of months after I was officially hired at the paper. Just our families attended the wedding, which was in Alice's parents' apartment in Parkchester, with the rabbi from my father-in-law's temple conducting the service. There was no honeymoon. I couldn't imagine taking off from work now that I'd finally been hired. Instead, we left for the new apartment in Greenwich Village that Alice had found.

A year or so before, Alice and I and some friends had walked east on Twelfth Street after seeing *Casablanca* or *The Maltese Falcon* at the Greenwich Theater. It was twilight on a summer Saturday. We passed a tiny garden with a black wrought iron fence in front of a brownstone. A Puccini aria was playing on a phonograph inside the house, and in the garden, wagging its tail in tempo, was a droop-eared basset hound angling for a pat from the passersby. The moment transfixed me—as it still does today, evoking in an instant the felicitous life I longed to lead.

Our first home wasn't a brownstone flat, but it was on Twelfth Street between Sixth and Seventh avenues, just across from St. Vincent's Hospital. It was a one-bedroom apartment on the fifth floor of a six-story brownish

building. The landlord had scraped and stained the floors, installed new
kitchen equipment and cabinets, and painted the walls white. The windows
looked north over the gardens of the Thirteenth Street brownstones and
there was plenty of light. The rent was $125 a month, precisely one week's
salary, the prudent standard.

Greenwich Village then looked much as it did in its bohemian heyday
twenty and thirty years earlier. Three-story red-brick taxpayers right out of
Edward Hopper lined Sixth Avenue. Painters, picture framers, and other
artisans worked in these walk-ups. There was a tiny Dial Bookshop just two
doors from our building, and around the corner a taxidermist with the rear
end of a white horse proudly on display in the dusty window. Just a block or
two south were the old artists' haunts, Patchin and Milligan places, where
e. e. cummings had abandoned capital letters. At night, student nurses from
St.Vincent's necked with their boyfriends in the backseats of cars parked on
Twelfth Street.

We furnished the apartment in the cliché of the time—austere Danish
Modern with reproductions of Picasso and Chagall bought at a shop on
Eighth Street next to the sandal store. Alice brought her piano and we
merged our books, which were pridefully displayed on shelves in the living
room next to the lamp tree. We even had a car, a blue Nash Rambler that
looked like an overturned bathtub I'd bought used for $250 and parked on
the block. I was twenty-one. Alice had just turned twenty.

Today, two people that age self-consciously setting up life like grown-ups
would seem bizarre. Perhaps it did even then, but we were oblivious. And it
was a good life. Alice had found a job as an editorial assistant at a trade magazine for popular music retailers called *Music Vendor.* It was run by an aging
lefty intellectual who called himself Max Gilman and had offices across from
Carnegie Hall. Alice made $80 a week, so between us we earned more than
$200. Today, $200 will get you a nice dinner for two with a middling bottle
of wine at any of a half-dozen Italian restaurants on the East Side of Manhattan. In 1959, you could have a couple of martinis and perfect sirloins at
Peter's Backyard or the Steak Joint in the Village for $20 or so with a decent
tip. You could see off-Broadway productions that are still talked about, like
The Threepenny Opera, The Iceman Cometh, Uncle Vanya, or Genet's *The Balcony* for $6 or $7. Besides Lotte Lenya, the cast of *Threepenny* included Bea
Arthur, Ed Asner, and Jerry Orbach, but no one had heard of them then.

Jason Robards was Hickey in *Iceman* at the Circle in the Square in Sheridan Square.

The flaw in the perfect picture was that I had to work nights, a routine that my body could never adjust to, even at twenty-one. I'd drag home from the paper about 8:30 each morning just as Alice was putting on her Capezios to go to work. I experimented with every kind of sleeping and eating arrangement. For a while, I'd try going to bed almost at once, hoping to get six or seven uninterrupted hours, have a light breakfast, and then try to eat a regular meal about 8:00 or 9:00 PM, before heading to the *Post* at midnight. That didn't work. I'd doze off for two or three hours, then be up, and collapse again about 5:00 PM. Alice would have to rouse me from my coma at eleven so I could get to work. Then I tried staying up as long as possible. All that accomplished was that I spent hours fighting sleep and feeling awful.

Food was an insoluble problem. I had a continuous bad stomach and nothing tasted right. I subsisted for months on turkey drumsticks Alice brought home from the Carnegie Deli washed down with Beaujolais. Toward the end of my lobster period, I was living mostly on macaroni and cheese, one of the few dishes I could digest.

Compounding the misery, from Saturday morning until I went back to work Monday night, I'd have to try to function as a normal human being, not a vampire consigned to the darkness. I'd sleep a few hours Saturday morning, then try to keep going until midnight, hope to sleep until seven or so Sunday morning, enjoy the day and Monday, then go back underground. Try as I might, I never found the trick. Once, we bought a subscription to a series of Sunday night concerts by the Budapest String Quartet at the Ninety-second Street Y. We'd settle into our seats, the Budapests would strike up the first chords of one of Beethoven's late quartets, I'd gaze at the gold curtain behind the players onstage . . . and conk out. It happened at every concert until we just gave up.

During the week, my tortured slumber was punctuated by the din of pile drivers. The Village was being gentrified, as the new catchword had it. Edward Hopper's red-brick taxpayers were giving way to sleek white apartment blocks with names like the John Adam, which, as it happened, was going up *thump, thump, thump* right outside my windows. Work started each morning just as I arrived home to kiss Alice on her way out the door.

Eventually I worked myself off the lobster shift and migrated to the day side, working on series and, finally, as the assistant day city editor. Now I encountered the daylight world of the *Post*, which in its way was as exotic as Al Davis's realm. The paper boasted the top Negro reporter in the country, Ted Poston, a tall, raucous black man who fearlessly went South to cover big civil-rights stories. And it had some of the top women reporters anywhere, including Fern Marja Eckman and Helen Dudar, who specialized in spectacular, months-long trials all around the country. There were investigative reporters who almost single-handedly toppled Robert Moses's autocratic development empire, and political reporters who were more pols than the people they covered. And there were the denizens of the "poets' corner," talented feature writers like Gael Greene and heavyweights like Irwin Ross, who wrote some of the paper's most impressive series. The UN was covered by Joseph P. Lash, an old New Deal disciple who later wrote a string of best sellers about FDR and Eleanor Roosevelt.

8

GOOD-BYE, DOLLY

AND THEN THERE WAS Mrs. Schiff, rarely glimpsed in the city room, but a pervasive presence. The proprietress was famous for her "Dollygrams"— story ideas, critiques, and directives that would arrive at the city desk typed on flimsy yellow half sheets by her loyal secretary Jean Gillette, who invariably noted "dictated but not read" over Dolly's simulated initials. One celebrated Dollygram read: "I constantly hear water running in Otto Preminger's penthouse next door. What could this be?" What, indeed? Another time, she wrote: "Why do we waste space showing men's tie knots in pictures? All men wear ties and everybody knows what a tie knot looks like. From now on, all pictures of men should be cropped under the chin." Without parsing the Freudian implications of the command, the news editors dutifully followed orders for the next couple of weeks, until Dolly forgot about it.

For a time, Dolly decreed that all datelined stories had to carry a reporter's byline, not just the *Special to the Post* slug we'd slap on them. No one had the nerve to tell her that there was no reporter for most of these stories, which were cobbled together by rewrite men from clips and a phone call or two. If she wanted bylines, she'd get them. One of our favorite new correspondents was one **FELIX PYE**, the namesake of Bill Carr's cat, Pyewacket, from *Bell Book and Candle*.

Mrs. Schiff, still a beauty, fastidiously coifed, and with a regal manner, came from a celebrated banking family, but she ran the *Post* like a neighborhood candy store, perhaps in keeping with the paper's role as the champion of the poor and oppressed. When she entertained important guests in her office, she'd send down for sandwiches from the luncheonette on the ground floor of the *Post* building and serve lunch on paper plates.

Dolly liked to match the sandwiches to the presumed ethnic tastes of her guests. Adlai Stevenson got roast beef on white with the crusts cut off. Hamill got corned beef. Abe Beame, the tiny future mayor, got salami on rye. Once, Meade Esposito, the Democratic party boss from Brooklyn came for lunch. Dolly served him a meatball hero. "Thank you, Mrs. Schiff," he said. "When you come out for lunch to the Jefferson Club we'll be sure to serve you matzo ball soup"—as if Dolly had ever met a matzo ball.

Harebrained as some of her ideas were, Mrs. Schiff could act boldly. The year I joined the paper, she scandalized the party establishment when, on the day before the gubernatorial election, she scrapped the *Post*'s endorsement of Democrat Averell Harriman and came out for Republican Nelson Rockefeller, who conveniently enough won. Four years later, she broke with her fellow newspaper owners and made a separate peace with striking unions, putting the paper back on the street a month before its competitors.

I spoke to her only once while I worked at the paper, but a couple of years after I left for *Newsweek,* she invited me for a drink at her penthouse apartment on Sixty-fourth Street and Lexington Avenue. I found Mrs. Schiff dressed in a Pucci outfit with an iced bottle of Pouilly Fuisse near at hand. She wanted to talk about the *Post*. What did I think of the drama critic? How about the comic strips? Didn't I think Mark Trail and Mary Worth were showing their age?

In the midst of my defense of Mary Worth, she suddenly asked, "Do you know the Duke of Windsor?"

I was tempted to borrow from Evelyn Waugh's *Scoop* and reply, "Up to a point, Mrs. Schiff," but I resisted the impulse and simply said no.

"It doesn't matter," confided Dolly, "he's a nitwit."

The conversation worked its way through another bottle of Pouilly Fuisse, before Mrs. Schiff asked me if I'd come back to the *Post,* eventually to succeed Paul Sann, whom she had installed over Wechsler. I told her I was flattered that she had so much confidence in me, but that I thought I had a good future at *Newsweek* I wanted to pursue.

Years later, I heard about another Dolly observation that plainly topped my Duke of Windsor moment. At a *Post* staff party, she suddenly blurted to one of the editors, "Just because FDR was in a wheelchair, it doesn't mean he was paralyzed *that* way. I know."

Work on the day side city desk introduced me to the exquisite boredom of routine newspaper work. The lists compiled at the exact same points in

the shifts, the story conferences, the updates in the weather, and stock blurbs
for each replated edition, the whole numbing ritual. It dawned on me that
my dreams of a lifetime as a newspaper pro had a profound flaw: I'd been at
it barely three years and I was bored already.

I distracted myself by writing articles for the *Post*'s Saturday magazine section and short profiles for the Daily Close-up column, which was derided
around the paper as the Daily Far-Away. My method was simple enough. I'd
write about people I was interested in and wanted to meet. It was impossible
to meet my pet subject, and that's what made him my favorite. Even more
than four decades ago, J. D. Salinger was already celebrated as a literary
recluse, stashed away in tiny Cornish, New Hampshire. He never talked to
journalists—or anyone outside his secretive circle—and his enablers never
talked to anyone about him. A long and increasingly arch story would
appear unheralded every couple of years in the *New Yorker* over his name,
and then the silence would resume.

I dutifully called the usual suspects: William Shawn, the murmurous
editor of the *New Yorker*, Salinger's literary agent, and other insiders. Shawn
gave me the most polite brush-off—"Mr. Salinger simply doesn't want to be
written about," he said in his whispery voice—and the others were brusque.
After a week or so of asking around, I had nothing. And then I made one
final call. I remembered that the *Post*'s library had a directory of weekly
newspapers around the country. So I looked up the names of the towns
around Cornish and found the *Claremont Daily Eagle* nearby. Soon I had the
editor on the phone, a pleasant fellow named Nelson Bryant, who later had
a long run as the outdoor columnist for the *New York Times*.

"Have you ever had anything about Salinger in the paper?" I asked.

I could hear him chuckling. "We don't have a clipping file like you big-
timers," he said. "Just the bound volumes of the paper. I'll look through
the last couple of years. Call me tomorrow and I'll tell you if I've found
anything."

"You're in luck," said Bryant, when I called the next day. Despite myself,
my heart started to beat faster. And when he told me what he'd discovered,
I almost passed out.

It turned out that the *Eagle* ran a high school column, and the year before,
at the local malt shop, a sophomore named Shirlie Blany had scored an all-
time, all-world exclusive: an interview with Salinger, the first and the last. It

was full of unheard of biographical giblets. And she had written it up for the *Eagle* in a style that sounded remarkably like Holden Caulfield's sister Phoebe.

> Jerome David Salinger is a tall, foreign-looking man of 34 with a pleasing personality. He was born January 1, 1919, in New York. He went to public grammar schools while his high school years were spent at Valley Forge Military Academy. During this time he was writing.
>
> His college education included New York University, where he studied for two years. With his father, he went to Poland to learn the ham shipping business. He didn't care for this, but he accomplished something by learning the German language.
>
> Later he was in Vienna for ten months. But he came back and went to Ursinus College. Due to lack of interest he left in midyear and went to Columbia University. All this time he was still writing.
>
> He later worked on the liner *Kungsholm* in the West Indies as an entertainer. He was still writing for magazines [the *Saturday Evening Post, Esquire, Mademoiselle,* and others] and college publications. At the age of twenty-three he was drafted. He spent two years in the Army which he disliked because he wanted all of his time to write.
>
> He started working on *Catcher in the Rye,* a novel, in 1941 and finished in the summer of 1951. . . . The book is the story of a troubled adolescent boy. When asked if it was in any way autobiographical, Mr. Salinger said: "Sort of. I was much relieved when I finished it. My boyhood was very much the same as that of the boy in the book and it was a great relief telling people about it."

Soon after the *Post* piece ran, *Publishers Weekly* duly tipped its cap to my coup. When *Time* did a cover story on Salinger a couple of years later, the magazine not only quoted from the interview, but tracked down Shirlie Blany, by now married to a sailor and living in Newport News, Virginia. I got a fresh tingle from my sole contribution to American literary history.

After the Salinger story, I interviewed the young playwright Edward Albee, whose one-acters *The Sandbox* and *The American Dream* had just opened at the Cherry Lane Theater on Commerce Street in the Village; the young writer John Updike; and Nina Simone, the morose jazz singer and pianist. Doing these pieces helped, but I couldn't really escape the truth that for all my precociousness, I was stuck on the desk at a second-rate newspaper with no real hope of doing more than scaling the *Post* masthead.

Just as the reality of my situation at the *Post* sunk in, my life changed dramatically. A decade before the Vietnam War, the military draft was a looming presence in the plans of young American men. To circumvent the draft, some joined reserve units, going on active duty for six months, then spending the next couple of years drilling or shuffling papers at an armory two days a month and for two weeks in the summer. The hitch was that Cold War crises could prompt reserve call-ups and draft speedups—indeed, my pal Jack Schwartz wound up feasting on iguana during survival training in the Panama Canal Zone as a result of one now-forgotten dustup.

I couldn't imagine taking two years out of my career to serve in the army, but I was fit enough to pass the physical and there was only one option left: fathers were automatically deferred. So, for my own selfish reasons, Alice and I decided that we'd forgo birth control. If she got pregnant, so be it. If she didn't, I'd face the draft and take my chances. She got pregnant almost immediately, and in mid-October 1960, we were all set for the birth, which was going to be overseen by the same obstetrician who had delivered Alice just twenty-one years before. The blue Rambler had long since expired, so I borrowed my father-in-law's Dodge sedan for the drive to Jewish Memorial Hospital way up in Washington Heights and warned my bosses at the *Post* that I might have to bolt at any time.

The call finally came. I phoned the doctor and we raced to the hospital, where he soon joined us. After examining Alice, he met me outside her room, held up his thumb and index finger barely an inch apart, and shook his head.

"She's only dilated this much," he shrugged. "It's going to be hours. I'm going to sleep and I suggest you do, too."

Next morning, hardly anything had changed. In those pre-Lamaze days, prospective fathers weren't part of the jolly birthing team, they were simply nuisances. No one talked to them or even acknowledged their presence. I hung around the waiting room, so unnerved that I couldn't read any of the

*Saturday Evening Post*s lying around, or even sit down. Late in the afternoon I heard a rhythmic sound and searched the room for the source. Finally, I realized that the mysterious beat was coming from my own knees, which were knocking together out of sheer terror. I lurched along Broadway until I found an Irish saloon, where I downed three bourbons in fifteen minutes. Now in a merciful alcoholic haze, I weaved my way back to the hospital. I was sure the worst was going to happen because my motive for becoming a father was impure. God was going to punish me, and Alice and the child were going to be collateral casualties.

After a labor that dragged on for more than twenty-four hours, the doctor told me I had a son, and that I could see him through the nursery window in a few minutes. I was standing in a daze outside the nursery when a nurse came toward the window cradling a small bundle in her arms. When she held up the baby, I almost fainted. Confronting me through the glass was a tiny red-faced monster, its head tapering like a dunce cap, its features all smooshed together. Instead of a neck, the baby had a swollen red band under its chin. My premonition had been right: The draft dodger and his wife would spend their lives raising a deformed cretin.

Of course, there was nothing wrong with John Robbins Kosner. The long, tight run through the birth canal had produced the temporary swelling around his neck. The gentle tug of the forceps had briefly distorted his face. Within a few days, he had become the beautiful baby he was meant to be, and we took him home to Twelfth Street to the tiny Portacrib that barely fit in our apartment.

Within seventeen months, John had a brother—and his advent had profound consequences for Alice and me, our marriage, and my career. One child was as much as we could handle, so when Alice became fertile again after John's birth, she began taking the birth-control pill Enovid, which had been put on the market by Searle, a pharmaceutical company based in Chicago. She'd get a supply each month from our neighborhood drugstore just down the block on Sixth Avenue. The pharmacist was a friendly gray-haired man out of central casting whose only claim to fame was his niece, Lesley Gore, the teenager who had a hit with "It's My Party (and I'll Cry if I Want To)."

In late spring Alice picked up her latest supply of Enovid and noticed a curious thing. The pills were identical to those she'd taken two months earlier, but strikingly different from the month's batch she'd just finished. Was Searle making two different versions of Enovid? Or had the lovable but inept druggist slipped her the wrong pills? If the pills weren't Enovid, Alice was almost certain to be pregnant. In those pioneering days, the hormone dosages in birth-control drugs were so strong that if the treatment was interrupted the patient became superfertile.

From my desk at the *Post,* I got on the phone to Searle and quickly learned that the firm made only one version of Enovid. Then I confronted the druggist, who dismissed the idea that he'd given my wife the wrong prescription. Perhaps if he could see the bottle the pills had come in? But, of course, Alice had discarded the bottle before she realized the pills had looked strange, so there was no evidence.

Now it was July, and we headed to Chatham on Cape Cod for a short vacation. Nearly as soon as we got there, Alice went for a pregnancy test at a local medical office. She dropped off a urine sample, and we were to return in a day or two for the result of the rabbit test. I waited in the car with John, who was barely eight months old, while Alice went inside for the verdict.

"The rabbit died," she said with a tight smile when she came out.

While we weren't looking, destiny's wand had waved once more. The confirmation that we would have two children within seventeen months began what was to be the most difficult period in my life, one so full of stress and heartbreak that I survived it only with a ruthless and nearly pathological suppression of my own feelings.

My marriage to Alice had thrown my mother into a severe depression reminiscent of the one that had engulfed her after her own mother's death just before I was born. My father's career as a salesman had guttered out in a series of flop jobs and now he was eking out a living checking up on thieving store help for a security company. And, of course, they had no savings to speak of. Sometime during John's first year, my mother found traces of blood when she undressed. She said later that her first thought was that her menopause had miraculously suspended and that she'd got her period again. All though her life, Annalee had been meticulous about her health. But now—perhaps because of depression, perhaps because she had an inkling of what was to come—she did nothing. Then she began to feel pain and found her abdomen was swollen and tender.

By the time she went to the gynecologist the ovarian cancer was beyond hope for her survival. So now we found ourselves in a situation of almost unspeakable complexity and anguish. Annalee would have to have electroshock treatments to ease her depression enough so that she could be treated for a cancer that was certain to kill her anyway. We had no money and no influential relatives or friends who could connect us with top doctors. My father loved my mother so much he simply unraveled. It all fell to Selda and me. Somehow, we found our way to a wonderful surgeon named Baldwin at Doctors' Hospital on the Upper East Side. I can picture myself at the *Post* talking to him on the phone after the surgery more than forty years ago.

"Edward, we got everything we could see," he said. "But there are microscopic seedlings that we can't detect and in cases like this they spread the malignancy." Annalee, he said, had perhaps nine months to live and they would be full of pain.

Thus began a long, downward spiral for my mother, briefly interrupted by a few upticks and small setbacks that could have only one resolution. Anyone who has cared for a terminal cancer patient knows the drill: the doctor's orders that get scrambled, the IV that fails to be connected, the private-duty nurse who doesn't show up, the weekend crisis when the attending doctor is unavailable. My mother's doctor was an innovator in the use of chemotherapy, and when he suggested that she would be an appropriate subject for testing an experimental drug, I consented. There probably wouldn't be anything to gain, but there plainly was nothing to lose.

In mid-February 1962, my mother was all but dead, but her heart beat on. She couldn't or wouldn't let go. The painkillers were losing their sway, and she was often in agony. Selda had been secretly stashing sleeping pills that Annalee had been too far gone to take, and one evening her husband, Nat, and I decided we could no longer let her suffer. While Selda guarded the door to the room, Nat and I tried to get enough pills into Annalee to kill her. Leaning over my mother, I couldn't believe I was actually doing what I was doing, yet I knew it had to be done. But our amateurish efforts failed, and Annalee suffered on for another forty-eight hours. It snowed overnight before her funeral, and the Westchester hillsides were a dazzling white in the morning sunshine as we walked back to the cars. Cliched as it was, I couldn't get Joyce's coda—*And the snow fell on all the living and the dead*—out of my mind.

* * *

Barely a month after my mother's funeral Alice felt twinges and we hustled off to Beth Israel Hospital downtown. But, once again, she'd gotten ahead of herself and we found ourselves sitting around all night waiting for something to happen. Finally, at dawn, I went back to Twelfth Street to get some sleep, instructing the nursing station to call me as soon as Alice went into labor. But nobody called, and I was snoozing away when an intern rang early in the afternoon to report that we had a boy. We named him Anthony, for Annalee.

Anthony's birth forever shaped my views on abortion, an issue I had to deal with for decades as editor of *Newsweek*, *New York*, and the *Daily News*. In the early 1960s, *Roe v. Wade* was still a decade away, and abortion was so rare that it verged on myth. Everyone knew someone who knew someone who knew an abortionist somewhere in Pennsylvania or Minnesota, or a woman who'd gone to Sweden to dispose of an inconvenient pregnancy. Anthony was certainly inconvenient—and inadvertent, the result of a pharmacist's incompetence. Alice's psyche was always frail, and having two children seventeen months apart when she was just twenty-three was a risky burden. Had abortion been as commonplace in the summer of 1961 as it is today, I suppose we would have flushed Anthony the moment the rabbit died.

In the 1970s at *Newsweek,* I had long and painful discussions about *Roe v. Wade* with the young feminists on staff. I told them I recognized that abortion all-but-on-demand was probably valid social policy, but I insisted on the parallel validity of Alice's and my experience. Had abortion been available, our son simply wouldn't exist. Any woman who had an abortion had to acknowledge that she was doing away with a life of immeasurable potential, committing an irrevocable act. Some of the young women accepted my argument, but most believed I was simply missing the point.

After my mother's death, we did all we could for my father, who was bereft. Alice found a larger apartment in our building with a room for the boys, and I went back on the desk at the *Post*. By the fall, I'd begun to bounce back from all the pain and pressure of the past months. Then the truculent typographers' union struck the New York newspapers, and I was suddenly out of a job.

The older and more enterprising hands at the *Post* quickly found temporary spots at local radio and television stations or on one or another of the interim newspapers that quickly sprang up. But I really knew no one outside my own paper and was left standing when the music stopped. After a week, I checked in at the Newspaper Guild office and collected my first strike benefits, sixty bucks or so. When I came home to Alice and the two babies, I felt like the robin returning to the fledglings in the nest with an empty beak.

After a couple of weeks, it was clear that the unions and the united front of publishers were dug in for a long siege. I was frantic because I was convinced that the *Post,* the weakest of dailies, would never survive an extended strike. I'd be jobless and broke with a wife and two infants to support. Then the phone rang.

It was Stan Opotowsky, the *Post*'s virtuoso rewrite man and desk hand. He and some pals, correspondents for London papers based in New York, were setting up a broadsheet strike paper called the *Chronicle,* to be printed on the presses of a weekly in Westchester about an hour's ride from the city. Stan wanted me to be the city editor.

The *Chronicle* lasted only about ten days, and that's a good thing, because after the first week, I passed out from exhaustion. But I learned more about newspapering in that fortnight than in my last years at the *Post*. I learned, for example, that most newspaper stories are composed of a few nuggets of fresh information atop long paragraphs of background. I'd been concerned that the *Chronicle* had no clip file. "Relax, I've got it right here," said Stan, patting a stack of papers from the out-of-town newspaper stand in Times Square. "Everything you need for national and foreign stories is in the *Sun*."

He meant H. L. Mencken's old paper, the *Baltimore Sun,* which was then notorious for running endless stories on just about anything. Sure enough, each *Sun* article was a trove of background material for our daily gleaners. With smuggled wire copy from a buddy at the AP, a couple of telephones, a pile of out-of-town papers, and a few deft rewrite men, something that looked and read very much like a real newspaper could be fabricated each day basically from scratch.

The real revelation to me was watching the Brits make up the paper long before the makeshift stories were written, edited, and set in type. Instead of cropping photographs with the rulers and triangles Americans used, they simply curled the pictures with their hands and calculated the dimensions in their heads—three columns by five inches, say, or one column by three inches. Then they wrote out headlines in various sizes with matching white-on-black reverse subheads and sent all the copy off to the composing room. On deadline, they used these prefab elements to lay out lively, elegant pages. Except for Opotowsky's performance the morning the Spring Hill miners were rescued, I'd never seen such nonchalant skill.

Not long after the *Chronicle* folded, Dorothy Schiff made another of her bold moves. Without warning, she broke with her fellow publishers, settled with the printers' union, and got the *Post* back on the street while her shuttered competitors seethed with frustration. I was thrilled to be back, but I knew this was just a reprieve and that I had to move on. Indeed, it would be irresponsible for me to cast my lot with the *Post*. I had a wife and two children and an impoverished father, a widower. Even if the *Post* tiptoed past this strike, it was ultimately doomed, would probably be the first to go. For all the logic of my analysis, I hadn't a clue what to do next. And then that wand waved again.

Working day side, I had become friendly with Helen Dudar, who was the closest thing the paper had to a literary type. Helen, thin and dark with her hair plaited in a braid down her back, came from Island Park, a hamlet just across the channel from Long Beach. But she somehow had transformed herself into a sophisticated woman who liked to read Françoise Sagan in French during downtime on the rewrite bank. Helen had covered a sexy murder trial in Boston, where she'd met a writer for the *St. Louis Globe-Democrat* named Peter Goldman. They had a commuter courtship for a year, then married, and lived in St. Louis before settling in New York. One day, Helen and I went for lunch at a restaurant in a converted firehouse a few nondescript blocks from the *Post* in what is today chic TriBeCa. I told her all my worries about the future.

"Peter's writing in the national affairs department at *Newsweek,* and he says there's an opening," said Helen. "Why don't you send a letter to his editor?"

My father, Sidney Kosner, as a young man in his Ivy League best (although the closest he ever got was selling umbrellas at the Yale Bowl on a wet football Saturday), circa 1932.

At 23, as a *New York Post* rewriteman, 1961.

The editor in chief of *The Campus* (third from left, back row) with the staff at City College, 1957.

With Al Davis (*left*) and Paul Sann, checking the front page of the first *Post* printed after Dorothy Schiff broke the publisher's united front and resumed publishing, April, 1963.

With President Gerald Ford in 1974 after Nixon's Watergate fall (Oz Elliot second from left).

With Kay Graham at the 1976 Republican National Convention in Kansas City.

Editor of *Newsweek*, 1976.

With Jimmy and Rosalyn Carter after the Camp David Accords, 1978.

With bodies of rebels slain by Southern Rhodesian troops, 1977.

With Israeli Prime Minister Menachem Begin, 1978.

The *Newsweek* Wallendas mourn the death of Karl Wallenda, 1978.

With Rupert Murdoch, center, and Roy Cohn at Cohn's birthday party at the Seventh Regiment Armory in New York, February, 1981.

With Pete Hamill at *New York* magazine, April, 1980.

With New York mayor Ed Koch at the 1980 Democratic National Convention in New York.

With Lally Weymouth (*left*) and Jim Hogue and Julie at the 1980 Democratic National Convention in New York.

Editor and publisher of *New York* magazine with "Mr. Peepers," wife Julie Baumgold, 1988.

Michael O'Neill

Editor in chief of *Esquire*, 1994.

With Mort Zuckerman at the *Daily News* before it all turned sour, 2000.

Daily News news meeting (with Michael Kramer, *right*), 2003.

Designing page one of the *Daily News* on September 11, 2001, with the headline IT'S WAR.

9

"Relax, Kid, It's Only a Twenty-five-Cent Magazine"

I KNEW THAT THE slick Ivy Leaguers at *Newsweek* would have no use for a kid *New York Post* rewrite man from CCNY. Helen's husband, Peter Goldman, after all, was a Williams man and had been a Nieman fellow at Harvard. But, as before, I had nothing to lose. So I sat down and carefully drafted a facile-but-not-too-facile, modest-but-not-too-modest letter to Lester Bernstein, the national affairs editor, and mailed it to his office. And heard nothing. After a week or so, I decided to call him. When I phoned on Monday, I was told he was off. At 10:00 AM Tuesday, I was told he hadn't come in yet. At 4:30, he'd left for the day. *They're ducking me,* I thought, unaware of *Newsweek*'s gentlemanly work routine in those days.

Finally, I reached Lester only to be told he'd never gotten my letter. So I did my best to re-create it, and eventually I was invited up to *Newsweek* one afternoon for a chat. Exactly on time, I checked in at the reception desk and sat down to wait. In a few minutes, a thin blonde in a long peasant skirt, white blouse, and sandals padded out to greet me. She had a long braid that ran down her back to her waist. *Even the secretaries at* Newsweek *went to Sarah Lawrence,* I told myself.

Actually, Lester's secretary was a middle-class girl from Queens named Eleanor Roeloffs. Years later, she married Montgomery Clift's brother Brooks and moved to Atlanta, where she worked as the secretary at the *Newsweek* bureau, getting to know the people around the governor, whose name was Jimmy Carter. When Carter ran for president in 1976, Eleanor covered the campaign, and when Jimmy became president, Eleanor transferred to the White House beat at *Newsweek*'s Washington bureau, where she gradually molted into Eleanor Clift, the queen of the Sunday morning TV political gab shows.

Lester was warm and friendly and offered me a one-week tryout in the national affairs department, the news magazine equivalent of my one-nighter at the *Post* five years before. This time it didn't make sense to try to practice. I knew that at *Newsweek* the writers were called associate editors, but beneath the glossy title they were essentially rewrite men, fashioning their stories from "files"—long reports—sent in by the correspondents in the field and from newspaper clips and other "research." If there was anything I didn't need practice in it was rewriting.

When I showed up at 10:00 AM on Tuesday, July 30, 1963—four days after my twenty-sixth birthday—none of the other writers were there yet. Eleanor showed me to a cubicle occupied by a vacationing writer named Jake Underhill. It was filled with family pictures and enough orange and black memorabilia to make it obvious that Jake was a Princeton man and proud of it. Gradually, the other writers drifted in and I was introduced to Frank Trippett, a big man with bushy black eyebrows and an equally thick Mississippi accent; Jacquin Sanders, a smiling little man who wrote novels; Russ Chappell, a quiet buttoned-down fellow who whipped out the devilish *Times* of London crossword puzzle and rapidly inked it in; and Peter, one of the most gentle and talented people I've ever met, who looked as if he should be teaching political science at his alma mater.

I couldn't imagine how Eddie—as everybody at the *Post* called me—could ever fit in with this group. Nor could I figure what to do after I'd reread the *Times* I'd brought with me and absorbed every word in the new issue of *Newsweek* given to each writer. In fact, there was nothing to do. Stories for the next issue wouldn't be assigned until later in the day, the files for these stories wouldn't start coming in until late Wednesday or Thursday morning, and the deadline wasn't until Friday afternoon—an eternity away on the city desk of a daily.

This was my first taste of the news magazine routine that I would come to love—the slow slide into the week with the long, boozy lunches, the almost imperceptible increase in the pace until Friday morning when the writers would actually write their stories in a burst of industry, then, spent, wait for Bernstein to edit their pieces and send the copy up front to the top editors for more fiddling.

Eventually, Lester gave me my story—my one shot at escaping the grubby *Post* to this Arcadia of big-time journalism. Maybe Bernstein was pulling for me, or maybe that invisible wand waved over me again. In any case, I was blessed in the choice of my first assignment. It was about the influx of hill-billies to the slums of Chicago, where an insurance magnate with a pencil mustache named W. Clement Stone (later a big Nixon buddy) was trying to help them. More to the point, it would be based on a file by Hal Bruno, one of the magazine's most talented bureau reporters. Hal's file ran to nearly thirty pages and it was crammed with all the color and quotes any rewriteman could want. So all I had to do was refine this cornucopia into a lively, fluent thousand-word piece. I polished my story to a high gloss and turned it in on Friday morning.

Just before dinner on Friday, Bernstein gave me a short to write about a move in Congress to give American presidents seats in the Senate after they'd completed their terms. The lead for that one popped into my head even before I'd rolled the paper into my typewriter: *The familiar figure, grayer now, rose at a Senate back bench. His left hand thrust into his jacket pocket, his right index finger stabbing the air, John F. Kennedy was telling the U.S. Senate why* . . . Despite all the talk about how news magazine editors rewrote everything the writers rewrote in the first place, both my stories went through essentially untouched.

When I showed up at *Newsweek* on Saturday morning, I was hoping Lester would have something encouraging to say. But about 10:30, the atmosphere suddenly changed. The phones started ringing and Bernstein and the other editors began scurrying around. Gradually, the word filtered back to Nation: Phil Graham, the brilliant, manic-depressive husband of Katharine Graham, whose family owned the *Washington Post* and *Newsweek,* had blown his brains out in a bathtub at their weekend farm in Virginia. This was a catastrophe, not just in terms of personal loss, but for the destiny of the magazine and the company, which Phil ran. Finally, Lester called me in. Apologetically, he explained there could be no thought of my future at such a moment—could I perhaps come back for another week sometime that summer?

Phil Graham's suicide struck *Newsweek* and the *Washington Post* like a thunderbolt, although his behavior had become increasingly odd. The *Newsweek* editors were especially bound to Graham: He had engineered the sale of the magazine from the Astor family in 1961 for $9 million and installed the current leadership. It was Phil who inspired the *Newsweek* editors and gave them the resources to challenge *Time* for supremacy in the news magazine competition after years as a lackluster also-ran. (It would take *Newsweek* years more to achieve parity with *Time*—at least in journalistic terms, although *Time* still holds a substantial advantage in circulation and ad revenue.) Thirty-five years later, Phil's widow, Katharine Graham, told the story of Graham's tormented spiral into suicide in her brilliant memoir *Personal History*. But on August 3, 1963, I knew nothing of that; to me, Phil Graham was a spectral figure whose death meant that I'd have to go through yet another tryout.

Barely a month later, I showed up again—and once again John Kennedy played a critical role in my nascent *Newsweek* career, as he would in the months to come. This time my assignment was a controversial new book by the conservative gadfly Victor Lasky titled *JFK: The Man and the Myth,* the first serious effort to debunk JFK, who had gotten mostly hagiographic treatment since winning the presidency from Richard Nixon. Bright and early Friday morning, I turned in my piece, then wrote another stylish short. I was hired on the spot at an annual salary of $13,500, fully $1,000 more than I was making at the *Post,* overtime included, the equivalent in 2005 of more than $80,000. I was terrified, but for the first time I truly believed I might have a real career in journalism after all.

Newsweek was a scary Eden for me. Its offices at 444 Madison Avenue, a tan brick tower on the west side of the avenue between Forty-ninth and Fiftieth streets, were smack in the middle of what was then the glamorous advertising district. Across the avenue was the New Weston Hotel, where one of Mary McCarthy's upper-class college beauties commits suicide in her book *The Group,* and a block north was 480 Madison, a futuristic office building that housed both *Look* and *Esquire* in their heydays. Atop the *Newsweek* building was the magazine's logo in red neon with the time and temperature, a midtown landmark.

The magazine was a big enterprise. The masthead listing the editors, writers, bureau correspondents, researchers, and other hands filled a full column of agate type. Some of the names were so exotic—a senior editor named Arnaud de Borchgrave, a researcher named Lourdes Blanco-Fombona—that I quickly understood that I wasn't in Washington Heights anymore.

Like *Time,* from which its editorial formula and all its operations were cribbed, *Newsweek* segregated tasks as formally as a beehive. The magazine was divided into front-of-the-book (national, foreign, and business news) and back-of-the-book (science, medicine, religion, education and such, and the arts) sections. The front-of-the-book departments were run by senior editors, each with a half dozen writers and a comparable number of fact-checkers, or "researchers." There were two senior editors for the back of the book, who supervised the section editors and researchers for each specialty. With only the rarest exception, the editors and writers were men and the researchers were young women. There were two managing editors—one for the front and one for the back—who reported to the editor in chief, who read the final version of every word in the magazine each week, including the picture captions. The magazine had a big Washington operation and bureaus in more than a dozen cities in the U.S. and overseas.

Phil Graham had memorably called each week's *Newsweek* "the first, rough draft of history," but it was actually an extravagant refining process in which a vast amount of raw material—ideas, reportage, data, transcripts, and photographs—laboriously excavated by the bureaus was shipped to New York, where it was even more laboriously winnowed and compressed into about 60,000 words. Only a fraction of the stories proposed each week actually made it to the story list and only a fraction of those survived into the issue.

Correspondents routinely transmitted long files to writers who might use no more than a colorful descriptive phrase or a quote. The writer's version of a story frequently emerged unrecognizable from the senior editor's type-writer. Then that version was passed up to the next rung in the line of command, where that pooh-bah might touch it up or, as often happened, order a complete rewrite of the senior editor's rewrite. Then the editor in chief might work over the results. All the while, the researchers were meticulously fact-checking every name, initial, date, statistic, and God-knows-what-else in the piece. Their fact changes routinely resulted in whole paragraphs having to be recast.

Most of this work was crammed into about thirty-six hours beginning Friday morning and ending when the issue closed after midnight Saturday night. And, of course, news had a way of breaking late, necessitating the drastic overhaul of finished stories and sometimes of the whole front of the magazine. How *Newsweek*—and *Time*—get published week after week and with such sustained quality is a testament to human ingenuity, stamina, and a deep strain of collective masochism.

None of the stories—even the reviews—carried bylines. The idea, conceived at *Time* by Henry Luce and Briton Haddon, was that the magazine was written in a homogenized, omniscient voice—the Voice of Authority, as it were. (These days, only the *Economist* in Great Britain carries on the mono-tonic tradition.) And the magazines did have authority. It's hard to imagine now, but in the early 1960s there was virtually no national news presence in America. The *Wall Street Journal* was circulated nationally, but it really was a business paper in those days. There were the evening news shows and occasional documentaries on the TV networks. But there was, of course, no all-news radio—WINS in New York pioneered the format in 1964—no cable news, no *USA Today*, or national editions of the *New York Times*. *Life* and the *Saturday Evening Post* were still around, but their influence was melting. The cover of *Time* (and to a lesser extent *Newsweek*) was a weekly assertion of significance—the ultimate validation of a politician, mogul, writer, movie star—and, most significantly, a trend. Weeks of feverish speculation preceded *Time's* choice of its Man of the Year (later modified to Person of the Year in the interest of political correctness).

By the early 1960s, Henry Luce was little more than a patriarchal figure at *Time,* but the magazine still clung to its partisan Republican allegiance. *Newsweek* was more liberal—easier on Jack Kennedy, plainly sympathetic to the civil-rights revolution the Reverend Martin Luther King was leading in the South. *Newsweek* loudly touted its columnists, including Stewart Alsop, Joe's more modulated brother, and tried to exploit the perception that *Time* copy was slanted by the founder's politics.

NEWSWEEK SEPARATES FACT FROM OPINION

proclaimed its slogan on everything from billboards to pencils. In fact, *Newsweek's* liberal politics suffused the magazine the very same way *Time's* predilections leached into its stories; but nobody seemed to care, and FACT FROM OPINION was one of the most effective magazine slogans ever coined.

I soon began to penetrate the permeable membrane that separated the

Newsweek culture from the life other mortals led. *Newsweek* never produced the literature that the indentured novelists at Time-Life churned out, like William Brinkley's *The Fun House,* with its dread martini test for prospective fact-checkers. But *Newsweek* had a full cast of characters whose escapades were invariably more entertaining than the copy they wrote or edited.

One back-of-the-book senior editor had a phobia about having his shirts laundered. So he simply bought new ones when he ran short and kept the dirty ones in smelly bags piled high in his office. Another insisted on keeping his office pitch black, with only a single lamp creating a small circle of light on his desk, at which writers had to sit waiting for him to eviscerate their pieces. The sports editor walked out of his office one morning and was never seen again; in 2004, his son, now a grown man, was still looking for him. A back-of-the-book writer quit without telling anyone, leaving a sheet of paper in his typewriter with the lament, **I can't write this story**. The science editor couldn't put out his section one week because he'd fallen out of a tree and broken his right arm. Another time, in a drunken fit, he tried to take a swing at his boss, missed, and fell to the floor, unconscious. Early arrivals often found one of the magazine's most brilliant writers curled up in a clothing closet, blissfully sleeping off last night's toot.

Eccentricity—or simple weirdness—was as often as not matched with brilliance. Peter Goldman would spend days meticulously typing notes from files and clips and then write flawless 4,000- and 5,000-word narratives on deadline without ever looking at the notes. The art critic, Jack Kroll, and the music critic, Hubert Saal, might fuss for days over routine reviews, then turn out cover-story-length obituaries of Picasso or Stravinksy in a few hours that were as definitive as anything published anywhere in the world the next week. Writers at the magazine used to think of themselves as gigolos, skilled professionals paid to perform exquisite acts on demand.

The top editors at *Newsweek* were called the Wallendas, after the circus troupe whose members operated without a net despite their propensity to plunge to earth from the high wire. At *Newsweek,* the deadly G force wasn't gravity, it was Kay Graham, who liked to replace her top executives with alarming frequency. As Lester Bernstein once said, "Kay must have loved her editors—she made so many of them."

* * *

There were three Wallendas, and they couldn't have been more different. Gordon Manning, the managing editor for the front of the book, was a manic ex-newspaperman from Boston. Kermit Lansner, his back-of-the-book counterpart, was often described as a West Side intellectual, which meant that he was Jewish and could tell the differences among Irving Kristol, Irving Howe, and Norman Podhoretz (the honorary third Irving), all of whom lived on Riverside Drive not far from Kermit in a building that became known as the College of Irvings. At the top of the Wallenda pyramid was Osborn Elliott, Newsweek's hawk-nosed, high-WASP editor in chief, who affected red suspenders and was called Oz. The Newsweek oral tradition had it that during his first days at the magazine, Frank Trippett, the national affairs writer from Mississippi, encountered Elliott in the elevator.

"Oz Elliott," said the chief, thrusting out his hand.

"Ah's Trippett," drawled Frank, pumping the proffered mitt.

Gordon Manning was revered and reviled for his uninhibited cascade of ideas—many good, a few unspeakable—and for the relentless pressure he put on correspondents, writers, and editors to excavate one more fact, one more quote, one more anecdote, and then cram it into an already jam-packed story. He was an energetic figure with bright eyes, fluttery hands, and a dramatic, flutey voice who would have made a good minor character for Dickens. Gordon delighted in factoids—inconsequential yet somehow beguiling bits of information that gave a news magazine story a sense of insiderness and faux authenticity. *Over a salad of field greens studded with gobbets of pungent Stilton, the summiteers sat down to shape the fate of the world* is the kind of sentence Manning liked to see in Newsweek stories.

He decorated the margins of manuscripts and galley proofs with questions, exclamations *(No! No! No!),* and directions. Peter Goldman once came in on a Saturday morning to find his elegantly crafted story festooned with scribbled cocktail napkins paper-clipped to the galley proof. Gordon had run out of copy paper and made do with supplies from the Waldorf bar. And he had a language all his own. A story short on factoids needed "more raisins in the rice pudding." If, as frequently happened, a writer missed the point, Manning would haul him in.

"Show the reader the arrows to Toyland," he'd command and wave the wretch back to his cubicle.

Manning had served his own apprenticeship under Elliott's predecessor, John Denson, a querulous newspaperman who invented the "Denson crop," a style of radical picture cropping in which nearly every feature of the subject's face was eliminated but the eyes. It was hard for readers to tell who they were looking at, but a Denson crop did give routine headshots an artificial intensity.

Gordon liked to tell the story of being summoned into Denson's presence with a researcher to hear the editor's dissatisfaction with a cover story that had just reached his desk. Denson had a habit of grinding his teeth when he was upset, and he was very upset with Manning.

When the chief subsided, Manning and the girl retreated to Manning's office.

"What was he chewing on all that time?" she asked.

"My nuts," said Gordon cheerfully.

Once, I had to write a routine five-line caption for a picture of a boat that had sunk in the Cape Cod Canal on Manning's home turf. The first version came back from Gordon with two questions: How far from Barnstable did the sinking occur, and what's the name of the Coast Guard cutter that responded to the mishap? I got the answers, inserted them in the copy, and sent the caption up front again. It came back with yet another query. I answered it and sent him the third version. A researcher came to my cubicle: "Gordon wants to see you."

When I walked in, Gordon was holding the caption like a dead mouse.

"Now, Ed," he said, quite seriously. "How deep was the channel where the boat sank?"

"I don't know how deep the water was," I replied, "but I do know the frigging caption is five lines deep, and I'm not fooling with it anymore."

To his credit, Manning took my defiance with good grace.

When Gordon left *Newsweek* to become a producer at NBC, he was serenaded by a group of Nation writers to the tune of "The Battle Hymn of the Republic":

I have seen him scribbling edits on a thousand tattered blues
As he's thumbing in the color and he's stamping out the news
He only has two biases—the gentiles and the Jews. . . .

Gordon's back-of-the book counterpart, Kermit Lansner, was his opposite in nearly every respect. Manning commuted from Westport in true *Man in the Gray Flannel Suit* fashion; Lansner lived in his West Side brownstone with his wife, Kay, a well-regarded painter. Tall and passive where Gordon was short and manic, Kermit had a kind of shambling elegance and a musical voice. He had come to *Newsweek* from *Art News* (his detractors liked to sneer that Kermit had been the night city editor of *Art News*) and sometimes acted as if he'd dodged out of the rain into 444 Madison one day and suddenly found himself running half a national news magazine. "It's all madness!" he'd often exclaim in the middle of a complicated discussion about the direction of a story. He had a more polished aesthetic sense than anyone in the place, but he had little patience for layout meetings. "Big pictures, little pictures— that's your choice in news magazines," he'd proclaim and slouch in his seat. By intellectual bent, Kermit was a counterpuncher. He'd rarely venture his opinion first, but could spot the flaws in others' notions and deftly destroy them. He brought an essential sophistication, not only to *Newsweek*'s cultural coverage but also to every part of the magazine.

In a Wallenda shake-up in 1970, Kermit suddenly found himself editing *Newsweek,* and it was a disaster. The very contemplative, reflective qualities that had made him such an effective counterpoise to Manning and Elliott were fatal in the top job. For one thing, Kermit had no feel for breaking news, the big stories that prompt news magazine editors to tear up the week's issue and start over in a hot rush of adrenaline. Lacking news instincts, Kermit feared the news. When George Wallace was a paralyzed by an assassin's bullet while campaigning for president in Laurel, Maryland, Lansner insisted on sticking with his scheduled cover—a canned shot of the Kremlin heralding an upcoming summit meeting. He had to be browbeaten into leading the magazine with the Attica uprising, the bloodiest American prison riot in decades. But, as it happened, Kermit's finest moment came when he saved *Newsweek* from disaster by keeping what looked like the biggest story of the year out of the magazine.

Karl Fleming, a darkly handsome, vibrant Southerner, had been *Newsweek*'s top domestic correspondent before he left to run an alternative weekly in Los Angeles, where he had been based. One day, Karl showed up at *Newsweek* with a dazzling exclusive—D. B. Cooper's own story. Cooper was the mysterious hijacker who'd seized a Northwest Orient Boeing 727 airliner in November 1971 and parachuted from the tail ramp somewhere over Washington state with twenty-one pounds of $20 bills strapped to his body. Cooper had never been seen again and was already a hero of American folklore.

Fleming was offering his scoop to Kermit on condition that *Newsweek* run it without rereporting it. He gave Kermit forty-eight hours to decide—and warned that if Kermit turned it down, he would go across town to Time-Life. "Wait till the word gets out that you had first crack at *Time*'s big sensation and turned it down," he told Lansner. Kermit was already under fire over the lackluster magazine he was putting out. The D. B. Cooper sensation could save him. Passing it up and getting scooped by the competition would surely finish him.

To his eternal credit, Lansner stood up to the excruciating pressure. He told Fleming he wanted twenty-four hours to check the story as thoroughly as he could and then he'd make his decision. Meanwhile, one of the magazine's top writers starting cranking out a cover-story version and the art director designed a D. B. Cooper cover.

On Friday afternoon, Bill Cook of the San Francisco bureau got hold of the passenger manifest from the flight Cooper had hijacked. Armed with a photo of Cooper supplied by Fleming, Cook went from house to house in the area around Portland, Oregon, where the flight originated and showed the image to Cooper's fellow fliers. He called Saturday morning to report that not one recognized the man in the picture. But the crucial call came a few hours later.

Among other vivid details, Fleming's Cooper related how he'd stared at the land beneath the starry skies as he stood poised to jump from the rear of the 727.

Now, over the telephone squawk box on Kermit's desk, Henry Simmons, a former science editor now in *Newsweek*'s Washington bureau, was calling in.

"It's balloon gas, Kermit," cried Simmons. "It's all balloon gas!"

He had gone to the Federal Aviation Administration, which files weather reports sent in every three hours by small airports all over the country. Following the path of the Cooper flight, he'd checked the reports from the airstrips Cooper had flown over that night.

"It was overcast," said Simmons triumphantly. "Nobody could have seen the ground or the stars!"

And so Lansner sent Fleming packing with his world exclusive—which turned out later to have been a hoax by two con men who had simply gone to the public library, cribbed details from old local newspapers, and then written it up as D. B. Cooper's own story. By the simple act of *reporting the story,* Kermit had saved *Newsweek* from a fiasco that would have stigmatized the magazine for years. As with Stan Opotowsky's cool professionalism handling the mine rescue at the *Post* more than a decade earlier, I never forgot the lesson of Kermit's courage and common sense in a tight corner.

During his short tenure as editor of the magazine, Lansner constantly found himself having to pick the least worst of a set of unappetizing options. To his credit, he regularly made the right poor choice. "What else could I do?" he'd invariably say. "Look at what I was offered." What he never understood, but I grasped instinctively, was that it was the editor's job to make sure strong material was always available. The editor had to picture himself squirming at the end of the week, and squeeze, cajole, beg, or threaten early enough so that there was always a strong fallback project on tap if somehow the planned cover story fell through or was overtaken by events. "It's the best we had" was never good enough.

Oz Elliott was *Newsweek*'s Sun King—and not just for the rosy complexion nurtured by a lunchtime martini. Elliott was a charismatic editor with a commanding officer's snap and a real moral sense who drove *Newsweek* to transcend its DNA as the perpetual also-ran to *Time.* Oz came from an old but not especially well-to-do New York family, had followed the Buckley-St. Paul's-Harvard-U.S. Navy track, and started in journalism on the *Journal of Commerce.* After a successful stint at *Time,* Elliott had defected to *Newsweek* and become editor at just thirty-six. In the years before I came to the magazine, Oz had recruited a talented band of editors, writers, and correspondents, and it showed. Elliott made sure that he never—or, hardly ever—had to settle for "the best we had."

While *Newsweek* couldn't match *Time*'s staff in depth and intellectual resources, Oz's magazine was sharper, faster, and more inventive. The difference would be dramatically on display on big, breaking stories, where *Newsweek* excelled. With Elliott leading the charge, *Newsweek* was first to grasp the galvanic significance of the civil-rights movement sweeping the South. Just the week before my tryout, *Newsweek* had treated the March on Washington and Martin Luther King's "I have a dream" speech at the Lincoln Memorial as a transcendent moment in postwar American history.

Elliott could be chilly and aloof, especially if his orders were challenged or his enthusiasms unappreciated. He cared about staff morale, but he could use his editing pencil like a rapier. *ZZZZZ!* he'd scrawl next to a boring lead on a writer's story or the even more dread *MEGO!*—an acronym for My Eyes Glaze Over. Hard-to-parse passages earned a *HUH?* and rough ones an *AWK!* or an *UGH!*

Barely six weeks into my new *Newsweek* career, Lester Bernstein began assigning me political stories. The same thing had happened at the *Post.* Editors quickly recognized that I had a nonideological feel for American politics and sighed with relief that they'd found somebody to trust with the work. Early on, I'd realized that I'd never be able to master American political history from the start; so I decided to concentrate on the post-FDR period, starting with the 1948 election when Harry Truman beat not only Tom Dewey but also Strom Thurmond, running on the segregationist Dixiecrat ticket, and Henry Wallace, the head-in-the-clouds candidate of the Communist-led Progressive Party.

At *Newsweek,* my assignment on that third week in November 1963 was to work with the magazine's new pollster, Lou Harris, on a piece about the forthcoming Republican presidential primary in New Hampshire, a big test for Barry Goldwater, the Arizona conservative who was scaring the pants off the liberal Eastern wing of the party. I can't remember now how Harris's data showed Goldwater, Nelson Rockefeller, and Henry Cabot Lodge running in New Hampshire, where the first-in-the-nation primary was scheduled for early in the new year. But I do know that my piece was supposed to lead the Nation section (as we called it) and that Lester had already edited it on Friday by the time the writers headed over for a liquid lunch at the New Weston Hotel across the street.

The New Weston was one of the last stand-up bars, except for the *Lost Weekend* saloons that still drew morning and afternoon drinkers around town. The long, polished wood bar had a brass rail running along the bottom and green-leather booths lining the opposite wall. The generous drinks were poured by a laconic barman named Gus, who had a neatly trimmed mustache and an almost impenetrable Germanic accent. The Nation writers were convinced that he owned a dozen apartment houses in the Bronx and worked for the fun of it. I was standing with Peter Goldman, working on my second I. W. Harper—a taste acquired from

Betsy Luce at the *Post*—when Gus learned forward behind the bar and beckoned to us.

"You guys are with *Newsweek*, you should know this: The president was shot in Texas. They hit him in the hand," he said.

We dashed out of the bar and met another *Newsweek* staffer, who had been elsewhere, who told us Kennedy had been shot in the head and that it looked bad. Back at the office, writers, editors, and researchers were clustered around the black-and-white TV set. Moments before Gus the barman alerted us, Walter Cronkite had reported: "Here is a bulletin from CBS News. In Dallas, Texas, three shots were fired at President Kennedy's motorcade in downtown Dallas. The first reports say that President Kennedy has been seriously wounded by this shooting."

He updated his reports every few minutes, but the outcome was clear enough. Finally, at 2:38 PM, a choked-up Cronkite looked at the camera and said simply: "From Dallas, Texas, the flash—apparently official—President Kennedy died at 1:00 PM Central Standard Time, 2:00 PM Eastern Standard Time. . . ."

This was the biggest and most wrenching story I'd been involved in during my brief career. It would make a more dramatic tale if I'd gone through the next forty-eight hours fighting through my anguished tears to work on the assassination issue. But in fact I had no emotional reaction to it at all. I went numb, as I would while working on all the big stories I would deal with over the next forty years—including September 11, when I was editor in chief of the *New York Daily News,* within sight of the burning twin towers. A perfect professional detachment would overtake me, similar perhaps to the calm that steadies the surgeon's hand at the critical moment or firms the lawyer's voice for his summation.

All I could do was wait patiently for my assignment as Oz and his editors marshaled the *Newsweek* staff for the biggest story of their lives at the magazine. They tore up the issue, dispatched correspondents and photographers to Dallas, put the Washington and foreign bureaus to work, and alerted the printing plants around the country to gear up for a huge, late press run. When the story list for the issue was posted later on Friday, Peter Goldman was assigned to write the narrative of the assassination. My job was to write the history of the Kennedy administration—on deadline! I'd have files from the Washington bureau and help from the *Newsweek* library, but I knew immediately that the judgments and analysis would be mine. I was essentially on my own.

The other writers and researchers drifted home early, knowing that material would be pouring in overnight and that their real work couldn't start until Saturday, when all the stories would have to be written, edited, fact-checked, and laid out in time for printed magazines to reach newsstands around the country first thing Monday morning. I knew that my only hope was to stay all night. At 2:00 AM, I looked up from my legal pad and realized I was alone. The only sound was the water cooler turning itself on and off in the deserted office. Every hour or so I'd panic, certain that my instant history would look pathetically amateurish in the light of day. Hunched in my cubicle, I had concluded that most of the achievements of JFK's presidency would prove ephemeral. The enduring legacies would be the glamour that enveloped the Kennedy years, the legend of the Cuban Missile Crisis, and the Peace Corps—not a bad call for a twenty-six-year-old kid who'd just escaped from the rewrite bank of the *New York Post*.

The assassination issue was a triumph for *Newsweek,* distinguished by Goldman's brilliant narrative, and a moving essay entitled "That Special Grace" by Ben Bradlee, the magazine's Washington bureau chief and a Kennedy pal. (The personal and journalistic complexity of Bradlee's relationship with JFK would come to light only later.) The press run was interrupted Sunday morning so the magazine could be updated when Jack Ruby dodged out of the crowd in the basement of Dallas police headquarters and assassinated Kennedy's assassin, Lee Harvey Oswald. Elliott's cover choice—a compelling portrait of the martyred president—easily eclipsed *Time's* pedestrian picture of the new president, Lyndon Johnson, which many read as *Time's* back of the hand to JFK.

Bradlee was my collaborator—or, more accurately, I was his amanuensis—for my first *Newsweek* cover story early in the new year. The story was called "Jackie's New Life," and the cover showed her peeking out from the doorway of Averell Harriman's Georgetown home, where she had taken refuge after LBJ moved into the White House. The story was based entirely on a brief file from Bradlee, who had talked to Mrs. Kennedy and others close to her. The trick was that there were no direct quotes in the file. Indeed, the story couldn't even hint that *Newsweek* had spoken to anybody at all. It was all divine writ. Even so, I buffed the piece to a high sheen and couldn't help being pleased when Bernstein complimented me on it on Saturday afternoon.

"I think I just made a sow's ear out of a sow's ear," I said modestly.

I was sitting smugly in my cubicle an hour later when one of the researchers handed me a green file from the Washington bureau.

"Well, kid," it read, "I didn't think you started out with a sow's ear, but you sure didn't finish with one. Great job!" It was signed, "Ben."

Lester, it turned out, had played back my flip remark to Bradlee. I was mortified. But I gathered from Bradlee's generous and debonair message how much I had to learn if I was going to be making a career among pros like him.

From then on, stories about the Kennedys became one of my specialties. When the Warren Commission report came out in September 1964, I was assigned to glean all the facts about Lee Harvey Oswald, which appeared in two different parts of the report.

Poring over the material, I learned for the first time how inadequate were the FBI's vaunted field investigation reports. Bureau agents did indeed interview hundreds of people who'd known Oswald, but there was no coordination among the G-men. Agent X had no way of knowing about intriguing leads that Agent Y had picked up in his interviews and couldn't follow up with the subject he was questioning. So the FBI amassed mountains of information without any sense of pattern or direction—an approach that, judging from the scathing post-9/11 critiques of the bureau, still held true nearly forty years later.

The Kennedy assassination was still gripping three years later when William Manchester published his big book authorized by the Kennedy family. Manchester, a Marine veteran and onetime *Baltimore Sun* reporter, had known JFK since the war and was thought to be a trusted family chronicler. But something had gone wrong: suddenly the Kennedy family was marshaling all its clout to force Manchester and his publisher, Harper & Row, to delete troublesome passages from his manuscript. In fact, Manchester had already made major changes in the book, which originally all but blamed Lyndon Johnson for Kennedy's murder. It wasn't entirely clear what the latest fuss was about, but it was a sensation at the time, and Oz tossed the grenade to me.

It dawned on me at once that because *Newsweek* had only a token bureau in New York, I'd not only have to write the story, I'd mostly have to report it myself. We did have a few advantages: A *Newsweek* editor named Jim Cannon knew Manchester from the *Sun* days and took me to see him in Middletown, Connecticut, where he was teaching at Wesleyan. Oz Elliott was a chum of the editor in chief of Harper & Row, Evan Thomas, the son of Norman Thomas, the great American socialist. Thomas had us over for chicken sandwiches (on white with the crusts cut off) at his desk in a building conveniently around the corner from *Newsweek*. These intimate contacts with two of the principals in the furor were what news magazines live for. Unfortunately, tea with Manchester and chicken sandwiches with Thomas yielded nothing really useful. The heart of the story was the passages the Kennedys were trying to suppress, and author and publisher wouldn't really talk about them. So there I sat on late Friday—less than twenty-four hours from deadline—trying to cobble together a cover story out of color notes.

By 11:00 PM I knew that I wouldn't be able to make this turkey fly. Then the phone rang. The raspy voice on the line identified himself as Dick Goodwin, the Kennedys' literary *consigliere*.

"I understand you're doing a piece on the book, Ed," said my new best friend, who invited me to meet him at Robert Kennedy's apartment at UN Plaza, a new luxury high-rise on the East River.

I got to the flat around midnight to find Goodwin sitting on the sofa, drinking brandy. He offered me one and almost at once excused himself to take a call, leaving me to wander around the room. It was full of family photos, but the furnishings could charitably be described as cheesy—hardly an outsider's idea of Kennedy glamour.

When Goodwin returned and we began to talk, it was obvious that the brandy I found him fondling wasn't his first of the evening. But he made perfect, chilling sense. The pressure of doing the JFK book, he said, had overwhelmed Manchester. "He started calling his wife 'Jackie,' and his daughter 'Caroline,'" reported Goodwin. I could use what he told me, but I couldn't say that I'd met with him and I had to attribute it all to Kennedy family sources.

Goodwin's message was that the unhinged writer had put all sorts of nutty stuff in the book and the poor Kennedys, who had authorized the work, now had the desperate task of getting it out of the manuscript. Manchester, who denied that he'd gone around the bend, was trying to portray—"spin," we'd say today—it as a censorship battle pitting the heroic truth-teller against the selfish enemies of history.

Then Goodwin dramatically left the room again and returned with a big wad of galley proofs—the Holy Grail!

I was salivating into my snifter. "What you've told me is really fascinating, Dick," I said, trying to sound as ingenuous as I could. "If you'll give me an hour with the galleys, I know I can find a lot of examples of what you're taking about."

"I can't do that, Ed," he replied.

Over the next fifteen minutes, I tried every argument I could muster to coax the galleys out of his grip. Nothing worked.

When I was as frantic as he wanted me to be, Goodwin made the offer he'd planned from the start: "I'll read to you from the galleys and you can take notes."

So Goodwin read selectively—very selectively—from Manchester, and I scribbled down some passages that must have sounded shocking at the time. The only one I recall had Jackie looking into a mirror on the day of her husband's funeral and being distressed to spot a fresh set of wrinkles around her eyes.

When Goodwin had leaked his last, I beat it out of UN Plaza, dashed back to the office, and began rebuilding my cover story around the fresh nuggets I'd collected. I broke for a couple of hours' sleep and was back in my cubicle hammering away when Lester and the writers strolled in after 9:00 AM. When they asked what had happened, I told of my post-midnight tryst with Goodwin and the Rémy Martin.

A few hours later, my telephone rang and it was the now-familiar raspy voice.

"Ed, I hear you're telling people you met with me last night and that I was drunk."

I had a *klong*—a *Newsweek* term for a sudden rush of shit to the heart—but then instinct took over, and I came up with my first ever nondenial denial.

"Dick," I said, without even a gulp, "only the two of us were there and we know you weren't drunk, so how could I have said something like that?"

He grumbled, but accepted my lie.

* * *

With the Jackie cover story in early 1964, I knew I could do the work at *Newsweek,* and a little of the tautness went out of my neck. The Wallendas knew it, too. Before I had a chance to enjoy my fledgling confidence, they handed me my next task—not simply a cover story, but an ambitious special project. In the spring of 1964, LBJ had launched his War on Poverty, with Kennedy brother-in-law Sargent Shriver in command. My job was to create, organize, edit, and write a multipart report on poverty in America. I read everything I could find, directed the bureaus to visit poverty pockets around the country, interviewed Shriver and his team in Washington and academics in Cambridge. I assigned myself the tone-setting lead piece and a tail piece describing how the poverty war was actually going to be waged.

"Poverty amid plenty is the paradox of American life," read my lead sentence, and, not having read Marx, I thought I'd hit on an original formulation of the problem. For the cover, the editors chose a picture of a conveniently beautiful young Appalachian girl with a fetching smudge on her cheek—a Madison Avenue fantasy of poverty in America borrowed from Dorothea Lange and the Great Depression.

All the elements of the package were written and edited by Friday afternoon of cover week except my coda on how Shriver proposed to fight LBJ's war. I sat down to knock it off, and for the first time in my life, I simply couldn't write a story. After a couple of hours, I decided that what I needed was a decent night's sleep. I'd be back in the office at seven Saturday morning and have the piece on Lester's desk by the time he came in at 9:30 or so.

Next morning was worse. However I tried, I couldn't get past the first paragraph. At 11:00, my Brooks Brothers button-down was drenched in flop sweat and I knew what I had to do. I slipped into Lester's office and stood in front of his desk. He looked up, expecting to hear that my piece was ready.

"Lester," I said. "I've let you down. I just can't write the story. So let me resign and I'll try to get my old job back at the paper."

"Relax, kid," he said cheerfully. "It's only a twenty-five-cent magazine."

Open sesame! In a flash, I realized why I hadn't been able to write a coherent story about how the War on Poverty would be fought. The poverty warriors themselves didn't have a clue. *It wasn't my fault, it was theirs.* I went back to my cubicle and polished off the article in less than an hour. It basically said that Shriver & Company were full of ideas and good intentions but had no clear strategy—in capsule, the verdict that would be rendered years later when Johnson's ambitious effort finally petered out.

I never forgot that episode. In the most disarming way, Bernstein was telling me it was only journalism—that there were limits to how much clarity we could bring to confused and confusing reality. And I also learned that if I made a sustained and conscientious effort and still couldn't understand something in the news, it was simply too murky or unresolved to get straight. Henceforth, in writing, editing, or directing the reporting of a story, I would never be shy about saying I didn't understand something. It's remarkable what you can learn when people are forced to explain something that everyone else professes to understand.

News magazine writing—certainly in the '60s and '70s—was a craft unlike any other in journalism. It required an unerring eye for what was interesting combined with a keen sense of organization and an almost poetic gift for compression. An ideal news magazine story found the perfect narrative arc with no digressions or doubling back. Every sentence was a string of facts or a pithy quotation. And every story had its ration of color touches—those gobbets of tangy Stilton in the field greens salad at the summit—readers would never find in most newspapers.

Thanks to the fact-checking, news magazine articles were literally accurate —at the least, the names and the chronology were right—although the fundamental thrust of the story might be slanted or tendentious. Some accomplished journalists couldn't write a news magazine story if life itself were at stake, and some otherwise unheralded scriveners were wizards at it. "He's just not gaited for the work," Lester said of one highly touted prospect who flunked his tryout.

I felt then—and still do—that, at its best, news magazine journalism was a marvelously effective medium. A well-turned *Newsweek* story would harvest all the salient information from many sources and puree it into an easy-to-digest narrative, analysis, or profile. An hour or so spent with *Newsweek* or *Time* each week could keep a reader up on everything from politics to the latest wrinkle in medical research or theology. And the well-machined prose itself gave pleasure.

The very slickness of the news magazines and their self-conscious air of omniscience offended many newspaper people. After Bradlee left *Newsweek* to run the *Washington Post*, he delighted in needling Elliott and the rest of us as a bunch of high-priced dilettantes who cribbed their stories from the papers when they weren't busy downing three-martini expense-account lunches. For all their repetitiousness and lack of polish, the newspapers had a kind of honesty and knobby authenticity the news mags could never achieve—or so the argument went.

Even as I was starting out at *Newsweek*, Cassandras were foretelling the death of news magazines. Like the dinosaurs—a favorite metaphor of all doomsayers—they were done for. Forty years later, *Newsweek*, *Time*, and *U.S. News* have a combined circulation of about 9 million, publish more than 6,000 pages of advertising each year, and turn a handsome profit (at least *Time* and *Newsweek* do).

Having made my escape from the *Post*, I wasn't inclined to waste much anxiety on the prospects of *Newsweek*, even though it was increasingly dawning on me that I could have a very bright future there. And I did. Over the next dozen years, I rose through the ranks at the magazine, progressing from writer to editor of the national affairs section and on to the Wallenda high wire. I wrote more than a score of cover stories, created a new section on the cities, and worked on all the magazine's big projects, including an innovative 1967 special report called, quaintly enough, "The Negro in America: What Must Be Done," and a later investigative package, "Justice on Trial," both of which won National Magazine Awards.

I met all the American presidents from Nixon to the first Bush, dozens of other politicians, nabobs, and moguls, and got to see a lot of America and the world. I probably learned more about how to manage people—and how not to manage them—than I did about journalism. And I learned a lot about myself, not all of it becoming.

When Oz Elliott called Peter Goldman, our colleague Larry Martz, and me into his office early in 1967, we had no inkling of the scope or recklessness of what he had in mind. From their founding, the news magazines had never indulged in explicit editorializing. Few readers were in the dark about how Luce's *Time* felt about the great issues and personalities of the day, but they still had to get the message for themselves from the slant of the stories, the choices of covers, pictures, and headlines. *Newsweek* let its columnists give their opinions, but the magazine itself took no stands, at least overt ones. Now Oz proposed to change that. We were going to do an advocacy issue in which *Newsweek* would draft its own program for black advancement in America. More precisely, Goldman, Martz, and I were going to dream up that program. We were aghast.

The task was impossible! Who were we to devise solutions for a problem that had tormented the country since its birth? We were journalists, not policy analysts! (Today we would have said policy "wonks.") It was, to invoke Kermit, madness! Oz listened patiently to our panicky mewling and told us to think about it for a couple of days and then come back for another talk. When we returned, Peter, Larry, and I were even more frozen in our determination not to undertake Oz's pet scheme. We had rehearsed our arguments and we delivered them with passion and lucidity. Once again Oz respectfully heard us out. Then he gave us a lesson in leadership that I can still evoke at will.

At the Harvard Business School in the 1970s—and today, for all I know—there was a conceit called "The Valley of the Shadow of Death." All big deals and projects ultimately found their way there, and it was at this critical point that the leader had to push past his alarmed followers' entreaties to turn back—and spur them onward to salvation. Oz wasn't fazed by our faint-heartedness. He looked from one to the other of us seated around him. "I understand how you feel, but we've got to do it!" he said, pounding his fist into his open palm. More stage fright, another pounded fist—and we were embarked.

Much of what we proposed was from the conventional liberal syllabus, but we did come up with one original notion—a literacy program starting before kindergarten. It foreshadowed many of the initiatives in the decades to come.

Writers and midlevel editors didn't often venture out of the office, but when they did, the experiences were all the more vivid for being so rare. The 1968 presidential campaign was the most inflamed in modern American history, and I was able to escape my cubicle to follow Robert Kennedy as he careered across the country like a man under a spell. Lyndon Johnson had abdicated after barely defeating Gene McCarthy, the first antiwar candidate, in the New Hampshire primary. RFK, who had hung back when McCarthy challenged LBJ, now jumped into the race.

The Kennedy campaign was a punishing cavalcade of eighteen-hour days spent on whistle-stop train trips (self-consciously reminiscent of Harry

Truman's give-'em-hell 1952 upset of the starchy Thomas E. Dewey) and motorcades through rapturous ghettos. RFK first rode a revived Wabash Cannonball through Indiana. There was a lunchtime rally at the Soldiers and Sailors Memorial, a huge Mussolini-worthy monument in the center of Indianapolis where secretaries squealed at Bobby in his shirtsleeves. A night-time motorcade inched through the streets of Gary while hundreds of black teenagers ran alongside the cars, whooping and hollering as Kennedy waved distractedly and flashed his boyish off-center grin.

A few weeks later, we were in Portland, Oregon, where Kennedy faced off against McCarthy, whose chilly moralism somehow appealed to the New England roots of the Oregonians more than Bobby's fervor. On the morning of primary day, William vanden Heuvel, Kennedy's state campaign manager, was the picture of despair as he made his rounds toting a couple of clean shirts for the candidate in cellophane bags. Vanden Heuvel knew he was involved in a historic episode, the first election ever lost by any Kennedy, and that he would forever be associated with the outcome.

In a top-floor suite at the Benson Hotel, Richard Nixon spent primary day in a better mood, although he was going to lose the Republican primary to Nelson Rockefeller. ("Battling Nelson did it!" exulted *Time* next week.) Nixon knew he was going to win the Republican nomination and that he stood a good chance of defeating whoever the Democrats ran to succeed Johnson. To pass the time, he had a fresh reporter scheduled every forty-five minutes throughout the day. When *Newsweek*'s turn came, my colleague and I thought at first the suite was empty. A freshly pressed suit hung eerily on a door. Then we spotted Nixon. He was seated in a barrel-shaped club chair, his arms wrapped around his legs, which were pulled up to his chest. He looked like a troll hunched under a toadstool in a fairy tale. With crisp pre-cision, he outlined the coming presidential campaign culminating in his election. His analysis turned out to be right, although he couldn't know that Kennedy would be dead in a few weeks and that the Democratic convention in Chicago would be a nightmare of hatred and violence.

After Oregon, Kennedy made what would be his last trip, a whistle-stop campaign through the dusty agricultural towns of California's Central Valley. At each stop, a few hundred farm workers gathered reverently at the bunting-draped railing of the last car as the train drew to a halt. The reporters clambered down to watch, among them the magisterial columnist

Joseph Alsop, a fat finger holding his place in the volume of Thucydides he carried everywhere.

Kennedy made the same speech, with its Camus quotation—"Perhaps we cannot make this a world in which children no longer suffer. But at least we can reduce the number of suffering children"—wherever he went, but he always managed to salute each burg for its world-renowned artichokes or Brussels sprouts. By the end of the day, he was so punchy that he didn't known whether he was in Turlock or Merced and bade fervent farewell to wherever he thought he was. Then it was back onto his chartered Boeing 727 for the flight to Los Angeles and his election-night appointment in Samara.

In those days before AIDS and sexual-harassment codes, that Kennedy campaign was one of the randiest ever seen. Bloody Marys were always available before takeoff, after takeoff, and during takeoff, and there was so much late-night scampering around that it's a wonder any stories ever got written and filed. Every once in a while these days, I catch a glimpse of an oh-so-serious talking head on TV and flash back to the young blonde sneaking off with the hard-boiled *Washington Post* political reporter down some dim hotel corridor. Such behavior would scandalize today's journalism police, but it all seemed harmless and charming in its day.

Barely five years after the Kennedy assassination, reporters never let a candidate out of their sight during the '68 campaign. I would have been following Bobby through the kitchen of the Ambassador Hotel in Los Angeles on primary night, but I had to go home to Alice. I'd been on the road for a week, during which she'd had to entertain her parents, who had retired to Florida and were up for a visit. On Sunday, I thought of changing my plans and remaining in L.A., but Alice sounded so forlorn on the phone that I didn't have the heart to stay away any longer. So I flew back to New York and went to the office on Tuesday. That night, I tried to stay up to watch the primary coverage to the end, but I was still exhausted from the trip and packed it in after it was clear that Kennedy had won California.

Alice, who was up early to get the boys off to school, told me the news when I got up. I rushed to the office to prepare for another Kennedy assassination issue, but by three o'clock I felt so terrible that I had to go home, where I went right to bed. I believed that for the first time in my life I was having an emotional reaction to a big story—the assassination of Robert Kennedy had literally floored me. I slept fitfully that night. Next morning, I felt even worse. Alice brought me a glass of juice and suddenly stared at my chest.

"You've got red blotches all over," she said.

Then I realized that my reaction hadn't been emotional after all; I'd been incubating a case of German measles caught from the kids, and now the evidence was undeniable. For the first time since I'd gone to work on *The Campus,* I missed working on a big story because I was too sick to lift my head up off the pillow.

In the run-up to another presidential campaign, I found myself flying around Florida in an Art Deco DC-3 with John Lindsay, the liberal Republican mayor of New York, who had switched parties and was running in the Democratic primaries. Lindsay was a favorite of Oz Elliott's, so much so that I'd had to buff his glory in two *Newsweek* cover stories. The first stop was South Beach, the low-rent retirement haven in Miami Beach for thousands of New York Jews. Lindsay had become anathema to many of them because he favored a low-cost public housing project that would bring many blacks to Forest Hills in Queens. As Lindsay and his aides paraded down South Beach's main drag, a plane flew overhead dragging a banner reading **LINDSAY MEANS TSOURIS**—"trouble" in Yiddish.

When we stopped outside a popular deli, an angry little man came barreling out of the crowd and raised his fist to slam Lindsay in the back of the head. Mindful of the assassinations, I threw myself between the little man and the candidate and pushed him away from Lindsay, who campaigned on as if nothing had happened.

Pat Vecchio, a New York cop who acted as the mayor's bodyguard, grabbed my arm and pulled me aside.

"Why'd you do that?" he grumped.

"He was going to slug the candidate," I explained, pleased with my civic intervention.

"So what? It would have been a great headline for Lindsay," replied Vecchio with a grasp of politics plainly superior to mine.

After a long day prop-stopping through Florida, Lindsay's plane was finally heading back to the starting point, Miami. The mayor was always described as "patrician" and people were always complaining that he was too starchy, so he rather ostentatiously loosened his tie and joined the small press party in the back of the DC-3 for a just-us-guys drink. Among them was

Hunter Thompson, who had inexplicably joined up and had been trotting around with us all day toting his own personal six-pack of beer. As Lindsay awkwardly bantered with the reporters, Thompson suddenly leaned forward, fixed the candidate with an earnest look, and said:

"Mr. Mayor, why are you such an asshole?"

Lindsay stared at Thompson as if a giant cockroach had materialized before him, and the ersatz bonhomie evaporated in a heartbeat. Undeterred, Hunter flashed that gonzo grin of his and hoisted another brew.

In 1969, after six years at *Newsweek,* I got to edit the national affairs section, the flagship of the magazine. This was, by far, the hardest job I ever had, poised as it was between my staff, the thoroughbred writers and researchers of the Nation section, and my bosses, the cranky, quixotic Wallendas. It was my first taste since college of managing people, and my first opportunity to put into practice the leadership impulses that I'd been marinating over the years. In this, I was powerfully influenced by the Kennedys—or, more precisely, by the emerging myth of Kennedy activism. To my mind, it was the leader's job not simply to solve problems, but to *anticipate* them and find solutions even before his followers recognized that there was a problem to solve. The practical benefits of this approach were evident. The perils should have been equally apparent, but I was too callow to see them.

Outwardly more assured than I had any right to be, I drove the staff hard and myself even harder. The section was better than it had been in years, but the atmosphere could be tight. I knew what had to be done and how it had to be done, and I didn't waste a lot of time explaining why. People told me I terrified them in meetings because I was always three steps ahead. I had an influential and articulate ally in Peter Goldman, but some of his colleagues chafed under the taut rein. One summer, I returned from a month's vacation on Cape Cod to find a huge picture of Peter—who had run the section while I was away—taped to my office door.

Trouble at home made my life as fraught there as at the office, although I never mentioned it to anybody. My mother had spotted Alice's eggshell psyche the first time she'd met her. "Don't marry a sick girl," she cautioned. But I rationalized away her warning as a jealous mother's desperate ploy to hold on to her boy. Now, raising two young children with a husband consumed by his work was taking its toll on Alice. What had begun as a skittishness about crossing big open spaces or driving through tunnels metastasized into a classic case of agoraphobia. Alice became convinced that she would lose control and collapse if she walked on the street or rode in an elevator. She became essentially house-ridden, although she would venture out clutching my arm if the trip couldn't be avoided.

Alice was no stranger to mental problems. He mother, an elementary-school teacher in the Bronx, was prone to manic fits and depressive sieges. When she was on a high, my mother-in-law would go on shopping sprees or reorganize all the closets in their two-bedroom Parkchester flat, babbling away the whole time. Then the switch flipped. She'd creep into her bed in the dark and turn her face to the wall, not uttering a word or eating a morsel for days. Alice's mother was one of the first bipolar patients treated with lithium salts by Dr. Nathan Kline at Rockland State Hospital. The dosages were huge in those pioneering days, and they stabilized her frantic mood swings. But over time, she began acting strangely in other ways. One day, she became convinced that the spoons in her kitchen cabinet were sending her messages in secret code. Eventually she became totally gaga. After her death, an autopsy showed changes in her brain tissue that today would be recognized as signs of Alzheimer's disease.

For a few years, a string of psychiatrists had been treating Alice for anxiety and depression. I had the same symptoms, but without the agoraphobia. One day in 1969, I looked at a picture of myself just taken at the magazine for publicity use. Staring back at me was a despairing man in black-framed glasses who looked a lot older than thirty-one. His eyes were haunted. I decided I needed to see a psychiatrist, too.

It sounds odd, and it didn't always feel that way, but the next eighteen months were a treat for me—a graduate school at which I took a master's degree in a subject that had always fascinated me: myself. I was as introspective as the next narcissist, but I had been striving as long as I could remember, and I'd never had time—or made time—to think through, or even fully feel, the conflicted emotions that had gripped me since childhood.

The doctor was relatively young and his approach was eclectic. I quickly learned what should have been obvious: I was such a good talker that—without intervention—I could have prattled on for months camouflaging everything important with swirls of words out of a Steinberg drawing. But the doctor had seen that act before, and soon enough he stepped in. One evening, I was gassing on about how happy I could be if only Alice weren't so hobbled or my job weren't so stressful or whatever. If, if, if . . .

"If my uncle had tits, he'd be my aunt," the doctor said simply, and that stratagem evaporated.

I trained myself to remember my dreams and became quite adept at winkling out their emotional content rather than parsing their narratives, which were often beguilingly ingenious. Once, I volunteered a pat interpretation of a dream.

"If that's all it's about, why go to the trouble of dreaming it?" he asked. Point taken.

I had recurrent dreams of a huge jetliner looming over the city and slowly floating down, and of flying like a bird over the harbor and the skyline, which I came to recognize as precursors of mopiness (frequent) or exhilaration (rare). One night, I had a vivid dream of walking through a cemetery and nearly tripping over a femur sticking out of a grave. I didn't need any help deciphering that one: I had reached the point where I either had to go deep into my love for my parents and my discomfort with them or shy away from the treatment. For a few more sessions I tried to press on, but it was hopeless. I simply couldn't will myself to excavate the painful deposits. The patient had to be so miserable and tormented that he had no choice. It wasn't an elective course.

Aborted as the therapy was, it worked to a remarkable degree. Perhaps it was because, after feeling yoked to my family responsibilities and my nerve-racking work, I felt that I was finally catering to myself. Perhaps it was the central insight I'd found in the treatment. My first preoccupation in my talks with the doctor had been my yearning for perfect intimacy—that sense of utter love and companionship in an inhospitable world.

"This is what I mean," I said one day, holding my hands before me, the pointed index fingers pressed seamlessly together.

"Why should you expect to have that?" the doctor asked.

Over time, I came to understand that, like everyone else, I was essentially on my own and had to make the best of it. Trying to replicate my childhood bond with my mother wasn't the answer. Simply identifying the root of my throbbing sense of loss remarkably disarmed it. I felt better.

My situation made me an obvious candidate for the kind of office romance so available at *Newsweek* in those days. Here was a group of men in their prime working in a hermetic setting with a group of well-bred young women, nearly all of them unmarried and many quite attractive, whose basic job was to serve them. The majority of the girls—and they hadn't yet morphed into the young women of the feminist vocabulary—came from families with money, some of which they spent each week on psychotherapy or four-day-a-week psychoanalysis. The magazine routinely rented hotel rooms on Friday nights for writers and editors working too late to get home to the suburbs, making illicit love—or sex—more convenient.

The concept of sexual harassment hadn't yet been codified, and some of the men were predatory hounds. One editor in particular was notorious for practically stalking the shifting objects of his affection. A young writer called me one night to report that an important *Newsweek* editor was even then staring up at the window of a researcher the writer was dating. What should she do? I told him to tell her to ignore the editor and he'd go away. She did and he did. Some of the office flings turned into real romances and led to happy marriages, after the man got his divorce. For a number of the young women, the office affairs, unsatisfactory as they might be, were a rite of passage that may have done them more good than harm—unfashionable as it is now to suggest that.

Out of cowardice or a sense of self-preservation, I resisted the temptation, although at times I ached with longing and occasionally made an ambiguous pass. With success as national affairs editor, I knew I was on track to be a Wallenda—perhaps to get to the top of the high-wire pyramid—and I didn't want to be gossiped about that way. When I first strayed, it was away from the office and the people who worked there.

But I wasn't immune to office intrigue. One day, Lester Bernstein, who had become a Wallenda, called me in and closed his office door. Oz Elliott, it turned out, had privately agreed with Ed Diamond, a senior editor who oversaw Science, Education, Medicine, and all the other noncultural back-of-the-book sections, to elevate Diamond to the Wallenda wire. Diamond was a high-energy editor, but Lester and many of us hated his harum-scarum style. Ed thrived in chaos and was happy to create it when it suited him. More to the point, Diamond was a natural rival for Bernstein—and for me down the road.

As we met, Diamond was on his way to Moscow on a reporting trip, but before he left, he couldn't resist leaking the news of his promotion to a researcher he fancied, even scribbling the new pecking order on a napkin for her. She, in turn, couldn't keep the big news to herself, and soon the magazine was buzzing with the word. Had Diamond kept his mouth shut, his promotion would have been proclaimed to the staff as a fait accompli on his return. Instead, Lester had time to maneuver. We were soon in Oz's office telling him that it was, of course, his prerogative to give Diamond any title he liked, but that we wouldn't work with him as a Wallenda. Others felt that way, too.

This put Elliott in a miserable bind: two of his best people were challenging his decision to reward a third. To rescind the promotion would be to break his word to Diamond; not to would cause a rebellion. Oz hated to have his authority questioned, but he folded. When Diamond returned from Moscow and heard the news, he left the magazine (and turned up years later as a valuable contributor for me at *New York* magazine).

This and other episodes gave me an understanding of life in the media that guided me for decades. I realized that big-time journalism was like *La Ronde,* Arthur Schnitzler's turn-of-the-century play about the liaisons of a string of interconnected characters. If you lasted long enough in journalism, you'd hire people who'd fired you, be fired by people you'd hired, find yourself working for people who'd been your colleagues or subordinates, and bossing people who'd been your bosses. "Always be nice to them on the way up because you may meet them on the way down," my father used to counsel, wisely, as always.

As a journalist it was my good fortune to work in national affairs at *Newsweek* during the years when it seems the nation itself might be self-destructing. Besides the assassination of JFK, the murders of Robert Kennedy and Martin Luther King happened on my watch, as did the Harlem, Watts, and Detroit riots, the shooting of George Wallace, the Moon landing, Chappaquiddick, the Vietnam War, the antiwar crusade and the campus riots, Richard Nixon's landslide over George McGovern, and the Watergate scandal that brought Nixon down.

Watergate began horribly for *Newsweek,* but ultimately became one of its finest hours. Bradlee's *Washington Post* owned the story from the beginning, leaving Max Frankel's *New York Times* Washington bureau pathetically trying to catch up. *Time* and *Newsweek* were out of the early running, too, which

Bradlee never tired of pointing out to Kay Graham and Oz. By now, I was managing editor of the magazine and slowly we began to gain some traction.

We quickly realized that the magazine's traditional way of running things simply didn't work in the Watergate world of exploding scoops and tantalizing leads. The news magazine's great advantage in a huge evolving story like this was its ability to synthesize great gobs of news and present it in coherent weekly installments, a continuing narrative. But *Newsweek's* weakness was inherent in its strength: in a story as volatile as Watergate, the magazine risked being overtaken by events, its latest chapter rendered irrelevant or off-track by a late-breaking newspaper scoop. So we improvised, establishing an ex-com of New York writers and editors who convened each morning for a squawk box telephone conference with Mel Elfin, the Washington Bureau chief, and his increasingly plugged-in Watergate reporters. That way, we could discuss the latest wrinkles in the story and, more important, try to plan for contingencies.

There are any number of metaphors for running a news magazine, which must close all copy by Saturday evening and then run on presses all over the country—and the world, for that matter—so that more than 3 million copies reach newsstands and subscribers starting Monday morning. Steering a huge ocean liner is one: you've got to start turning the rudder well before the great vessel responds and settles into a new course. But I prefer the image of the high wire. Your choices shrink with each step in the editorial week. You can't stop, and at a certain point you can't turn back. If you want to be able to make choices late, you've got to build those options into your progress—with Plans A, B, or even C expressed in alternate page layouts for the issue, multiple cover possibilities, even provisions for emergency press and shipping schedules.

With Watergate, we could never know when a major development might break over the weekend, forcing a drastic overhaul of the issue. The infamous Saturday Night Massacre, when Nixon fired Watergate special prosecutor Archibald Cox, leading Attorney General Elliot Richardson and his deputy to resign rather than carry out the order, happened just a week after the Yom Kippur War between Israel and the Arabs, and once again we had to scramble. It was nerve-racking, and as the story stretched over the months, the task seemed to be endless. Amid all the tension and confusion, I discovered that I had a compass.

Early on, I was seized by the conviction that Nixon would be driven from office. I simply knew the outcome in my gut. It was the first time I'd ever felt such certainty about the direction of a big story, and nearly thirty years would pass before I felt that way again.

Between March 26, 1973, when *Newsweek* published the first cover, rather daintily headed **THE WATERGATE MESS**, and August 9, 1974, when Nixon gave his last weird salute and choppered off from the south lawn of the White House, we published more than thirty cover stories on the scandal. There were cartoons by the cover editor, Bob Engle, showing the embattled president as Laocoon wrestling with serpents and Nixon barely staying afloat at sea in a life preserver. There was Nixon standing like George C. Scott as Patton before a huge American flag proclaiming, "I am not a crook." There were Haldeman and Ehrlichman in their shades looking like banana republic goons out of *State of Siege.* There was John Mitchell and Rosemary Woods, craggy Judge John Sirica, slick John Dean, and Congressman Peter Rodino, as alert as a sparrow.

On July 16, 1973, on a rare day off, I was out at the beach with Alice listening to a portable radio when a previously unheralded presidential staffer named Alexander Butterfield told Senator Sam Ervin's Senate committee that Nixon had taped himself in the White House. Back in the office next morning, I told Bob Engle to scare up a tape recorder with reels that rotated atop the machine. Then I had the Washington bureau photographer, Wally McNamee, rent a small plane and get permission to fly briefly over the White House. (You could actually do such things in those days.) Engle photographed the tape recorder and Wally shot the White House from the same bird's-eye perspective. There were no design computers with their magical effects in 1973, so Engle had to use a retouching technique called a dye transfer. He seamlessly grafted the tape recorder reels onto the roof of the mansion and *violà!*—the White House as tape recorder.

The result is my favorite cover of the more than one thousand I oversaw at *Newsweek, New York,* and *Esquire* and the thousand-plus page ones we churned out at the *Daily News* during my time there. (Thirty years later, the American Society of Magazine Editors chose it as one of the fifty best covers of all time.)

But Watergate was a reporting, writing, and editing challenge, not a graphics exercise. Most of all, it was a test of stamina. In those days before overnight shipping and e-mail, transmitting documents was more Pony Express than Federal Express. The transcripts of the Nixon tapes prepared for the congressional hearings and legal cases were a sensation, revealing the president, for one thing, telling his attorney general, "I don't give a shit. I want you all to stonewall it, let them plead the Fifth Amendment, cover up, or anything else, if it'll save it—save the plan." But before we could write and edit the story and design a cover, we had to get hold of the goods and read it.

Often, the only way to get the material to New York overnight was to "pigeon" it. A Washington staffer would take the stuff to National Airport and arrange for a stewardess on a New York–bound flight to bring it along. A New York staffer would meet her at LaGuardia and deliver the transcripts to Peter Goldman's doorstep and mine, where we found them when we got up at 6:00 AM. We'd have it all read when we met at the office at 9:30 for the squawk box conference with Washington. We'd drag back to our homes in time for a couple of drinks and a late dinner and fall exhausted into bed— only to wake up at 6:00 AM. to be greeted by a fresh pile of transcripts.

As the story moved into the courts, the special prosecutor's office, and Congress, *Newsweek*'s Washington bureau began to break big news. On the day three Republican senators called on Nixon to tell him he had to quit, two of them reported to *Newsweek*'s chief congressional correspondent, Sam Shaffer, with a better verbatim account than Woodward and Bernstein's; and one of them, Hugh Scott of Pennsylvania, took notes for Sam. Another reporter, John Lindsay, brought John Dean's lawyer, an old pal, up to Top of the Week to tell us what Dean was going to testify to. A third got a Supreme Court justice to walk him through the Court's deliberations on the Nixon tapes case.

One night, I dozed off in front of the TV, to be roused by Charles Sandman, a Nixon loyalist on Rodino's House impeachment committee, brandishing a copy of *Newsweek* at a late hearing as he denounced our work to the nation. There were other Nixon scandals that came to the surface in the midst of the Watergate frenzy—and I learned a valuable lesson from one of them. At one point, the Washington bureau came up with what I thought was a second-tier story about tax trouble Nixon's daughter Tricia, who had been married at a splashy White House wedding, and her husband, Eddie Cox, were having over a minor Florida land deal. As was standard practice, we gave Nixon's press secretary, Ron Ziegler, a heads-up on the story on Saturday before deadline. Rather than treat the tax story as the minor flap we thought it was, Ziegler went on the attack. He issued a formal White House statement denouncing *Newsweek* for the article—which hadn't yet been published—and warning of the consequences. We scratched our heads and went to press. When I came back to the office after the weekend, my first visitors were the chief counsel of the Washington Post Company and a top *Newsweek* business executive.

"You guys better have that story nailed down," said the lawyer, sounding remarkably like Snively Whiplash from the *Bullwinkle* cartoon.

I assured him that we did, my fingers crossed under my desk. Soon afterward, we found out why Ziegler had so overreacted. It turned out that the president himself had big-time tax problems. He had taken a huge deduction for the value of his papers donated to the federal government, although such deductions had been outlawed, and he owed hundreds of thousands in back taxes and penalties. Ziegler had gone ballistic over Tricia's taxes to try to scare us away from her father's.

The lesson I took from this episode reinforced my earlier experience with the indignant producers of *Twenty-One* and served me well in years to come, helping me win a reputation as a news prophet of sorts: whenever a story triggers a disproportionate response from its subject, it is *always* a signal that a far bigger story is waiting there to be exposed.

With Goldman writing the weekly Watergate installments and the Washington bureau chipping in ever more useful reporting, *Newsweek* pulled away from *Time* and was broadly recognized as the magazine leader on the story. Syndicated research done soon afterward found more people reading each issue of *Newsweek* than *Time,* so we had a larger audience even though *Time* had a million more subscribers than *Newsweek* did.

Finally, the pressure became irresistible, and on Thursday, August 8, 1974, Nixon acknowledged what I'd known all along would happen: he resigned in a brief televised speech to the nation. Next morning, after his tearful farewell to the staff and paean to his sainted mother, he flew off to San Clemente in disgrace. On Saturday, we put the finishing touches on the issue, and on Sunday morning I flew to Nantucket to join Alice and the boys on vacation. People always harp on how incestuous big media can be. There was irrefutable proof of that aboard the twin-engine commuter plane that morning. Seated right behind the managing editor of *Newsweek* on the plane was the chief editor of *Time,* Henry Grunwald, and his wife, heading for their home on Martha's Vineyard.

"How many pages did you do on Nixon?" I asked Henry.

"We held it to thirty-six," he said.

"We did forty-eight," I said, and smiled to myself.

Although my title was managing editor, I had effectively been running the magazine for more than a year. Oz Elliott had first given up the editorship in 1970 when he moved over to lead the business side and handed the pencil to Kermit Lansner. But Oz never really was comfortable on the other side of the church-state divide, nor was Kermit up to editing the magazine. Just before the Democratic convention in 1972, Kay Graham exercised her prerogative, reinstalling Elliott as editor in chief and giving Kermit a column, for which he was equally unsuited.

Oz stormed back in a burst of energy. He resolved a bitter legal conflict over opportunities for women at the magazine by promoting a bunch of experienced researchers to be writers. He introduced a new weekly essay to be written by readers and outside contributors and hired Shana Alexander and Bill Moyers as columnists. But Elliott's enthusiasm waned over the months, and with his implicit approval, I found myself making most of the day-to-day decisions that shaped *Newsweek*.

As Watergate heated up, these decisions were increasingly significant. Shortly after noon on Saturday, October 20, 1973, we got the first word of the impending Saturday Night Massacre. I rang up Oz, who was at his weekend place in Stonington, far up the Connecticut shore.

"He no here. Go beach. Be back soon," reported his Asian houseman.

So we crashed a new cover and briefed Oz when he checked in later in the afternoon.

On Tuesday morning, Gibson McCabe, the convivial, old-school president of *Newsweek*, came into my office.

"I just want to thank you for what you're doing for the magazine," he said simply. He didn't have to say more.

10

Madam Dragon

IT WAS DURING THIS time that I first began to have regular dealings with Katharine Graham, who inspired both authentic admiration and profound anxiety around *Newsweek*. She had an office at the north end of one of the editorial floors and was an occasional visitor at story conferences and lunches for newsmakers and corporate chieftains held at Top of the Week, the sleek entertaining rooms designed by her pal Pei on the forty-second floor of the *Newsweek* building.

Kay had gone through a splashy New York phase starting in the mid-1960s, when Truman Capote staged the Black and White Ball in her honor at the Plaza Hotel—a storied gala for an elect 540 that mingled Rockefellers and Rothschilds with Andy Warhol, Frank Sinatra, Norman Mailer, and Tennessee Williams—the birth of a new café society. In the early 1970s, she became a walking advertisement for the designer Halston, who dressed her in ultrasuede. But no matter how many Halstons she wore, Kay never seemed to be in her element in New York.

She was a Washington creature, more at home with Ben Bradlee and the *Washington Post* than she'd ever be with Elliott and the rest of us at *Newsweek*. She had already made her name as an off-with-his-head sovereign by dispatching a number of men who fell out of favor while running the Washington Post Company, which owned a number of TV stations and paper mills besides the newspaper and magazine. But after installing Bradlee, she rarely fiddled with the editorial management of the paper. At *Newsweek*, she did the opposite.

I found her scary. She was a tall, edgy woman with a resonant voice and an aristocratic accent that drawled out the syllables in *e-nor-mous, mar-va-lous,* and *ex-traor-din-ary.* Elizabeth Peer, a *Newsweek* editor and great fan of

Mrs. Graham, could do a pitch-perfect Kay exclaiming *Un-fuck-ing-be-lieve-a-ble!* that would send tingles up the spines of her colleagues. Mrs. Graham knew everybody important and you had to be up on your Joes, Henrys, Andrés, Macs, and Scoops, or quickly be exposed in conversation as a hopeless hoople. It was impossible to sustain a facade of news magazine omniscience with a woman who entertained Washington's grandest at her Georgetown mansion. And she didn't just feed them—she talked to them all the time and was full of inside dope far dishier than anything in *Newsweek*'s celebrated Periscope.

Kay's tics and foibles were balanced by her unflagging commitment to journalistic excellence at both the newspaper and *Newsweek*. Unique among the people I worked for over the years, Mrs. Graham never talked about editorial budgets or the risks of offending powerful interests or big advertisers. There was only one issue: how could *Newsweek* be better, quicker, more thoughtful, more rewarding to its readers? I'm afraid those of us who hadn't really worked at many other places failed to grasp how rare and precious her approach was.

Of course, what made Kay most fearsome to me was the certainty that my destiny was in her fidgety hands. Over the months, it became increasingly clear that Oz was falling out of her favor. Perhaps she was just bored with him. In any event, she began confiding her dissatisfaction to me, sometimes with an *un-fuck-ing-be-lieve-able* roll of the eyes. These conversations made me painfully uncomfortable. I respected Elliott and was as loyal a number two as could be imagined, but I knew she was right. I tried to deflect her with bland remarks like "You have to decide what you want to do," that neither betrayed Oz nor made me look like a fool who didn't see that changes had to be made.

In the first week of June 1975, I found myself in Paris on my first overseas trip for *Newsweek*. It was nobody's business that this was my first trip ever out of the country, not counting sales meetings in the Caribbean. In fact, the heir apparent to the editorship of a great international news magazine was such a provincial that he didn't even have a passport, a dirty little secret that required some fast talking on my part to secure one for the trip.

Before landing in Paris I'd made a reporting trip through the Middle East with Arnaud de Borchgrave, *Newsweek*'s chief foreign correspondent. Arnaud was a trig, compact guy with a perpetual tan who was a Belgian count of some sort and inevitably was known around the magazine as the Short Count. He was famous for his intrepid exploits. Once, he returned from Vietnam toting his helmet with a conspicuous bullet hole near the temple. Oz laid on a triumphant welcome for him in the lobby of the Newsweek Building, complete with a parading bagpiper. De Borchgrave was in Kay Graham's permanent purdah because he had abetted Phil Graham's philandering in the manic days before his suicide—or so Kay thought. His politics made him suspect to some on the staff; Arnaud was relentlessly anti-Soviet and people thought he was too cozy with Arab potentates at the expense of Israel.

Whatever his sympathies, de Borchgrave was very plugged in, and we were greeted as warmly in Israel as we were in Egypt, Syria, Lebanon, and Jordan, where King Hussein had us to lunch at his rather modest palace in Amman. The king had arranged for a Royal Jordanian Air Force helicopter to pick us up at the Allenby Bridge across the Jordan River from the Israeli-occupied West Bank for a quick trip to the sandstone ruins of Petra. Soon I was sitting between two young Jordanian pilots in their dashing jumpsuits as the Alouette helicopter darted into the air. Each had a map in his lap, and they were arguing in Arabic through their headsets and gesticulating wildly. It dawned on me that a nice Jewish boy from Washington Heights was flying over the Dead Sea on Friday the 13th with two Jordanian space cadets who were lost in their own country. Looking out the window, I spotted a sinuous watercourse in the desert that corresponded exactly to a feature on the map and pointed it out to the pilots. *Allah akbar!* The pilots got their bearing and we soon reached Petra.

Before the trip ended, Arnaud arranged audiences with Hafez Assad, the ruler of Syria, and Egypt's Anwar Sadat, who soon made peace with Israel and was assassinated. He was succeeded by his deputy, Hosni Mubarak, who took notes like a clerk at our interview. The dour Assad made me a gift of a pack of lung-busting cigarettes and had little useful to say. That may help explain why he held on to power in Syria for another twenty-five years. Mubarak rules Egypt still.

Mrs. Graham was in Paris for a meeting of the board of the *International Herald Tribune,* of which the Washington Post Company was part owner. She suggested that we meet for lunch at Lasserre, the iconic three-star restaurant on the Avenue Franklin Roosevelt not far from where I was staying at the Plaza Athenee on the avenue de Montaigne.

I was determined to be punctual, so I carefully plotted my path from hotel to restaurant and set out with time to spare. It was a sparkling day. I was edgy, of course, but exhilarated, too. Here I was strolling in the Parisian sunshine on my way to lunch at one of the world's great restaurants with one of the world's most powerful women, who was surely going to talk to me about becoming editor of one of the world's most important magazines. *Pas mal!*

Then I realized with a *klong* that I'd somehow wandered astray. It was getting very close to the appointed hour and I was lost—a nightmare scenario so clichéd I couldn't believe it was happening to me. Stifling the panic, I stopped a couple of passersby and tried to follow their French directions. Finally, I got a fix on my destination and started running along the rue Jean-Goujon to the intersection with avenue Roosevelt. I dashed into the lobby of the restaurant and rode up in the tiny elevator. Sweating and frantic, I made my apologies to Mrs. Graham—who didn't really seem all that glad to see me—and sat down.

The next ordeal was ordering. I could decipher the menu well enough, and I should have given our orders to the captain and the wine steward. But I wasn't sophisticated enough to realize that ordering in English was perfectly appropriate, so I sat mute while Kay ordered food and wine in assured but flat, American-accented French. All I remember from the lunch was glimpsing the fabled Andre Malraux across the room—"He has lunch here every day," confided Kay—and the *coup de theatre* of Lasserre's ceiling sliding open to the sky to let out the smoke from the cigarettes of Malroux and others. However unpromisingly the lunch started, I must have acquitted myself all right because she ended the meal with a promise that we'd talk further back in New York.

We met again several times, and finally her plan was set. She would essentially fire Oz, although he would keep his title as editor in chief until he found something else to do. I would have the title of editor, move into Oz's old office, and have full authority to run the magazine, although I'd keep Elliott in the picture about my plans. She was going to give him the word on Monday. I was to say nothing to anyone outside my family.

I tried to stay calm over the weekend and pretty much succeeded until late Sunday, when Oz called. He'd got wind that something was up although he professed not to know what. Could we meet for a drink? We wound up in a nearly deserted Chinese restaurant not far from his apartment at 10 Gracie Square overlooking the mayor's residence, Gracie Mansion. It was a long way from Lasserre.

Now I was torn between my obligation to Kay Graham and my loyalty to Elliott, whom I admired more than anyone at *Newsweek* and who was about to be blindsided by the proprietor. Under the circumstances, I felt I had to tell him what was in store. As a fig leaf, I made him promise that he'd act with her as if he knew nothing—our meeting, of course, had never happened.

Inevitably, when Mrs. Graham broke the news, Oz acknowledged that he knew what was coming, and she doped out that I was his source. Kay was furious with me—the first time I'd felt the icy blast of her anger. It soon got worse. In those days, and for all I know still today, *Newsweek* did not offer contracts to its top editor; he served at the proprietor's pleasure and there would be no golden parachute when the fall inevitably came. Because I was young and had progressed up the ranks from lowly Nation writer, I was making a modest salary as managing editor. I wanted a significant raise to take responsibility for the magazine and I had another issue: Alice and I had no money to speak of, we had two sons in an expensive private school, and we could barely afford the co-op apartment we'd bought with a loan two years earlier. As editor of *Newsweek,* I should be able to entertain important news sources at home, and I needed money to fix up the place. I had no agent or lawyer to represent me—that wasn't done at the magazine—and so I handled the negotiations, such as they were, myself. At an early point, I made the mistake of telling Kay that I wanted to discuss "a package" of salary and other considerations, and she exploded. Her sovereign attitude was that she and *Newsweek* were doing me a favor by letting me run the magazine and I'd better be damn grateful, not haggle over money. I hadn't even edited my first issue and I'd already twice provoked the wrath of one of the most fearsome bosses in journalism—not an auspicious beginning. But my appointment had already been announced, and she couldn't easily fire me before I started, so the issue was resolved.

Achieving a goal that had long seemed improbable thrilled me, but my joy was shadowed because my father hadn't lived to see his adored boy's name at the top of the *Newsweek* masthead. After my mother's death in 1962, my father had never once thought of remarrying. Instead, he lived on in their apartment in Washington Heights and strung along a succession of widowed lady friends. My father had no money and no prospects, but his charm had never deserted him, and these women fell all over themselves to feed him and even launder his handkerchiefs and underwear. Every Sunday, he would pick up John and Anthony and take them around town even as he had taken me thirty years before. Although he chain-smoked cigars, drank Scotch, and had always lived on a diet that would be considered near-suicidal today, Sidney had never spent a day in a hospital. Then, toward the end of 1974, he showed up one weekend with a stricken look on his face. Ben, his identical twin, had died of a heart attack in California.

"I'm finished," said my father, the most optimistic man I've ever known.

"Nonsense," I insisted. "Your health is fine. What happened to Benny has nothing to do with you." But I felt a pang of fear: twins know.

Indeed, they do. From that day on, my father's health began to deteriorate. He never had a heart attack, but he began showing symptoms of heart failure, which he first misread as heartburn and dosed with handfuls of Tums. Finally, early in 1975, he agreed to go to the doctor, and it soon became clear that he could no longer live by himself.

Here, I made a decision out of weakness and selfishness that I've never stopped regretting. I should have taken my father into our new home so he could live more comfortably and be cared for. But between the pressure of my job and Alice's emotional brittleness, I couldn't find a way to do the right thing. So Aunt Selda helped find a place for Sidney in a residence for old people in Long Beach. I rationalized that my father would have company and regular visits from Selda, Freda, and the rest of us on frequent Sundays. The new arrangement seemed to be working for the first few months. Then one night I got a call from my father that nearly broke my heart. He was feeling weaker and weaker and didn't know what to do. I told him to hold tight until the morning, when we'd come out and take care of everything. I was tormented all night by feelings of helplessness and remorse.

Next day, we got Sidney into Long Beach Hospital, where Selda had worked for years as a volunteer and knew everyone, and hooked him up with a young cardiologist. Under his care, my father gained strength and he looked a little better each time we visited. On Thursday, April 17, I arranged to take off from work, and Alice and I went to Long Beach to see Sidney.

This time we found him transformed: His skin had a pink glow and his eyes shone with uncommon serenity. I knew something was wrong, but the cardiologist insisted that Sidney was improving so much that in a day or so he could be transferred to the intermediate-care facility adjoining the hospital and ultimately return to the senior residence. Whatever the doctor said, I drove back to the city convinced that I might have spoken to my father for the last time.

Late that night, the young doctor called to say that we had better come back to Long Beach the first thing next morning. We got there just in time to hear a code blue on the hospital's public address system. I rushed to Sidney's room. Just before someone closed the door in my face, I got a glimpse, that I wish I hadn't, of doctors and nurses bent over him. After a time, the young cardiologist came into the waiting area and suggested we go for a walk outside.

"You know, Edward," he said solemnly, "I was certain he was getting better and he'd be up and walking around next week."

"I knew what was going to happen," I told him.

"How?"

"You've known him for a couple of weeks," I replied as gently as I could. "I've known him for nearly forty years."

Of all the condolence notes I got, the one from Kay Graham was the most heartfelt and the most consoling.

11

"THE DOGS LIKE THE DOG FOOD!"

BECAUSE OF VACATIONS AND other complications, I didn't formally take over *Newsweek* until Labor Day, and my reign literally started with a bang. On Friday, September 5, a twenty-six-year-old disciple of madman Charles Manson named Lynette Alice Fromme, who was called "Squeaky," pointed a .45-caliber automatic at President Gerald Ford in a park in Sacramento, California. She was tackled by Secret Service agents and charged with trying to assassinate the new president even though her gun wasn't loaded.

This was a sensational story, with its echoes of the assassination of JFK and the murders of his brother and Martin Luther King only seven years before. The country was just recovering from the trauma of Watergate, and now Nixon's successor was in a freaky waif's gun sights.

There was no question that this had to be a cover story and what the image on that cover had to be. "It didn't go off," read the headline on my first "official" edition of *Newsweek* over a picture of a wild-eyed Squeaky after her capture. The magazine had just come out when Saul Bellow— perhaps American's greatest living writer and *Newsweek*'s cover boy just two weeks earlier—was on television denouncing the magazine for glorifying Squeaky by putting her on the cover rather than a picture of her targeted victim, Gerald Ford. To me, the news, not some misplaced civic impulse, dictated the choice, and I defended the magazine as best I could. Stirring the pot is a good strategy for magazines, but I'd rather my debut week had passed without such drama.

For the next week's cover, we retreated to a safe, lifestyle subject, "Who's Raising the Kids?," but four days after that bland offering hit the stands, I was confronted with another sensation. Patricia Hearst, the blond and beautiful publishing heiress who had been kidnapped by a radical gang nineteen months before and, as Tania, had joined them in bank robberies, was captured by the FBI in San Francisco. Ordinarily, I'd have been thrilled with such breaking news, but as soon as I got the bulletin my heart sank. Just two weeks after Squeaky Fromme, I'd have to put another violent young radical woman on *Newsweek*'s cover. Just to compound my discomfort, the cover editor, Bob Engle, had worked his magic and scored an exclusive color picture of Tania, her clenched first raised in defiance after her arrest by the feds. It would make a blockbuster cover, and I could just hear Saul Bellow clearing his throat.

The Squeaky and Tania covers in my first three weeks on the job sent a powerful signal that this was no longer your father's *Newsweek*. But the truth was these choices were dictated by the news, not any agenda of mine. Oz, Kermit, or any other editor of the magazine would have been compelled to make the same decisions. I did have a carefully thought-out plan to freshen up *Newsweek,* but it certainly didn't entail glorifying radical criminals. But you can never fight the news when running a newspaper or news magazine, and responding properly to the news was making me and *Newsweek* controversial in a way I never intended but could not escape.

It got worse. The next month, the culture staff began pushing for a cover story on a young singer from Asbury Park, New Jersey. The country had barely heard of him, but his charismatic talent was erupting in his third album, *Born to Run,* named after his anthem. His name was Bruce Springsteen. A *Newsweek* writer had gotten close to him, we had great pictures, and we were about to introduce him to America and the world. What I couldn't know was that *Time* magazine was playing catch-up on the story and a *Time* writer was working a classic hustle on the man who ran *Time,* Henry Grunwald.

Henry was a cultured refugee from Hitler who had worked his way up the pecking order at *Time* from gofer to chief editor. Around the office, his nickname was "the horny avocado," a nod to his rotund shape and reputed roving eye. In those days, *Time* staffers haughtily refused even to acknowledge that *Newsweek* existed. Still, there was muted concern in *Time*'s carpeted corridors that high-brow Henry would be at a disadvantage, at least in covering popular culture, to *Newsweek* and its new editor, who was just thirty-eight. Just as Karl Fleming had squeezed Kermit about D. B. Cooper, the *Time* writer warned Grunwald how embarrassed he'd be to be scooped by *Newsweek* on the biggest sensation in pop music since Bob Dylan. Grun-wald grudgingly relented and determined to beat the upstarts.

The result was that both American news magazines came out on Monday, October 22, 1975, with covers starring a young singer unknown to almost every one of their combined 7 million subscribers. Everyone from Johnny Carson to the journalism reviews fell all over themselves with glee. If anyone doubted that the news magazines were lost in their own dream world, here was the proof. What a hoot! Almost overnight, T-shirts bloomed with one cover on the front and the other on the back. The twin issues sold out. (Nearly thirty years later, you can find them on eBay if you look diligently enough and are willing to pay top dollar.)

Newsweek and *Time* were fair game, as they were a couple of times each year when they sported the same cover subject. Still, the puzzlement and ridicule betrayed a fundamental misunderstanding of what the magazines do. Even in the mid-1970s, there was scant direct competition in the media. As they do today, CBS, NBC, and ABC each had evening newscasts using essentially identical formats. But even the surviving tabloids in New York, the *Daily News* and the *Post,* then had such different audiences and aspirations that they really were not competitors. Aside from the network news-casts, *Time* and *Newsweek* were the only head-to-head competitors in big-time journalism. Part of the exhilaration and anxiety of putting them out was the frisson each Monday morning when the editors and staff of each saw what the competition did with basically the same raw material. Given the symmetry of their formats, it would be remarkable if the news magazines didn't come up with the same choice of newsmaking personality, breaking news story, or trend several times a year. But readers and critics just couldn't—or wouldn't—absorb that simple truth. And when the matchup involved an obscure entertainer with a funny name, there was no containing the hilarity.

The Springsteen cover *was* part of my plan. Almost from the start, *Time* and *Newsweek* worked from a predictable syllabus. Year after year, the cover stories involved big breaking news, politics, and business with a sprinkling of medicine, religion, education, sports, writers, artists, and an occasional movie star. Once or twice a year, *Newsweek* or *Time* would produce a "big act," a special report like Oz's "The Negro in America" or "The Arts in America."

In the bitter aftermath of Vietnam and at the peak of the Watergate furor, *People* magazine made its spectacular debut in the spring of 1974. During its first year, *People* did cover stories on Martha Mitchell, Henry Kissinger, Jackie Onassis, Gloria Steinem, Pat Nixon, and Mark Spitz, the Olympic phenom, to name a few, the new celebrity mix. *Sixty Minutes* was luring bigger and bigger TV audiences with a journalistic blend of big-time interviews, investigative stories, and pieces about entertainers that put the audience in the room with the stars. Across the media, the fascination with celebrity that now engulfs us was beginning to build. Liz Smith debuted her column in the *Daily News*. Starting with *Jaws* and *The Exorcist*, Hollywood was turning out blockbuster movies that became newsmaking events in themselves.

I had made my reputation at *Newsweek* as the hardest of the "hard" news guys. But I now felt in my gut that the very definition of news was evolving, and that the news magazines had to find a way to thrive in the new environment. I was convinced that sociological trend stories—the supposedly more sensitive "New Man," single mothers, the aging of America—were more newsworthy than the latest chieftain of General Motors and more interesting to the readers, too. It was not a scheme to turn *Newsweek* "soft"— less focused on hard news—but rather to recognize that a news magazine had the whole spectrum of modern life as its rightful purview. We would continue to excel in hard news, especially big breaking stories, but if the choice was, say, between Rocky (Nelson) and *Rocky* (Sly Stallone), I'd go with the champ. At least, that was my instinct.

Similarly, I felt the editorial ranks of the magazine had to be shaken up. When Elliott returned for his second term, he made few changes in Kermit's masthead, especially since he had installed many of the editors in his first term. It was time for the next generation to take charge. I named new editors for the national affairs, foreign, and business sections, chose the first woman senior editor to oversee the noncultural back of the book, and picked a new man to run the arts sections. Nobody was fired. The business editor became a columnist, and the cultural editor became the theater critic and did movie reviews and cover stories as well. I knew how to spot talent: four of the editors I put in place went on to edit magazines of their own, including *Newsweek*, the *New York Times Magazine*, *Business Week*, and *Working Woman*.

After a shakedown period, the new team got traction and the magazine showed new energy and flair. Better, *Newsweek* began to identify new stars—the gargantuan tenor Luciano Pavarotti, the fashion designer Diane von Furstenberg—who are still world-famous three decades later. When *A Chorus Line*, the groundbreaking musical, opened on Broadway, there was star Donna McKechnie high-stepping on *Newsweek's* cover, and when big-money fever first infected major league baseball, Oakland pitcher Vida Blue made the cover, too, in the oval on a greenback usually reserved for U.S. Grant. But that didn't mean the magazine was stinting on the old syllabus. More than 40 percent of the covers in my first year were on national politics, and there was a classic big act, a self-portrait of America pegged to the bicentennial of the Declaration of Independence on July 4, 1976.

The real sensation was published three months earlier. Bob Woodward and Carl Bernstein, the *Washington Post* reporters whose work had toppled Nixon, had just finished the follow-up to their 1974 best seller, *All the President's Men.* Although Nixon had been banished nearly two years before, Woodward and Bernstein and their publisher, Simon & Schuster, were skittish about a backlash against *The Final Days,* and knew first publication in a respected news magazine would provide a firewall of sorts. Given the corporate connection with the *Washington Post,* the obvious home for the excerpts was *Newsweek.* Simon & Schuster wanted us so badly that serialization rights were priced at just $65,000. Practically overnight, Peter Goldman and I read the manuscript, which was strewn with amazing scenes, among them Nixon, drunk late at night, talking to the portraits in the White House and later kneeling to pray with Henry Kissinger in the president's hideaway study near the Oval Office.

Simon & Schuster was ruled by Dick Snyder, a notorious autocrat. The serialization rights were handled by a young woman named Joni Evans, who was destined to become the next Mrs. Snyder (and who divorced him in a headlined case that provided years of gossip). Prickly as Snyder could be, we quickly struck a deal to run two long excerpts in *Newsweek,* the first to appear on March 29, 1976. The hardcover books were not to go on sale for a week after that. Now all we had to do was agree on the text of the two installments.

Bob and Carl came to New York and we met on a Monday morning in my office to cull the excerpts, which Peter Goldman had already provisionally carved out of the galleys. And then the trouble started. Woodward was as calm and cooperative as could be, but Bernstein, for all his bad-boy charm, could be snarky and mulish. We had contracted to take material from throughout the book, and Goldman had deftly extracted most of the juice from the manuscript and blended it into two exciting sections. Bernstein thought Peter had done too good a job. "You're raping the book," Carl complained, and it suddenly dawned on me that the deal was coming apart before our eyes. Bernstein had to agree with what we were doing, and he had dug in his heels. We tried to bridge the gap but made no progress by the time we separated for lunch.

Peter and I were despondent when we rejoined them an hour later. Bernstein looked as adamant as ever, but before we could say anything, Woodward spoke.

"Let's agree to agree," he said mildly in his midwestern monotone.

Neither Peter nor I knew what that meant, if anything, but it sounded good. Woodward had obviously subdued Bernstein, and we soon settled on the excerpts.

For the next ten days the project was handled at *Newsweek* like a batch of nuclear secrets. A tiny cadre of staffers copyedited the text, ordered illustrations, laid out the pages, wrote headlines and captions, and designed the cover. A press release describing the cornucopia of scoops in the first except was drafted and was to be issued Sunday afternoon, setting the stage for the magazine to hit the stands Monday morning.

But when I picked up the newspapers outside my door at 6:30 Friday morning, I got a *klong*. Liz Smith, the gossip columnist, had somehow got hold of our excerpts, and there were most of our precious scoops splashed in the pages of the *Daily News*. If such a thing happened today, I'd consider it God-sent publicity; magazines and TV news shows now routinely ballyhoo their goods days in advance. But in March 1976, I considered it a calamity. And I had good reason: our excepts had carefully put Woodward and Bernstein's shocking nuggets in context with an eye to forestalling criticism that they were exploiting a president's downfall for tabloid fodder. And now here it was—fodder for the biggest tabloid in America!

Once in the office, I convened a crisis meeting and decided to release to the press the full text of both excerpts to offset the tabloid effect. The story got huge play around the country. *Newsweek* got credit, but I feared all the exposure would doom our hopes for a big newsstand sale. On Monday, my son John, then fourteen, had the day off from school, and he joined me for a walk around our neighborhood around 10:30 to see how the issue looked on the stands. The first news dealer we approached had no copies of *Newsweek*.

"Didn't get your delivery yet?" I asked him.

"Nope, all sold out," he said with a puzzled look.

The story was the same at the next newsstand and the next and the next. *Newsweek* was sold out everywhere. At the office the next morning, I learned the astonishing news that the magazine had sold out around the country by noon on Monday—more than 300,000 copies snatched up within a few hours. The circulation director had rejected my suggestion a week earlier to pump up the press run. Now the magazine couldn't go back on press because in those primitive days the color ads for each issue were printed separately well in advance and the supply had been exhausted. Still, for all the histrionics, the exercise had been a triumph.

There was more drama to come. A *Newsweek* staffer walking back from lunch on Thursday spotted stacks of the Woodward and Bernstein book in the window of one of the big bookstores on Fifth Avenue. Others confirmed that the book was all over town, in breach of our contract with Simon & Schuster that forbade any book sales until the following week.

I got *Newsweek*'s house counsel, Ed Smith, to bring a copy of the contract to my office and we called Dick Snyder on the speaker telephone.

"Dick," I said, "the book's on sale all over."

"So?" he replied.

"So that violates our contract," I shot back.

He went into a long explanation of how the books had to be shipped from the printer earlier than planned to avoid an imminent teamsters' strike, and how the bookstores must have opened the cartons by mistake.

"I understand, Dick, but we had an—"

"What do you care?" he cut in. "You've sold out all your magazines."

"A contract's a contract, Dick," I said.

"Sue me, baby!" Snyder shouted and hung up.

For Christmas, I sent Snyder a parody of *Time*'s annual Man of the Year issue—a *Newsweek* cover with his picture on it, his quote, and the headline Asshole of the Year! I didn't talk to him for years, turning my back on him at parties until he finally made peace.

It turned out to be a classic demonstration of my theory that media life is just one long performance of *La Ronde*. After our mano a mano, Snyder became a chum and then a good friend, as he is today. Thirty years after the episode, he told me the real story of what had happened:

Hundreds of thousands of copies of *The Final Days* were being printed when Snyder got a call from Edward Bennett Williams, the chief outside counsel of the Washington Post Company and the capital's premier fixer. Kay Graham had just seen the final manuscript of Woodward and Bernstein's book, and she wanted changes made. Snyder didn't know what her changes were, but he was sure they'd weaken the book. Dick also heard from another *Washington Post* lawyer that the company planned to enjoin publication of the book unless Simon & Schuster complied. Snyder stalled for time and consulted his own lawyers who told him, he said, that, under the law, if he could ship just one volume from the printers to a bookstore, Graham would be powerless to thwart him. So he moved up the shipping date, and *The Final Days* was published unscathed. The tale about the impending teamsters' strike was just a cover story he cooked up to keep me in the dark. He'd broken his contract with me, but in his own mind he'd saved the book.

Long after the fact, I also learned how Tony Schwartz, a young writer for a countercultural magazine called *New Times,* had gotten the excerpts from Kitty Kelley, who grew up to be the pop biographer of Sinatra, the Bush clan, and others. Unable to use them in his monthly, he let Kitty pass them on to Liz. Tony confessed when he joined me at *Newsweek* as a writer (and subsequently followed me to *New York* and to *Esquire*).

In the bubbly wake of *The Final Days* and other coups, *Newsweek* was riding high and so was I. Newsstand sales and overall circulation were up and so were advertising pages. Bob Campbell, a retired Air Force general who was president of *Newsweek,* took me for a celebratory meal at a fancy corporate lunch club high up in the Pan Am Building. He beamed, raising his martini to clink mine.

"Well, Ed," he said, "the dogs like the dog food!"

I'd never heard editorial success put quite that way, and I never forgot it.

12

"POOR CLAY"

BY THE END OF the year, I found myself in the middle of another media sensation that turned out later to be a star turn from *La Ronde* featuring Katharine Graham, Clay Felker, and Rupert Murdoch. Felker was one of the princes of New York. His fame derived from his creation a decade earlier of *New York* magazine, first as a Sunday supplement to the *New York Herald Tribune* and then, after the *Trib* folded, as a slick weekly. Felker had taken the notion of the city magazine, until then a bland chamber of commerce monthly puff sheet, and reconceived it as a sassy weekly, the sophisticated voice of the capital of the world. Felker's *New York* invented upscale service journalism—where to find the best bagels, how to have cracked heirlooms mended—and lavished resources on making the information definitive. There were smart columns on politics and Wall Street, near-pornographic restaurant reviews, literate and acerbic critics for the movies, theater, and music. But what made *New York* legendary were the feature articles by Tom Wolfe, Jimmy Breslin, Gloria Steinem, Julie Baumgold, Gail Sheehy, and others—paragons of the New Journalism.

Clay was a Midwesterner from Missouri, where his father had edited the *Sporting News,* and he had worked at *Life* and *Esquire* before starting *New York.* He was tall and pale, with a sly, crinkly smile and a soft Middle Border accent. He wasn't particularly talkative, but his reputation was so incandescent that any random remark was taken as the ultimate insider's word. Clay liked to give big parties at his chic duplex—it was literally a loft with the bedroom cantilevered over the great room—on East Fifty-seventh Street, where he'd stand against a wall with his arms crossed over his well-cut blazer, looking as pleased as Gatsby, another Midwesterner, at the mob of New Yorkers who'd turned up. Over the years he had become close with another out-of-towner, Kay Graham.

For all the admiration it attracted, *New York* was never really very profitable, and Felker was often at odds with the magazine's board of directors,
who represented the people who had invested in the start-up and owned
stock in the company. Felker was an editorial genius, but he was no publishing paragon. Any profit the magazine managed to eke out was pumped
back into editorial and big dreams. One involved buying the *Village Voice,*
the first "underground" newspaper, founded by Norman Mailer and others
in the late fifties. The scruffy *Voice,* as it happened, was owned by another
prince of the city, Carter Burden, a handsome fellow with a formidable pedigree who dabbled in politics. Felker swapped Burden a 35 percent stake in
New York for the *Voice,* which Clay planned to turn into a national weekly
for young hipsters. And without giving the board much of a say, Felker spent
millions launching a West Coast version of *New York* called *New West,* with
separate editions in Los Angeles and San Francisco. An expeditionary force
of editors and writers was dispatched to the coast, put up in fancy digs, and
equipped with rented Alfa Romeos. Inevitably, *New West* went far over
budget. And Californians showed a remarkable lack of enthusiasm for the
new magazine bestowed on them by the carpetbaggers from Gotham.

So Felker found himself in a crisis with his board. His solution was to find
backers to buy the magazine for himself. One of the people he turned to was
Murdoch, the Australian who had already parlayed his father's small paper in
Adelaide into a nascent media empire back home and in London. Murdoch
had made his first foray into American publishing in 1973, when he bought
a newspaper in San Antonio. The next year, he started the *National Star,* a
supermarket tabloid competing with the *National Enquirer.* Two years later,
Rupert paid Dorothy Schiff a pittance—$30 million—for the *Post* and
quickly began remaking it into an antic Fleet Street tabloid. Playing the soft-
spoken, slightly bewildered Aussie, Murdoch let Felker believe he would help
him. But the more Rupert looked into the deal, the more he realized how
disgusted the board was with Felker and how ready they were to sell to him.

Clay didn't twig to what Murdoch was up to until it was too late. Desperately, he turned to his great friend Kay Graham. His plan was simple: the
Washington Post Company would outbid Murdoch for *New York,* which
would join *Newsweek* in a magazine division at the company. It all had to be
done nearly overnight because Murdoch was closing his grip on Felker's
jewel. Much as she wanted to, Kay couldn't just do the deal—she had to clear

it with her executives, especially Peter Derow, an ambitious young Harvard MBA who had taken over the business side of *Newsweek* and was being groomed for bigger things at the mother ship. Derow knew Felker's reputation for whispering in Kay's ear and her reputation for heeding kibitzers. He told her that he'd quit if she brought Felker into the company. She blinked.

Carter Burden and his 35 percent stake in *New York* turned out to be the fulcrum of the deal. Burden was spending the holidays skiing in Sun Valley. As the clock ticked, Felker tried to put together new financing, but Murdoch seized the moment. With a New York lawyer (and friend of Burden's) named Peter Tufo and a check for $15 million, Rupert hopped a private jet, mushed up to Burden at a ski lodge, and sealed the sale. Back in New York, I fielded a series of tearful phone calls from Mrs. Graham. "Poor Clay," she kept sobbing, "poor Clay."

The sale of *New York* was nearly as much an ordeal for me as it was for Felker. The Media section at *Newsweek* had scheduled a cover story on Murdoch and the battle for the magazine. The writer was one of our best, but the problem was he didn't know—couldn't know—as much as I did about the real story of Murdoch's triumph. It was the kind of story that had to be written and edited with infinite sensitivity—with a safecracker's sandpapered fingertips. The trick was figuring out what had to go in and what could be left out, knowing that *Time* was also working on the story and would delight in embarrassing Kay if at all possible.

So I got out the old emery board and spent a long Saturday working on the Murdoch story, which was running with a cover that parodied one of Rupert's Fleet Street tabloids: **PRESS LORD TAKES CITY!** screamed the headline on the *Daily Splash*.

It was long after eight before I could leave the office, and I was late joining Alice for dinner with my old elementary school friend Tom Baer and a friend of his at an East Side restaurant named the Coup de Fusil, the gunshot. I could have been shot from a cannon when I sat down at the table, frazzled and exhausted and somehow angry that I'd had to put so much effort into making Felker's folly publishable. Facing me across the table was a beautiful woman with exquisite greenish eyes downcast by sadness. Her name was Julie Baumgold, and she knew Tom through *New York*, where she had been one of Clay's star writers and Tom was Felker's contract lawyer.

I had been in love with Julie's writing for years. She wrote in a voice that was at once knowing, confident, and elegant, and she managed to get so close to the people she profiled that some of them were never the same. And yet the pieces were appreciative, often affectionate. Julie's writing was so *big* that I always pictured her as a tall, bronzed blonde. Blonde she was, but Julie was no Amazon. She was, in Clay Felker's words, a pocket Venus.

I gulped down my first martini and ordered another. The talk turned inevitably to Felker's loss of *New York* to Murdoch. Julie was distraught. She and other writers were going to quit rather than work for the barbarian Rupert. The strain of the week and that second martini combined to unhinge me. Somehow, I decided that I had to lecture Julie about real journalism: stylish and sophisticated though it might be, *New York* was still just a feature magazine that instructed people about where to find the best cappuccino. It was arrogant of the *New York* writers to feel that their work was so exquisite that only the sainted Clay Felker could edit it. And so on.

I saw tears in Julie's eyes, but she didn't stalk way from the table, as she had every reason to do in the face of such loathsome behavior. When Alice and I got home, I sobered up and realized what a monster I'd been to a talented woman whose only sin was to have lost the magazine she loved. I knew that I'd have to apologize as soon as I could the next morning, but I was further tormented by the possibility that she and Tom were lovers (they most definitely were not) and that my morning call would find them in bed together suppressing giggles at my clumsy effort to atone. Still, I knew I had to make that call. And when I did, Julie later told me, she thought she was dealing with a crazy man.

Perhaps the real explanation for my bizarre behavior that night was that I'd had a *coup de foudre*—a thunderbolt of love—at the Coup de Fusil. As it happened, I didn't see Julie again for nearly six months, and I'm quite sure she had nothing to do with the collapse of my marriage.

As I settled into my stride running *Newsweek,* Alice and I became more and more estranged. She had always done writing on the side, first romance stories for a pulp magazine called *True Love,* then feature pieces for the *Daily News* Sunday rotogravure magazine, and a biography of William Jennings Bryan for teenagers, but she never really established an independent career. Her latest therapist reinforced her growing conviction that my career was responsible for the marginality of hers. Many women would have thought being married to the editor of *Newsweek* was rewarding in itself—going to the White House and glamorous dinners at Kay Graham's, traveling overseas and being plugged into everything that was going on in the world. But Alice felt the life was keeping her from developing her talents, suffocating her.

Soon we were at an impasse. Finally, one night she said she'd remain my wife only if I agreed that she would have nothing to do with my career—no dinners, no travel, no nothing. I thought about it for a moment, realizing that what I said next would change my life, one way or the other. "Let's break it up," I said, surprising myself more than Alice. Since it was almost July 4, we decided to keep our plan to go to the beach for the weekend and deal with the new reality after the holiday.

On Tuesday, July 5, I found myself back at my *Newsweek* desk, essentially a single man for the first time in nearly twenty years. I glanced at my red leather *Economist* desk diary and found I had two choices for lunch: the Bonn bureau chief, who was in town, or a book party for the writer Rex Reed at Elaine's. The Bonn bureau chief was a decent enough guy, but it was no contest. At lunchtime, I directed the *Newsweek* driver to head uptown.

At Elaine's, I decided that I needed—hell, I deserved—a vodka. I asked the bartender for an Absolut and ice, but she said she was only pouring wine. I whipped out a five and offered to buy an Absolut when Elaine herself intervened and got me my vodka. After a few gulps, I moseyed through the crowd, greeted the guest of honor, and got on the buffet line, where waiters were spooning out the pasta shells and other staples of Elaine's. Clutching my plate, I looked up and realized that standing next to me on line was Julie Baumgold, more beautiful than ever.

For some reason, she didn't flee at the sight of me and we joined the actresses Polly Bergen and Sylvia Miles and some others at a table. Around two, the lunch broke up and I offered to drop off Julie on my way back to the office. It turned out that she lived nearby, on Eighty-fifth Street just off Central Park, and we were there in less than five minutes. When I got back to my desk, it suddenly dawned on me that now that Alice and I were separating, I had to start *dating*. But who?

The television sensation that year was *Roots,* which gave the term "miniseries" to the language of entertainment. *Roots* was based on Alex Haley's account—later tainted by plagiarism—of tracing his ancestry to the West

African enclave of the Gambia. A huge audience had been mesmerized by Haley's saga, which touched off a nationwide fad for finding one's own roots and prompted a *Newsweek* cover story. Sitting in my office the week the story was on the stands, I realized that I had only the sketchiest idea where the Kosiners and the Fishers had come from in Europe. "The caves," as my mother characterized my father's roots, didn't offer much guidance, so I decided to dig up the story myself.

Since "Fisher" was coined by an Immigration officer, my only hope was "Kosiner," and the only person I'd ever heard of outside my own family with a similar name was the Polish novelist Jerzy Kosinski, the celebrated author of *Steps* and of the Holocaust nightmare novel *The Painted Bird*. I'd read the books, but I'd never met Kosinski and I set my assistant (whose name, Nina Posnansky, made her roots clear) to finding him. She quickly located him at Yale, where he was teaching literature and was a fellow of Davenport College.

When I had Jerzy on the line, I explained my quest, and his reply made my heart beat faster.

"Of course, I can tell you all about the family," said Kosinski in his staccato, accented English. "The Kosiners are descended from a long line of wonder rabbis in Lithuania. In the eighteenth century there was a schism. Some of them converted to Catholicism, moved down into Poland, and started calling themselves Kosinski."

He went on and on, embellishing the saga with fascinating detail as I scribbled madly on a yellow legal pad.

"This is beyond anything I could have hoped for," I burbled. "I can't thank you enough."

"I'm glad I could help," said Jerzy modestly.

I was euphoric when I put down the phone—and smug, too. Such a savvy reporter was I that with one well-placed telephone call I'd unlocked the mystery of the Kosiners! And what a tale! David Halberstam and half the distinguished journalists I knew claimed descent from Lithuanian wonder rabbis. Now I had my own pedigree.

A few years later, I was introduced to Kosinski at a party. I thanked him again for the wonderful gift of the roots of the Kosiners. "We must be cousins!" I exclaimed. "Could be," deadpanned Jerzy.

Then, in the gentlest possible way, Kosinski, who was born Jerzy

Lewinkopf in the Polish commercial city of Lodz and was a renowned fabulist, explained to me that he had made up the whole saga of the Kosiner/Kosinskis, wonder rabbis and all.

"But why did you do it?" I asked him, more bemused than angry.

"It made you happy, didn't it?" replied Jerzy, and of course he was right.

Every con depends on the mark's greed—for riches or sex or, in Eddie Kosner's case, for roots. Kosinski had made me deeply happy and I instantly forgave him. In fact, Jerzy became a good friend and remained so until he took his own life in 1991.

Julie was the first one I called for a date, and I cunningly suggested dinner a week later at a refined French restaurant in the east fifties called Le Cygne, the swan. That was a success, and to show my cosmopolitan discernment, for our second date I booked a Japanese table at another of my favorites, Nippon, then as now one of the city's premier Japanese restaurants. I was seeing other women, too, but I felt more attracted to Julie each time we met. But before the romance got far, I left town. Long before my breakup with Alice, I had planned to take the month of August as my vacation, a traditional perk for the *Newsweek* editor. Now, I couldn't very well spend it with Alice, so I decided to book a *Newsweek* grand tour, using the opportunity to travel abroad, as I should have long before becoming editor.

Five days after my fortieth birthday, I left New York, as free as I'd ever been. The trip took me to Japan, Korea, Singapore, Bangkok, and Hong Kong and then on to South Africa and Southern Rhodesia, as it was then called, where the white farmers were facing Robert Mugabe's black fighters and bloodthirsty allies from neighboring Mozambique. I ended up in Paris and then took one of the first Concorde supersonic flights back to Washington, where I spent the night in Georgetown with an old flame of sorts. Attentive but not importunate, I checked in by telephone with Julie along the way, the first time spraddled on a tatami mat in a serene ryokan in Kyoto.

There is no form of travel as gratifying as a grand tour by a news magazine pooh-bah. Because the magazines are published everywhere in the world, everyone wants to meet the editor. The bureau chiefs in your ports of call book the best suites in the prime hotels, lay on cars and drivers and meetings and meals with prime ministers and moguls, writers, architects, TV stars, anyone who might interest the chief. Before you leave, the staff prepares a briefing

book on everything and everybody you're going to encounter, and the State
Department and CIA are happy to pitch in, too. The visiting bigfoot need
only behave himself—and the bureau chiefs are discreet wizards at cleaning up
after those who don't. Because everything is so well planned, it's possible to
stop for three or four days in a place like Bangkok and spend nearly every
waking hour meeting everyone worth meeting. It spoils you for any other
travel the rest of your life.

In Bangkok, we were invited to dinner by General Kriangsak Chomanan,
the head of the proud Thai armed forces. In their civilized way, the Thai military tended to play political musical chairs in the autumn, when aging gen-
erals were compelled to retire. Well in advance, the next prime minister
would be designated and given a few months to get organized for the "coup."
General Kriangsak knew he'd be the man starting in November, and he was
thrilled to meet the editor of *Newsweek* and my traveling companion, Rick
Smith, the Asian editor for our international editions. He not only invited
us to his palatial home outside the capital, but produced his incoming
defense minister—a tiny, solemn man in a black suit whose name sounded
like Upadeet—and insisted on cooking our dinner himself.

So there we sat, around a mammoth lazy Susan at the general's dining
room table, while a TV set blared American cartoons dubbed in Thai and Mr.
Upadeet sat mute, his feet barely touching the floor. The general ladled up
one course after another, all the while holding forth on his plans for the new
Thai government. The food was exquisite, but a little of the Kriangsak
Weltanschauung went a long way. And there was a problem: both Rick and I
were single and, in those pre-AIDS days, eager to sample Bangkok's frisky
nightlife before the curfew. Talking our way out of the general's feast required
all our ingenuity, but we made it back to the bar district before lights out.

The Asian leg of the trip ended in Hong Kong, then still a British crown
colony but with operatives of the mainland Communist regime conspicuously active. Over meltingly tender chicken cooked in clay, one of them, a
newspaper editor, regaled me with tales of a famous guest who had preceded
me. "Oh, yes," he said, "I remember Katharine Graham—*Madam Dragon!*"
How well I knew.

My last day in Hong Kong was a Sunday, and I spent the afternoon
cruising Victoria harbor on a pleasure junk used every weekend by Smith and
some colleagues. One of them took a picture of me reclining on the deck with

a cold beer, a man insufferably pleased with himself and his surroundings. Then I flew off to South Africa, where I was greeted by our Johannesburg correspondent with big news from back home: Elvis Presley had dropped dead at forty-two in the bathroom of Graceland, his home in Memphis.

I checked in with the office where my deputy, Ken Auchincloss, was running the magazine while I was away. Ken was Groton and Harvard and had no need to ask Jerzy Kosinski about his roots. His father had been a lifer at *Time*, and Ken was to the manner born, a blithely adept amateur of journalism. He was smart as a whip and an elegant writer, and he relished being a contrarian. I asked Auchincloss what the magazine planned for the Presley issue, which was certain to be a sellout on the newsstands, and was stupefied by his reply.

"We're just discussing that now," said Ken. "Some people think it should be a cover story, but I don't. We have a really important piece on the Panama Canal that I really think we have to do on the cover."

I almost gagged, but I held my tongue. News magazines run like military units, with a clear chain of command. When the commander is away from the fray, he doesn't try to countermand the leadership in the field.

"Well, it's your show," I said with false heartiness. "But if you do take a vote, my proxy's for Elvis."

As it turned out, my distant proxy didn't count for much. *Newsweek* went with a cover on Bert Lance, Jimmy Carter's louche head of the Office of Management and Budget, and blew a major moment in American popular culture—and a certain sellout on the newsstands.

13

THE FALLING WALLENDA

I COULDN'T KNOW IT at the time, but that summer marked the high point of my trajectory at *Newsweek*. The very qualities that spurred my success at the magazine—my decisiveness and my conviction that the magazine had to be more popular—led to my undoing. For one thing, as *Newsweek* prospered, I became even more confident in my own judgment. For another, I let my fascination with popular culture deteriorate into a reflexive tic. It was one thing to herald such enduring talents as Steve Martin, Springsteen, Pavarotti, Woody Allen, Willie Nelson, and John Belushi. But Jacqueline Bisset in a wet T-shirt touting a dog of a movie called *The Deep*? John Denver? Suzanne Somers in the first "jiggle TV" show *Three's Company*? Robert Stigwood, the florid-faced Australian rock impresario? Disco's Donna Summer?

Each of these covers in a run of more than one hundred issues of *Newsweek* might be justifiable. But the cumulative effect was inescapable. For all the heavyweight covers the magazine published week after week, the impression gained traction that *Newsweek* on my watch was getting soft.

Perhaps had I been older or had failed somewhere else earlier, I might have picked up the signals and quickly countered the perception. But the core requirement in running an important magazine or newspaper—or anything else, for that matter—is to have confidence in one's own judgment. Whenever hard decisions have to be made, there is always somebody in the room offering the easy way out—the shred of doubt that can be inflated into a red flag, the counsel of delay that can be nursed into cancellation. *Better safe than sorry* is one management mantra, but so is *No guts, no glory.* Consistently choosing the right course is called sound judgment.

So my instinct—and my arrogance—led me to disregard the whispers. At dinner at Kay Graham's home in Washington one night, Joe Alsop, the

Mandarin columnist who was one of Kay's most influential confidants, took me aside.

He looked at me over the rims of his half glasses and said in a fatherly way, "Don't let the magazine go soft, boy."

I assured him that I wasn't—and wouldn't—but I was oblivious to a warning a more accomplished courtier would have recognized for what it was. Not until I was banished from the realm and reflected on my fall did I understand that Katharine Graham's world was a court with all the intricate etiquette, Byzantine politics, and nuanced signals so familiar to the favored nobles at the Sun King's Versailles. Indeed, I could have saved myself much anguish if early on I had got hold of the best guide to survival at a place like *Newsweek* or Condé Nast—Baldassare Castiglione's Renaissance classic *The Book of the Courtier*.

The supreme courtier was, of course, Ben Bradlee, who had many of the qualities touted by Castiglione, including, as I discovered at a party in East Hampton two decades later, a lovely singing voice. Ben was always well turned out in his bold Jermyn Street striped shirts, his hair slicked back Palm Beach–style in wings behind his ears. He was always elegant, even—especially—when most profane. He called the proprietor "Katharine," the name only insiders used to show their intimacy with the sovereign. He could blaspheme at her and sass her, too, but he always told the world how fortunate he was to serve the Graham family, journalism's royalty. No matter how high he soared, Ben *never* mistook himself for an owner—the supreme act of lèse-majesté.

I had no such charm and I had a tin ear for conversation at a court high on obliqueness. Kay was addicted to indirection. If she asked, "What did you think of this week's *Time* cover story on gerbils?" she really meant, *It was brilliant—why didn't Newsweek do it?* If she asked, "How is Rod doing as chief of correspondents?" she really meant, *I can't stand him—get rid of the guy.* A disarmingly casual remark by the Duke of Alsop was as close to a direct order as I was ever going to get from the sovereign.

My way of running the place also began to grate on some of the troops. I drove them hard, and not always in a direction they wanted to go. I was impatient, and I could be abrupt and sarcastic. Oz had been, too, but perhaps because he was older or perhaps because he was more at ease with himself, the staff was more willing to take it from Elliott. And there was the problem of people's ambitions.

In the first few years of any new administration, the staff is caught up in the common pursuit. People are energized by the new direction and are busy jostling for position in the evolving pecking order. But when people find their seats and the enterprise settles into its cruising speed, the scheming for advancement only intensifies. In later years in other jobs, I learned how to deal with the editor or writer with an inflated sense of his or her talents and possibilities. I never dashed their hopes—unless I wanted them to leave—but talked positively, if vaguely, about what the future might hold. There would never be a fixed date, but always a gauzy promise of another chat in six months or a year to see how things looked then. It worked remarkably well.

But two years or so into the *Newsweek* job, I lacked subtlety and guile. If pushed to it, I was likely to tell someone their dreams of glory wouldn't materialize on my watch. This approach has the virtue of honesty, but it's a foolproof way to make people realize that they're never going to achieve their dreams so long as you hold on to your job, giving them good reason to want to see you gone.

Too late to do me any good at *Newsweek,* I stumbled into a management insight that served me well later, particularly at *New York* and the *Daily News.* At the last minute, I found myself having to make a tour of some of *Newsweek*'s domestic bureaus. I always sorted through my in-box before such trips and took care of any pending business before leaving town. But there was no time for that on this trip. I returned ten days later dreading all the unresolved issues I'd left festering in that box on my desk. And then a remarkable thing happened: when I went through the pile, I discovered that nearly all the issues had been settled or had become moot while I was away. The chief of correspondents had figured out on his own how to make a complicated personnel switch; the editorial controller realized that the big cost overrun in the photo budget was really just a typo in his printout; the disgruntled writer had found a new job and was leaving.

Thus was born what I call the Robert F. Wagner School of Management. It was named for Bob Wagner, a kindly, near-somnolent politician who enjoyed three very successful terms as mayor of New York in the late 1950s and early 1960s without ever seeming to make a decision. The Wagner school was the antithesis of the hard-charging New Frontier style I'd so admired. Making many hard decisions was like surgery—you didn't do it unless and until you had to. More often than not, a satisfactory resolution presented itself before you got around to settling something.

The Wagnerian approach to hard-news decisions would be disastrous, of course, but even there it had its applications. People are always telling the editor he must commit to running a story he has doubts about because the competition has it or the source will clam up or some such. The most notorious recent example of this was Dan Rather's fiasco with the spurious Bush Air National Guard memos—rushed on the air because *USA Today* was supposedly hot on the same trail. In many cases, these pressures turn out to be specious and there really is another day—or perhaps only another hour—to perfect the decision.

Also too late, I learned the benefits of seeming not to hear something said in a meeting, or forgetting it, or acting as if the issue was so complex one couldn't really understand what to make of it. These stratagems had to be used sparingly—no one was going to believe that the chief was a deaf, absent-minded doofus—but they could be helpful in stalling until a mess resolved itself or in buying extra time.

Within a few years, I encountered another remarkably effective management trick that I could never bring myself to use. I glimpsed it first from Roone Arledge, the genius TV innovator who took first *ABC Sports* and then *ABC News* to the top. Arledge simply never returned phone calls from people who worked for him and many who didn't. Nor were his whereabouts clear. When he ran *ABC News* and *ABC Sports* simultaneously, he maintained offices at each headquarters but was rarely at either. People looking for him at news concluded he must be at sports. Anxious producers gazing at his empty sports desk assumed he was at news. So underlings would line up outside both his offices toward the end of each day, desperately hoping for a few words with the chief. Roone was so hard to find that most people simply made the decisions themselves. Since most of the people who worked for Arledge were able, they generally made good decisions—just what the elusive Roone wanted.

John Evans, an effervescent Welshman who had been an alcoholic and a barrister and ran Rupert Murdoch's magazine empire for a while, never returned any calls—except Rupert's. "When they can't talk to me, they do it themselves," he once told me cheerfully. "If it's really a crisis, they call five times and I get back to them."

* * *

None of these tricks of the trade were available to me as my sure grip on *Newsweek* began to falter. It is a natural law of leadership that one bad turn inevitably provokes another. Early in 1978, hoping to score another *Final Days* coup, we bought serialization rights to a Watergate memoir by Bob Haldeman, Nixon's bullet-headed White House *consigliere*. The revelations in Haldeman's book *The Ends of Power* couldn't compare with Woodward and Bernstein's, but they were fresh. As we had done with *The Final Days,* a small special unit handled the Haldeman material to prevent leaks, since the chief virtue of the excerpts was their exclusivity.

I knew something was wrong on Thursday night of publication week, when I brought Julie back to her apartment after dinner and, in those days before cell phones, checked my answering service. The operator told me I had more than a dozen messages, most of them flagged urgent, and my heart dropped. My first call back was to Peter Goldman, who told me the bad news: our precious Haldeman excerpts were going to be splashed all over a newspaper next morning, four days before *Newsweek* would be published. The really bad news was that the newspaper was Ben Bradlee's *Washington Post,* our rival in the court of Katharine the Great. So we had not only lost our exclusive, we had been scooped by our corporate sibling. Had the roles been reversed, I doubt that *Newsweek* would have stolen a *Washington Post* exclusive and run with it. And if we had, Bradlee would have screamed bloody murder. But Bradlee sensed he could rape us with impunity—and he was right.

I took a Valium—my first ever—and contemplated the next day, which figured to be excruciating. The spectacle of fancy-pants *Newsweek* getting scooped by Ben's intrepid paper was just too delicious to leave alone. I'd be barraged by media questions: Now that the news was out, was *Newsweek* even going to bother publishing the excerpt? How could this have happened? Did Bradlee even tell Kay Graham what he was going to do? If not, why not? If he did, what did she say? Wasn't it all humiliating?

In the office next morning, I made a decision—and again stumbled into a priceless media management insight. I knew that if I started answering questions from the press, the story would hemorrhage. At the same time, I knew that simply saying "no comment" was too lame to contemplate. So I had all the calls referred to a *Newsweek* PR woman, who was authorized to quote a single sentence from me: "We've had better days and we will again."

Miraculously, every reporter was satisfied by the quote. No one pursued the embarrassing questions I'd conjured up the night before in my Valium-cushioned reverie. In fact, most of the stories used my quote as the second paragraph, setting a tone of plucky grace under pressure by *Newsweek* in the maelstrom. The simple lesson I learned is that many reporters don't really want to dig into a story—they want a bite of red meat. If you toss them one, they'll snap it up and dash off in another direction, tails wagging.

I later got the scoop on Bradlee's scoop. It turned out that Nancy Collins, a tall, glamorous blonde on probation at the paper, determined to save her job by getting hold of the book, which was being bound at a plant in Pennsylvania. She told her plan to the editors at the Style section, who cautioned her not to steal the book. So Collins snuck into the plant, "borrowed" a copy, Xeroxed as much as she could, then returned the purloined volume and hightailed it back to Washington. In the spirit of *La Ronde,* Collins later became a useful contributor of celebrity interviews for me at *New York* magazine and *Esquire,* just like Tony Schwartz, who had scooped us on *The Final Days* in 1976.

Alice and I had quickly worked out our divorce settlement because there was so little to divvy up. We were divorced under the "old" New York law, which provided lifetime alimony for the wife but required no division of assets. Had the law passed just three years later been in effect, I would have had to dispose of our apartment and the small stash of Washington Post Company stock I'd managed to accumulate, and essentially split the proceeds with Alice. This would have added up to hardly anything. The apartment, what real-estate brokers call a classic six, with spacious dining room and maid's room on the Upper East Side, was worth barely more than the $50,000 I'd paid for it four years before. And it carried a $20,000 mortgage. The *Washington Post* stock—which has since split several times, and nearly reached $1,000 a share in the summer of 2004—was selling for well under $50 a share. So the timing of the divorce was one of those unscripted episodes that invisibly shape one's future. Even with the salaries I earned in big jobs over the next quarter century, I'd never have been able to re-create such valuable assets today.

Instead of a division of community property, I agreed to pay Alice a generous slice of my income as alimony and helped her find and furnish an apartment just two blocks from mine. We shared custody of John and Anthony, who split their time at each place.

In the summer of 1978, Julie and I set out for France. We hadn't discussed marriage, but the trip was plainly an audition of sorts. My run as a roving bachelor had lasted barely nine months. I'd spent time with a number of attractive, accomplished women, but I quickly lost any enthusiasm for that life. All the women wanted to marry or remarry, and I felt it was unfair to keep seeing them if I had no desire to tie myself down again so soon. By the spring of 1978, I knew I felt differently about Julie. She had survived two years that would have devastated anyone without her fierce resilience— marriage to a neurosurgeon, a miscarriage, divorce after just nine months, and the death from cancer of her father, who had built Baumgold Brothers into one of the world's leading diamond concerns and whom she adored. And then she'd lost *New York,* too, and *Esquire,* where she'd been a contributing editor.

The trip in a tiny rented Renault took us from Paris to Normandy and then down through the Loire to Les Baux near the Mediterranean and on to Marseilles, stopping for a night or two at romantic châteaus with side trips to three-star restaurants along the way. It was going to be carefree and elegant— a taste of the life I'd never led. The reality was so different it was comical. Put two willful people with no sense of direction in a tiny car on the jammed back roads of France in the middle of July and ax murder is just one option—and by no means the most drastic.

We were often lost and nearly always late—inching behind trucks and campers on narrow roads threading through one provincial town after another. Once, we were so far behind schedule that we had to put up in a dreary hotel in the middle of the ancient university city of Montpelier, where we were the only guests in the vast, dismal dining room. Back in the equally dismal room, we had a fight at 3:00 AM so horrific that we finally fell asleep certain that at dawn we would split up and drag back to New York separately.

But somehow, when the morning came, we got back in the Renault and headed south—except that we couldn't escape Montpelier. We left the hotel, drove onto the road that encircles the city, missed the sign for the AutoRoute—and found ourselves back at the hotel. A second pass produced the same result. Obviously, it wasn't our destiny to break up—or even to get out of Montpelier alive.

On the third try, we somehow hit the AutoRoute, and that night we found ourselves standing on the eerie white escarpment of Les Baux, the primeval mining site of aluminum ore, or bauxite. The moon and stars seemed close enough to harvest from the sky.

"Is there anything you'd like to ask me?" said Julie, her green eyes fixed on me.

By then I knew that she had brought along on the trip the text of a short cable to her mother. It read AISLES AGAIN, and she was poised to send it the minute I asked the right question. But I held off the inevitable until we were back in the States. We set the date for November, just seventeen months after my first marriage ended.

The ceremony at Julie's mother's apartment on Fifth Avenue was modest enough and the honeymoon consisted of a night in a suite at the Carlyle, three blocks from our apartment. That turned out to be just as well, because the *Newsweek* guests at the wedding brought the first word of one of the weirdest—and ultimately biggest—stories in years. In a dystopian community in the remote jungles of Guyana on the northern coast of South America, followers of a charismatic American cult leader named Jim Jones had been found dead. The *Newsweek* crew had managed to wedge a short story into the issue closing that night.

The story turned out to be the Jonestown Massacre. On my wedding day, following Jones's orders, more than 900 of the cult members, including more than 270 children, had swallowed Kool-Aid laced with cyanide. Anyone who refused or tried to escape was shot by Jones's henchmen.

Once the pictures of the mounds of corpses and the eyewitness accounts began flowing out of Jonestown, the magnitude of the story became plain. It was simply one of the most bizarre chapters of modern times, a saga of human brutality and folly unmatched in this age of cults. Today, cable news would feast on Jonestown. In the late 1970s, it was the kind of pop cultural sensation that *Newsweek* ought to own. And own it we did, publishing a special report dozens of pages long that evoked all the drama, mystery, pathos, and sheer lunacy of the grotesque episode.

Sitting at my desk directing the Jonestown coverage, I felt like the conductor of a magnificent symphony whose instrumentalists are responsive to the leader's every baton shiver or the virtuoso commanding the mighty

Wurlitzer organ at Radio City Music Hall. It's the same feeling of sublime assurance a great athlete must have at the decisive moment of a big game. Amid the adrenaline rush, I began to hope that such a star turn by the magazine might reverse the tide that I sensed was running against me. Tone-deaf though I may have been to the oblique language of Kay's court, I knew my *Newsweek* history, especially the fate of my predecessors. I knew I'd be dispatched sometime, but I desperately didn't want to be blindsided, as Oz and Kermit had been. So I tried to enlist an ally in Peter Derow. Kay was so infatuated with Derow's business smarts that she'd brought him back to run *Newsweek* after he deserted to take a big job at CBS. I asked Peter to give me a heads-up if he got the sense that I was in trouble with Mrs. Graham, and he solemnly promised he would. So I didn't panic when Kay suddenly suggested that we spend a day together in New York.

The problem, as it emerged from her circuitous conversation, was that I wasn't delegating enough responsibility to others, forcing too many decisions to end at my desk and generally gumming up the works. This, as I later figured out, was her euphemistic way of saying that while I was, of course, a brilliant editor, I was a lousy manager. I thought I was a terrific manager. If I insisted on making decisions, it was because things turned out better that way whether the issue was the editorial budget, a bureau hire, or the next week's cover. And yes, I was going to read every word of every week's issue, just as Oz and Kermit had; that's what a news magazine editor did.

Had I been more sophisticated, I would have eagerly embraced all her criticisms and remedies and then simply gone on as I thought best. But I felt compelled to justify myself and show her where her analysis was off base. I did agree to some Band-Aid changes, but I don't think the day went the way she'd hoped it would. Afterward, some suggested that Kay was just trying to set me up—*I tried so hard to help him before I had to fire him*—but I think she was genuinely trying to save me.

A few months later, Julie and I found ourselves playing Rosencrantz and Guildenstern in one of Kay's most baffling theatricals. A "stiffy," one of those fancy invitations, showed up in the mail bidding Mr. and Mrs. Edward Kosner to dinner at the Graham mansion in Georgetown a few weeks hence. Nothing more was said about it, and when Julie and I arrived, we were startled to learn that the dinner was for us. "Oh, yes," one of the guests told us during drinks. "That's how my invitation read—in honor of you two" and a

French diplomat who was retiring to Paris. We tried to cover our embarrassment at being clueless guests of honor only to suffer a second shock: the Frenchman and his wife were seated at our hostess's table, while the other two honored guests were relegated to a table as far from Kay as the dimensions of the room would permit. Somehow, we survived the evening and retreated exhausted to the Madison Hotel. "What was that all about?" Julie asked in the car. I was sure I knew, but I didn't have the heart to tell her.

But Derow was silent through the spring, so I forced myself to tamp down the sense of foreboding that gripped me when I awoke each morning and stayed with me through the day. Were people avoiding me in the corridors and at the endless run of office parties that were part of life at the magazine? Stay cool. Besides, Julie and I were going to be leading a *Newsweek* delegation to China at the end of June, and there were endless preparations for the visit, a rarity in those days. Nobody gets fired in the middle of an official trip to Peking, right?

But one day when something or other went wrong, I realized with a clutch of the guts that I had lost control of the mighty Wurlitzer. My confidence was compromised, and I simply didn't know what to do next to save myself. That's when I gave way to the conviction that I was doomed at *Newsweek*.

Whatever my torment, I still had to publish a magazine each week, and at the beginning of June I made the most fateful cover decision of my life. One obvious choice was Pope John Paul II, who was going on a historic pilgrimage to his native Poland. But in just a few months the pope would be making his first visit to the U.S. for, among other ceremonies, a Mass at Yankee Stadium, and that seemed to me the right occasion to put him on *Newsweek*'s cover. So for the upcoming issue, I planned a big inside story on John Paul with dramatic color pictures.

The week before, Julie and a friend had taken me to Times Square to see a ballyhooed new horror movie called *Alien*. It starred the tall, imposing Sigourney Weaver as Ripley, crew member on a spaceship who squirts a flamethrower as she battles a really nasty monster that bursts out of the bodies of her comrades and chases her around the vessel. Ridley Scott, a brilliant Brit, had directed *Alien*. It was the first big movie of a summer that was going to offer a run of blockbuster horror and sci-fi pictures. So I decided to order up a cover story on the trend. It turned out to be my last.

On the afternoon that ***HOLLYWOOD'S SCARY SUMMER!***

appeared, I got a call to come to Derow's office. I greeted Peter with a smile, but he looked as if his dog had died, and I fell silent.

"Katharine is asking for your resignation," he said.

The plan obviously was for Derow to do the deed, sparing Kay the confrontation, but I wouldn't have it.

"If she's going to fire me," I said, "she's going to have to do it herself."

In her office down the hall, Kay looked as if *her* dog had died, too. But she said what she had to say, and, when I asked, informed me that my successor would be Lester Bernstein, the man who'd hired me at *Newsweek* sixteen years earlier. And so the media merry-go-round spun on. (Lester himself was dispatched two years later, just after *Newsweek* won several National Magazine Awards.) Afterward, I went home and broke the news to Julie, who was rock-solid as always in a crisis, and to John and Anthony.

Over the next several months, I went through the classic stages of mourning—denial and isolation, anger and depression. The last stage—acceptance—took years. Mercifully, we had the perfect setting for the denial and isolation stage. In the mid-1960s, Julie's parents had bought a weekend retreat in Redding, Connecticut, about sixty-five miles from the city in leafy Fairfield County. The compound had a Dutch Colonial main house, a guest cottage with its own sauna, a near-Olympic-size swimming pool, and a Har Tru tennis court. Redding had a huge lawn surrounded by towering maple, elm, and fir trees that created a natural amphitheater of heart-stopping beauty. Ten minutes in Redding and your pulse would slow and the city and its anxieties would evanesce in the fragrant sunlight. Julie had taken me there one winter weekend when we were courting, and she always said that it was Redding I'd really fallen in love with. After we married, we made the guest cottage our own. Julie's mother and brothers would fill the main house on the weekends, but for now we were alone with my sorrow.

For the first few days, the phone rang all the time—colleagues and friends calling with their condolences. Sighing or straining to be optimistic, they meant well, but most succeeded only in making me feel worse. One of the first callers was Pat Moynihan, whom I'd first met a decade before when he was a professor at the Harvard-MIT joint center for urban studies and I was starting *Newsweek*'s new section on the cities. Pat had risen from Hell's Kitchen (and a year at CCNY) to fame as a pioneering social thinker, U.S.

ambassador to India and the United Nations, and, after his election in New York three years before, to be the only true intellectual in the U.S. Senate. One of his greatest achievements was his prescient 1965 report on the plight of the Negro family, which we had misread and savaged at *Newsweek*. We had met only a few times, but now Pat was calling to offer his farm upstate in Columbia County if I needed to get away—a kindness I could never forget.

Denial and isolation quickly gave way to anger—a burning fury that would shake me awake in the middle of the night. My brain seethed with manifestos to Kay Graham railing against the despicable way I'd been treated. *How could you have done this to me? Why didn't you just say you didn't like the direction of the magazine? I would have corrected it. Why? Why? Why?*

Of course, I never sent the letters, nor did I encourage pals who called regularly to trash Kay—it would be a sign of weakness to join in. Soon enough, I tried to focus on my situation. It wasn't promising. I had just turned forty-two, and my professional reputation was badly scuffed. The conventional wisdom soon took hold that I'd been fired because I'd cheapened the magazine and been harsh to the staff, the kind of talk that would make others reluctant to entrust me with their magazines. What's more, news magazine editors and writers live in an insular world, like cops and marines, and I was hardly known outside *Newsweek*. I had met other editors when I was asked to join the board of the American Society of Magazine Editors, but to their publishers and owners I was simply another guy Kay Graham had canned.

In Kyoto on my Asian trip two years before, I'd visited a famous fifteenth-century Zen rock and sand garden, and now I saw it as a metaphor of my quandary. The isolated tapering stones stood for other magazine and publishing companies, each full of ambitious people scheming and struggling to reach the top of their own rock. None of these strivers was going to invite in a potential rival like me at a high level. Only an owner or chief executive might do that, and I didn't know any except Kay Graham.

While I was pondering my lot back in the city, Dick Clurman, an old-school news magazine guy, chief of correspondents at *Time*, and one of Oz's closest friends, took me to lunch in the Grill Room of the Four Seasons, the big-time media canteen.

"You're a commanding officer," said Dick. "We've just got to find you a command."

Clurman knew just what to say to a humbled editor, and he raised my spirits. But securing that command was another story. The only lead I had was one of the first calls I'd got in Redding. Dick Wald, a top executive at ABC News, asked if I'd consider working as a consultant on one of their shows, *20/20*. The program was supposed to be Roone Arledge's answer to CBS's supremely successful *60 Minutes,* but it had gotten off to a disastrous start. Arledge had many brilliant brainstorms, but he had his clunkers, too, and this was one of them. He had teamed Harold Hayes, a good-ol'-boy former editor of *Esquire,* with Bob Hughes, an Australian raconteur and polymath who was the art critic of *Time* magazine. The TV audience was stupefied by this garrulous duo and they were promptly yanked off the air and replaced by Hugh Downs and Barbara Walters. Now, with a new producer, the show was trying to redeem itself. My role essentially was to hang around and offer magazine-editor insights on *20/20* segments as they were produced.

With nothing better—actually nothing else—to do, I accepted, and turned up at the ABC News broadcast center near Lincoln Center after Labor Day to discover that nobody involved with the show knew I was coming or what I was supposed to be doing. I had no desk or office or telephone. The show was broadcast live on Thursday nights, but segments were added, killed, expanded, and contracted all the time, and figuring out where to be when was almost impossible. The producers who turned out the segments were gypsies themselves whose only tangible achievement was a tape reel of their best pieces.

I was achingly uncomfortable in this new world. I was spoiled from my years in an agreeable office with an attentive assistant and an ordered day of meetings and good lunches. Now, if I was lucky, I'd be able to locate the office or editing room where a *20/20* segment was being hatched and could cadge a corned beef sandwich and a ginger ale from the cellophane-wrapped trays that turned up every so often. For the line producers, the hours were uncountable: as a rule, it took an hour in the editing room for each broadcast minute of a *20/20* piece. Routinely, a producer would spend twelve hours cutting a story only to be told that two or three minutes had to be added or subtracted. And then the segment might get dumped for something sexier just a few hours before airtime.

The physical discomfort wouldn't have meant much had I anything to

offer. But I quickly learned that story elements fundamental to print journalism hardly mattered in TV magazine shows. One segment I kibitzed was
devoted to Donna Summer, the disco queen I'd put on the cover of
Newsweek three years before. Tom Hoving, once the head of the Metropolitan Museum of Art, now a TV talking head, was the "correspondent" on the
segment, which consisted of a tape of Summer performing and interviews
with her and her parents back in the Middle West. "She's hot! She's new!
She's disco!" cried Hoving, or some comparable gibberish, and the piece
began.

After the rough cut ran, I gingerly pointed out that it left out some good
stuff—how old she was, how much money she'd made from her hit records,
and her biography, including the fact that she'd left home at seventeen to
appear in the German company of *Hair*. The *20/20* execs respectfully agreed.
"Find the writer and get him to work it in," said one, and went back to mas-
saging one of the performance cuts. You couldn't publish a magazine profile
of Summer without the elements I'd mentioned, but for a TV piece all that
really mattered was the pictures: great tape, great segment.

Late one Friday afternoon, Arledge actually materialized at his ABC News
office, and his top deputies, Geraldo Rivera, and I joined him for a drink.
The shoptalk was mostly about how an upcoming Barbara Walters interview
with King Hussein could really be held to eight minutes whether Barbara
squawked or not. In those days, the evening news shows ran at 7:00 PM, but
all the networks fed the programs to their affiliates at 6:30, and the silent
screens on the console behind Roone showed the anchormen mouthing the
news—Walter Cronkite on CBS, Roger Mudd on NBC, and Frank
Reynolds on ABC.

About twenty minutes into the shows, I saw all eyes in the room lock on
Mudd's screen. Bright orange flames were leaping into the sky from the deck
of some sort of boat. Roone punched up the sound in time to hear Mudd
report there were no injuries in the barge fire on the Mississippi.

In the newspapers the next day, that fire might make a one- or two-para-
graph short tucked at the bottom of a column. But flames made great TV—
their rapt eyes testified to that—and Roone snatched up the phone on his
desk to make sure his evening news at seven would have comparable tape.

The image of some of TV's top news producers mesmerized by a barge
fire has stayed with me over the years. Like a great TV shot, it says it all.

Television is about the pictures and the logistics of getting those pictures on the air, not the words. It's the nature of the beast, and the reason that, since Walter Cronkite, so few print people have ever made the transition to TV news. I certainly got the TV tingle sitting in the control room on Thursday nights when the director said, "We're on the air," and the show began. But I realized that *20/20* really didn't need anything I had to contribute. So just after Thanksgiving, I thanked Dick Wald for paying me so well to kibitz and ended my TV career.

Now I was really desperate. The cruel reality was that I couldn't promote myself into the kind of job I was qualified for; I had to wait for it to come to me, if it ever did. After a few weeks, I became convinced that I had to get back to work as soon as I could and that nobody was going to offer me anything. Then, out of the ether, I was approached by the people who ran the CBS magazine group. Along the way, CBS had acquired a mixed array of monthlies ranging from *Woman's Day* to *Popular Mechanics,* and Bill Paley, who still ran the company, was pressuring his underlings to bring in somebody to tune up the indifferent editorial content. I'd actually wangled an interview with Paley earlier in the summer that led to a dead-end conversation with Bill Leonard, who was running CBS News. Six months later, with no other prospects, I became the editorial director of Paley's magazines. I asked for a contract but was turned down. The pay was a bit more than half what I was making at *Newsweek.*

Everyone at CBS was as nice as could be to me, but the job wasn't much. The editors of the magazines, which also included *Field & Stream* and *High Fidelity,* reported not to me but to their respective publishers. My role, it quickly became clear, was to encourage and cajole them into putting out better magazines. I had always been a line officer, with specific responsibility for producing something. Now, for the first and only time in my career, I held a staff job—I was a glorified kibbitzer. And for the first and only time in my career, I woke up in the morning without looking forward to going to work.

There was one provocative interlude. The head of the magazine group wanted to buy *Saturday Review,* a once-proud but now anemic journal of ideas and the arts, and it fell to me to make the editorial case for the acquisition at a meeting to be run by Paley himself, who plainly had the last word. The publishing side ran up elaborate charts and I rehearsed my spiel. Copies of recent issues of *SR* were on the table as the meeting began, with cover stories like "Whither NATO?" and "Secrets of Sleep," or their equivalent. Paley idly leafed through the pile, a look of deepest boredom on his still-handsome, tanned face.

When the presentations were finished, Paley fixed his chilly eyes on me and asked simply, "Do you think this magazine is interesting?"

I was tempted to fall back on, "Up to a point, Lord Copper." But I resisted and blathered on about how the magazine could quickly be sharpened up.

Paley harrumphed and pressed on: "Can anyone give me a good reason why we should bother with this?"

Nobody really could. In an instant, he had cut to the salient issues—and the CBS purchase of *Saturday Review* mercifully died on the spot. Paley hadn't become Paley and stayed Paley all these years by accident.

14

Deus ex Murdoch

NOT LONG AFTER THAT doleful episode, my office phone rang late one
dark winter afternoon, and I picked it up to find Rupert Murdoch on the
other end. Without any foreplay, he wanted to know if I'd be interested in
talking to him about taking over *New York* magazine. Julie had never accepted
my argument that I couldn't do much more than wait for a big job like this
to come to me, but I knew what I was talking about. Here was the proof.

In three short years, Murdoch and his lieutenants had made a mess of
Julie's old magazine. The star writers and editors had quit after the takeover,
and Rupert had to parachute in a band of Aussies and Brits from the *Post*
and elsewhere in the empire just to get the magazine out. Then he installed
Jim Brady, a savvy American who had worked for John Fairchild at *Women's
Wear Daily* and as publisher of *Harper's Bazaar*. Brady had helped develop
the *Post*'s infamous "Page Six" and he'd been putting out *New York*'s equivalent, "The Intelligencer." As publisher, Murdoch had hired Joe Armstrong, a
Texan who liked to wear cowboy boots with his business suit and had a born
salesman's easy charm. I'd first met Joe when he was Jann Wenner's publisher at *Rolling Stone*. Joe had fallen out with Wenner, and I'd tried to set
him up on the *Newsweek* business side, but those boots weren't made for
news magazines.

After about six months, Brady was replaced by John Berendt, a talented
but unprepossessing editor who had put in time at *Esquire* (and would later
write *Midnight in the Garden of Good and Evil*). Not long after I was fired at
Newsweek, Armstrong fired Berendt and made himself editor *and* publisher.
He tried manfully, but this hadn't worked, either, and the magazine was
being put out by an informal troika of writers and editors with predictable
results. The advertising was going soft and so was the circulation.

I didn't know all this when I went to talk with Murdoch on a sunny Saturday morning in February, but I had read *New York* since the first issue and I knew how far it had fallen. The magazine that gave the world Tom Wolfe's "Radical Chic" had recently published a cover story called "The Windiest Corners in New York."

Murdoch was still relatively new to New York, but he had a sumptuous apartment in one of the best co-ops in Manhattan, 834 Fifth Avenue at Sixty-fourth Street, just across from the red-brick Arsenal building that fronts the Central Park Zoo. (Nearly twenty-five years later, in a classic trope from *La Ronde,* Rupert made page one of the *Times* when he paid a record $44 million for a Rockefeller triplex in his old building.)

I was well prepared for my conversation with Murdoch. I had simple, clear ideas about how to bring back *New York,* many of them from Julie, who knew the magazine better than anyone except Felker. Instead of trivial nonsense like windy corners, *New York* had to focus again on the personalities and issues that New Yorkers care about. Stylish name writers had to be recruited, the service coverage had to be reinvigorated, the hodgepodge typography had to be scraped off *New York*'s classic look. Everything from photos to captions to headlines had to be executed better—the magazine had to be edited, not assembled. It would likely take six months to start winning back alienated readers and advertisers, but there was no question it could be done. *New York* had a model of success. It didn't have to be invented, just excavated.

Murdoch was whip-smart with an attractive manner, polite and soft-spoken. Rupert spoke *Strein*—that's how the word "Australian" sounded when he pronounced it, and his accent made it hard to understand much of what he was saying. But I got the drift because, remarkably, Murdoch ticked off all the points on my *New York* list before I had a chance to recite them myself. At that moment, I knew that I'd be able to do the job for him.

After my *Newsweek* experience, I was determined to have a contract, and I enlisted Tom Baer to negotiate it for me. The pay was better than I was getting at CBS, but not yet what I'd been making editing a news magazine, and there weren't really many issues to resolve. Early on, Tom made a suggestion that was to change my life, although it seemed like a grace note at the time.

"You know," said Tom, "Clay always had a provision in his contracts giving him the right of first refusal if the magazine were ever put up for sale."

The holder of such a right had to be given a chance to match any offer for *New York*. I told Tom that with Murdoch as the owner, this option was simply an abstraction—he had never sold any property he'd inherited or acquired.

"So what?" said Tom. "Let's ask for it, anyway. Maybe he'll feel it's as worthless as you do and give it to us."

Murdoch did indeed grant the option. The whole deal was wrapped up in a couple of days. On Friday, six days after we'd first talked at his apartment, Murdoch came uptown to his lawyer's office from his base at the *Post's* relocated plant near the Brooklyn Bridge to sign my contract in person, a courtesy I recognized and appreciated. Then, before heading back to Australia, he bought *Cue* magazine, *New York's* only competition, and fired Armstrong.

With the contract signed, I now had to go crosstown to the CBS offices in Times Square and quit the job I'd taken just six weeks before. The CBS magazine bosses were dumbstruck and angry, and they didn't relish having to tell Paley that their trophy editorial director had jumped ship for Murdoch. But I pointed out that I wasn't under contract (they had refused to give me one) and that I couldn't pass up the chance to edit an important magazine like *New York*, no matter how diminished it had become.

I was encouraged by my first dealings with Rupert, but the prospect of working for him was daunting. He had a fearsome reputation. *Private Eye,* the London satirical magazine, ridiculed him as the Aussie "Dirty Digger," and each day's lunatic *Post* front page reinforced Murdoch's grotesque image. But if I was ever to climb back on the media carousel and redeem my reputation, I would have to start as a Murdoch minion.

Only years later did I learn the real story of how I'd come to be rescued by Rupert from *Field & Stream* and *Popular Mechanics*. It turned out that his first choice for *New York* had been Don Forst, who had started with me on night rewrite at the *Post* and had worked on the *Boston Herald American,* a tabloid Rupert had picked up along the way. But Don had just taken over as editor of *Boston* magazine, and felt he couldn't leave. He suggested me. Murdoch wanted to have me checked out, and he turned to Howard Rubinstein, the best-connected PR man in the city. But Rubinstein knew only one person at *Newsweek,* Susan Agrest, a former researcher who reported city stories as part of the magazine's tiny New York bureau. As it happened, Susan was the best friend of another young woman I'd briefly romanced after breaking up with Alice and before I began courting Julie. The woman and I had parted on good terms. When Rubinstein played back to Agrest all the horror stories about me at *Newsweek,* she told him to disregard them: I was a fine editor and a good guy with many admirers at the magazine.

When I finally pieced together that story, I shivered. None of us can know the invisible forces that can determine some of the most important turning points in our lives. What if Forst had suggested someone else for *New York?* Or if Rubinstein's call had gone to someone at *Newsweek* who'd felt badly treated by me? Or if I'd acted dishonorably to Susan's friend? My call from Murdoch would never have come, and I'd never have known that I'd missed out on a job I was born to do.

* * *

Now the first step was to meet my new charges. Armstrong had packed up his stuff on Saturday, and I arranged to join *New York*'s managing editor and the art director on Sunday at the offices on Second Avenue and Forty-first Street, just around the corner from the Art Deco palace then occupied by the *Daily News.* Joe had used Clay Felker's old office, invariably described in the coverage of Felker's fall as opulent, wood-paneled evidence of the great editor's grandiosity. It was actually a comfortable room with a sink in a Formica counter on one side and a tiny bathroom. I found a pet stuffed bear on the windowsill overlooking bleak Fortieth Street.

Laurie Jones, the managing editor, and Roger Black, the art director, looked forlorn that Sunday afternoon. The last months of Armstrong's reign hadn't been much fun. Laurie, once Miss Kerr County in Texas, had risen from copy editor to wield the managing editor's mighty clipboard at *New York.* Everywhere in the magazine world except at *Newsweek* and *Time* the managing editor is the woman or man who makes the trains run on time, the personnel director, office manager, and production honcho. But as Armstrong lost touch, Laurie had been making major editorial decisions.

Roger Black, another Texan and an improbable graduate of the choir school of New York's starchy St. Thomas Episcopal Church, was a brilliant typographer, who had been giving his subordinates a nearly free hand in laying out the feature stories. The result was a magazine that looked inventive but incoherent. Having barely survived Armstrong's term, Laurie and Roger were understandably worried about what Rupert had foisted on them—me. I tried to be reassuring.

The next day I met the staff, who assembled in the magazine's dining room—another fabled Felker extravagance—looking like dazed survivors climbing out of the rubble after an earthquake. I introduced myself to them, answered what questions I could, and tried to dispel the look of abject panic I detected in more than a few eyes. Whatever the truth of the hard-guy reputation that trailed me from *Newsweek,* I was determined to be as benevolent a boss as I could be. Nobody would have the least excuse to call me a prick ever again.

My new mellowness was tested soon enough when I casually asked what the magazine had planned for the next week's cover story.

It turned out to be a disquisition on the supposed dangers to city dwellers of microwaves from transmitters and the like. My heart sank further when the cover was proudly shown to me—an insanely busy cartoon of New Yorkers cowering before the infernal emissions. Not wanting to spook my new charges, I restrained the impulse to scream, and told them mildly that I'd read the piece overnight and we'd discuss it next morning.

Much as I hated it, I'd already decided to run the microwave cover, figuring that it would be better to get the first issue out without upheaval and use the time to make sure the next several covers were stronger. Besides, I told myself, everyone out in magazineland would understand that in my first week I had to go with whatever was in the inventory. That was my plan until I got home that night and showed Julie the cover.

"You can't use *that!*" she said, as if addressing an imbecile. "Everybody's going to be watching what you do with your first issue of *New York*. It can't be a cartoon about microwaves."

She was right, of course. The microwaves cover was almost as bad as windy corners as a signal that *New York* had regained its old stride. My first cover had to be on the news—whatever that turned out to be.

In fact, there was a big story going on in New York: a rash of murderous attacks on policemen. So Tuesday morning, I called in Laurie, Roger, and Nick Pileggi, the magazine's crack crime reporter, and told them Monday's cover was going to be "The War on the Cops." They went pale.

"But it's already Tuesday morning and the magazine closes Thursday night," said Laurie, looking genuinely stricken.

"That's easy," I replied. "At *Newsweek,* we crashed cover stories in less than twenty-four hours. We've got plenty of time."

"We've never done anything like this around here," said Roger.

"Not to worry," I soothed. "Magazines always have covers. I've never seen one come out with a blank one."

I told Black to round up a foolproof photographer, a couple of models, and a cop uniform, and arrange a shoot late that night on a subway platform. I told Pileggi to pull together a 2,500-word piece, and I told Laurie to get the rest of the issue closed as efficiently as possible to clear the decks for the late cover. They left my office shaking their heads—Rupert had indeed inflicted a madman on them—but I knew all would be well.

As indeed it was. "The War on the Cops" was no National Magazine Award winner, but it sent the right message to the staff as well as to subscribers and advertisers. The next several covers were on the mark as well. Late in April, I put a late self-portrait of Picasso on the cover pegged to a giant retrospective opening at the Museum of Modern Art, and was rewarded by a phone call from Murdoch to tell me how much he liked it.

The call illustrated a trait of Murdoch's that his detractors either never knew or willfully ignored. Although he was indelibly identified in New York with the tabloid *Post* and *National Star,* Rupert published newspapers and magazines across the spectrum in Australia, including *The Australian,* the country's only national quality broadsheet, which he founded in 1964. In Britain, besides the tawdry *News of the World* and *The Sun,* Murdoch owned a share in a London production company that turned out many of those Masterpiece Theatre Brit-lit extravaganzas.

Indeed, Murdoch was just getting started building the intercontinental media colossus he named News Corporation in 1980. Over the next two decades, he took over the *Times* of London and the *Sunday Times,* more Australian papers, the *Boston Herald American* and the *Chicago Sun-Times,* bought the 20th Century-Fox film studio, the TV stations that form the nucleus of today's Fox Network, *TV Guide,* and HarperCollins book publisher and started Sky satellite TV and Fox News.

He believed in horses for courses—that media properties had to be suited to their audiences—upmarket, mid-, or downmarket. However much he relished tabloids, he knew that *New York* was an upmarket magazine and ought to look and read like one.

Besides getting the magazine back on track, my first weeks were spent shoehorning *Cue* into the pages of *New York*. *Cue* was an oddity, a magazine that grew from a seating sheet for theaters into a useful fortnightly listing guide for entertainment and the arts in the city. The articles in *Cue* weren't much, but it had a couple of hundred thousand loyal subscribers and was the closest thing to a direct competitor *New York* had. Shrewdly, Murdoch understood that by gobbling up *Cue* he could strengthen the appeal of *New York* and kill off the competition, all for a couple of million.

And, typically, Murdoch didn't shortchange the readers. Instead of just plastering a miniature *Cue* logo on *New York* somewhere, he directed me to add twenty new pages a week to *New York*'s regular complement and fill them with the most accurate and complete listings we could devise. *New York* published fifty issues a year, so we would be giving readers a thousand additional pages each year. It also turned out that *Cue*'s celebrated listings were compiled by a handful of overworked staffers and were riddled with errors. So between the thousand new pages and the listing reinforcements we had to hire, Rupert was spending another million annually.

But it paid off. *New York*'s subscription rolls swelled with the addition of the *Cue* readers and newsstand sales instantly jumped by 50 percent. For the first issue of *New York* incorporating *Cue*, I wanted a cover story with an entertainment slant, and I was able to get my old *Post* pal Pete Hamill, now a polished magazine writer, to profile Frank Sinatra, the first of many wonderful pieces he wrote for me at *New York*, *Esquire*, and the *Daily News* over the next quarter century.

It was already clear to me that *New York* was on the way back, but the advertisers were standoffish. The big department stores never lavished ads on Felker's *New York*, but once he was history some of them developed retroactive admiration for him and were frosty to Rupert's magazine. And then there was the urban legend about a Murdoch conversation with Marvin Traub, the potentate of Bloomingdale's. When Murdoch pressed Traub to advertise in the *Post*, Traub replied, "But Rupert, your readers are our shoplifters"—or so the story went. It never happened, of course. In fact, the demographics of *Post* readers were closer to the *Times* than the *News*, and Rupert offered a $10,000 bounty to anyone who could prove the colloquy ever happened. But as a metaphor, the shoplifter story was irresistible and it lives on to this day.

As it happened, Traub was one of the first skeptical advertisers I had to try to win over. He showed up with his entourage early on and played Scrooge. Traub was riding high in those days. Bloomingdale's was being celebrated as a model of hip retailing, and he was its guiding genius. He and his underlings faced me in a circle in the *New York* dining room, grilling me about my plans for reviving the magazine. Traub's crossed arms and sour expression made clear to everyone in the room that he was unimpressed with my answers.

The problem was that I was telling him the truth: I had no sexy secret formula for reviving *New York*. I was simply going to make everything about the magazine better: the ideas, the cover stories, the writers, the headlines and captions, the design, the listings, even the crossword puzzle on the back page. Week by week, issue by issue, the magazine would be transformed, and everybody would know it. In six months, all the qualms about *New York* would be forgotten.

I told him a story I'd heard about Chuck Noll, the pro football coach who'd taken over the lowly Pittsburgh Steelers in 1969. The team was one and thirteen in his first season but made the Super Bowl four times between 1974 and 1980 and won more of them than any other coach's team. Noll's simple rule was that every time he replaced a player on the roster, it was with a better player. Over time, the incremental upgrade in every element of the Steelers—the offense, defense, special teams, and coaches—made them champions.

A few weeks later, I did the same dog-and-pony show for the crusty executive responsible for all the pages bought by Revlon, one of our cornerstone advertisers. He looked as dubious as Traub, and in desperation I offered a challenge.

"Make a note in your pocket diary to call me six months from today," I said. "I guarantee that you'll tell me that everything I've said was going to happen *did* happen."

I'd forgotten all about that conversation one morning in the fall when my assistant told me the man from Revlon was on the phone.

"You asked me to call you," he said. "You kept your promise. The magazine is everything you said it would be."

I had indeed transformed the staff, recruiting able new editors and filling *New York* with the work of gifted, sophisticated writers like Julie, Marie

Brenner, Michael Daly, Pete Hamill, and Michael Kramer. They would be joined later by Michael Gross, John Taylor, Tony Schwartz, Patricia Morrisroe, Jesse Kornbluth, and others who developed real followings among readers and their fellow journalists.

The revitalization of *New York* fed off the astounding transformation of the city in what came to be known as the Roaring Eighties, the second Gilded Age. In the midseventies New York was engulfed in debt and crime. The city essentially went bankrupt and Washington turned its back, the moment immortalized by the *Daily News* wood:

FORD TO CITY: DROP DEAD

New York was rescued at the brink by Governor Hugh Carey, financier Felix Rohatyn, and labor leaders headed by Victor Gotbaum, but the financial collapse deeply wounded life in the city. Strapped, city hall cut back on garbage collection and the streets were strewn with refuse. The subways broke down. Public school pupils huddled in drafty hallways for want of classrooms. Desperate crackheads unleashed a murderous crime wave. Cooperative apartments on Fifth Avenue that would sell a generation later for $15 million were given away for $250,000. New York's very survival seemed to be in doubt—or, at least, that was the journalistic take on it.

The worst was over by the start of the 1980s, but it was hard to tell by the quality of everyday life. One of the early covers I did was a graffitied wall that read **WOUNDED CITY**. Not long afterward, Nick Pileggi penetrated the surreal triage system the police had evolved to deal with the thousands of crimes committed every day. The cops still investigated homicides, of course. But armed robberies were pursued only if the stickup man actually fired his gun. If you were robbed by a mugger who held his fire or was armed only with a knife, detectives wouldn't bother. Burglaries would be recorded for insurance purposes, but kiss your TV or computer good-bye. Your car, too.

Still, the first, faint signs of revival could be spotted if you looked hard enough. In its heyday, *New York* had been celebrated for its stories about clever new neighborhoods, but the magazine hadn't been able to do any for years because every neighborhood in the city was deteriorating, even the Upper East Side, where the sidewalks were crumbling and the streets full of potholes. But now the trendies were pouring into the Lower East Side, the vanguard of the legions that would turn the loft blocks of SoHo (South of Houston) and TriBeCa (Triangle Below Canal) into New York's improbable new gold coast.

And the new cast of characters who were to dominate New York life into the nineties and beyond were beginning to find their way into the papers. The three most conspicuous were each media monsters in his own way: Donald Trump, the pompadoured young builder from Queens who was slapping his name on skyscrapers all over midtown; George Steinbrenner, the bullyboy owner of the Yankees who was buying players and firing managers on the back pages of the tabloids every time you looked; and Mayor Ed Koch, the flyover people's idea of a gabby New York Jew, who was blustering his way to national fame. Then there were the moneymen and their trophy wives: Henry Kravis and Carolyn Roehm, Saul and Gayfryd Steinberg; the Tisch brothers; the sleek designers Ralph Lauren and Calvin Klein, both up from the same lower-middle-class Bronx neighborhood; and the art stars, among them Julian Schnabel and Ross Bleckner. Restaurants like Le Cirque and Mortimer's were practically private clubs for the flaunting new rich, who were promptly proclaimed *Nouvelle Society* by John Fairchild in his acerbic *Women's Wear Daily*, the newsletter of the eighties beau monde.

A crowd like this was more than any Gotham editor could dream of—inexhaustible fodder for profiles and snarky "Intelligencer" items. And now *New York* again had the writers who could capture the mingled romance and repulsiveness of such a crew in deft pieces that were at once celebrations and send-ups.

In my first year on the job, Julie and I were invited to Roy Cohn's birthday party. Cohn was a grotesque New York figure who had first made his name with G. David Shine as henchmen for Senator Joe McCarthy during his Communist-hunting crusade. Cohn had then become a lawyer in private practice and a small-time corporate wheeler-dealer. He had been tried three times for some shenanigan or other by New York's incorruptible Robert Morgenthau, then U.S. attorney. He'd beaten the rap each time, but a malign aura of corruption hung over him. True or not, Cohn did every-thing he could to cultivate the notion that he was connected—to the Mob and to ultraconservative Reaganites.

His sinister appearance helped. A closeted homosexual, Cohn was always tanned to a mahogany turn, and there was a deep crack down the front of his nose that looked as if it had burst on the grill, like a hot dog. He was close to George Steinbrenner and liked people to think he was part of Murdoch's inner circle, although Rupert professed to find him creepy.

His birthday party was staged amid the Tiffany glass splendor of the Seventh Regiment Armory on Park Avenue in the sixties. Joey Adams, the old gagman, was the master of ceremonies, and he set the tone.

"Welcome to Roy Cohn's birthday," shpritzed Joey. "If you're indicted, you're invited."

Sure enough, there was Steinbrenner, who'd been suspended from baseball once for making an illegal campaign contribution to Nixon and would be again for hiring a gambler to dig dirt on one of his players. At another table, recognizable behind his tinted glasses, was Carmine DeSapio, the last boss of Tammany Hall, who'd once left a mysterious eleven thousand dollars in cash in a taxicab and who had later done two years in a federal pen for bribery. Other past and present miscreants were scattered around the room, and many rose to croon testimonials to Roy on his big night.

What made *New York* so much fun to do was the fact that it could be newsy, but it didn't have to furnish the news magazines' weekly syllabus. Instead, the magazine could jump on big local stories—the murder of John Lennon outside the Dakota, the first big insider-trading scandal, the brutal rape of a jogger in Central Park, the death of Andy Warhol—and deliver the definitive narrative that readers came to expect from *New York*.

Our only imperative was to be provocative and interesting. And since New Yorkers were interested in practically everything, I could interpret the mandate as broadly as I wanted. Most weeks, *New York* delivered the local goods, but it was never parochial. Marie Brenner was dispatched to London for a cover story on the wedding of Prince Charles and Diana Spencer. Julie went to the 1980 Republican convention in Detroit and came back with a cover story on Ronald Reagan's "total woman," Nancy. Movie stars made the cover, and so did Cindy Crawford, one of the first supermodels.

The core of *New York*'s offering was the trend stories—some profound, some frivolous—but all somehow compelling to the audience. The cover lines told the stories: Downward Mobility, Forever Single, Couch Potatoes,

Second Thoughts on Having It All, Home Is Where the Office Is, Social Climbing, Attitude, Restaurant Madness, Living in Tight Spaces, The New Puritans, Forget the Hamptons, Now It's Country Chic. The covers were clever photo-cartoons, most of them conceived by the imaginative Jordan Schaps.

The first cover story on AIDS, by Michael Daly, appeared in *New York* in June 1983, and the first major piece on the club drug ecstasy, by Joe Klein, in May 1985. The cool look of *Miami Vice* made the cover that same year, a few months before David Blum named new young Hollywood stars "The Brat Pack."

Stories on revitalized areas from the Lower East Side to Long Island City in Queens and Columbus Avenue in Manhattan—"The New Left Bank"— to Battery Park City gave yuppies a head start on homesteading in the next hot neighborhood. The glories of old New York were celebrated, too, in year-end special issues, among them "The Unseen Beauty of New York," and my favorite, "You Must Remember This," an homage to the city not quite beyond recall. For that issue, Neil Simon hymned the Automat, Cleveland Amory evoked the Stork Club, and Gay Talese wrote a paean to Moondog.

For all the attention to trends and nostalgia, the magazine routinely delivered state-of-the-art service pieces on which writers and editors might labor for months before the material was meticulously fact-checked. "How to Complain" was a definitive manual for the victimized. So was "Tenants' Rights" and "Co-Op Tyranny." "The Repair Guide" told readers where to get Aunt Mildred's prized bone China teacup fixed and where to find the artisan who could make the scorch mark on a silk blouse disappear. And "The Best Doctors in New York" became a perennial best seller.

Word got around in the business that people were doing good work at *New York* and, incredibly enough, having a good time. As in Felker's day, the magazine became a magnet for talent. One unheralded star turned out to be a tall, fidgety woman named Lally Weymouth, who happened to be Kay Graham's daughter. Lally was Kay's oldest child and should have been her heir apparent at the Washington Post Company. But perhaps because she was a woman, perhaps because her embrace of left-wing causes during a romance with the polemicist Alex Cockburn made her seem flaky, her brother Don was installed at the company.

Lally was casting about for work in journalism. Both she—and Kay—

were afraid I'd hold the mother's sins against the daughter, but, of course, I never would. With little experience, Lally did a superb job covering the Newport trials of Claus von Bulow, whose rich wife wound up in a coma after a mysterious insulin injection. One trial ended just a day before *New York*'s deadline, and Lally was certain she'd never be able do her 8,000-word cover story in time.

"Don't worry about anything," I told her. "Rent a limousine. Take all your notes and write in the backseat while the guy drives you to New York. Bring in what you have, and we'll help you get it in shape."

"I've never done anything like this on deadline," wailed Lally.

But she did, and her work helped launch her career.

Over the years, whenever I ran into Kay Graham around New York, she would always thank me for nurturing Lally, and Lally would tell me how her mother had concluded that she'd made a mistake when she fired me. I never knew whether to believe that, but Kay was very complimentary to me in her autobiography and once told the *Wall Street Journal,* "Ed is a brilliant editor and he did a wonderful job at *Newsweek.* During Watergate, he instinctively knew what was going on, and he produced a succession of important covers."

One afternoon, Anthony Haden-Guest, a writer whose connections were sometimes better than his stories, brought in another Brit, a skinny young woman with bobbed hair and a formal, almost solemn manner. Her name was Anna Wintour. She'd worked in London on *Harpers & Queen,* come to *Harper's Bazaar* in New York, and survived a stint at Bob Guccioni's women's magazine *Viva.* Laurie Jones, the managing editor, and I put her right to work as fashion editor.

Anna Wintour—or *Ahna,* as faux insiders insist on calling her—has become an icon in magazines and in the world of fashion, the rail-thin, imperious editrix of *Vogue* and scary central character in a best-selling roman à clef, *The Devil Wore Prada.* The only scary thing about her in 1981 was the relentless energy, focus, and talent she brought to her work. Before she even started, she transformed the slovenly corner where her predecessor had toiled into an immaculate workspace of white Formica, with fresh, neatly aligned marking pens.

For her fashion issues, she'd present me with meticulous storyboards in which every page and spread was sketched out in precise detail, with scouting Polaroids attached of the clothes to be shown. One season, the theme was the marriage of downtown art and fashion, an original concept in those days. She recruited top New York artists like David Salle, Jean-Michel Basquiat, Alex Katz, and Red Grooms to paint backdrops against which her fashions were photographed. For the first time, *New York* had fashion pages more striking and innovative than those in *Fashions of the Times* or even *Vogue* itself. Confronted with such a bounty, I could only nod my head gratefully and turn Anna loose.

Over the next two years, Anna did extraordinary work. She put together a small team, including a stylist named Jacques Dehornois, a fastidious little man who decorated her layouts with arrays of old eyeglasses and regimental ties strewn over bath towel racks that made the pages look both elegant and mysterious. When, after a year, she said she wanted to produce all the magazine's lifestyle pages, including special issues on interior design and entertaining, I readily agreed. These, too, were stylish and inventive, although Anna had an inexplicable mania for putting shots of beady-eyed red snappers in every food issue.

Anna hadn't been at the magazine long when Ralph Lauren came to lunch in *New York*'s paneled dining room, where we romanced advertisers and chatted up newsmaking figures in the life of the city. I had never met Lauren before, although Julie had done the first story ever on him for the men's fashion paper *Daily News Record* in 1968, when he was starting out as a tie designer. Now, at lunch, Lauren suddenly turned on Anna, who was sitting demurely across the table from him. She'd failed to pay enough attention to his designs in her last fashion issue—or so Ralph felt. Eyes downcast, she took her punishment for a few moments until I cut Lauren off. "I'm not comfortable with this and I'm going to change the subject," I told him, and he fell silent. He obviously realized that he'd been out of order because an hour after he departed, a torrent of roses from Ralph appeared at Anna's desk.

Early in the game, I'd realized that all an editor had to do when he found an extraordinary talent like Anna was to get out of her way and let her work. Years later, in an interview with a British magazine, I compared her to a great soprano or tenor, a natural wonder who appears once every generation or so, a Callas or a Pavarotti.

The double doors to my office were always open, and everyone in the newsroom could watch me and my visitors. When Anna came to see me she always emerged with the go-ahead to pursue whatever plan she'd brought with her. Inevitably, more than a few people concluded that I was infatuated not only with Anna's talent, but also with Anna herself and that we were having a romance. If that were the case, I wouldn't have been the first editor of *New York* to find love in the office, but there was nothing to it. Every so often we'd have lunch, and the experience of sitting next to Anna on a banquette at The Four Seasons or Le Cirque was tepid enough to dash any libidinous fantasies.

Before we married, Julie had said she might not want to have children. This suited me. To have a child meant a lifetime of responsibility and vulnerability to catastrophe. John and Anthony were surviving adolescence without calamity, and I felt that I'd done my duty to propagate the human race. But when Julie changed her mind, I knew I couldn't object. It seemed to me that every woman had the right to try to have a child, and any man who married a childless woman was obligated to help. On Bastille Day 1981, our daughter was born three weeks early, but perfect.

We named her Lily, not a popular name at the time. When Lily went to nursery school a few years later, there were two other Lilys in her class. This was puzzling until I remembered that *Masterpiece Theatre* had done one of its miniseries on the actress Lillie Langtry, the mistress of Edward VII, a show obviously popular on the Upper East Side.

The revival of New York and *New York* slowly began to pay off. My contract provided for a bonus based on a percentage of *New York*'s operating profit, so I regularly got a copy of the magazine's financial snapshots—called the "flashes"—that were sent to Murdoch. The flashes were part of the rigorous system Rupert used to track every one of his properties. Each week, Murdoch got a thick binder that reflected the latest results of each operation, and he read every one of them and remembered what he read. Because of the *Cue* expense, New York lost money in my first year, but turned profitable the next. Each year into the mideighties, the operating profit grew. Then, as the boom took hold, the magazine really took off.

My profit participation aside, I had always been interested in the business side of magazines—rare among editors in those days. Perhaps it was because I was a salesman's son. At *Newsweek,* I was friendly with many of the salespeople, and I was fascinated by how they sold the magazine to advertisers. I steeped myself in the arcana of syndicated research—the statistics on how many readers supposedly see each issue of a magazine and all the social and economic data about them. In the seventies and eighties, some people considered it unseemly for an editor to be so interested in a magazine's business life. But I was simply ahead of my time. Today, magazine editors are expected to help flog ads and to take a hand in circulation strategy as well.

When I joined *New York,* the business side was being run by a young woman named Cathie Black, who had been Armstrong's deputy. She was an alumna of *Ms.,* the feminist magazine started by Gloria Steinem that had made its debut as an insert in *New York* in 1972. Cathie would go on to have a long and prosperous career as a magazine executive—and we would have a *La Ronde* moment in the late nineties—but this was Cathie's first big job, and we worked together like Mickey Rooney and Judy Garland putting on a show in the backyard.

Approaching the end of my third year at *New York,* I suddenly realized that the magazine's fifteenth anniversary was just months away—late April 1983—and we had to make a splash. The problem with anniversary issues is that they have to be special but somehow in sync with the magazine's DNA. The last refuge of desperate editors is an anthology of the magazine's best articles or a hoked-up array of the ten, fifteen, twenty, twenty-five biggest, best, worst, most expensive, weirdest, richest, most beautiful people, places, things—you name it. Nothing like that would do this time.

Some of the photo editors at *New York* had come to know the men who were about to publish a coffee-table book called *A Day in the Life of America.* Dozens of top photojournalists had covered the country, recording the great and small happenings on a designated day. The resulting best seller would spawn a long and lucrative run of spin-offs. Why not our own *A Day in the Life of New York?*

The plan for the issue evolved over the next several weeks. We would cover the day not only in photographs but also in articles, by the magazine's top writers, that illuminated the high and low life of the city over twenty-four hours. Pulling it all together would be a narrative by Pete Hamill that would render the actual events of the day with all the statistics of birth, death, crime and punishment, stock trades and sports scores, hours of sunlight, and inches of rain (if any).

We settled on a day—March 1—and went to work. Michael Daly would start on midnight patrol with anticrime squad cops. Michael Kramer would join an ambitious young deputy mayor at city hall; Tony Schwartz would take up the story down at the World Financial Center with a top American Express executive; Julie Baumgold would chronicle new society with lunch at Le Cirque; Jenny Allen would spend a long afternoon with a welfare mother in Harlem; Marie Brenner would take us to the Metropolitan Opera, where young soprano Linda Zogby was singing Mimi in *La Bohème.* Finally, Nick Pileggi would be at Beth Israel Hospital overnight for the birth of a brand-new New Yorker. The photographers would cover these scenes and dozens of others, from a near-deserted Bronx elevated station in the dawn's early light to Katz's delicatessen on Houston Street.

We had an alternative date in case of rain, but so much would have to be reorganized that a postponement would be catastrophic. For one thing, we'd negotiated with the Met to bring up the houselights during the café scene of *La Bohème,* so our photographer could snap an unmatched single shot of the great packed hall during a performance. I checked the weather before bedtime on February 28. Rain was in the forecast, but there was no telling how much or when. I drifted in and out of sleep through the night, listening for the sound of raindrops on the top of the air conditioner that jutted out one of the bedroom windows. Nothing. The forecast was wrong!

At about 5:00 AM, I heard the first dread plop and then a steady thrum of rain. I hid in bed for another hour or so, then dragged myself to the window. The streets were slick, and a dreary day was dawning. I felt like an inconsequential version of Ike on D-day trying to decide whether to send the landing craft toward the misty Normandy beaches.

Finally, I decided we'd gone too far to call it off. There was a chance the weather would lighten up. If it poured all day, we couldn't very well celebrate *New York*'s big anniversary with *A Rainy Day in the Life of New York.* We'd just have to try again. It was only money.

The god of journalism smiled on us. The weather cleared up through the morning hours, and the sun actually peeped out briefly in the afternoon. When we reviewed the film a couple of days later, we found that virtually all of it was usable. We decided to rephotograph a couple of big scenic shots in good weather, and dutifully acknowledge the substitutions in the introduction to the special issue.

Part of the charm of working for Murdoch was that you never knew when you would hear from him. I could have three conversations with him in a single afternoon and then not get another call for two or three months. It all depended on whether there was something he needed to know from you. However long the gap between calls, it was like talking to a certain kind of friend—the conversation always picked up as if there'd been no interruption. Murdoch checked in one morning in the midst of the big anniversary issue.

"I'm calling from Switzerland," said Rupert in a conspiratorial whisper, "and do you know what's in the next room?"

I confessed that I didn't.

"Hitler's diaries!" murmured Murdoch.

"I didn't know that Hitler kept a diary, chief," I piped up, feeling again like a character in *Scoop*.

"That's just the point," said Rupert. "Nobody did. How big a story do you think this is?"

To my credit, my answer was prescient.

"Well, chief," I said, "Hitler's diaries would be one of the great stories of our time—if they're authentic."

That was the beginning of the great Hitler diaries fiasco, a hoax that eclipsed the great scam autobiography of Howard Hughes a decade before. I'd been involved in *Newsweek*'s coverage of the Hughes fraud, and I'd learned a valuable lesson that turned out to apply to the Hitler scam.

A writer named Clifford Irving and his pal Richard Suskind had concocted the Hughes book in 1971. Irving claimed that he'd taped a hundred hours of secret interviews with the mad billionaire. Actually, he and Suskind had cobbled the book out of the clips and the stolen manuscript of a memoir by one of Hughes's trusted enablers. They'd sold the hardback, paperback, and magazine serial rights for $1.4 million, confident the wacky recluse would never leave his Bahamas hideaway to repudiate the book. Irving had even forged Hughes's signature on the contracts, using a sample of his handwriting from an old *Newsweek* cover story. But Hughes confounded the fraudsters. He was so furious at their effrontery that he held a press conference over the telephone and the scheme collapsed. The feds and investigators from the New York district attorney's office traced Irving and Suskind to the sunny Mediterranean isle of Ibiza and swooped down.

Working on the Irving story at *Newsweek*, I'd arranged to talk with one of the young New York assistant district attorneys on Ibiza. The ground rule was that he'd answer my questions yes or no, but wouldn't volunteer any information. The tale of how Irving and his pal actually worked hadn't yet been revealed, and I was full of ingenious theories about stolen Hughes files and other arcane sources used by the scammers.

The investigator waved off all my leads.

"It's really very simple," he said.

I ignored him and pressed on.

"No, you don't understand," he said impatiently. "It's very, very simple."

What he was trying to tell me was that the great Hughes caper consisted of Irving and Suskind simply reading everything they could find on Hughes and putting it into the first person. The D. B. Cooper hoaxers who had fooled Karl Fleming had done the same thing—turned newspaper clips into first-person narrative.

Murdoch and others could have saved themselves a lot of grief if they'd channeled the Hughes episode, but they were too dazzled by their world scoop. The German magazine *Stern* first told the world about the sixty-two dark-bound volumes, which were aboard a plane carrying Hitler's possessions that crashed near Dresden in the last days of the Third Reich. An East German general had hidden them away for three decades. Then the diaries were smuggled to the West one volume at a time by a memorabilia dealer named Konrad Kujau. *Stern* had paid more than $4 million for the Hitler diaries and was selling rights to newspapers and magazines around the world. Murdoch wanted the diaries for his London *Sunday Times*. He was calling me because my old colleague and friend Maynard Parker was there for *Newsweek* and Rupert wanted a line on Maynard.

Eventually, the *Sunday Times*, *Newsweek*, *Paris Match*, and Italy's *Panorama* bought in, and Murdoch had the Hitler scholar Hugh Trevor-Roper, Lord Dacre, authenticate them. But just as the *Sunday Times* was going to press, the scheme unraveled. Doubts about the diaries were everywhere, but *Newsweek* ran its story anyway. In a desperate effort to protect the magazine, Maynard Parker wrote the notorious kicker on the cover story: "Genuine or not, it almost doesn't matter in the end."

When the hoax was finally unraveled, it was as simple as the Hughes and D. B. Cooper scams. Konrad Kujau, the "memorabilia dealer," hadn't smuggled the diaries to the West—he'd written them himself, aping Der Fuehrer's handwriting. Most of the entries were lifted from a book of Hitler's speeches and statements. The banality of some of the others—*Must not forget tickets for the Olympic games for Eva*—should have been a giveaway. But the real clue to the fraudulence of the Hitler diaries was hiding in plain sight. The sixty-two books were bound in synthetic leatherette. Now, would the master of a military cult with the greatest leather fetish of all time inscribe his precious *pensées* in books bound in leatherette? You didn't need to be Trevor-Roper, who incidentally couldn't read German, to answer that.

Murdoch's reputation being what it was, the Hitler diaries became just another page in the legend. But poor Maynard carried the epic embarrassment of his horrendous *Newsweek* kicker to the grave.

15

MORT 'N' FRED

I WAS IN STRIDE at *New York* in 1984 when Mortimer Zuckerman approached me to move to Washington to edit *U.S. News & World Report,* which he'd just bought, along with more prime real estate, for $164 million from the magazine's staff who had taken over the ownership from the family of the conservative founder, David Lawrence. I'd first met Mort when he came to New York in the early eighties after he bought the *Atlantic Monthly* in Boston, along with its own prime real estate on Arlington Street facing the Public Garden.

Zuckerman was an émigré from Montreal who had all sorts of graduate degrees from Harvard and had already made his fortune as a real-estate developer based in Boston. He was jokey, a little geeky, always looking for women. In time, he wound up dating or having affairs with nearly every accomplished unmarried woman in New York—among them, Diane Von Furstenberg, Nora Ephron, even the feminist Gloria Steinem, who, as it happened, shared with Mort an unheralded passion for ballroom dancing.

Although he said he yearned to marry and have children, Zuckerman always seemed to wind up with older women. He prized his dog Stockman, a Labrador named after a Reagan economic adviser who disclosed Ronnie's covert deficit strategy in an *Atlantic Monthly* article that caused a sensation. The incumbent editor of *U.S. News,* a good old pro named Marvin Stone, decided to leave when the sale closed and was gone in a few months. I had already run a news magazine, Julie loved New York life, and Lily was newly enrolled in a fancy nursery school, a major coup at the time. But I told Zuckerman I'd be willing to make the switch if we could cut a deal.

Mort talked about a big salary, but I didn't really care about that or pricey perks because I would be at the office all the time, and taxes would eat up a lot of the pay, anyway. What I needed was capital. Although I'd been working for twenty-five years, I had accumulated no money to speak of. Alimony for Alice and tuition for John at Stanford and Anthony at Yale took care of that. So I told Zuckerman that I needed a highly unconventional deal and that I'd understand if it was too ingenious for him.

The idea was that if I met certain agreed-to objectives (circulation, ad pages and revenue, editorial distinction) at the end of a three-year contract, I would have a stake in an earned bonus that I could let ride in a new contract or take off the table. Thus, if I were successful, I would have the one thing I needed and wanted—not just a salary, but some money to invest or use as I wished.

I also had many ideas for the magazine. The most basic was that *U.S. News* would never be able to challenge *Newsweek* and *Time* for breadth of coverage, presentation, or (because of its earlier deadlines) in breaking news. Given the historic circulation edge the other two enjoyed, *U.S. News* could never top them in readers or ad rates (although it could carry more and cheaper ad pages than its competitors). My notion was that his magazine could model itself on Britain's *Economist* and become the smartest, most analytical news magazine, read by the elite. This more desirable upscale audience would allow the magazine to command ad rates higher than its circulation would otherwise merit. I didn't mean to change *U.S. News* so much that it would be unrecognizable to its loyal readers, but to give it a distinction beyond its bland conservatism.

And Zuckerman wanted me. In talks at his apartment, he was bright, funny, and flattering, a charming suitor. He insisted time and again that he would be spending most of his time doing real-estate deals in New York and would take little hand in the magazine except for his back-page columns. Still, rethinking the magazine was a snap compared to negotiating a contract with Zuckerman and his partner and *consigliere,* Fred Drasner, a dem-dose guy from Far Rockaway who had been Zuckerman's tax lawyer, which meant he was a very smart man.

Zuckerman and Drasner were an odd-couple pairing of Jewish archetypes. Mort, who hadn't yet switched to contacts, was the classic scholarly Jewish son who could easily be imagined in yarmulke and sidelocks hunched over his Hebrew texts in a nineteenth-century shtetl study house. Drasner was the kind of smart mouth you'd see hanging outside a candy store in poorer Jewish neighborhoods all over New York, jingling change in his pants pocket, making small-time bets on college basketball games, and trying to get laid.

Together Mort 'n' Fred, as they soon came to be known, were a crack team, brainy and ruthless. The takeover of the genteel, iconic *Atlantic Monthly,* founded by New England intellectuals in 1857, resulted in bitterness and ugly litigation with the publisher and longtime editor Robert Manning, who lost his job. The takeover of *U.S. News,* with its even more valuable real estate, ended up in a lawsuit against the current staff—the sellers—by the magazine's retired staff, who felt they had been screwed.

There was a lot at stake for me: if I took the job, I'd be uprooting my family and subletting my New York co-op. Fortunately, I had my friend and lawyer Tom Baer, who knew how to deal with Mort 'n' Fred.

I was under contract to Rupert Murdoch and would never leave unless he released me. Still, I didn't want Rupert to read about any of this in Liz Smith's column before he heard it from me. So I called him and told him I wanted to see him. He said he was coming to *New York* for the Christmas party and we could talk beforehand. When Murdoch showed up, I closed the double doors to my office and told him I would never break my contract with him, but I wanted to explore Zuckerman's offer.

"Of course," said Murdoch. Then he proceeded to tick off the reasons I'd inevitably decide not to go with Zuckerman.

"First of all, you've done that," said Rupert. "Secondly, Zuckerman's an amateur and you won't like working for an amateur. Besides, Julie loves New York, and you wouldn't want to drag her away."

In thirty seconds, Murdoch had perfectly analyzed the situation.

The negotiations stretched out endlessly—another Zuckerman tactic—and Mort never called Julie, which might have clinched the move. Still, it finally seemed that the deal would get done. One afternoon, Drasner was supposed to fax Baer a multipoint deal memo that would outline the actual contract. When the fax arrived, I determined that all the provisions were as agreed—except one. Baer called Drasner, who said one of his secretaries had made a mistake and a corrected version would soon be faxed. That one duly arrived. The faulty paragraph had indeed been fixed, but this time another provision had been changed.

With that, the deal began to unravel. The complicated arrangement that would give me the chance to earn my capital stake—the main attraction for me—entailed a letter of credit that *U.S. News* would buy. Unlike money put in escrow, the funds covered by a letter of credit would be untouchable in litigation. Zuckerman was never really comfortable with that expensive novelty and very quickly the whole thing came apart.

A few hours later, the phone rang in my office at *New York.* On the other end, I heard a sepulchral voice. My charming suitor had been transformed into a dumped teenage swain morosely replaying the circumstances that led to the breakup. Finally, I had to get off the phone or start blubbering myself. Rupert had, of course, been right.

Had I gone to *U.S. News,* Michael Kramer would have been at my side as chief political columnist and confidant. Like Julie, Michael had been an early recruit at Felker's *New York.* He left to run a magazine about journalism called *More,* then returned to write the political column "The National Interest" a year before my advent. The column had a distinguished pedigree: Richard Reeves and Ken Auletta were two of his predecessors. Kramer was as versatile as anyone I've ever worked with, able to write with equal fluency about grubby doings at city hall, presidential politics, defense, and foreign issues from Peking to Moscow to El Salvador. He had a big following of insiders, and it was a special treat for me to work with him. Having someone of Kramer's talent and sophistication meant I could get any political story executed with speed and savvy, an imperative for a magazine with *New York's* ambitions.

One day in 1987, Michael showed up in my office to tell me that he was going to work for Zuckerman as the chief political writer and columnist for *U.S. News.* He felt that no matter how good his stuff in *New York* was, it was still a local magazine, and he wanted a national audience and a chance to appear on *Meet the Press* and other big-time TV showcases.

Now I had to find someone to replace him—a political writer as deft and well connected as Kramer and someone whose own political views were a good fit with mine. There was no shortage of accomplished applicants, several of them aces at commentary. Another option was Joe Klein, a compact, bearded author of books on Woody Guthrie and a Marine unit in Vietnam who had a reputation as a superb reporter and had written for *New York* over the years. Lately, Klein had been doing pieces on politics and music for

Rolling Stone. I was dithering over my choice while shaving one morning when WINS reported some big political story breaking in Iowa, the site of the first caucus of the upcoming presidential campaign. I realized that the analysts I was considering would be doing what I was doing: reacting to a bit of breaking news. But an ambitious hound like Klein would have got wind of the story the night before and called me from the airport on his way to Des Moines. So I picked Klein, one of the best choices I ever made. He did superb work for *New York*, then went on to become rich and famous as "Anonymous," the author of *Primary Colors*, the roman à clef about Bill Clinton that caused a sensation a decade later.

Inevitably, there were a couple of *La Ronde* twists to the Kramer-Klein switch. Michael eventually deserted Zuckerman to become the political columnist for *Time*, then rejoined me working for Mort at the *Daily News* at the end of the nineties. A Klein career move in the early nineties cost me one of my closest friendships, and he eventually took over the political column at *Time* that Kramer had once written. *Plus ça change.*

16

GODS AND MONSTERS

PART OF THE FUN of editing *New York* in the eighties were the glimpses it afforded of the grotesque figures of the Age of Greed. Donald Trump was by no means the richest or the shrewdest of this gang. He was simply the best at shameless self-promotion because he genuinely believed his own lies. By the early years of the millennium, he had morphed into a bloated caricature of a caricature with his unreality TV show, his signature line—*You're fired!*— his weird pageboy comb-over, and his third wife, the gorgeous model Melania Knauss. But in the late eighties he still had some of the boyish bridge-and-tunnel charm he'd brought from Queens. Established with three casinos in Atlantic City, he started choppering people from the press and show business to the big heavyweight championship fights at the Convention Hall across from his Taj Mahal. Julie loved the fights and she loved writing about Trump, so we found ourselves the guests of Donald—the papers invented "The Donald"—and Ivana for three Mike Tyson fights.

The routine was always the same: Liftoff at dusk in Trump's helicopter from the downtown heliport on the Hudson, the hop to Atlantic City with Donald or Ivana holding court, a vast buffet dinner in one of the hotel's banquet rooms, and then the march through the casino to ringside next door at the Convention Hall. The cast of characters varied, but Norman Pearlstine, the chief editor of the *Wall Street Journal,* and his wife, the writer Nancy Friday, who liked to wear a spiky metal dog collar, were often aboard, along with the soon-to-be-second Mrs. Trump, Marla Maples, with a friend in tow as a beard. Jack Nicholson and Norman Mailer turned up at one bout and so did Muhammad Ali, murmurous and trembling with Parkinson's, at another.

The high point of the evening was always The Walk, led by Trump through the casino with its ersatz gilt and mirrors, ding-ding-dinging slot machines, and raucous craps tables. As Donald strode though the great room, the sea of gamblers parted. They waved, they bowed, they thrust copies of his latest book—on sale everywhere in the hotel—to be autographed. "Way to go, Donald!" they'd cry. "You the man!"

Here were thousands of working people gambling away their hard-earned money into the bulging pockets of the country's most famous multimillionaire, and they were cheering him. Trump had somehow persuaded them that he was one of them—only taller, better looking, with an ex-Olympic skier for a wife, and with a slightly better head for business. It was a true marvel of American capitalism.

The only problem with these junkets was that the ostensible reasons for going—the championship fights themselves—were a joke. Tyson had been boxing as a pro for about three years, and he was a feral creature. For a while, he'd lived in a high-rise next door to the offices on *New York* magazine, and I would sometimes see him at night lounging against the wall near the entrance to his building, waiting for his posse. Now, in the ring, he was a terrifying force of nature—especially against opponents like Michael Spinks, Carl "The Truth" Williams, and ex-champ Larry Holmes, who had shown up for a payday. Iron Mike chased Holmes around the ring for three rounds and finished him off in the fourth. Both Spinks and The Truth were knocked out in a minute and a half of the first round of their bouts. Trump's fans, who had paid as much as $250 for a ticket, had hardly sat down before the referee was counting out the recumbent Spinks and Williams. But they took it with good grace; being able to say they were there seemed to be worth the price of admission.

Flying back to Manhattan after one fight, I found myself sitting in the back of the chopper across from Jack Nicholson and Mailer. Norman not only had written brilliantly about boxing but he used to spar in the gym and liked to assume a pug's affect. Nicholson was a fight buff, too, and tonight Nicholson was reminiscing about going to the fights in Mexico with John Huston in the old days. The conversation was harmless and charming, and later I gave Julie a few overheard quotes for a piece she was doing on the fight for *New York*.

After the magazine came out the following week, we were having dinner with friends at Primavera when Julie was summoned to the phone. She came back to the table in tears. Furious that his chat with Nicholson had turned up in *New York,* Mailer had tracked her down at the restaurant and excoriated her. She was innocent, of course—I'd been the eavesdropper—and now it was my turn to be furious at his abuse of my writer, and of my wife.

It didn't take long for the next confrontation. Every month or so, Alice Mason, an East Side real-estate woman who knew the value of publicity, gave a dinner party in her rental apartment on Lexington Avenue and Seventy-second Street. Alice's dinners were infamous. She'd pack her flat for an endless, claustrophobic cocktail hour, then scatter her guests to three or four smallish rooms for the food, which was barely edible. But Alice had a formula. She had a core of regular guests who were surrogate hosts and there was always a big-name guest of honor—postpresidential Jimmy Carter was a favorite—and a mix of recognizable faces from *nouvelle société,* show business, and journalism. Reliably as Old Faithful's gusher, most of the guests would read their names a few days later in Suzy's column in *Women's Wear Daily.* For a while, Julie and I were on Alice's A-List.

With all the publicity about her big-bucks co-op sales and her dinner parties, Alice had become quite grand. Only Julie knew—and Alice surely knew she knew—that in the bad old days, she'd been the humble ballroom dancing partner of Julie's Uncle Eddie.

The invitation to another Alice Mason dinner came early in 1989, not long after I'd fractured the fibula in my right leg ice skating with Lily in Central Park. On the appointed night, I somehow managed to get the trousers of my dinner suit over the cast on my leg, picked up my cane, and headed downtown with Julie. I'd just hobbled into Alice's packed drawing room and grabbed an anaesthetic drink when I found myself face-to-face with Mailer.

"Norman," I said as affably as I could, "if you ever have a problem with something my wife has written, take it up with me. You made Julie cry."

A storm cloud swept over his face.

"Let's settle it outside," growled America's greatest living writer.

At first, I thought he was making fun of the whole silly business, but he was deadly serious.

"Norman, I'm a cripple with a cast and a cane. Why don't you just kick me over and stomp me right here?"

He growled something and turned away.

It was well known around town that Julie was the unbilled author of a frequent column in the magazine called "Mr. Peepers' Nights." The title reminded people of the character Wally Cox played on fifties TV, but Julie's conceit was that Peepers was an elderly gent who liked his beakers and went everywhere, casting his alert Presbyterian eye on all the fools and frauds who passed for social New York in these gaudy days. In one Peepers, she threw away a sly line about the delights of an Alice Mason dinner—and we were never invited again.

By 1986 I had worked with four different publishers in my half-dozen years at *New York,* so when Murdoch's minion John Evans took me to lunch at The Four Seasons and asked whether I'd like to be editor and publisher of *New York,* I knew my answer before the remains of the crab cakes were cleared away. I had only one reservation: I didn't want to be a figurehead. I would take the job only if it was understood that I'd really be running the business side as well as the editorial side of the magazine. I'd be responsible for the cover of *New York* and the bottom line, too. It was rare for one man or woman to hold both titles on an American magazine, but Murdoch had been a pioneer in turning editorial types into business executives. I knew everything about both the business and editorial sides of *New York* and I was certain I could do a good job.

At first blush, there would seem to be endless problems in combining the roles. The major one was how could an editor and publisher maintain the sanctified separation between church (editorial) and state (the business side) so dear to the ethics of magazine publishing? Wouldn't I be susceptible to selling out editorial for a plump ad contract? Wouldn't I truckle? These are the kinds of questions that provide fodder for endless journalism school panel discussions, but in the real world the answer was simple: No, I wouldn't. Common sense was an unerring guide. The magazine's greatest asset was its editorial integrity. Compromising it would be the most destructive thing a publisher could do. I ran church and state at *New York* for the next seven years—leading the magazine through a still-unsurpassed run of profitability—and never once had a conflict-of-interest problem.

I used to joke that if anyone saw me talking to myself in my office, it would be the publisher chewing out the editor for taking such a long lunch. Still, for appearances' sake, I commandeered a second office on the floor occupied by the publishing side. I would spend the morning in my editorial

office, then walk downstairs after lunch and meet with the ad sales, circulation, production, and promotion staffs. After a while, it was clear that this
charade served no point, so I met with both staffs in my editor's office. I hap-
pily gave the second-floor space to my publishing deputy, Larry Burstein, a
crack ad salesman and a good staff manager. Because work is really play for
adults, the new challenge of perfecting business strategy and tactics was a joy.
Indeed, mastering a new syllabus kept me from getting bored running the
editorial side year after year.

New York is a deceptive magazine. When the editorial is tuned properly,
it looks as easy to put out as it is to read. But a glance at the magazine during
some of the down periods it's suffered over the years shows how shallow and
unrewarding it can be in the wrong hands. The business calculus is no less
complex. *New York* is a city and regional magazine, but, in my day at least,
more than fifty thousand of its subscribers lived outside the New York area.
There were big pockets of readers in California, Florida, Texas, and Illinois
—all of them worthless to *New York*'s essential advertisers, local retailers and
restaurants. These local advertisers were charged different rates depending on
the scope of their operations. But the magazine also had another ad con-
stituency: high-end national advertisers, among them Estee Lauder and
Ralph Lauren, BMW and Range Rover, luxé resort hotels, and expensive
vodkas and single-malt Scotches. For these advertisers, the gross circulation
numbers were less important than the demographic characteristics of the
readers—their income, education, and career tracks.

All these elements—editorial snap, big local audience, and affluent demographics—had to be kept in equilibrium for the magazine to thrive. And the
real key to making money at *New York* was the willingness of the readers to
renew their subscriptions year after year. With loyal subscribers, *New York*
didn't have to spend the vast sums many other magazines did to enlist new
readers to replace those who dropped out. In the late eighties, *New York* attained
what I liked to call an actuarial renewal rate: the only readers who didn't renew
were those who died during the term of their subs. When couples divorced,
one partner kept the subscription and the other bought his or her own.

As a result, as New York boomed, *New York* regularly recorded operating
profits of $8 to $9 million a year on total revenues of less than $50 million.
This was a margin of nearly 20 percent, unheard of for a weekly and three
times the margins earned by *Time* and *Newsweek*. Murdoch was happy.

Profitable and prestigious as it was, *New York* was a tiny outpost in the News Corporation empire. Rupert kept expanding all through the eighties, and the company produced remarkable innovations. In 1983, Murdoch pioneered satellite television in America. Calculating that vast expanses of the western U.S. were too rugged and sparsely settled for cable operators to wire, he started selling receiving dishes that could pick up programming from a satellite orbiting the heavens. The dishes were expensive, but that wasn't the real problem. They were three or four feet across and persisted in getting blown off the roofs of the dish subscribers' homes, sometimes taking the roofs along for the ride. This first stab at Sky TV bombed, but two decades later Rupert was the master of a satellite TV realm that encompassed big swathes of China, India, Italy, Spain, the U.K., and, thanks to his stake in DirectTV, the U.S.

Three years later, he put Barry Diller, a college dropout who was easily the brainiest and the ballsiest executive in Hollywood, in charge of his fledgling fourth TV network, Fox. Diller recruited two young hotshots, Garth Ancier and Stephen Chao, a Harvard guy who'd worked for the *National Enquirer* and had a fresh brainstorm every fifteen seconds. Murdoch flew some of his magazine editors out to California to meet with Diller and his crew. We sat mesmerized in Barry's office on the 20th Century-Fox studio lot as Chao spun off a string of wacky programming ideas. I had no clue that I was present at the creation of what we know today as reality television. The only one of Chao's ideas I remember was the germ of the show that became *Cops,* the videotaped adventures of real cops around the country arresting dope dealers, drunks, and wife-beaters, and still a popular show on Fox. The rest of Chao's ideas sounded even more improbable at the time, but I'm sure many have found their way on the air by now.

At about the same time, Murdoch bought a group of profitable trade magazines from Bill Ziff, many of them covering the travel business. With the magazines as a point of departure, John Evans developed a visionary hotel reservation system. Using a terminal provided by Murdoch, travel agents could scope out rooms and amenities at thousands of hotels and resorts and order up faxed photos of the accommodations to show clients. The system anticipated today's Expedia—owned by Diller!—and other sites on the Web where travelers can look over potential destinations and shop for bargains. Long before the Internet made his system obsolete, Evans sold it for Murdoch for a handsome profit.

With so much going on in an empire stretching over three continents, Murdoch began holding meetings of his far-flung crew in Aspen, where he had a beautiful hilltop ski lodge. The meetings were held every two years in June, when the slopes are bare of snow but exquisite nonetheless. They would mix speakers from the world of ideas and politics with presentations by the editors or publishers of Murdoch operations. Trying to resurrect his reputation, Richard Nixon showed up at one meeting and stood on an empty stage with only a microphone for more than an hour, talking about everything from China to the next NFL season. The British politician David Owen was there, too, and Paul Volcker and Professor Charles Murray, a leading conservative social thinker.

Some of the presentations by Murdoch's people were fascinating, too. At one meeting, the scamps from the *Sun,* Murdoch's London tabloid, left copies of their paper on every seat in the auditorium before they spoke. When they were finished, they asked the audience if anyone had noticed anything different about the paper. Nobody had, except one fellow who asked why the normally topless Page 3 girl was dressed to the chin as a Canadian Mountie. It turned out that all the content in this edition of the tabloid had been lifted word for word and picture for picture from the *Sun*'s sober-sided sibling, the *Times* of London, but with *Sun*-style headlines and captions. Their point was clear and didn't even have to be enunciated: readers judged the journalism in a newspaper by its format and reputation, not the actual stories themselves.

Watching Murdoch work an Aspen meeting was a revelation. He'd have a quick breakfast with one fellow, move on to another, have lunch with a half dozen, meet others at cocktail time (though he hardly drank), take dinner with another group, and circulate afterward. Many of the staffers at the meeting, especially the Australian newspaper people, had worked for him for decades. They knew his foibles and worse, but had a matey affection for him. They felt that he cared about them and could be trusted—remarkable, especially for a proprietor so reviled outside his own company.

New York surged in the late eighties. The Dow Jones Industrial Average peaked at 2,722 on August 26, 1987, but the atmosphere was so ebullient that nobody paid much attention. Developers tripped over each other to erect high-rise apartment houses along First, Second, and Third avenues

on the East Side, and new buildings started going up on the West Side of
Manhattan for the first time since the Depression. So much real-estate
advertising poured into *New York* that we had to publish special (and very
lucrative) thirty-six- and forty-eight-page sections to accommodate it all.

Nouvelle société got the fever and passed it on. The masters of the universe
(the phrase Tom Wolfe lifted from Alphonse Daudet) and their trophy wives
or proud survivor spouses were out every night at one benefit or another,
angling for social supremacy. Women's fashion took on some of the madness
of the days of Louis XV, when courtiers hobbled along in great bulging skirts
called panniers and staggered under elaborate coiffeurs decked out with
model sailing ships. The new set's pet designer was a tall, quiet Frenchman
named Christian Lacroix, who dressed them in the gaudy colors of the sunny
Midi, clunky costume jewelry, and short hooped skirts. The women pranced
about looking like dancing lamb chops.

Bergdorf Goodman, the city's swankest department store, flew Lacroix to
New York. His designs would be sold exclusively at its Fifth Avenue emporium, and a benefit fashion show was to be staged as the first event ever at
the new glass-walled Winter Garden of the World Financial Center, hard by
the twin towers of the World Trade Center. The event would be the apothe-
osis of new society in the new Gilded Age, and Julie decided to mark the
moment with a cover story in *New York*.

The gala was scheduled for Tuesday night, October 20. A runway was
threaded through the towering palm trees newly planted in the Winter
Garden, and the models practiced catwalking in their Lacroixs. Then, just
hours before the big show started, the stock market crashed. The Dow went
into free fall until it had lost 25 percent of its value, igniting fears of a new
depression. But the moguls in their black ties and their wives in their favorite
Lacroixs seemed oblivious. They oohed and aahed and applauded raptur-
ously as the models twirled and flounced. Hunched over the railings of the
walkways ringing the atrium, stock traders from the brokerages in the World
Financial Center gazed down at the spectacle as their world seemed to teeter
on the brink. Julie called her cover story "Dancing on the Lip of the Volcano," and it was a classic.

For all the hand-wringing, the economy shook off the crash like a
Labrador retriever fresh from the surf. But by the start of the nineties, recession took hold and Murdoch felt the squeeze. From the start of his career,

every big Rupert acquisition had prompted gloomy predictions that he'd finally gone too far. This time, the stories might be on target. In 1988, Murdoch had paid crafty old Walter Annenberg $3 billion, essentially for *TV Guide,* the largest-circulation magazine in the country. In the U.K. the next year, he bought the publisher William Collins and merged it with Harper & Row to form HarperCollins, then launched satellite Sky TV, which was costing a fortune.

No one will ever know how close Murdoch came to losing his company. By one account, it all hinged on a Pittsburgh banker. Had he insisted on calling in a $10 million loan—a pittance—the dominoes would have started tumbling to bankruptcy. Others claim the tale was hyped to enhance Rupert's swashbuckling legend. All I know is that the more pressure Murdoch fell under, the more grace he showed. Early in the drama, he gave a lunch for the editors of his magazines, which included, besides *TV Guide* and *New York,* the monthlies *Seventeen, New Woman, Soap Opera Digest, Premiere, Automobile,* and *Mirabella,* started by Rupert for Grace Mirabella after she was dumped as editor of *Vogue* for Anna Wintour.

One by one, the magazine publishers delivered their grim ad sales forecasts, which meant the profitable books would make far less money and the losers would lose even more. I've seen other owners explode in red-faced, profane fury at such news. Murdoch simply smiled and said, "I know how difficult these times are for you, and I want you to know how grateful I am for all you're doing."

He was almost apologetic later when he called me at *New York* and asked me to reduce the magazine's regular complement of editorial pages by four. It soon became plain that the magazine group's profit-and-loss statement was being dressed up. The unheard of was happening: Murdoch was going to sell some properties. (In 1988, he'd had to give up the *Post,* but that was because new cross-ownership rules forbade him to own a newspaper and a TV station in the same market.) Suddenly, the right of first refusal that Tom Baer had wangled into my contract more than a decade ago might be worth more than the paper it was typed on.

This put me in a ticklish position. Murdoch obviously was looking to sell the magazines as a group. Would my option on *New York* apply in a group sale? What if *New York* was essential to any sale, and my efforts derailed a deal that Murdoch desperately needed to do? That certainly would end my career with News Corp. And what if I tried to buy *New York* myself? Could I raise enough capital to bring it off? And could I succeed in running *New York* as a stand-alone magazine competing with big magazine divisions that could negotiate preferential paper and printing contracts and offer group ad buys? I didn't even know precisely how to value *New York* in any sale.

I approached all these questions methodically. The most important one was whether my option had standing in a group sale. Using Bill Zabel's law firm, which Tom Baer had helped found and which had helped in my divorce from Alice, I got an opinion that it did. This was based on a New York real-estate case in which the sale of a parcel of land was blocked by the owner of an option to buy one component. Satisfied with this, I talked to several investment bankers about how much I'd have to raise to make an offer for *New York*. Based on the industry multiple of the magazine's profits, we calculated that *New York* should be worth about $75 million in an auction environment. But the fundamental question was whether, if I managed to buy *New York*, it was realistic to try to operate the magazine myself. I concluded that the best course was to sell my right of first refusal back to Murdoch for as much as I could get.

Murdoch had chosen Marty Singerman, who had been the publisher of *New York* and head of the magazine group, to handle the negotiations. Marty had joined Rupert as a circulation man when Murdoch launched his supermarket tabloid the *National Star* and had become a loyal News Corp. lifer. He was a lovely man, and he had become my friend as well as a boss.

Awkwardness was built into the situation and it didn't take long to manifest itself. Murdoch made an offer that was a fraction of what Tom and I were looking for. Now I found myself sitting across the desk from a friend who'd turned into an adversary, arms crossed and mouth set. No matter how much Marty liked and respected me, in the pinch he was Rupert's man. It was just business, a distinction I've always understood that has saved me from misreading professional judgments as personal ones.

Soon we were at an impasse, and Murdoch wheeled in one of his most trusted moneymen, Stan Shuman, a pillar of the investment house Allen & Co., who had been in for years on all News Corp. business. Stan was a tall, handsome man with silver hair and a winning just-us-guys manner. By standing firm, I'd forced Rupert to double his offer. Stan told me the number and insisted there would be no more.

Now I was in a quandary. I still felt the option was worth more, but I had no taste for trench warfare. I didn't want to be a fool by accepting less than I should, but I also didn't want to be a fool by losing out on that elusive pot of capital I'd been seeking for a decade.

One Saturday morning in late spring 1991, Julie, Lily, and I drove to Redding for the weekend. Cruising along the winding Merritt Parkway, I dithered over what to do, but as I unloaded the car I had an epiphany. I pictured in my mind a two-column story in the business section of the *New York Times* reporting that Tina Brown had accepted X million dollars for her right of first refusal in the sale of *New York* magazine. That sounds like a good deal for her, I thought—and for me. I called Tom to tell him to accept the latest Murdoch offer.

Now Marty Singerman could be my friend again. He handed me the check from Rupert with a note that read, "With great pleasure—you earned it all!" and a warm handshake.

The windfall changed my life. For the first time I had a financial cushion to handle any emergency. More than that, I now had every working editor's talisman: fuck-you money that would enable me to walk away from any job that suddenly turned ugly. I treated myself to a little silver Miata roadster— no Morgan, but good enough for scooting along the leafy byways of Fairfield County. I bought zero-coupon bonds maturing in time to cover Lily's college expenses, and temporarily stashed the rest of the money in Treasury securities.

17

Amateur Hour

THE BUYERS OF *NEW YORK* and the other magazines turned out to be a group of people I'd never heard of who were financed by Henry Kravis, one of the charter barbarians at the gate in the world of leveraged buyouts. Periodically, Kravis assembled pools of money from his loyal investors. The money would be used to buy up companies, run them for a while, then take the enterprises public to recoup the original investment. The Kravis operators would get management fees and still control the businesses with a sizable minority interest after they cashed out the rest. The trick was to buy properties at the right figure, then cut costs and spur revenues so that margins, and hence the value of the properties, grew and could be cashed out at a rich price.

The Kravis operation that bought the magazines was called K-III and was run by three executives who had gotten rich on the sale of Macmillan, the publishing house, to buccaneer Robert Maxwell (who later committed suicide by jumping off his yacht). Their plan was to build a diversified magazine publishing empire comprising both consumer and trade books. To give this mixed bag of obscure but profitable publications (among them *Dog World* and *Soybean Digest*) some cachet on Wall Street, K-III paid Rupert $650 million for *New York* and most of the other Murdoch magazines.

The chief of K-III was a man named William Reilly, the former boss of Macmillan, who liked to wear white-collared Turnbull and Asser shirts and ride around town in a stretch limousine. But it was Kravis I met with first after the sale went through. Reared in Oklahoma, the dapper, Napoleon-sized Kravis had become one of the rulers not only of Wall Street but also of *nouvelle société*. He was married to the designer Carolyn Roehm, had a vast apartment in 740 Park Avenue, probably the best building in Manhattan, a weekend retreat north of the city with an indoor riding barn the size of a college basketball arena, an estate in the Dominican Republic, and a membership on the board of the Metropolitan Museum of Art, to which he had contributed the $10 million Kravis wing.

I told Kravis that he would enjoy owning *New York* but had to understand that the magazine would be writing about his friends and people he did business with.

"If people think you somehow have control over the editorial content, your life will be hell," I said. "Every time you go out to dinner, somebody at the table will complain about something in the magazine and expect you to take care of it. If you're smart, you'll do what Rupert did. When somebody would complain, he'd throw up his hands and say, 'Those madmen at *New York*! They're out of control, won't listen to anybody.' It worked every time."

Kravis nodded noncommittally, and we went on to talk about *New York*'s future.

It was clear from the start that Reilly and his colleagues were amateurs in the slick world of consumer magazine publishing. They had to operate *New York* and the others, but what really animated them was the prospect of goosing the operating margins so that when they took the company public in five years or so the stock price would make them and Kravis even richer. There was a big problem: Reilly was counting on real cost savings at *New York* and the other Murdoch magazines. But everyone—except K-III—knew that Murdoch ran an extraordinarily efficient operation. And any fat that might have escaped Rupert had been stripped away in the previous six months as the magazines were buffed up for sale. So big savings were out of the question. The only alternative was to boost revenues, but the recession, which hit magazine ad sales particularly hard, made that impossible.

To supervise the magazine group Reilly chose a beefy character named Harry McQuillan, who looked like he'd once been a Notre Dame linebacker and who had run the textbook division at Macmillan. Unlike the Murdoch men I'd worked for who genuinely enjoyed being involved with *New York*, McQuillan cared only for the bottom line, which now was about half of what it had been in the glory days of the late eighties.

Anyone with experience in magazines knows that editorial quality alone can't generate sustained ad growth. Of course, a celebrity editor like Tina Brown can draw added pages from advertisers like Estée Lauder when she shows up at the *New Yorker*. But if the economic climate is poor, the ad momentum dies, as Tina learned in her failure with *Talk* in the midnineties. The editor's responsibility is to make sure his magazine is so good that it's eligible for a bigger share of advertising when times improve, as they inevitably do. This was too nuanced for poor McQuillan, who fretted over the weekly ad-page counts.

A year after K-III bought *New York,* Tina did in fact show up at the *New Yorker* and began generating the kind of chatter she memorably christened "buzz." Tina had blitzed the slick magazine business in 1984 when she took over the revived yet moribund *Vanity Fair* and made it a hit through sheer force of will and talent—and millions of dollars from Si Newhouse, whose idea it was to bring back the stylish slick, which had flourished in the twenties and early thirties. Among other things, Tina paid her writers so much that I had to double the rates we at *New York* were paying for cover stories. By the time she left for the *New Yorker, Vanity Fair* had rung up losses of $100 million or more.

In another curious turn of the carousel, I could have been the first editor of the revived *Vanity Fair.* Newhouse had long nursed a yen to buy the *New Yorker,* the best and most important magazine in America, but was rebuffed by the family owners. Frustrated, he decided to create his own *New Yorker* by disinterring *Vanity Fair,* which had gone out of business in 1936.

Out of the blue one day in 1982, Alexander Liberman called and invited me to lunch in the Grill Room of The Four Seasons, then the canteen and hiring hall of the magazine world. Liberman was an art director and noted sculptor who had become Newhouse's éminence grise and counselor at Condé Nast. His title was editorial director, and he had a hand in everything from hiring and firing editors to the layouts for every page of every Condé Nast slick. Liberman had a special émigré charm. A tallish, handsome older man with bristly eyebrows, Alex spoke softly and musically but preferred to listen. Like Jacqueline Onassis, he'd gaze at you as you blathered on as if you were the most brilliant person he'd ever met. Alex was so stylish that he dressed the same way every day. A white shirt, plain black tie, and a Paul Stuart suit, black in the fall and winter, tan poplin in the spring and summer. People used to speculate that he had only two suits, but I suspected he had a dozen in each shade in his closet and rotated them through the month.

Now, Liberman wanted to talk about bringing back *Vanity Fair,* which, as it turned out, Si was more enthusiastic about than Liberman was. I was too young to have read the original, but years before, I had come upon a coffee-table book of selections from the magazine, devoured it, and regularly gave copies as gifts. The new *Vanity Fair* was to be a stylish magazine of reportage and the arts, a kind of monthly *New Yorker,* but with more flair. I told Alex that I thought it would be hard to find an advertising market for such a magazine. But my main reservation was that I was having such a good time putting out *New York* that I couldn't imagine retreating into an office somewhere for nine months to hatch a start-up, no matter how glorious its lineage. I suggested that they sign up Tom Wolfe as the emblematic editor of the new *Vanity Fair* and let his sensibility set the tone. A Tom Wolfe magazine could be a commercial and artistic success.

Eventually, Newhouse and Liberman chose Richard Locke, a former editor of the *New York Times Book Review,* and the first issues were very lit'ry. They featured Gore Vidal, Diana Trilling, Marianne Moore, Francine du Plessix Gray (Liberman's stepdaughter), and other worthies. The magazine evolved a style of lugubrious black-and-white cover portraits of writers like Philip Roth and Susan Sontag, who seemed to be picking their noses. Locke was soon gone, replaced by Leo Lerman, a gentle Condé Nast aesthete who wasn't suited for the work, either.

Liberman and Newhouse came calling again, but I wanted no part of it. It's a good thing: I never could have worked the magic Tina did when she arrived shortly from London, where she'd been editing *Tatler.* By the October 1984 issue, *Vanity Fair* boasted "Raquel Welch Pumps Gold," "Jessica Lange & Sam Shepherd," "Teenage Suicide Pact," "Gossip of Houston," John Updike, Jesse Jackson, and others. Tina was on her way.

The next year, Newhouse finally got the *New Yorker* for $185 million, or $200 million, depending on which account you read. To seal the deal, Si made various representations about the independence of the magazine, much as Rupert had made guarantees about the *Times* of London and the *Sunday Times* when he bought them. Newhouse kept on William Shawn, Harold Ross's sainted deputy who'd been editing the magazine for more than three decades, for two more years. Then he unceremoniously dumped Shawn and replaced him with Robert Gottlieb, himself a sainted book editor at Knopf (also owned by Newhouse) and celebrated collector of women's plastic handbags from the fifties. Gottlieb tinkered with the magazine for five more years. And then one day Tina Brown was the editor of the *New*

Yorker. At *New York,* we welcomed her to the job with a mock *New Yorker* cover drawing featuring Tina as Eustace Tilley.

The *New Yorker* wasn't really a competitor of *New York*—it was a national magazine that had some "Talk of the Town" pieces about the city, reviews of New York cultural events, and some listings. But *New York* was getting submerged in all the buzz about the new *New Yorker*—never a good thing in the ad world. At *Vanity Fair,* Tina had perfected a repertoire of promotional tricks, and she was using them all now. With much fanfare, first copies of each issue were hand-delivered to the doorsteps of big-time media types and other supposed influentials on Sunday nights, as if the contents were so hot the privileged recipients couldn't wait for their regular subscriptions. Newsstand copies started popping up each Monday at drugstores and supermarkets around town. And Tina staged flashy lunches with *New Yorker* writers and people in the news bloviating about the issues of the day.

K-III had been keeping *New York* on short rations, and I told Reilly and McQuillan that we had to strengthen the magazine in this new environment. Grudgingly, they budgeted an extra $200,000 for added writers and pages, but the money was quickly rescinded. Reilly and McQuillan weren't in the magazine game, they were desperately trying to play the big-money game.

From the start, the editors and publishers of the old Murdoch magazines were encouraged to invest with their new masters. Reilly held a meeting for the group in which he sketched the rosy financial future of K-III, scribbling upward-thrusting lines with a Magic Marker on a big pad of paper propped on an easel. While K-III would show operating losses for years to come, he said, there were tax-loss carry-forwards, and the real figure to watch was EBITDA—earnings before interest charges, taxes, depreciation, and amortization were deducted. K-III's properties would throw off big cash flow, and that's the number the markets would use to value the company when it came time to go public four or five years hence. Insiders like us could buy shares now at $5 each. When the payoff came, those $5 shares would be worth $35 or possibly $50; it was hard to say precisely what Reilly was forecasting. As Reilly worked away on his easel, I couldn't help thinking of the hustling promoters of old, scribbling dreams of wealth on tablecloths for the dazzled prospects. I had bought as much as I could of News Corp. stock, but now I signed on for just enough K-III shares to show my loyalty to the team.

* * *

Joe Klein had done a superb job as Michael Kramer's successor covering politics for *New York*. He was the first to realize that William Jefferson
Clinton—the five-time governor of Arkansas who'd turned the 1988 Democratic convention catatonic with a marathon speech—was the class of the
1992 field. Joe published the first major cover story on Clinton in *New York*
early in the year and was ridiculed by the pack for getting out front. I knew
Joe was right in the spring when I watched Clinton perform at one of a series
of candidates' breakfasts run at the Regency Hotel on Park Avenue by a
couple of political operatives. A number of Clinton's challengers for the
nomination had already done this dog-and-pony show, and it was clear from
the moment he opened his mouth that he was in a league of his own.

With Klein, I was looking forward to the conventions and the fall campaign
—*New York* would have the leading-edge coverage that would get the magazine a lot of attention. Then one Monday morning, Joe walked into my
office with an unusually serious look and said, "We've got to talk." I got a
klong—any experienced editor knows that expression combined with those
words means bad news. And the news turned out to be worse than I could
imagine. Without a trace of embarrassment, Klein told me that he was
leaving *New York* to be the chief political writer and columnist for *Newsweek*,
which was being run by my protégé and close friend Maynard Parker. By
taking off this way, Joe was breaching the code. Political writers swap jobs
before the campaign starts or after November. As a matter of course, they
never change allegiance in the middle of a presidential election.

On those rare occasions when I really hate what's going on, I take off my
glasses. Staring at the blur that had just been Klein, I said, "You mean to tell
me that you and my friend Maynard got together and cooked this up, and
didn't even have the courtesy to let me know what you wanted to do?"

"I know what you mean," said Joe, "but we knew how you'd take it."

"And you were right," I replied. "Look. You're not a slave here, and you're
not under contract. Everybody's entitled to try to get a better job. But you
and Maynard know this kind of thing just isn't done in the middle of a presidential campaign."

I told Klein to clean out his office, and I called Maynard and told him I'd
never speak to him again.

I was deeply hurt by Parker's betrayal. Over the years, Maynard had been the protagonist of a Perils-of-Pauline melodrama at *Newsweek*. A big man with awesome energy and stamina, Maynard had had an unconventional path to the top at the magazine. Reared in a middle-class suburb of Los Angeles, he'd gone to Stanford, served with the military in Vietnam, and then joined *Life* as a reporter. He soon found his way to *Newsweek* in Asia as a correspondent and bureau chief. When I became editor of the magazine, I brought him back to be my national affairs editor. I had tried to guide and help Maynard the way Oz Elliott had helped me, and he'd worked his way up the masthead since I'd left.

Around *Newsweek*, Maynard was known as "Mad Dog" for his propensity to rev up one story after another, "scrambling the jets," in newsmag talk, to switch cover stories at the last minute. He was politically more conservative than most of the *Newsweek* editors. Kay Graham was known to have her doubts about Parker's "soundness," and the Hitler diaries fiasco hadn't helped his cause. I'd counseled Maynard that he'd ultimately get to run the magazine, but I'd had to hold his hand time and again when things looked bleak. Now I felt that my reward for being a good friend was what passes for treachery in the magazine business.

Klein went on to do fine work for *Newsweek*, and John Taylor, one of *New York*'s top staff writers, ably took over the political beat, although he couldn't match Joe's sources. Over the months, mutual friends tried to patch it up between Maynard and me, but I wouldn't budge. Every time I read one of Klein's pieces in *Newsweek*, I'd get angry all over again. Finally, on September 13, 1993, Maynard telephoned and I took the call.

"If Rabin and Arafat can shake hands at the White House," he said—I was actually watching the ceremony on my office TV when Parker called "don't you think we could have lunch?"

I agreed that the statute of limitations had run out; we were friends again.

I didn't know it when Maynard called, but 1993 was to be my last year at *New York*. I felt increasingly uneasy with the management. I had uncommon autonomy and a contract that was probably too rich for the K-III crowd, with its ample salary, profit participation, and leased top-of-the-line Lexus. When the contract next came up for renewal in the spring of 1994, I had a sense there'd be trouble. Whatever my instinct, there were no red flags from Reilly and his crew. Just the opposite. As the twenty-fifth anniversary of *New*

York approached in April, Reilly proposed marking it with a gala dinner in my honor at the Metropolitan Museum of Art, such a popular setting for new-society celebrations that John Taylor had spoofed it as a Party Palace in a *New York* cover story not long before.

Staging a dinner at the museum gave it real cachet, but there were complications. The Met had strict rules covering everything, including the number of guests in the American Wing, which couldn't top about 250. This meant making the guest list would be a delicate exercise, sure to offend many people who expected to be invited. What's more, Henry Kravis had his own list, and he was, after all, not just one of the hosts but the proprietor. In the end, we managed a sparkling list, and on the afternoon of the big event I was in the *New York* dining room, doing the even more ticklish task of trying to seat the dinner, when I was summoned to the phone.

It was Kravis, and he had more on his mind than placement. It turned out that *W,* the slick monthly fashion magazine published by Fairchild's *Women's Wear Daily,* was doing a big spread on the lavish houses where Henry and Caroline Roehm disported themselves. *W* had already photographed Caroline's mammoth riding barn, and now the magazine was flying a photographer over their vast spread in the Dominican Republic. Kravis rightly figured that a picture of his gigantic hacienda would make him look like an imperialist pig. He wanted me to call John Fairchild, who owned the magazine, and get him to kill the story.

Now, Fairchild was a fearsome figure in the mingled world of fashion and new society in New York. He ruled his empire of trade publications like an old-fashioned press lord, rewarding friends and punishing those whose fashions or personalities somehow offended him. For years, Fairchild treated certain designers—among them Geoffrey Beene, Pauline Trigere, and John Weitz—as pariahs whose names were never to be mentioned in *WWD* or *W.* Suzy, the last of the society columnists, wrote for Fairchild, and she, too, could flatter, humiliate, or banish at her or Fairchild's whim.

I had always gotten along well with Fairchild. Julie was, after all, an alumna of John's *Daily News Record,* and he was always very gallant to her. Every once in a while, he would come uptown to have lunch with me at The Four Seasons. He invariably took the subway, priding himself on his old newspaperman's Spartan tastes.

Kravis's idea was that I should threaten Fairchild that *New York* would do a hatchet job on him unless he backed off on the Kravis takeout. It was ludicrous, of course. I had never threatened anyone that way in my career, and if I was going to start now, John Fairchild was hardly the one to target. He was a lot tougher than Henry Kravis and his crowd.

I told Kravis I'd have nothing to do with his scheme. "If you want to try to muscle John Fairchild, you'll have to do it yourself," I said. "I'd never make a call like that—to him or anyone else."

Kravis harrumphed and subsided. I'd worked for the fearsome Murdoch for thirteen years and he'd never issued any inappropriate commands or even borderline requests. Once, he observed mildly that Marie Brenner had been a little harsh on Cornelia Guest, the daughter of his social pal and *Post* gardening columnist CZ Guest, who was making a splash around town as the latest deb of the year. "She's only seventeen," he said, and he was right. Another time, he expressed concern about a piece Julie was contemplating on Claudia Cohen, a gossip columnist of sorts and the daughter of the feared Bobby Cohen, who controlled all the newsstands at airports and terminals around New York. "In this business, you don't want Bobby Cohen for an enemy," he cautioned, but Julie had already decided there wasn't enough new to say about Claudia, and the issue was moot.

The dinner was all that I'd hoped. A genuinely glamorous and accomplished crowd turned out, and the photographers jostled each other to shoot all the media stars. My old suitor Mort Zuckerman, who had bought the *Daily News* out of bankruptcy, made the strobes spark, but he was quickly upstaged by Murdoch, who had just reclaimed the *Post,* touching off a tabloid war that still rages in New York.

Standing at the lectern in the soaring Englehard Court of the museum, the cultural heart of New York, I could spot Murdoch and Mailer at the candle-lit tables, Anna Wintour and Donald Trump, Clay Felker, Bill Buckley, Kravis and Sonny Mehta, Kurt Vonnegut and Gay Talese, the editors of America's great magazines, and dozens more—rulers of media, the arts, and commerce in the city. Felker was seated at an antiseptic remove from Murdoch. Kay Graham's daughter, Lally, was there, too.

"There are old loves in this room that will never die," I told the crowd, "and old wounds that will never really heal. But Scott Fitzgerald was wrong: There *are* second acts in American lives and third acts—and plenty of encores." I knew what I was talking about, but on that triumphant night I had no inkling of how faithfully my life would ultimately track my own speech text.

One of the stars at the dinner was Sonny Mehta, the chief of Knopf, probably the most distinguished publishing house in the country. Sonny was a Sikh who had come first in his class at Cambridge and gone on to success in London publishing. He'd been imported by Si Newhouse when Robert Gottlieb left Knopf to edit the *New Yorker*. Mehta was a mysterious fellow, dark and dapper with a small goatee, a chain-smoker and Scotch-sipper who seemed to inhabit his own bubble of intrigue. He'd take a writer to lunch and then hardly talk, letting the silences run until the poor author started babbling to fill the dead air. He often ignored messages, and even some of his own writers were crazed by his elusiveness. His editing was often invisible or nonexistent, but he had faultless taste for books that would sell—literary and commercial fiction and nonfiction, too. To be published by Knopf was a novelist's dream.

Julie's first novel, *Creatures of Habit,* a romance and knowing social satire of New York in the early nineties, had not only been accepted by Knopf—a coup in itself—but Sonny himself chose to be her editor. Early in the game, they had gone to dinner to talk about the book; then they came up to our apartment to continue going over the manuscript. I stayed out of the way in our bedroom, but late in the evening I heard a commotion and ventured out to investigate.

There I encountered a scene that could have been lifted from the book. The most exalted figure in New York publishing was hunched on one of the steps to our sunken living room with a bloody handkerchief pressed to his nose while Julie struggled to restrain our black mutt, Sunday, a stray who had come out of the woods in Redding one Sunday morning. Unaware of Sunday's quirks, Sonny had bent over to pat her and had been rewarded with a nip. It wasn't really the poor dog's fault; she had been abused along the way and snapped at anyone who got too close, especially strangers. Distraught, Julie shepherded Sonny to the emergency room at Lenox Hill Hospital, where they waited until 3:00 AM for Mehta to be patched up.

Sonny—and Julie's novel—survived the episode, and the book was published in the spring. She was soon the guest of honor at a glamorous party of her own given by the Lauders at Mortimer's, the clubby hangout for social people on the East Side. If there was a single moment when Julie and I together seemed to be thriving in our careers, it was that spring.

* * *

Claeys Bahrenburg, the head of Hearst's magazine division, had brought the model Lauren Hutton, once a *Newsweek* cover girl, to the dinner at the museum. One day in the late summer, he invited me to lunch at "21." Bahrenburg was one of the last of an endangered publishing breed—big guys who liked their shooters and silver bullets and looked right in lime-green slacks appliquéd with little whales. I'd known him since he had sold ads for *Cosmopolitan,* one of Hearst's biggest titles, along with *Good Housekeeping, Harpers Bazaar, Redbook,* and, incongruously, *Esquire,* the fading men's magazine.

Although "21" had lost much of its luster as a power spot after many years of atrophy, lunch in the front room downstairs next to the bar with its weird array of hanging airplane models still had a touch of the old we're-all-big-timers-here appeal As a hiring hall, "21" was a distant second to the Grill Room of The Four Seasons, but inviting someone in the business to lunch there could still make the guest suspect that something was up. After a gossipy tour of the magazine business, Claeys suddenly said, "How would you like to be the editor of *Esquire?*" I should have seen it coming, but I was blindsided by the question. At moments like that, I'd do the analysis in a heartbeat, and I heard myself reply, "Under the right circumstances, it might be something I'd want to do."

I think Bahrenburg expected me to laugh off the offer, which I probably should have done, and he seemed surprised and relieved by my answer.

I'd probably made up my mind that I wanted the job the moment he asked. If I was bored at *New York* after thirteen years of "Summer Pleasures" issues and "Fall Previews," I would never admit it. I've always felt real accomplishment comes only with good work sustained year after year. I sneered at the idea of burnout. Like the characters in Julie's novel, I'm a creature of habit, and I loved nearly everything about my life at *New York.* But I couldn't totally dismiss the notion that dealing with something new would be good for me. And I really was uncomfortable with the K-IIIs.

I conjured up a new life: I saw myself in my tweed sports jacket with leather elbow patches having drinks with John Updike or Phillip Roth in the lobby of the Algonquin, then heading back to the office to edit Norman Mailer's brilliant take on Bill Clinton. Freed of the weekly grind, I'd be able to channel all my energy and smarts into compelling monthly issues that would reestablish *Esquire* in the magazine pantheon. My ego was piqued, too: how many editors could do a news magazine, a city slick, and a monthly with a proud literary tradition in a single career?

It was a fantasy, of course. *Esquire* in 1993 was little more than a husk of the great magazine founded sixty years before by Arnold Gingrich and brilliantly led in its heyday sixties by Harold Hayes (who, in another turn of the carousel, after being dumped at *20/20,* had become my successor as editorial director of the CBS magazines). After he lost *New York,* Felker, an *Esquire* alumnus, flopped with a misconceived fortnightly version. Then, in 1979, two whiz kids from Knoxville, Tennessee, named Chris Whittle and Phil Moffitt showed up and bought the magazine.

Whittle and Moffit had started a business putting out student guides while at the University of Tennessee; that venture grew into a custom publishing outfit they named 13-30 for the demographic they were targeting. Whittle, an irresistible salesman who sported bow ties and a crafty Middle Border charm, was the business brains of the enterprise. Moffitt, with a small brush mustache and introspective manner, was the editorial hand.

Esquire, which was losing $5 million a year, almost sank them until they completely reinvented it as a marketing machine, with each issue devoted to a theme, like travel or fitness, that would appeal to a specific category of advertisers. Within a few years, *Esquire* was so thick with ads that it looked like a catalog. It was like shooting adrenaline into a doomed patient—the poor soul could be made to twitch, but the treatment couldn't be sustained. The first couple of travel issues might work for readers or advertisers, but the approach eventually turned predictable and tiresome. Before the inevitable happened, Whittle and Moffitt split up. Phillip got *Esquire,* which he turned around and peddled to Hearst for an astounding $86 million. Chris renamed 13-30 Whittle Communications and started Channel One, a television service that pumped an hour-long news program—with commercials! —into school classrooms on TV sets thoughtfully provided by Whittle. (After I left K-III, Bill Reilly bought Channel One from Chris.)

Buying *Esquire* never really made sense for Hearst, whose specialty was women's service magazines like *Good Housekeeping.* Frank Bennack, who ran Hearst, and his deputy, Gilbert Maurer, were shrewd operators, but they were no more immune than others to the lure of owning an iconic magazine and, more to the point, making it great again.

When Bahrenburg called me, *Esquire* was being edited by Terry McDonnell, a gruff veteran of *Rolling Stone* and two other magazines aimed at men, *Outside* and *Men's Journal.* Terry's solution was to give *Esky* a he-man, Montana persona to compete with *GQ*'s appeal to what's become known in the new millennium as metrosexuals, straight young guys who worry a lot about their clothes and grooming.

I found the magazine so uninteresting that I'd stopped looking at it, although I'd read it since Hayes's day and still got a complimentary copy in the mail each month. In fact, I had to get Claeys to send me a year's worth of back issues to familiarize myself with *Esquire* before I could think about what I might do with it. I tried to scope out the magazine's vital signs: the circulation —subscribers and newsstand—and the ad page trends. I also discussed the Hearst overture with friends. They all thought I was nuts even to consider it. Why leave *New York* for a doomed enterprise?

At my second meeting with Bahrenburg, I told him that I had very specific requirements for a deal to edit *Esquire,* and if they were unrealistic, we'd just as well end the courtship. When I told him what I wanted—including a five-year contract—Claeys didn't blink. That should have told me how desperate Hearst was to save *Esquire* and that I should have skittered away—or asked for a lot more.

Now I started planning how I could rejuvenate *Esquire,* and Tom Baer began trying to turn the terms into a contract. I rationalized that I really didn't have to make a final decision until we saw whether the actual contract could be drafted.

We are all hostage to our experience, and we tend to approach new problems the way we've solved old ones. At *New York,* I'd stripped the magazine back to its core elements and then tried to burnish them to their original sheen. At *Esquire,* I wanted to bring back brilliant writing, revitalize its heritage in fiction, and make the service journalism so good the magazine would be indispensable to its target audience. The old *Esquire* always had important women writers and readers, and I thought the new *Esquire* could appeal to women, too, while maintaining a clear identity as a men's magazine. I had no doubt that I could make the editorial pages of the magazine vibrant again, and that circulation and ad page gains would inevitably follow. Circulation—especially newsstand—and advertising had always been strong when I ran *Newsweek* and *New York.* I had the touch, or so I thought.

Bennack and Maurer liked my plans, too, and by mid-October the contract was ready to sign. I was bound to K-III until the next spring, so now I had to tell Reilly I wanted to leave and see if he'd release me early, although Hearst was prepared to wait if he balked. I made one of those "we've got to talk" calls to Reilly, and I think he suspected something when I showed up at K-III's elaborate offices in midtown. I told him about the *Esquire* offer, and that I wouldn't try to use it as a negotiating ploy for a new deal with him. I really wanted to edit *Esquire* and hoped he'd release me from my contract, but I'd of course stay to the end if he insisted. Bill said he understood how I felt, but asked for the rest of the day so he and his colleagues could decide whether to make a counteroffer anyway. He called after lunch to say they'd decided to release me from my contract and to wish me luck.

Now came the hard part—telling all the people at *New York* that I was leaving them. During my years there the magazine had enjoyed a stability it had never experienced before. After the initial shakedown in 1980, the surviving staffers and the new hires settled in for the long haul. Once in a while, we would lose a writer to Tina at *Vanity Fair,* and both Kramer and Klein had gone on to the news magazines. After more than a decade with me, Laurie Jones, the managing editor, had doubled her salary at *Vogue,* and Dick Babcock, the skillful articles editor, had left to edit his hometown *Chicago* magazine. But I found able replacements for them, and the masthead rarely had to be tinkered with. Without being told, people on staff understood how rare it was for a magazine to have such a run.

There was no frenzy and chaos. Cover pieces and special issues were well planned, and when a story had to be crashed, sure hands like Hamill, Michael Daly, and John Taylor turned out faultless copy on deadline. I showed up every morning around 9:15 and left at 6:30, and the only people who stayed late were those who liked to hang around the office. Many writers and editors felt their time at *New York* was the best they'd ever had or would have in the business. I thought often of a phrase John Cheever wrote in a letter to me after a cover story and lunch at *Newsweek,* "a sunlit clearing in the forest." *New York* would be the only time in my career when I could run every aspect of a publication to my own taste, and I was proud of the result.

On my last day, Bill Reilly invited me to a valedictory lunch and asked to go to Le Cirque, where I was a regular and he wasn't. I got to the restaurant on Sixty-fifth Street off Park Avenue before Reilly and found Richard Nixon standing outside the entrance. Inside, Sirio Maccioni, the *patron,* rubbed his hands together and explained apologetically that the corner banquette in the front of the restaurant where I usually sat was spoken for today. "President Nixon is having President and Mrs. Reagan to lunch," he said, almost beside himself with anticipatory pleasure. Sirio had thoughtfully set up for me a round table for two almost in the laps of the presidential party. "You'll be able to watch everything," he said.

Nixon waited outside until his guests arrived, then ushered them to the L-shaped banquette. He seated himself on the short leg of the L with Nancy between him and Ronnie on the long leg. When Reilly showed up, he did a double take. "Am I seeing what I think I'm seeing?" he asked.

It was easy to eavesdrop on the conversation on the banquette. Never much for small talk, poor Nixon tried one gambit after another but kept coming back to golf. Nancy gazed at him as he droned on, with the same rapturous expression she always beamed at Reagan, who said little. When the menus were presented, Nixon said, "Let me recommend the *goujonettes* of sole—they're a specialty here." I don't remember what they ate, but I was struck by the scene. Where but in America could two men who'd had such tumultuous political careers wind up chatting about golf over a leisurely lunch as the afternoon idled away? As lunch wore on, Reagan seemed to lose even more interest, content to stare placidly out into the restaurant as he chomped away. None of us knew it then, but his Alzheimer's was well advanced.

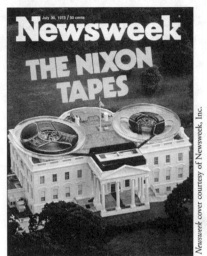

June, 1973: My favorite cover.

January, 1964: First cover story.

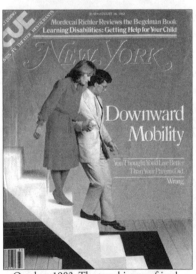

October, 1983: The trend is your friend.

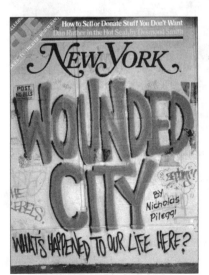

November, 1981: The bad old days.

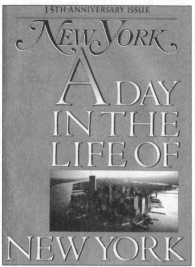

April, 1983: Renaissance.

October, 1987: Gilded age.

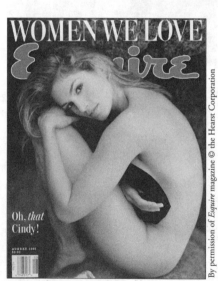

August, 1995: Beyond beauty.

August, 1994: Bombshell.

December 14, 2000: The fortieth page one.

September 12, 2001: Prophetic.

April 10, 2003: End of the beginning.

18

EDSQUIRE

ESQUIRE WAS A FIASCO, but like so many debacles it started out promisingly enough. After I signed the contract, Bahrenburg walked me over to the magazine's offices a few blocks from the Hearst castle on Eighth Avenue and Fifty-seventh Street. "You're going to like the offices," he promised. Actually, I was sure I was going to hate the offices. After working for nearly thirty years on the East Side of midtown, I dreaded the move to the far West Fifties, then a wasteland of nondescript office buildings on desolate streets. Without telling Julie, I'd detoured one Saturday morning on the way to Redding and drove past the *Esquire* offices on Fifty-fifth Street between Seventh and Eighth avenues. The façade of the building had been redone, but still looked dreary. It was a childish reaction, and I shrugged it off, or tried to.

But Claeys was right. Terry McDonnell had drafted his friend François de Menil, of the art-collecting de Menils, to design the *Esquire* offices, and he had done a splendid job—all high-tech industrial chic, a bright and appealing place to put out a great magazine. The staff was waiting for me in the glass block-walled conference room. The magazine was limping along, and they had the same tremulous look on their faces that I'd encountered at *New York* on my first day there. But they were reassured by the hiring of what the *Post* liked to call a "high-profile editor" that Hearst was committed to *Esquire* and wouldn't sell it or fold it out from under them. I introduced myself, shook hands with each staff member, and told them we were going to succeed and have a good time doing it. They didn't look persuaded.

Bahrenburg and other Hearst big shots had urged me to clean house, but I decided to do what I'd done at *New York*. I'd meet and evaluate each editor and writer before deciding who would be part of the new regime. The survivors were happy to tell tales about McDonnell, who had been moved downstairs in the building to be editor of Hearst's small outdoor title, *Sports Afield*. He was remote and cranky, they said, had a mean temper, and sometimes threw things at them—nothing I hadn't heard before.

As much as I liked the offices, I was pleasantly surprised at the quality of my new subordinates, led by Terry's deputy, David Hirshey, a onetime sportswriter who had toiled at the *Daily News* back in the early eighties when Felker had been installed to put out an afternoon edition that turned into a disaster. Dark and energetic, David had even more hair than I did and a deep love and understanding of *Esquire*. The other articles editors were literate and sophisticated. And the design director was Roger Black, who had worked for me at the start at *New York* and had gone on to become one of the world's stellar typographers and designers, having redone *Newsweek*, much of the *New York Times*, the *Baltimore Sun*, and many papers abroad.

Soon I began to feel giddily optimistic about my new magazine. My plan was simple enough: I'd try to reinvigorate *Esquire* by reconnecting with its roots both from the Hayes era and the Whittle and Moffitt days. Some of the changes were cosmetic—introducing a redrawn version of *Esky*, the magazine's leering little figurehead, to the upfront "Man at His Best" section of short items—but the rest were substantive. I'd fill the feature well each month with a half dozen strong pieces, some topical, some quirky, by established, skilled writers. When compelling short stories were available, we'd publish them. On other months, we'd print a sampler of short, effective excerpts from new novels by name writers. The service section of the magazine would be called the "*Esquire* Guide." Each issue would be devoted to a single topic: extreme sports one month, everything you need to know about your heart the next. Over time, these individual guides would add up to a serial encyclopedia of rich information about everything important in a man's life. Finally, the fashion coverage of *Esquire* would again coach men in contemporary good taste, not simply flaunt goofy designs in bizarre layouts.

Both *Esquire* and *GQ* depended on celebrity covers to sell the magazine, and I knew I had to play that game. But I was determined that the stories that went with the covers would be real journalism about celebrities, not just soufflés. Julie followed me to *Esquire*, of course, and so did some of my other top *New York* writers, including John Taylor and Michael Gross, so I knew the strategy could be brought off. I'd even have a gossip column of sorts—the work of Jeannette Walls, a striking redhead who survived a Dicksenian childhood with her hippie parents in West Virginia, put herself through Barnard, started at *New York* as one of my assistants, and then made the "Intelligencer" column required reading.

Even though I started in late October, the antediluvian production and distribution schedules of monthly magazines meant that my first real issue wouldn't be published until mid-February and dated March. My highest priority was to make that first issue a big seller on the newsstands, the signal that the new *Esquire* was connecting with readers again. This should have been easy enough because the magazine had been selling barely 85,000 copies each month with B-list actors like Harvey Keitel out front.

My choice was simple enough: Tom Cruise was coming out with a new movie in the spring, teaming up with even prettier boy Brad Pitt as a pair of bloodsuckers in *Interview with the Vampire,* based on the Anne Rice novel. Without knowing it, I'd chosen the newsstand champ; Cruise's face on the cover sold more issues of more magazines than anyone in Hollywood. I had the touch!

The story of that Cruise cover turned out to be a playbook for the insane and pathetic game magazines have to suffer to wrangle movie stars on their covers in hopes of selling thousands of extra copies. Cruise was the king of the newsstands, and his PR handlers acted as if they were representing Louis XIV. Heading the Cruise operation was the fearsome Pat Kingsley, who had ruthlessly and effectively controlled press contact with Cruise for as long as anyone could remember.

No, Cruise would not pose for a cover shot, although we offered the artistry of every name photographer in the world except Annie Leibowitz, who worked only for Condé Nast. No, there were no production shots of Tom as a vampire from the movie that we could use. Cruise might talk to the writer, but the poor scribe couldn't bring up Scientology, his marriage to Nicole Kidman, or the persistent whispers that he was a homosexual and she was a lesbian. In the end, Cruise squeezed out a few unrevealing moments for the writer on the phone from the *Vampire* set, and we got an illustrator to imagine him with pointy canines for the lead spread of the story. At the last minute, the photo editor scrounged up a sepia-toned beefcake shot of Tom by Herb Ritts that had been used in Europe but never here and we went to press. The cover sold predictably well, the issue was well received by advertisers and the press, and I felt I was off to a good start.

Early on, I got Mailer to write not about Clinton, who knew better than to give Norman an interview, but about Madonna. The issue, with Madonna posed in front of a target in a black leather bikini and dog collar, was a news-stand sensation, selling more than 200,000 copies, an *Esquire* record. Even the fact that the multimillionaire star walked away from the studio with a $5,000 mink coat used in one of the shots and wouldn't give it back failed to squelch my euphoria.

The next few covers—starring Woody Allen, Jerry Seinfeld, and David Letterman—were big hits, too. We had fiction from celebrated American writers like Richard Ford, David Foster Wallace, and Annie Proulx—plus a story from the master, Saul Bellow. I even updated the revered old *Esquire* pinups. An innovative photographer named Timothy White came up with an ingenious way to electronically airbrush scanty costumes on all-but-naked photos of our era's most famous supermodels in the classic Varga Girl poses.

One by one, Naomi Campbell, Claudia Schiffer, Angie Everhart, and the rest signed on for the series. When her turn came, Cindy Crawford endeared herself to the photo crew. On her back in the studio, she whipped off her top and cheerfully announced, "Here they are, boys. These are my tits."

By the end of my first year on the job, everything seemed to be on track, but there were disturbing signs. Since funnymen Seinfeld, Allen, and Letterman had done so well, we followed with Jay Leno, who easily beat Dave in the nightly TV ratings. *Esquire* with Leno's big mug on the cover tanked on the newsstands. Ominously, ad pages, anemic under McDonnell, stubbornly refused to grow. And despite the new energy in the magazine, Hearst couldn't get readers to pay more than $7.95 a year for a new *Esquire* sub-scription, the lowest price of any major magazine. I did a little digging and discovered why: more than a quarter of the magazine's subscribers were geezers over sixty-five who'd signed on using those annoying Publishers Clearing House cut-rate stamp sheets.

The publishing side was a shambles. The publisher I inherited was fired and replaced by one of the biggest characters in the ad sales game, Ron Galotti. A brash little guy with bright eyes and supreme confidence that spilled over into arrogance, Galotti would later achieve pop culture immor-tality as Candace Bushnell's lover, Mr. Big, in the stories that became *Sex and the City* on HBO. He'd started at Hearst, jumped ship to Condé Nast, got fired there, and now was being taken back into the Hearst fold. I was thrilled. If anybody in the business could sell ads for *Esquire* it was Galotti. He lasted six weeks before he bolted back to Condé Nast (and later quit with Tina to found *Talk*).

To replace Galotti, I got my old deputy from *New York,* Larry Burstein, who was happy to leave his hot spot as number two on the business side at the *New Yorker.* When the band stopped in this round of musical chairs I was working with my third publisher in barely a year at *Esquire*—not a formula for success at even the most robust title, which *Esky* definitely was not.

Toward the very end at *Newsweek,* I'd felt that I was losing my grip on the operation, but I'd never before been involved with a failing enterprise. Besides the demographic bad news, I'd learned a lot, none of it encouraging. As I checked the monthly single-copy sales figures, I realized that there were barely a half dozen stars or personalities who could sell magazines for *Esquire,* and with Cruise, Madonna, Seinfeld, Allen, and Letterman, I'd used up nearly all of them in my first year. I tried a gamut of others, among them O. J. Simpson, Bruce Willis, Sharon Stone, Richard Gere, John F. Kennedy Jr., Pierce Brosnan as the new James Bond, Jim Carrey, and Al Pacino. Not one of them scored.

And wangling celebrities for the cover became even more excruciating. Sharon Stone, who was starring in a Western, would pose, but only if *Esquire* spent thousands flying her horse to Arizona for the shoot and only if she could be shot in a frumpy frontier granny gown. (She did cut a microscopic hole over one breast so sharp-eyed readers thought they got a tiny glimpse of nipple.) The devilish Tim Allen, who at the time had the number one television show in America, the number one movie, and the number one non-fiction best seller, agreed to wear a small, elegant pair of shiny red horns along with his dinner jacket for the cover shoot. Then his wife forbade him to and we wound up with a pointless picture of Mr. Potato Head in a tuxedo. John Travolta, another Scientologist and a pilot, agreed to pose sitting on the wing of one of his jets smoking a cigar, but not at the controls.

Every ridiculous demand and condition had to be negotiated with the sharky press reps for the movie studios putting out their movies. One exception to all the mendacity was Steve Martin, the odd, smart comic actor and writer (who first appeared on a magazine cover in 1978, when I put him on *Newsweek*). Playing off his lonely guy shtick, Martin helped us create an *Esquire* cover in which he was the only inhabitant of a desert island the size of a manhole cover, complete with a palm tree. The cover was witty and elegant—"Steve Martin Needs a Hug," was the cover line— and bombed on the newsstand.

Amid all the torment, being editor of *Esquire* had its pleasures. Twice a year Julie and I would go to Milan for the men's fashion shows put on by the designers, including Armani, Versace, Dolce & Gabbana, Romeo Gigli, and Jean Franco Ferre. For all of them, the men's collection was secondary to their women's line, but more than a few did substantial department store and fragrance business, so it made sense for them to keep up their men's lines. The problem with the shows was that the clothes the designers (except for Armani) showed bore no recognizable connection to what was actually manufactured and sold under their names. Instead, the men's shows were self-indulgent or cynical extravaganzas aimed at getting a rise out of the fashion press.

The editors of *Esquire, GQ,* and other magazines hungry for fashion advertising were expected to show up at every show, visit with the designers, and act as if they really cared whether Versace was showing pegged pants or Bermuda shorts or thong bathing suits or convict stripes on the runway. The shows were staged all over the city from ten or eleven in the morning until long after sunset, and in between the editors had to join their publishers at lunches and dinners romancing the suits who placed the ads for the designers' suits. Some of the shows were so goofy they were surreal. Vivienne Westwood, the British designer who had a tiny men's business, dressed up her models as Tango punks or Sun King courtiers. Ferre had all his bare-chested models sprayed with a garden hose before they pranced out on the runway. Gigli liked to take over odd places, like an abandoned Pirelli tire factory, to stage endless parades of models and members of the crowd wandering around like hippies waving huge sunflowers.

The saving grace was that this all took place in Milan, and occasionally in Florence. Milan is an all-business place, like Chicago, but it has some superb restaurants, La Scala, and an exquisite Four Seasons hotel in a former convent right next to the Versace palazzo. Before he was murdered in Miami, Gianni himself would serve pasta to his guests after the shows. He'd always make sure to have a few young Hollywood stars around; one night we ran into Leonardo DiCaprio wandering like a lost soul around Versace's huge garden. Armani, too, made sure the front rows of his shows were full of people like Liam Neeson and Pat Riley, the basketball coach with the slicked-back hair who wore only Armani on the sidelines.

One summer, Julie and I stopped in London on the way to the Milan shows. On the Sunday before we left, we drove down to Kent to the famous Sissinghurst gardens created by Vita Sackville-West and her husband, Harold Nicholson, in the 1930s. Ed Victor, the literary agent, lived in an old house on the grounds, and he had invited us to visit, along with the British writer Fay Weldon and her husband. We spent a resplendent afternoon touring the gardens and visiting with Ed's neighbor Nigel Nicholson, Vita and Harold's son and a distinguished publisher and memoirist in his own right. Mozart piped from Ed's sound system played over the gardens as the sun set on a perfect, civilized day.

Less than twenty-four hours later, we were in the garden of Versace's Milan mansion for the first show of the week. The theme was rap music, which was just gathering force. The models' path and a small stage for musicians were decorated with white placards that read **FUCK, SUCK, MOTHERFUCKER**, and like sentiments. As the boys started their promenade, a man and a woman dressed all in black with microphones attached to headsets began intoning the words on the cards. Instantly, I was plunged into a deep funk, slumped in my chair, chin nearly resting on my chest. A sharp pain exploded in my rib cage—Julie's elbow. "Snap out of it," she hissed. "You can't sit in the middle of the show looking like that." I put a smile on my face, as my father the salesman always counseled, and soldiered on.

That wasn't the worst of it. Before I'd left New York, a young woman from the *Times* named Robin Pogrebin had interviewed me for a piece she was doing on *Esquire*. She had just been assigned to the magazine beat at the paper, and this article would be her debut. Given the weak ad picture, I was worried about the story. On Monday morning, when the piece was due to appear, I called my assistant, Fran Kessler, who'd been with me from the start at *New York*.

"You're not going to like it," said Fran in a voice that sounded as if her best friend had just died. "Has *Esquire* Gone Out of Style?" read the headline. The story began by speculating that I'd miss my nice office with my collection of model vintage cars when I was fired and went on to list the reasons I'd be gone: ad pages down, circulation down, *Esquire*'s identity crisis. Blah blah blah. Pogrebin suggested that as a weekly editor I couldn't find the monthly rhythm, and that at fifty-nine I was too old, as she put it, "to speak to today's man." The article wasn't anything like the *Times'* usual toothless coverage of magazines. Rookie Robin was trying to make her mark—a bull's eye on my back.

The article turned up later in the *International Herald Tribune,* which the staff at the Four Seasons affixed in an attractive plastic bag on the door handle of every guest every day. So now my humiliation was complete. Not only had everyone in New York seen the piece, all my competitors and comrades in Milan in the men's fashion world had it hand-delivered to their rooms. There was nothing to do but hold my head up and get through the rest of the week, which I did. I'd been in the business long enough to know that Pogrebin's piece was a death sentence, but I also knew that in the worst of times the only thing to do was to press on, doomed as that course might be.

I got back to New York in time for a circus so gaudy that it diverted me from my own troubles. Earlier in the year, a book had come out of nowhere to leap to the top of the *Times*'s best-seller list and get everybody talking. It was a hilarious roman à clef about Bill Clinton called *Primary Colors,* written by "Anonymous" and published by Harry Evans at Random House. Whoever Anonymous was, he was a hell of a writer, and obviously someone who'd been close to Clinton as he ran for president in 1992. Guessing the author's identity became a journalistic obsession. Professors fed passages from the book into their computers along with samples from well-known writers, hoping to detect telltale sentence patterns that would nail the culprit. Certain scenes in the book reminded me of something, but I could never tease out what.

Finally, the *Washington Post* got hold of some galleys and identified the scribbled corrections on the margin as the handwriting of—Joe Klein, who had quit *New York* in the middle of the campaign to be Maynard Parker's political columnist at *Newsweek*. Klein showed up at a press conference at Random House wearing Groucho glasses with a big nose and mustache, but nobody thought it was funny.

Joe's argument was that he was just following an old literary tradition of pseudonymous political satire. Besides, he was a columnist, and he had told his boss, Maynard, what he was doing, although he made Parker promise not to tell *his* bosses or anyone else. The problem was that many people thought it was inappropriate for a national political writer who had first boosted Clinton then lambasted him to be lampooning the candidate in an anonymous novel. The fact that Joe worked for a national news magazine complicated everything. Outdated as the standard was, people somehow still expected the newsmags to separate fact from opinion—and columnists from novelists. It looked for a time as if Maynard might lose his job, too, but Donald Graham, who'd succeeded his mother at the Washington Post Company, stood up for him and the storm passed. Now I realized why some of the scenes in *Primary Colors* seemed faintly familiar to me—they were reworked from Clinton pieces Joe had written at *New York* before he quit.

Back at *Esquire,* the chaos on the business side spun on. Sniffing the wind, Burstein left for another job. The woman running Hearst magazines was Cathie Black, who had been my first publisher at *New York* so long ago. Cathie was a rangy blonde who could have been the principal of an up-to-the-minute Catholic girls' school. She had gone on from *New York* to work for Allen Neuharth on his innovative national daily *USA Today,* then worked for a newspaper trade association before being tapped by Frank Bennack as Bahrenburg's successor. Cathie had greeted me as an old comrade when she joined Hearst, but had grown chillier by the day as *Esquire*'s ad sales and newsstand circulation stagnated. Now Cathie chose a fellow *Ms.* alumna, Valerie Salembier, who had worked with her at *USA Today,* as Burstein's successor. I'd first met Valerie two decades before, when she was the first woman ad rep at *Newsweek.* Now she was my fourth publisher in fewer than three years at *Esquire.*

The classic advice counsels that when you're in a hole stop digging, and I thought I did. I abandoned much of my original scheme for *Esquire* and improvised. I ditched the "*Esquire* Guide" and the novel excerpts and all but gave up celebrities on the cover. The new idea was for smart trend stories, another staple of the classic *Esquire.* So Bruce Willis *et al.* gave way to "The Truth about Male Vanity" illustrated on the cover by an erect six-inch ruler with a scale that read eight and a half inches, and covers about the weird life of J. D. Salinger, and a heart fashioned of barbed wire with the headline "Divorce Is Good for You." These flopped, too, but I could never tell whether they failed on their merits or simply because nobody cared. At

Newsweek and *New York,* I'd been used to all-but-instant feedback from readers and people in journalism. Now, John Taylor, Julie, Pete Hamill, and others published some of their best work in *Esquire,* and it disappeared without a murmur.

Nothing I tried could reinvigorate *Esky,* and by the spring of 1997 the magazine had so few ads that it risked suffering pocket flop, the dread condition where a magazine is so thin that it droops over on itself in the rack at the supermarket checkout.

So I initiated yet another makeover, with a new design and new editorial elements. The ballyhooed debut of yet the newest new *Esquire* was all set. Inauspiciously, Valerie had sold only about two dozen ad pages for the premiere, including two precious spreads from Chrysler.

The car company was in the vanguard of a pernicious trend in magazine publishing. Chrysler insisted that none of its glossy ads could run in issues of magazines that had articles, pictures, or fiction the bluenoses in Detroit considered too gamy or controversial. If a magazine ran some outré stuff without flashing the orange light, all future ads would be killed.

I scheduled a wonderful short story for the big issue by the celebrated gay writer David Leavitt. It was called, "The Term Paper Artist," and it was about a gay guy who churned out term papers for straight college men in exchange for letting him blow them. Rust Hills, *Esquire's* veteran fiction guru, urged me not to run the story, but Will Blythe, his younger subordinate, lobbied hard for it. "The Term Paper Artist" was a deft, wry story with no explicit scenes. I had no qualms about running it—after all, this was 1997!—and I knew the ad side was vetting all the copy for the fastidious folks at Chrysler.

The morning after the magazine went to the printer, I turned on my office computer to find a blinking red urgent e-mail from Salembier. It turned out that the *Esquire* ad exec assigned to monitor the copy for Chrysler had gone on maternity leave and *no one* had vetted the copy until the publisher herself had looked at it after deadline and had a seizure.

We had a Hobson's parlay of unappetizing choices: We could alert Chrysler to *The Term Paper Artist* and have the company order us to kill the story or pull its ads; we could let Chrysler discover the story when the magazine hit the stands later in the month and risk the loss of all future advertising; or we could try to pull the story quietly and salvage the ads.

Putting out our reborn *Esquire* with two spreads of house ads and fewer than twenty real ads was suicidal. Killing the story on press with the inevitable outcry from gays and the quality-lit crowd was equally unthinkable. But something had to be done—in just a few hours.

Perhaps because I had been a magazine publisher myself, perhaps because I felt that as editor in chief my paramount responsibility was the magazine's survival rather than my own, I decided to sacrifice the short story to save the precious car ads. Just like Nixon in his final days, I chose what I felt was the least worst course. It was the biggest mistake I made in a long career.

It didn't take long for the storm to break over my head. Will Blythe quit in protest, and let the world know about it. Implausibly enough, I insisted to the press that I had killed the story because I'd had sudden second thoughts about its literary quality and its appropriateness for *Esquire*. I simply couldn't admit that I'd killed the story to save the Chrysler ads. Nobody was fooled.

I limped on after the cataclysm, but I knew it was over. One Friday morning, Cathie called me over to the Hearst castle and put me out of my misery. To this day, "The Term Paper Artist" disaster lives on in my entry on Google. As my successor, Cathie had lined up Art Cooper's deputy at *GQ*, David Granger. As I write this, Granger is still going strong in his eighth year as editor in chief of *Esquire*. He's done a far better job than I did. He's won more than his share of National Magazine Awards and gotten good reviews in the press. But from everything I can gather, *Esquire* has yet to turn a profit and, when I last checked, that introductory subscription price was still $7.95. Just the other day, I got a solicitation from *Esquire*. The price: $5.95.

Now I was sure my career was over. I felt it had been a pretty good run of nearly four decades. But at sixty, I was coming off a very public failure, and I knew nobody would hire me again. Under my contract, I would be paid by Hearst for the next eighteen months, and I had a comfortable nest egg, so I wasn't worried about money. What I was going to do with the rest of my life was another question, one I couldn't answer and didn't really want to think about.

This time I wasn't as tormented as I'd been after Kay Graham fired me. I replayed in my mind what I'd done wrong at *Esquire*. I knew that I hadn't turned stupid or incompetent overnight or over the three and a half years I'd worked for Hearst. I still had the same talent, sensibility, taste, and energy that produced such success at *New York*. To use Lester Bernstein's wonderful phrase, I wasn't "gaited" for the work at *Esquire*. I had put myself in a situation in which I was all but destined to fail. The lesson I drew from the sorry episode is that one has to pick one's jobs as carefully as Willie Sutton, the master bank robber, picked his. Tina Brown learned the same lesson. Backed by Si Newhouse's Medici millions, she had leveraged her talent to triumph at *Vanity Fair* and the *New Yorker*. On a conventional budget at *Talk,* all her artistry produced just another glossy feature magazine that no one needed. It lost $56 million. Tina didn't turn stupid overnight, either—the situation had been too much even for her.

I filled my new free time doing things I enjoyed and had never really had time for. We took a couple of wonderful trips, one of them a long drive through Scotland, where we toured castles and stayed at country inns, most memorably on the Isle of Skye. Back in New York, Julie was busy with another novel, this one an ambitious tale of one of the world's great diamonds narrated by Napoleon and his amanuensis, Count Las Casas, and I was mostly on my own. I started running around the Central Park reservoir early in the morning and having lunch with old colleagues and other chums at the Century. I read or reread whatever struck my fancy, the novels of Evelyn Waugh, the collected stories of Isaac Singer, history, and biography. What turned out to be the great tech bubble was inflating, and I began talking to my broker nearly every day. I moved in and out of companies I'd never heard of whose products I knew nothing about—JDS Uniphase was a favorite—and made money nearly every time. In good weather and bad, I spent a lot of time in Redding, enjoying its beauty across the seasons.

On many sad afternoons, I visited my friend Maynard Parker. A few months after I left *Esquire,* Maynard came down with a bad sore throat just as he was heading off to a magazine editors' and publishers' conference in Arizona. He stopped to see his doctor, who checked his blood and sped him to the hospital. Maynard, who neither smoked nor drank and worked out relentlessly at the Reebok gym, had contracted a particularly aggressive type of leukemia. Lally Weymouth, who had become a prolific contributor to *Newsweek,* arranged for him to be treated by the top specialists at Memorial Sloan-Kettering, but nothing worked. In the late spring of 1998, he had a stem-cell transplant. I saw him a few weeks later at Lally's July 4 party in Southampton, a wraith in a white linen jacket. He died not long after that.

Maynard had survived the Hitler diaries and *Primary Colors* to become a fine editor of *Newsweek,* but he couldn't overcome the final obstacle.

One part of my old routine that I never abandoned was reading all the newspapers, a habit I'd begun at the *Post.* Each morning at six, a loud thump outside our door announced the arrival of the *Times, News, Post,* and *Wall Street Journal,* and I dutifully worked my way through them all every day. Try as I might, I couldn't turn off the pattern of a lifetime. Indeed, my brain acted as if it hadn't heard that I'd been fired; as I read, it kept churning out ideas for stories, profiles, covers, columns, all sort of coverage.

Sitting on the scuffed Chesterfield in the dining room, it sometimes seemed incomprehensible to me that I wasn't working and that I'd probably never work again. Julie was obsessed with the idea that I'd ended my career with a failure and kept telling me that I somehow had to redeem myself. I reminded her, as I had eighteen years before, that I couldn't really find a job. A job had to find me.

19

SUNDAY, BLOODY SUNDAY

IT WAS NOW MORE than a year since Cathie Black had fired me, and I had no prospects. Then, one beautiful afternoon as I was reading under the towering maples and elms in Redding, the portable telephone rang. Implausibly enough, on the other end of the line was the barky voice of Fred Drasner, Mort Zuckerman's partner in their publishing ventures. Five years earlier, Mort 'n' Fred had swooped in and bought the once-proud *New York Daily News* out of the bankruptcy pit in which the crooked Robert Maxwell had left it. Zuckerman had made favorable (for him) new contracts with the paper's craft unions, smashed the editorial union, the Newspaper Guild, and fired many old-timers. Then they moved the *News* out of its landmark Art Deco headquarters on Forty-second Street, one of the most beautiful buildings in the city, into one of the ugliest, a tawny concrete monstrosity in the brutalist style briefly popular in the seventies. The building had once housed an ice-skating rink and the back offices of a bank. It was on Thirty-third Street near Tenth Avenue overlooking the railroad yards.

Actually, the first call I'd gotten in June 1997 after my ouster from *Esquire* had been from Zuckerman and my old friend Pete Hamill, who had become Mort's fourth editor in chief of the *News* in the six years he'd owned the paper. They wanted me to become the Sunday editor, but I turned them down. I'd learned enough from the *Esquire* failure not to jump into anything. Besides, much as I loved Pete, it would be awkward to have him as my boss.

Editing the Sunday paper was again what Drasner wanted to talk about now, but there was a twist that made it far more appealing. It turned out that Harry Evans had been trying to sell Mort 'n' Fred on a scheme to reconfigure the *Sunday Daily News* (as it was oddly called), in the spirit of the London Sunday papers like the *Sunday Times* and the *Observer,* into a nearly freestanding paper with its own editorial flavor. The new Sunday paper would have access to much of the staff of the daily paper, but it would have a significant crew of its own and would generate its own news and features.

This was a bold—and expensive—stab at solving a problem that had dogged the *Daily News* and other big papers for years. The Sunday paper generated fully a third of the *News's* revenue, but the circulation was eroding. No one expected the paper to recapture the circulation from its glory days after World War II and before television, when the *News* sold more than 3 million copies a day and 4 million on some Sundays. But by the late nineties, the daily paper was selling no more than 725,000 copies a day and the Sunday sale was about 100,000 more, even with steroid injections from sweepstakes and other promotional gimmicks. The trend had to be reversed, no easy task when the paper's main competition, the thin but lively Sunday *New York Post,* sold for half the *News's* $1 cover price.

Early the next week, I had lunch with Fred at a midtown Italian restaurant where the maître d' administered extreme unction to Drasner, a regular there. "What I want to know is whether you've lost something off your fastball," said Fred, affably enough. I assured him my hummer was still humming, and that I'd be happy to explore the Sunday idea with him, Mort, and Harry Evans, their editorial guru. That began weeks of conversations, mostly with Evans, about how this new Sunday paper could be brought to life.

Now I was genuinely torn. The appeal of creating a new paper—essentially a weekly—was powerfully seductive. So was the chance to go back to work, and to end my career with a success rather than the *Esquire* flop. But the negatives were scary. Working for Zuckerman was likely to end in tears. After bringing Hamill to the paper with much hoopla, Mort had dispatched him after only nine months as editor in chief.

Once again, friends urged me not to do it, especially those who knew the reputations of the paper's insular editorial hierarchy and of the mercurial Zuckerman.

Part of the attraction of the *News* job was working with Harry, an energetic little man, the son of a Yorkshire railroad train driver who had gone to work at sixteen and had become one of the finest newspaper editors of our time. Evans first became famous as the crusading editor of the London *Sunday Times,* the creator of its famed Insight Team of investigative reporters who broke the thalidomide scandal. When Murdoch bought the *Times* of

London in 1981, he lured Evans over as his editor with elaborate guarantees of freedom from editorial meddling by the proprietor, which Murdoch of course quickly subverted.

Soon enough, Evans and Murdoch were at war. In the gruesome endgame, Evans barricaded himself in his office, sending combat bulletins to the frenzied media while Murdoch's legal henchmen tried to pry him out. Inevitably, Evans capitulated.

In the midst of the Evans melodrama, Murdoch called me at *New York* magazine. He was concerned—or wanted me to think he was concerned—that I thought he'd savaged Harry.

"They all think it was about politics, but it wasn't," said Rupert. "I could have lived with his leaders"—the Fleet Street term for editorials—"if he got the paper out on time. And if his leaders were brilliant, I could have lived with the paper being late all the time. But the leaders weren't any good and the paper never closed on deadline. So, you see, he had to go."

Actually, Evans and I had crossed paths long before that. He was a chum of Clay Felker's and Kay Graham's, and one night in the late 1970s we were invited to dinner with Kay and Harry at Clay's windowed duplex on East Fifty-seventh Street. Drinks were long over and dinner nearly done when Evans finally showed up, mumbling apologies and excuses. Wherever he'd been, he made little sense and the dinner awkwardly broke up. Only years later did I learn that Kay had been tempted to replace me with Evans as editor of *Newsweek,* but both realized that it would be awkward to have a Brit editing one of America's premier news magazines.

After the Murdoch fiasco, Harry came to America with his bride, Tina Brown, who went to work on *Vanity Fair* while he invented the wonderful magazine *Condé Nast Traveler* for Newhouse. Harry quickly became one of Zuckerman's whisperers (Mort always has to have an offline kibitzer, or two or three), a role in which he replaced—Felker!

In time, Evans leveraged himself into the job of running Random House, one of the plums of publishing, although he hadn't had all that much experience in the business. At Random, Evans ratcheted up the hoopla. He started a beautifully produced literary quarterly, called aptly enough *At Random,* to plug his books and authors and ran lively panel discussions at chic Barney's. Eventually, Harry's free spending got him the boot from Alberto Vitale, a taut little ex-accountant who ran the business side of Random House for Newhouse. And before you knew it, there was Harry ensconced at Mort Zuckerman's side as editorial director of both the *Daily News* and *U.S. News*. And there was I ensconced at Harry's side trying to conjure this bold new freestanding Sunday newspaper.

This time around, Tom Baer was more successful in getting an acceptable contract out of Zuckerman and Drasner. Mort had pledged to pour fresh money into the Sunday paper. Just to avoid any misunderstanding, I insisted that the contract specify the job slots and salaries for my new Sunday staff.

Remaking a magazine or a newspaper is one of the joys of being an editor, an exercise of pure craft that blends intellectual challenge and commercial instinct. The trick is always to find the of-the-moment incarnation of the publication from within its genetic code. And make no mistake: all lasting magazines and newspapers have their own DNA. When an editor finds the right approach, new readers and advertisers are drawn to the reborn publication without alienating the vast bulk of traditional followers.

The *Sunday Daily News* was a different sort of problem than any I'd dealt with before. The paper was a big grab bag of material. There was the main news section with its dozens of sports pages, a feature magazine that mixed everything from profiles of gangsta rappers to recipes for casseroles, a first-rate TV guide, a sheaf of those annoying but valuable supermarket discount coupons, and, of course, the once-world-famous color comics. True to its shriveled roots, the paper still carried features that had run for as long as anyone could remember, most conspicuously the "Justice Story," a page rehashing bloody crimes, mostly from the '30s and '40s. Like the daily, the *Sunday News* was assembled, not edited.

What's more, out of inertia as much as anything, most of the newsstand and candy store owners insisted on wrapping the Sunday paper in those comics, as their fathers and uncles had done. So no matter how compelling a front page the editors might conjure up, readers found what looked like last week's or next week's or any week's *Sunday News* when they went out to buy the paper on Saturday night or Sunday morning.

Undaunted, I set out to reformulate the paper, creating two tightly edited and crisply designed feature sections: "ShowTime" for movies, pop music, and other entertainment coverage, and "LifeLine," totally devoted to service, including relationships, personal finance, gadgets and new technology, health, and a nosy troubleshooter for bilked consumers. The main news section was streamlined, with added gossip and a new "Ideas and Opinion" section showcasing commentary by provocative writers like Michael Kramer, who joined me to edit the section and write for it regularly. A fresher front page was designed with a vivid splash of red for the logo and teases for the new sections and features. I hired a small but gifted staff of writers to generate investigative and enterprise stories that would make each Sunday's paper distinctive. Then I had miniature versions of the paper made, so I could walk Mort 'n' Fred through their new *Sunday Daily News*.

The battle with the *Post* for readers was simple compared with the war inside the paper over this rump Sunday edition. The *News* had been run for years by what came to be known as "the permanent government," a clutch of veteran *News*ies. Talented, tough, and insular, they were a vigilant immune system that rejected outsiders or gobbled them up like stray microbes. The permanent government helped destroy Hamill, although many people on the staff adored Pete. Mort 'n' Fred installed Debby Krenek, a bright and hardworking woman whose main accomplishment at the paper had been to mastermind the *News*'s move from Forty-second Street to Thirty-third Street.

Krenek had been a news editor, a job unique to newspapers. A bridge between the top editors and the city, national, and sports editors, the news editors determine the display of stories in the paper and lay out the pages on the computer. Good news editors bring energy and sparkle to each day's editions, and Debby was a crackerjack. But she lacked the vision, flair, and other skills to run a great metropolitan tabloid, and the permanent government quickly formed a protective carapace around her.

Even before I started the Sunday job, the paper seethed with speculation —on-target, as it turned out—that I was being groomed to take Krenek's job. Her minders did their best to impede my crew, mostly to protect her but also because they loved the paper and genuinely thought this Sunday edition was a terrible idea. I knew what they were up to, and I also knew I would prevail because Mort 'n' Fred were behind me and because I was as good an editorial infighter as they were.

Still, the *News* was treacherous territory for any newcomer no matter how experienced elsewhere. My appointment had hardly been announced before a thin envelope turned up in my morning mail (which usually appeared sometime during the afternoon). When I opened it, I found a one-sentence note from Michael Allen, one of the half dozen members of the existing Sunday staff I'd inherited. He was resigning to take a job with the Associated Press. Allen wasn't just any staffer; he was the only African-American (born in West Africa, as it happened) on the Sunday team. I was familiar with Allen's work only through a sheaf of clips he'd sent me, including an assignment to cover Nelson Mandela in South Africa.

The *News* had a dismal record of dealing with its African-American reporters, a group of whom had sued the paper in an ugly episode just a few years earlier. I certainly didn't want to begin my new job by losing the only black reporter on the Sunday staff. Nor could I trust the editors on the daily to give me a fair appraisal of Allen's work. So without consulting anyone, I called him in and talked him out of leaving the paper.

"I know we're going to do good work here," I told him, "and you should be part of it."

Afterward, I proudly passed the word that I had retrieved an African-American staffer who had set his mind on leaving the *News*.

Oh, God!" exclaimed one midlevel editor. "We had a chance to get rid of that guy and *you talked him out of it?* Now we'll be stuck with him forever."

It turned out that Allen was a mediocre reporter who was later to reward my good deed by suing me and the paper for racial discrimination. His ingenious argument: I was such a clever white racist devil that I talked him out of leaving the *News* not only to deprive him of the chance to advance his career at the AP but also to keep him at the paper so I could discriminate against him.

Finally, early in 1999, I made my first appearance in the paper's newsroom. Actually, the *News* occupied two chambers the size of airplane hangars on the third floor of the building. Coming off the elevators, you first entered the space used by the editorial-page writers, the small business department, and the endless desks of the feature staff. A left turn took you into an even vaster room filled by the news and sports departments and the news and copy desks. Because it was Saturday morning, the rooms were all but deserted, the desks and aisles overflowing with stacks of old newspapers and other detritus. Only a few souls were stirring under the only relic of the paper's glory days—the bronze-colored four-sided clock that had hung in the old city room on Forty-second Street. The only daylight came through the grime on the windows high up on the wall that ran the length of one side of the news room.

The scene wasn't colorful enough to be Dickensian, but it was depressing anyway. The first newsie I met was Lou Parajos, the Sunday news editor, who had worked for the paper since boyhood (and who, in the weird way of the world, knew my cousin Leonard, the gifted comic book illustrator, from summers in the Adirondacks). Eventually I found Bill Boyle, the Sunday editor who was moving over to a big job on the daily. Bill was a black Irishman who never wasted a word. Extraordinarily able and devoted to the paper, he coexisted with the permanent government but never joined it.

I'd brought along a small notebook to jot down insights about how the current Sunday edition was put out, but of course I never used it. Instead, I spent the long day trying to master the *News*'s computer system. All the copy could be found on it—if you knew how to look for it—edited and sent to its next destination. With the right clearances, you could even read a story as the reporter was writing it or the desk editing it. You could write—or rewrite—headlines and sit at the elbow of one of the art directors and design the front page. When the time came to do page one, I stood around respectfully and watched Boyle and Arthur Browne, the prime minister of the permanent government, work out the page. I finally got home drained but exhilarated. Forty-one years after I stepped into the *Post* city room, I could still feel the special appeal of newspaper work, so fundamental compared to the slick magazine work I'd mastered.

After another Saturday session, Boyle handed me the con, and I was the editor the *Sunday Daily News* in fact as well as on the masthead. The new Sunday paper made its debut, and it was a success. Both readers and advertisers liked the new coverage and the new feature sections.

I didn't have to wait long for a big story. Early on a Saturday morning in July, we got word that John F. Kennedy Jr., his wife, the beautiful Carolyn Bessette and her sister were overdue on a flight piloted by John to Martha's Vineyard. For the first time since *Newsweek*, I found myself running a big story for a big-time news publication. It was as if I'd never been away. With Parajos's help, we tore up the paper just hours before deadline, adding a sixteen-page wraparound section devoted to the Kennedy story. For the next edition, we increased the wrap to twenty-four pages and added sidebars on every conceivable angle, including the first published description of the small plane's "death spiral" into the sea. The photo staff found a color photo for the front page of JFK Jr. and Carolyn dressed formally and glowing with youthful glamour. The headline read simply

LOST

Relations between the people who ran the daily and the new Sunday crew were arctic at best. I had got Zuckerman to agree to appropriate salaries for Kramer and some of my other top editors, which made them among the highest paid people at the *News,* where some staffers hadn't gotten raises in years, a sure trigger for resentment. Daily staffers who worked with the new Sunday paper were treated like collaborators by the permanent government. I sent my deputy to the daily news meetings, where he was made to feel less welcome than a spy from the *Post*.

One morning, Ed Fay, another *News* lifer who functioned as the enforcer for the permanent government, strode into my office, sat down, and started berating me over some faux pas or other committed by one of my team. I tried to deflect Fay's onslaught as politely as I could, but finally I'd had enough. To throw him out of my office would have made a spectacle sure to be amplified with relish in the *Post* next day:

TURMOIL GRIPS
SUNDAY *SNOOZE*

So I simply got up and walked out, leaving Fay fulminating at my empty chair. Later that day—in a scene out of a bad novel—Eddie ambushed me at the urinal in one of the *News*'s smelly men's rooms. "You know what you are? You're a baby," he snarled at his trapped victim. I couldn't believe that the carousel I'd been riding for forty years had deposited me in this situation, but there I was.

* * *

However her allies behaved, Debby Krenek was professional enough in our dealings over schedules and office space. But even Debby let her fury show one Saturday afternoon in early September of my first year on the job. The daily staff had prepared an ambitious series to promote reading in the schools, and the kickoff piece was supposed to lead the Sunday paper. Late that afternoon at Arthur Ashe Stadium in Flushing, Serena Williams became the first African-American woman to win the U.S. Open—forty-one long years after Althea Gibson had won the tournament's predecessor, the U.S. Nationals.

This was surely the lead story for the *Sunday Daily News,* especially because the *News* has the most African-American readers of any New York paper. I chose a picture of a beaming Serena hoisting her trophy, and then designed page one. In the midst of it all, one of the desk assistants told me Debby was calling.

"Ed," she said, "I just heard you're making Serena the lead. What about the reading project?"

I explained that I had designed a prominent panel on page one touting the reading series, but that I was indeed leading the paper with Serena's triumph.

"You can't do that!" she sputtered. "You've got to do the reading project. It's our big effort."

I told her that I understood her feelings, but the decision was mine— and I was going with Serena. "You're making a big mistake," she said and hung up.

On Monday morning, her chief deputy, Arthur Browne, who was called "Chucky" around the paper after the horror movie character, handed me a two-page, single-spaced memo detailing the crimes against journalism and the *Daily News* I'd committed by going with Serena rather than the reading project. I thanked Arthur for his concern and told him we'd just have to agree to disagree.

The Sunday paper acquitted itself well on other big stories, including the seizure of Elian Gonzalez, the Cuban boy who was transferred by federal agents from his relatives in Miami to his father on the island.

One Saturday morning, I was awakened by a predawn call.

"Elian's been snatched," a crazed voice cried.

It wasn't a madman, but Tom Raftery, a legendary figure at the *News,* the only one working the midnight-to-8:00-AM lobster shift, whose job it was to monitor the wires and the police radio and alert the editors to big stories breaking when nobody else was around. With Raftery's timely heads-up, we were able to do another special wraparound section that easily outshone the *Post*.

But for all the talent and ingenuity invested in the new Sunday edition, the circulation needle hardly budged. Editorial flair was only one element in that battle, less important than price, effective distribution, and creative promotion of the paper.

Still, my stock kept rising. Finally, early in 2000, Mort called Debby to his office in the Boston Properties skyscraper at Lexington Avenue and Fifty-second Street. When he told her she was being replaced by me, so the story was told, she ran out of his office in tears.

Although I was the new editor and we'd done this dance before, making a contract with Mort was as excruciating as ever. It got so bad that when Zuckerman called my home one morning, Julie got on the phone before I could and told him off.

"Stop torturing Ed," she commanded.

That may have done the trick. The contract Tom Baer finally worked out with Zuckerman's chief in-house lawyer, Marty Krall, had very few wrinkles. I had contractual authority to hire, fire, or transfer the staff, except for my deputy, Michael Goodwin, whose editorial page staff had won the Pulitzer Prize in 1999. Zuckerman had picked Goodwin, and I couldn't touch him without Mort's approval.

The contract was about to be signed one afternoon. I was meeting with Krall and the president of the paper, a savvy and resourceful *News* veteran named Les Goodstein, when Zuckerman called on the speakerphone. At one point, I told Zuckerman I had to know what he was paying Goodwin since I was administering the editorial payroll. The request seemed reasonable enough, but Zuckerman exploded on the other end of the phone.

"Don't raise your voice to me," I said sharply.

When the call was over, Goodstein and Krall rushed to congratulate me for standing up to Zuckerman. It appeared that only Pete Hamill and I had the temerity to tell him to knock it off. The episode became a footnote in the oral tradition of the *Daily News* tribe.

20

ZUCKERMAN UNBOUND

SPENDING A YEAR AND A HALF editing the Sunday paper made it possible for me to succeed on the daily. I knew my way around the paper and all its arcane and sometimes antiquated processes, the computerized editing and typesetting systems, the nightmare printing plant across the Hudson that produced color reproduction plainly inferior to even the undergraduate *Daily News* at Yale. More important, I knew the strengths and frailties of the big *Daily News* staff, and many of them had come to know me a bit and to be reasonably comfortable with me as their boss. To strengthen that bond, my first step was one I had taken at *Newsweek, New York,* and *Esquire.* I asked every member of the staff from top editors to desk assistants to write me a memo telling me what they did, what they wanted to do, and how the paper could be improved.

As much for symbolism as for my own comfort, I had Krenek's office redone. Pete had worked in an adjoining drab cell of a conference room with a row of tiny windows high on the wall. "I used to have to call my wife to find out what the weather was," Pete told me. Debby had hunkered down in a dimly lit room off the newsroom with dingy walls and carpeting and drawn venetian blinds obscuring her view of the staff and their view of her. Indeed, most of the time, it was impossible to tell if anyone was inhabiting the editor's office. I had a glass wall installed facing the news room, painted the walls white, and amped up the lights.

"It looks like you're in a stage set," one of the desk editors remarked soon after I moved in.

Precisely.

Julie had never visited the *News* while I was doing the Sunday paper, but now she came to pick me up one evening when we were going to a screening in midtown.

"I had no idea it was so big," she said. "And you're in charge of all of this?"

Yes, I was. A lifetime after I first set foot in the *Post* city room, I was back putting out a daily paper. It was remarkable how little had changed. Of course, there was no composing room, no copy boys folding up copy books for the rewrite men to roll into their Underwoods, no spikes to impale galley proofs, no clattering AP machines spitting out bulletins. The news room was studded with computer screens and keyboards at which the reporters clicked away, and it was festooned with hanging TV sets on which CNN or Fox News or NY1 flickered throughout the day. Instead of dusty packets of clips from the morgue, reporters did their research on the *News's* computerized library system or on the Internet. Editors and staffers e-mailed each other even if they were sitting just a few desks apart.

Yet the essence was eerily the same. Newspaper work, especially on tabloids, is essentially a repetitious exercise in fitting what happens on any given day into a set of templates familiar to generations of readers—the runaway taxi in Times Square, the blameless black youth shot by a panicky cop, the "beloved" bodega owner killed in a robbery, the embezzling company controller, the lottery winner who keeps his job, the teenage TV star hooked on drugs, and on and on. Deconstructionists like to call these templates "scripts." The task is to determine which template best fits the new material, evaluate its appeal from sensational to commonplace, then assemble the results into an attractive package of headlines, photos, and text. The trick is to recognize the minor specifics that differentiate today's account about the teacher who seduces her fourteen-year-old pupil from last month's version of the same script, then make sure the fresh detail enlivens the new story.

Left alone, newspapers and magazines default to a middling energy level; what needs to be covered gets covered just well enough to get the job done without embarrassing anybody. The editor's job is constantly to prod the beast, goading the reporters to gather detail and making sure that what's mined finds its way into the edited story. Leads can always be better tuned, headlines punched up; it's an endless process of sharpening the material. If the reporter hasn't advanced the story—found or provoked the next development—the desk editors have to do the job. And if they don't, the top editors have to bounce the results back down the assembly line for retooling.

The job demands constant focus and an almost juvenile zest for finding fresh inspiration in familiar yarns. And it requires unerring vigilance: a sloppy caption, the misreading of a reference in the clips, a garbled quote, anything in the dozens of stories and gossip items in any day's tabloid can jump up and bite you in the ass, resulting in embarrassment or a lawsuit. At any hour, the editor must be alert to the fragmentary bulletin on the wires or on TV that can signal a big story that will require remaking not only page one but also most of the front of the paper before deadline. Big stories have a way of breaking at inconvenient times—late on Saturday night when the jumbo press run for the Sunday paper is almost done, on holidays when the paper is being put out by a skeleton staff, on days when the paper plans to lead with a major investigative or enterprise story that's been in the works for months.

Big stories—what Johnny Bott, my first city editor at the *Post,* liked to call "Class A stories"—are easy enough to recognize. The problem usually comes with the not-quite sensation, the 6 or 7 on a scale of 10. There's inevitably disagreement among the top editors on how to play the story, but the wisest course always is to go with the news. On Wall Street, they like to say, "The trend is your friend." On a newspaper, never fight the news.

News judgment is essential, of course, but the most important quality an editor can have is simply stamina, to keep focus and energy day after day, week after week, year after year. A big-town tabloid like the *News* publishes three or four editions 365 days a year. To function, it has to have orderly pro-cedures: planning meetings punctually at 11:00 AM and 3:00 every after-noon, smaller updating meetings after each deadline, regular weekly sessions to plan and schedule investigating and enterprise stories, and other meetings for the daily and Sunday feature sections. These meetings tend to become ritualized, with the participants sitting in the same seats, droning or racing through their schedules, making the same lame jokes. It can be hard to keep paying attention and disastrous not to.

Civilians may marvel at the way top editors can withstand the unrelenting pressure of big-time journalism, but they miss the point. The real challenge isn't pressure, it's boredom. Besides, the only people who get to do these jobs are those who long ago found that they can handle the pressure the way big-league hitters can handle ninety-five-mile-an-hour fastballs. It's not a char-acter trait, it's instinct.

I wasn't worried about managing the *News*'s 350 staffers. My real concern was managing one man—Mortimer Zuckerman. I'll always be grateful to

Zuckerman for bringing me back to journalism after my *Esquire* detour, but he turned out to be the most peculiar—and in many ways the worst—owner I ever worked for.

Most rich people who dabble in journalism self-consciously try to make their hobby publications shine. Why else bother with a paper like the *News*?; it was never going to turn much of a profit. The reward for a billionaire owner would come in giving the working people of New York a popular newspaper that told them what they needed to know and that entertained them at the same time, a worthy alternative to Murdoch's right-wing *Post*. There was even a financial rationale for building up the *News*: the bigger price a stronger paper would fetch if Zuckerman ever decided to sell out.

But from the start, Mort and his partner Drasner ran the paper their way. They got the *News* at a distress price, destroyed the editorial union, slashed the staff, and boasted of how much money they plowed back into the paper.

Despite all the turmoil over the years, the *News* staff still boasted many veterans, who were understandably shell-shocked by the time I moved into the main news room as the sixth editor in chief in the decade Zuckerman had owned the paper. Keeping track of the "doughfaces" who preceded Lincoln in the White House—Polk, Taylor, Fillmore, Pierce, and Buchanan—was nothing compared with tracking Mort's roster of top editors.

I had a clear enough understanding of how my career with Mort was likely to end, but I was determined to give him no provocation. I wasn't like the woman who marries a habitual drinker or philanderer and is convinced that, unlike all the other women, she can reform him. Still, I thought I had the smarts and the experience to avoid many of the potholes my predecessors had blundered into. Mort let everyone know how much he admired me, and many of my new subordinates testified that they'd never seen him show such respect for an editor.

The script played out faultlessly for most of my years at the paper. The news cooperated, of course. No editor of a New York daily ever had the cavalcade of big stories we covered during my time at the paper. The run started with the first Subway Series since 1956, the year the Yankees played the Brooklyn Dodgers. The 2000 World Series had hardly ended with the Yankees trouncing the Mets when the presidential election between

George Bush and Al Gore ended in a deadlock. Before the last hanging chad was retallied, the *News* published an amazing run of forty consecutive page-one stories culminating in a shot of a triumphant George W. Bush on December 14, 2000, over the headline

HAIL TO THE CHIEF

Then came September 11—the first attack by foreigners on the continental United States since the war of 1812 and the biggest single news event in the 375-year history of New York—followed by the war in Afghanistan and the invasion of Iraq.

I folded the Sunday paper back into the main operation and transferred Michael Kramer and several other key Sunday people to help me on the daily. Some of them had been shunted aside years ago by the old guard, so returning to a front-row seat at the morning and afternoon news meetings was sweet vindication for them. I offered Arthur Browne a key role, but he soon departed to join Debby Krenek at an Internet start-up devoted to pets and pet products. Ed Fay, who'd had that tantrum in my Sunday office eighteen months before, sniffed the new wind and decided to work with me. I welcomed him without even the faintest nod to his bad-old-days antics. Michael Goodwin, the former editorial page editor Mort had installed as my deputy, proved to have enormous energy, solid judgment, and a good touch in the news room. Miraculously, it seemed that the permanent government had finally been vanquished and a new day was dawning at the *News*.

Still, there was the pervasive refrain "That's the *Daily News*"—a lament sounded whenever something went wrong. I felt that some of my predecessors had shown weakness by blaming Zuckerman for their every problem or frustration, and I hated the defeatist ring of "That's the *Daily News*." I vowed to discourage both the bad-mouthing and the poor-mouthing.

Zuckerman had constrained his editors by managing the payroll and insisting on approval of routine editorial spending. My new contract gave me authority to administer the budget; we'd settle on an editorial figure and I was free to spend what I wanted on individual staffers, projects, or stories so long as I stayed within the overall number. How naïve I was! By ordering budget cuts and layoffs, Mort quickly reasserted his mastery over editorial spending.

I was in the job barely a year before the demands came for cuts. Over the next two years, Zuckerman imposed hiring freezes, wage freezes, and layoffs (buyouts was the euphemism). Goodwin and I had to produce "hit lists" of people we proposed to dispense with. Mort kibitzed these lists, adding up the projected savings and effectively insinuating himself into editorial staff decisions just like in the old days.

What made me wonder about the whole sad spectacle was that the paper was doing pretty well. Periodicals are cyclical businesses. The flush years are inevitably followed by leaner ones before advertising spending rebounds. You're winning the game if your ad revenue outpaces the competition on the upswing and drops less than your rivals or the industry average during a down cycle—and the *News* was doing fine by that standard. Compared to the *Post*'s $20-25 million annual losses, Mort's paper was a roaring business success.

There was a larger issue. Zuckerman had scored a windfall on the sale of *Fast Company*, a Boston-based business magazine in which he'd originally invested about $20 million. With its New Age management mantras and thousands of pages of New Economy advertising, *Fast Company* ballooned each month to the size of an old Sears catalog. When Zuckerman marveled at its success, I urged him to sell it. I'm sure that my advice had nothing to do with it, but, just as the dot.com bubble was bursting, Mort unloaded it on the German publishers Gruner & Jahr for an astounding $350 million or more.

It seemed to some of us that the payoff had made all of Zuckerman's media dabbling—the *Atlantic Monthly*, *U.S. News*, and the *Daily News*—a resounding financial success. Without feeling that he was draining his lucrative real estate development business, Boston Properties, Mort could nourish *U.S. News* in its competition with *Time* and *Newsweek*, and the *News* in its struggle with Murdoch and his deep pockets. Instead, Zuckerman sequestered the proceeds from *Fast Company* in a charitable trust.

* * *

On Tuesday morning, September 11, 2001, I was listening to WINS, New York's all-news radio station, while shaving, as I did every working morning. I was a 1010-WINS addict because, twenty-eight years before, the station had given me the first word about the start of the Yom Kippur War, when

Egypt and Syria sneak-attacked Israel on the holiest day of the Jewish cal-
endar. That 8:00 AM heads-up enabled me to switch *Newsweek*'s cover on a
Saturday morning, a coup in those days before satellite transmission and
other modern technological marvels.

About 8:45 AM on September 11, WINS carried a weird eyewitness
account of a small private plane striking one of the World Trade Center
towers. I immediately thought of the air force bomber that had smacked into
the Empire State Building when I was a boy—another oddity. I put down
my razor, stepped into the bedroom, and clicked on the TV. I barely got a
glimpse of the column of black smoke swirling from the top of the north
tower before the telephone rang, the start of the worst day in New York's history and the most demanding day in my life as an editor.

I was hustling to leave the house for the office when the second plane
struck. Just as on the Friday afternoon thirty-eight years before when John
Kennedy was assassinated, I had no emotional reaction at all to the news. I
recognized the horror, but all I could really think about was getting out the
paper—if we could publish a paper.

Even in the first minutes after the attack, traffic into Manhattan was
being frozen at the ten bridges and three tunnels that connect the island to
New Jersey and the other boroughs. Nearly all the *News*'s editorial staff lives
outside Manhattan, many in New Jersey or far out on Long Island. So the
first question was whether we'd be able to assemble a staff to work the story.
Then, of course, there was the printing plant, which was across the Hudson
in New Jersey. Would the printers, a quarrelsome and unreliable crew in the
best of times, show up for work on this dangerous day? And, if we managed
to get them a paper and they managed to print it, would the deliverymen,
another untrustworthy bunch, drive the bundles to the newsstands?

My first glimpse at the news room reassured me a bit. None of the
senior editors had managed to get in yet, but a deputy was standing like
Horatio at the city desk, clipboard in hand, directing the troops into
battle. Across the room, the photo editors were marshaling their staffers at
Ground Zero.

Over the next few hours, a remarkable number of reporters, editors, and
desk hands found their way to the office, many with remarkable stories of
talking their way past roadblocks or hitching rides with cops or firemen
headed for the scene. Not long after that, ghostly figures began stumbling in,

reporters and photographers coated with ashes from the cascade swirling from the collapsing twin towers. One photographer was hurled through the air and landed under a fire truck, shattering both his legs. But he managed to get his pictures to the paper.

It became clear enough that we'd be able to put together a special eighty-page edition free of ads, and that the telephone lines over which the materials would be transmitted to the printing plant were working. The word from Jersey was that enough printers were checking in to man the plant. A single 10:00 PM deadline was set. Once the plant started up, it would just keep running, with perhaps one small replate. If that schedule could be met, the *News* could publish more than a million papers, 300,000 more than on a normal Tuesday night.

But how, over the next seven or eight hours, were we going to report, write, edit, and lay out those eighty pages recording the biggest story of our lives? Sitting for a moment in my office, I thought of Stan Opotowsky, with his feet up on the desk at the *Post,* the Chesterfield King dangling from his lip, scribbling the story list for the rescue of the Nova Scotia miners so long ago. I would be like Stan and get it done.

The first task was to assemble a story list that would not only cover every aspect of the city's deadliest disaster, but blend in the Washington and foreign angles plus the on-scene accounts from the paper's star columnists and the illustrations that would show how the towers were struck and why they collapsed. But the key to publishing the issue was to lay out the pages before any of the stories were written and edited and the photographs chosen. The page designs would be simple—one story to a page or spread with bold headlines and big pictures. That way, the editors on the news desk could design the "shells" of the pages and order up the headline and caption specs before the material that would fill the shells was available. Once the text of a finished story cleared the copy desk, it could be dropped into the waiting page with a keystroke.

The photographs were the heart of it, particularly for a tabloid that billed itself for decades as "New York's picture newspaper." Here, the trick was to cull perhaps two dozen emblematic images from the thousands that were flooding in from the *News*'s own photographers and brave freelancers. Once the "selects" were chosen, a flow had to be determined so the pictures played off each other to achieve maximum impact.

Astonishingly, there were hardly any gruesome images, far fewer than produced by a routine suicide bombing in the Mideast. So many of the victims had been pulverized that I didn't see a single shot of a body. But there were two striking pictures that touched off a fervent debate among us. One was a long shot of one of the towers before it collapsed. Clearly visible in the air were the hurtling bodies of several victims who'd been driven to jump by the flames at their backs in their offices above the point of impact. The other was of a neatly severed hand on the ground; it looked like a discarded white glove. Some of my colleagues were queasy about printing either of the shots, but I was adamant. "If you're going to tell the story, you've got to tell the story," I said. I was thinking of the watchword of Stanley Walker, the celebrated Jazz Age city editor of the *Herald Tribune*: "Better to know the truth than not." After the paper came out, the use of those pictures stirred quite a storm, and I found myself defending my decision to media writers from as far from Ground Zero as Paris.

I had a very clear idea of what the *News*'s page one picture should be, but there was no sign of it in the stacks of photos piled up on the long table in the conference room. There were countless shots of the burning towers and of spectral survivors fleeing the scene coated in ash. But there was not a single picture of one of the jetliners approaching or striking one of the towers. There had been terror incidents before, including a car bomb beneath the same World Trade Center in 1993 that killed six people and injured a thousand. It was the use of jetliners as airborne bombs that distinguished this attack.

"That's the picture," I told the photo editors. "It's got to be out there somewhere."

The photo was the only missing element because I knew from the beginning what the page one wood had to be. With the same conviction I'd felt about Nixon's inevitable Watergate fall, I knew that the terrorist raid on the World Trade Center was more than simply an attack on America. It was the start of the next war.

By late afternoon, the story list had been locked in, most of the pictures had been picked, and the news editors were busy laying out the so-far empty pages. Everyone left the glass-tiled conference room, and I sat alone for a moment staring at a big painting of New York Harbor that had been taken from the *News*'s magnificent old headquarters, a scuffed relic of past grandeur. The precarious enormity of what we were undertaking finally hit and a morose conviction washed over me: *This paper is never going to come out.* But I also knew that even if I was ultimately right, the only thing to do was to act as if my premonition was wrong.

And then, miraculously, all the pieces fell into place. The adrenaline level was so high that even normally fumble-fingered reporters turned in crisp, vibrant copy. The *News's* rewrite men and women, part of a proud tradition of virtuosi dating to the Depression, churned out vivid accounts of the day's death, destruction, and unrivaled heroism. One, Corky Siemaszko, wrote a brief, tone-setting introduction, the tabloid equivalent of a news magazine violin. Pete Hamill, who had rejoined the paper to write for me despite his treatment by Zuckerman and Drasner, contributed a harrowing account of his escape from the Ground Zero maelstrom and his reunion with his wife amid the carnage. And a few hours before deadline, the image I'd conjured in my mind of the death plane and the tower materialized from one of the photo agencies.

IT'S WAR

screamed the red, page one headline superimposed on the photo—and we went to press.

Everyone exhaled. Then my premonition suddenly and sickeningly seemed to be coming true after all. The authorities had sealed off the Holland and Lincoln tunnels and the George Washington Bridge. The *News* was printing hundreds of thousands of papers, but with the western gateways to the city blocked, none of them would be delivered. Both the *Post* and the *Times* had printing plants within the five boroughs, so their delivery was assured. Now, it seemed, no one would see our paper but the people who put it out. At the last minute, someone got through to Governor George Pataki, who leads the port agency that runs the bridges and tunnels. Pataki gave the word to open the George Washington Bridge to the *News* trucks. Other trucks made the long loop north to the Tappan Zee Bridge that crosses the Hudson to Westchester and then sped down to the city.

More than 1.1 million copies of the *News* were sold on September 12, and 50,000 papers that got to newsstands late were sold the next day, along with more than 1 million copies of the Thursday *Daily News*.

In a rare free moment over the next few days, I went on the Web and looked at dozens of 9/11 front pages of newspapers across America and abroad. Remarkably few papers had held out for the iconic image of the plane approaching or ramming the tower, and none that I saw invoked the war that was soon to begin with the invasion of Afghanistan.

The 9/11 edition of the *News* was on a very short list for the Pulitzer Prize in spot news the following spring. In the final judging, the prize went to the *Wall Street Journal,* whose staff was literally blasted out of the paper's offices next to the twin towers. The *Journal* writers and editors somehow managed to reassemble in apartments around town and published their paper the next day, a miraculous journalistic feat. We hated to lose the prize, but all of us recognized that no one could top the *Journal*'s once-in-a-lifetime accomplishment.

These were great days for the paper. The staff regained its pride, and what had seemed a perpetual stream of blind-quote bitching from inside the *Daily News* to the *Post* and the *Village Voice* all but dried up. Over time, people woke up to the odd realization that the paper was in the grip of *orderliness.* The *Daily News* became a good place to work again and we had our pick of applicants, many from the *Post,* who wanted to join up. But, nearly out of sight, a fresh threat was developing.

For all its Murdoch pedigree, the *Post* was a pallid presence in the first year of the new millennium. The circulation had settled at around 470,000, barely two-thirds of the *News*'s. The *Post* was printed on antiquated presses that turned out murky black-and-white papers. It sometimes seemed more ink wound up on the readers' fingers than on the smudgy pages. And most of the old **TEDDY THE TOAST OF TEHRAN** pizzazz had subsided into a goofy sensationalism that lacked wit and snap. The *Post* was being edited by a bright woman named Xana Antunes, who plainly was under orders to make the paper more appealing to women (and, therefore, to department store advertisers). The *News* crushed the *Post* on 9/11 and everybody knew it.

Even before the Trade Center attack, Murdoch himself acknowledged the truth to me. I was standing on a Georgetown sidewalk after Katharine Graham's funeral in July 2001, when I ran into Rupert, who greeted me warmly. "You've certainly given us a wake-up call," he said with a smile that crinkled his eyes into slits.

The *Post* had actually been up and stirring for quite a while. Murdoch had invested $250 million in a state-of-the-art plant in the South Bronx just minutes from Manhattan and convenient to Brooklyn and Queens, where most tabloid readers live. Into the plant went the best color presses money could buy and a management crew that could make those presses sing. By early 2002 the *Post* was turning out 700–800,000 papers a day filled with dozens of color photos, graphics, and splashy color ads.

The *News,* too, had built a new plant in the midnineties, an operation masterminded by Drasner. Papers all over the U.S., Europe, Asia, and South America sparkled with color pictures, but Drasner was convinced that only color ads were important to newspaper readers. So Drasner ordered presses configured so that color ads could be printed in the middle and back of the paper. Editorial color was restricted to the front and back pages, the inside front and back covers, and orphan spots inside when no ads were sold for those pages.

Drasner had put the *Daily News* plant in Jersey, separated from its core readers by both the Hudson and the East rivers. The *News*'s circulation in Brooklyn and Queens could be decimated any morning by a flat tire or a fender bender in one of the tunnels.

The spectacular color was just a third of Murdoch's *Post* strategy. The unfortunate Xana Antunes was promptly replaced by a gruff Aussie named Col Allan, who'd edited Rupert's splashy *Sydney Morning Herald*. Allan was celebrated for, among other things, pissing in his office sink. He had been a Falstaff of sorts to Rupert's princeling son Lachlan, who was running the *Post* as a warm-up to inheriting the old man's throne. (Lachlan wasn't counting the days. "They'll have to carry me out," Rupert was fond of predicting in his seventies. Tired of waiting, Lachan quit in 2005.)

Allan didn't try to top **HEADLESS BODY IN TOPLESS BAR**, but he did bring his own kind of antipodean swagger to the paper. When a Vermont senator named Jim Jeffords defected from the Republicans, Allan proclaimed him **BENEDICT ARNOLD JEFFORDS**, prompting head-scratching by many *Post* readers who'd never heard of Jeffords or the Revolutionary war hero turned traitor. In the run-up to the invasion of Iraq, Allan proclaimed the antiwar French **WEASELS!** and portrayed two diplomats on page one of the *Post* with varmint heads.

In the summer of 2001, the *News* started a giveaway tabloid called the *Express* that was handed out after 3:00 in the afternoon by colorfully garbed hawkers outside train terminals and busy subway stations. *Express* was designed not only to keep other giveaway papers out of the market but also to nibble away at the *Post,* once an afternoon paper, which still sold a significant share of papers later in the day. Murdoch used the *Express* as an excuse to cut the price of the *Post* in half. The *Post* in all its color glory now cost just a quarter to the *News*'s 50 cents. Coupled with all sorts of near-giveaway home delivery deals, the newsstand price cut started the *Post* on a circulation spree. Unless the *News* made a dramatic countermove the *Post* was on track to pass Zuckerman in total circulation in the next few years.

I knew the *Post*'s moves would eventually drive Zuckerman crazy. Mort had always viewed the *Post* with a combustible mix of scorn and envy. He was constantly saying he didn't want his paper to try to out-*Post* the *Post.* Mort would sneer at Rupert's paper and insist he wanted nothing like it. Still, soon after he bought the *News,* Mort was so smitten by the *Post*'s style that he hired the *Post*'s top editorial troika and installed them over their *News* counterparts. It was a stunt right out of *Citizen Kane,* when Charlie buys the all-star lineup of the rival *Chronicle,* except that Kane's mercenaries made his *Examiner* formidable and Zuckerman's *Post*ies were dispatched in short order.

Mort's confusion about the direction of the paper meant the editor's office had a revolving door. He inherited Jim Willse, who had seen the paper through the Maxwell debacle, but soon cut him loose. Then came Lou Colasuonno and his *Post* posse, who lasted barely nine months. Zuckerman then brought in a British editor named Martin Dunn, who had worked briefly for Murdoch in Boston. When his contract ended after three years, Dunn headed back to London. Pete Hamill was next. Pete is one of the great newspapermen of our time, but he's more a writer than an editor. Hamill's only experience as an editor—five weeks running the *Post* when it was owned by a lunatic millionaire named Abe Hirschfeld and eight months running an English-language daily in Mexico City—is memorable mostly for a grotesque photo of the exuberant Abe planting a kiss smack on a stupefied Pete's lips.

Hamill had very clear ideas of what the *News* should be: an updated version of the paper immigrants like his parents began reading right off the boat. Today's newcomers—Dominicans and Bangladeshi, Nigerians and Taiwanese—were fundamentally no different from his family, he felt, except that not all of them spoke English. These people needed help and information, not celebrity fluff, a notion that inevitably put him at odds with Mort 'n' Fred. Pete also liked the literary tradition of newpapers. After all, hadn't Dickens in his day published serials in the London papers? Hamill's reincarnation of Dickens was Norman Mailer. At Zuckerman's suggestion, so Pete said, Mailer's brief life of Jesus, *The Gospel According to the Son: A Novel,* ran in daily installments. (Unlike the original, it was no circulation sensation.) Pete and Mort's fling was destined to end in bitterness, and it did in less than a year. Then Mort promoted and fired Debby Krenek.

Still, nothing really could quench Zuckerman's thirst for somehow injecting some of that *Post* sass into his pages. Now, Zuckerman was confronted each morning by his competitor's gaudy twenty-five-cent circus of performing weasels.

There were no outward signs of Mort's restlessness. But, like a dog that can hear a high-pitched whistle inaudible to humans, I could sense what was coming. Rupert himself turned up on Charlie Rose's TV show to talk about his global media company, News Corp. In passing, Murdoch told Rose that sooner rather than later the *Post* would reach its goal of passing the *News* in circulation.

Murdoch always says what he means and means what he says. If you examine all the quotes he's given over the years in interviews, speeches, and meetings with stock analysts, the remarkable thing is how straightforwardly he describes his problems and his objectives. Murdoch's version of spin is to talk plainly. I knew that the *Post's* circulation drive would inevitably cause a crisis at the *News*. By the time the *News* reacted to the threat, it might be too late to stave off the *Post's* triumph. Inexorably, pressure would fall on me and my colleagues to somehow jazz up the pages in a desperate bid to sell more papers each day, the equivalent of a Hail Mary pass in the dying seconds of a football game.

Zuckerman had suspended the sweepstakes giveaways that had been a staple of the *News's* circulation strategy when I joined the paper. The sweepstakes were expensive, and the readers drawn by the giveaway melted away when the contests ended. But sweepstakes did sell papers at crucial stages of the two periods each year when the Audit Bureau of Circulation measures sales.

Now, whatever it cost, the *News* had to gun its own circulation. Once the Murdochs realized the *News* would never let itself be outsold, they might abandon their multimillion-dollar circulation mania and the battle would shift to another front.

But nothing changed, and soon enough, I felt the first faint tremor. Staff moves at the paper were invariably telegraphed through leaks to other papers. Thus, *Daily News* folk learned of big steps affecting their careers by reading "Page Six" of the *Post* or the gossipy media coverage in the snarky *New York Observer*. Debby Krenek found out that she was a goner in a *Post* gossip item, which Zuckerman first denied.

Early in December 2002, the *Observer* came up with a report that Zuckerman was bringing back Arthur Browne, the prime minister of the old permanent government at the *News*, who had left the paper after my advent, first to join that pets Web site and then for *Bloomberg News*. Many *News* staffers considered the talented but abrasive and quirky Browne a scourge, and trembled at the prospect of his return.

Under my contract, Zuckerman couldn't hire Browne (except for the editorial page) without my approval, so I called him to find out what was going on. My call prompted an extraordinary call back from Zuckerman.

"You can tell the staff Arthur Browne isn't coming to the paper," said Mort, "and you can also tell them this: For as long as you can walk, even with a cane, you'll be my editor of the *Daily News*. You're a grown-up. I love working with you, and you're putting out a great paper. I would never bring in anyone without your approval. I ask only one thing. If you ever decide to hang 'em up, please give me enough warning."

I was stunned by this extravagance. Finally, I had the presence of mind to tell him that I was thrilled and gratified by his words, and that I wanted to keep at it for a long time. Knowing Mort, I also wrote a quick memo to my files memorializing his vote of confidence.

I was now sixty-five, and my contract was due to run out in sixteen months. I knew that I didn't want to work forever but certainly through the spring of 2005. Tom Baer, my lawyer, regularly spent the winter holidays in Aspen, where Mort always skied, so we agreed that if he ran into Zuckerman, he would tell him that I wanted to re-up for an additional year beyond the current contract.

Sure enough, Tom encountered Mort on the Aspen slopes. He told him how thrilled I was by his words and that after the new year we wanted to talk about extending the deal for an additional year on the same terms. One would have thought Zuckerman would have said, "Sure, we'll take care of it when we're all back in New York." Instead, he turned frosty and blew Tom off.

"I don't even know when Ed's contract ends," he said. "I'll have to look it up."

When Baer reported the conversation back to me, it was like that moment on a long flight when the plane almost imperceptibly begins its descent to the airport. I knew it was the beginning of the end, but we rationalized that perhaps Zuckerman didn't want even to think about business while on holiday. Tom would take it up again after the new year.

He did—and got the same brush-off. So I wasn't totally surprised a few months later when I was summoned to Zuckerman's office with my deputy, Michael Goodwin. Mort, it turned out, was armed with stacks of *Daily News* issues we'd put out during the Iraq War. Zuckerman wasn't concerned with the war coverage, which had been outstanding, especially for a paper with no foreign staff and a tiny Washington bureau. Instead, he proceeded to critique local stories, referring frequently to notes he—or someone—had scribbled all over the pages. This lead was dull and that headline was flat and why was this story two paragraphs longer than it ought to be?

Mort was always pushing for investigative reporting, long narrative pieces, and lots of shorts—and Goodwin and I had been extraordinarily attentive—but he'd never before critiqued the paper in this way. Patiently, I explained to him that these local stories were in the back pages of our Iraq War papers. Nearly all the editors' efforts had been focused on the war, and the local coverage during these couple of weeks had necessarily been an afterthought. And besides, everybody was reading the war coverage, which was selling on the newsstands.

Afterward, I realized how bizarre the episode had been. What had prompted this weird critique? Why had Mort had my deputy join me in his tutorial? What the hell was he getting at?

I decided I wasn't going to let it pass. The next day, I called Zuckerman for another appointment, this one for just the two of us. My script was simple enough, and I delivered it without strain or any real emotion. Just a few months ago, he'd told me he wanted me to be editor-for-life, but now a new tone had set in. I would only do the job if both he and I were happy with the results. If he wanted to replace me, he knew how to do it. But I would not work in an adversarial relationship with him.

I also told him that this was almost certainly my last big editorial job and, especially because of my *Esquire* experience, I wanted it to end on a positive note. I didn't want to be the pathetic target of kamikaze attacks in the *Post* until I was dumped. "Do you want me to be your editor or not?" I said bluntly. "If you do, we have to work together as we have in the past."

Mort smiled paternally and assured me that he indeed wanted me to be his editor. Much as I yearned to be reassured, I couldn't shake the conviction that Zuckerman would try to force me out, perhaps humiliating me so much that I'd have to quit, forfeiting the remaining year and more of my contract. I promised myself that, no matter what, I'd never quit.

* * *

Toward the end of June, Zuckerman called with a peculiar request. He wanted me to schedule a meeting with my half dozen top editors and their equivalents on the publishing side to hear a "presentation" about the paper by Iain Calder. Now, Calder was another of Zuckerman's shadow cabinet of whisperers. A Scotsman, he had spent his career in the U.S. at the National Enquirer, the supermarket tabloid that made its name with Elvis sightings and alien scoops. Calder, it turned out, had actually been slid into retirement years earlier as the paper evolved into a celebrity scandal sheet with a quick checkbook that produced exclusive—and often mostly true—stories. Most people thought of Calder as a hack, but Mort thought he was a tabloid genius. When I became Sunday editor, I'd gotten some suggestions from Calder, and when I took over as editor, I had to send each week's editions to his retirement home in Florida. Calder would dutifully send me memos with suggestions for sharpening up the coverage. Invariably, his notions were based on false premises or they were tone deaf or flat-out wrong, and after a couple of months, the Calder connection sputtered out.

But he obviously was still whispering to Zuckerman. It dawned on me that he'd probably supplied Mort with the scribbled script for his critique of the local coverage in the Iraq War papers. Now I was being asked to recruit the audience for a full-scale Calder critique of the paper for my subordinates and colleagues on the business side. Zuckerman couldn't have contrived a more degrading ordeal for me if he'd tried.

I had two choices. I could refuse to participate and thus risk being fired for insubordination and forfeit nearly nine months of salary. Or I could sit through the Calder tutorial and then decide what I had to do. I knew exactly what the Calder show would be like: the single most humiliating moment in a long career with its share of embarrassments. I determined that I would listen calmly to Calder and muzzle myself. There would be no defensive explanations.

When I showed up promptly at 9:00 AM in the conference room at Zuckerman's sleek Boston Properties office, the rest of the audience was already assembled. Thoughtfully, they'd left the seat just to the left of the head of the table for me. The empty chair facing me across the table was also vacant, left for Mort. After a few minutes, Zuckerman led Calder into the room.

Iain was pale and a little shaky. Mort might not have told him that he'd be presenting to the dozen top editorial and business executives of the paper. He sat down at the head of the table with a big pile of the *Daily News* and a typed script of sorts. His hands shook and his Scottish burr quavered as he launched into an introduction full of smarmy flattery for Zuckerman as a great newspaper publisher. He kept referring to the *Daily News* as "we" and "us." Finally, he opened the top paper in his stack and turned to a routine story about the Brooklyn district attorney who was getting after a couple of judges in a borough long famed for corruption on the bench.

"Now, Joe Hynes strikes me as a crusading D.A. in the tradition of Tum Dewey and Roody Giuliani," said Calder, sounding more like Sean Connery than he perhaps intended. "Why don't we get behind him and promote him in the paper, make him our guy?"

Suddenly, Bill Boyle, the no-bullshit enterprise editor, spoke up. "Because Joe Hynes is a hack," said Boyle.

"Oh, I didn't know that," said Calder.

Next, Calder found a story on a back page in another edition about a *Daily News* program offering free screening for prostate cancer to men around town. "Now this is our own program," said Calder. "Why are we relegating it to such puny placement? We should play it up big!"

Despite my vow, I couldn't resist. "Iain, that was the fifteenth story we've done on that program in the past two weeks," I said quietly. "We've had page one banners, special supplements inside the paper, you name it."

"Oh, I didn't know that," said Calder.

Then he found a story featured in a color box across the top of page one about a murder suspect in a New Jersey jail who had written to the *Daily News,* prompting a jailhouse visit from a reporter to whom he confessed killing a young woman.

"Instead of **YES, I KILLED HER**, why didn't you make the headline **I DRANK HER BLOOD**?" asked Calder.

"Well, Iain," another of my colleagues put in, "a lot of our readers look at
the paper over breakfast. We talked about it and decided that's not what we
wanted to stick in front of their noses at 7:00 AM."

"I see your point," said Calder.

It went on that way for another half hour or so, and finally Calder subsided.
Zuckerman ended the meeting with lavish praise for Calder's insights. "Following his lead could help the paper better connect with its readers," said Mort.

As I rose to go back to the office, Mort said, "Ed, can you stay and meet
with me for a few minutes?"

"No, I'm afraid I can't," I replied and headed for the exit.

The endgame didn't take long. Over the July 4 break, I'd suddenly had an
inspiration: I'd fire Zuckerman before he could fire me!

He was obviously trying to force my hand. Instead of quitting, I'd tell him
that I would retire from the paper when my contract ended in the spring.
That way, the pressure would be off. If he wanted to replace me earlier, that
would be fine. He could pay me off without any messy litigation.

Right after the holiday, I made another appointment with Mort. I
reminded him that back in November when he told me he wanted me to be
editor-for-life, he asked that I give him long warning if I even decided to
retire. He seemed surprised but not really shocked. He said he hoped I'd help
him with the transition to the next editor and asked if I'd accept some sort
of consulting role later. I said I might and we talked about the *News* for a
while before parting.

Inevitably, my decision started another complicated negotiation with
Mort and Marty Krall about how my retirement would be reported in the
paper. First Mort was against any announcement, then Krall brought him
around. I sent him a draft. Mort rewrote it to praise me. Finally, the story
ran. Rather than quieting things down, the news drove the *Post* into a frenzy
of lunatic speculation about who would succeed me.

The star prospect was a character named Steve Coz, who had just been
shoved aside as editor of the *National Enquirer*—Calder's old paper—
where he'd worked since graduating from Harvard. With Coz beating the
drum (and Calder likely whispering him on) the *Post* trumpeted his every
move. Coz was in New York to meet with Zuckerman! His wife was seen

on the West Side pricing apartments! Mort had offered Coz a contract! Some of these stories were illustrated with color photos of Coz looking demented.

The *Post*'s mischievous message was clear: Madman Mort was just desperate enough to hand his paper over to this character!

After a while, even Keith Kelly, the *Post*'s rambunctious media reporter, couldn't keep this nonsense going, and the succession at the *News* dropped out of the papers. But not for long. Just as it had happened before to so many Zuckerman editors, I got the word about my successor from another paper. The *New York Observer* called to say it was going to publish a story next day quoting Martin Dunn, the Brit who had edited the paper for three years in the midnineties, then went home when his contract ended. Dunn told the *Observer* he was coming back to run the paper as editorial director and would be arriving in a couple of weeks.

Typically, Zuckerman himself never told me about Dunn, although he must have been hatching the scheme for weeks. After a week or so, he sent me a lame e-mail thanking me for my work. I knew it was time to hop off the carousel and write a book.

21

THE BIG SCREW

DURING MY LAST WEEK at the *News,* various emissaries dropped by trying to tease out exactly when I was leaving. They hoped to stage a formal farewell in the news room, a ceremony that by tradition ends with the departing worthy striding out to an ovation from the staff. I know they genuinely wanted to give me an affectionate send-off, but I had another idea.

Without saying so out loud, and trying not to be pretentious, I wanted my departure to be a metaphor of the transience of the journalistic life: *One minute he was here and then he was gone.* So I said good-bye privately and individually to many people I worked with. Then, after the first edition closed on Thursday night of my last week, I simply strolled out of the building, never to return. Next morning, early arrivals in the newsroom could glimpse my assistant packing up my pictures and files through the big window in my office.

Dunn showed up the next week. He took the title of editorial director but was in all but name the editor of the paper. Not long afterward, Arthur Browne—the Old Guard stalwart Zuckerman told me wasn't coming back to the *News*—turned up as editor of Mort's editorial page. Later, there were more layoffs and an embarrassing snafu in the Scratch 'n' Match sweepstakes game: a typographical error by the company that was running the contest led thousands of *News* readers to believe that they were winners, many of them of the $100,000 top prize. When the mistake was announced, readers clutching their worthless winning game cards besieged the paper until Zuckerman, who was sailing his yacht off the Galapagos Islands when the storm hit the *News,* announced a $1 million drawing for the losing winners.

Eighteen months after I left, Zuckerman brought in yet another new editor, a Brit named Michael Cooke, who had run papers in Canada and

Chicago. Counting Dunn's two tours, Cooke was Mort's eighth editor in the dozen years he'd owned the paper, and the *Post* immediately dubbed him the Cookie Monster. (By the fall of 2005, boosted by out-of-town sales, the *Post* trailed the *News* by barely 26,000 copies a day, and was actually ahead if the cut-rate bulk sales to advertisers and others were deducted from each paper's paid circulation. Within a few weeks Cooke was gone.)

Whatever my travails, I had lasted longer than any of Zuckerman's other editors. And I took satisfaction of sorts in the knowledge that I had pretty accurately anticipated how my *Daily News* adventure was going to end, although the timing surprised me a bit.

Now, with time to reflect, I had an epiphany. I realized that I had become an editor from childhood for a simple reason: it was my way of bringing order to my life. From the start, I had sensed the frailty under my mother's radiant sheen; and I had feared that my father, for all his salesman's assurance, was an ineffectual figure in the world. I knew our finances were precarious, and people in the family were always coming down with dread diseases. Each time the telephone rang in our little apartment, it could herald disaster. And so I collected my stamps and coins, my miniature soldiers and replica cars. I always carried a charm, a rabbit's foot or silver dollar, in my pocket. At night, I'd stack my change, quarters at the bottom, then nickels, pennies, and dimes, heads up, oldest first. I was in control of my collections, if nothing else. And as an editor, I felt a degree of control over other things.

An editor's world—a school, a town, a metropolis, the country, or the globe itself—is arrayed for him each day . . . and he puts it in order. Journalists often feel that they are at the mercy of events, but it's actually the other way around. Nothing can happen that the editor ultimately can't tame by deciding its placement in the daily, weekly, or monthly cavalcade. Of course, the order created is faux, a formulaic construct that holds its shape no longer than the next edition. But there's genuine gratification in the false sense of tidiness a well-turned newspaper or magazine can induce.

The irony, of course, is that journalism is a disorderly, even a rowdy trade. The best way to understand it is as one of those huge strip-mining machines, essentially a big screw mounted on tank treads. It reams away at the vein of coal or ore until there's nothing left worth gouging and spews its harvest out behind. It is mindless and relentless, a perfect machine whose only purpose is to get all the good stuff.

Grasp the operation of the Big Screw and you're an expert on journalism, eligible to participate in those boring panel discussions and write soporific essays in journalism reviews.

Journalists will pursue President Bill Clinton's behavior with an intern as avidly as they went after Nixon on Watergate or Ronald Reagan's Iran-Contra disaster or Bush's Scooter Libby crack-up. They will zealously torment limousine liberal mayor Mike Bloomberg about his antismoking drive in New York just as they hound right-winger Rush Limbaugh about his pill-popping. Martha Stewart gets the full tabloid treatment about her greedy stock dump no less than Jack Welch, caught in a humiliating divorce row that exposed his ludicrous retirement prerequisites. None of these targets gets better treatment because of their perceived politics.

The Big Screw instinctively heads for what it craves: conflict, deceit, hypocrisy, greed, mendacity, violence, and vulnerability—the periodic table of news elements. And once the strip miner finds a mother lode, there is no stopping it. Typically, the machine is turned on by a thin rumor, a muzzy tip, an outright lie, but if something of substance lurks just beyond the surface, the Big Screw will inevitably find it.

Journalism is remorselessly efficient at detecting vulnerability. A good reporter can recognize fear in the voice on the phone. Or the hesitation that lasts a beat too long in answering an outwardly benign question. Or the glib answer that just slightly contradicts an earlier smooth reply.

In the *Alexandria Quartet,* Lawrence Durrell wrote about a journalist who always looked as if something was happening around the corner and he wasn't going to get there in time. But the real journalist is the one you know is going to ferret out something that you don't want known. Once such a reporter—or, more often, a pack of them—goes after you, nothing will save you. Big people in trouble turn to PR wizards whose "crisis counseling" is supposed to help them through the worst. But for all their savvy, these sorcerers rarely can help clients protect their secrets. Indeed, their advice invariably is to tell the truth contritely, make a splashy charitable contribution, and hope the press will get bored and turn on another unfortunate.

If politics is no safeguard against the Big Screw, then neither is being a journalist, even a distinguished one. The disaster at the *New York Times* touched off by Jayson Blair's depredations is proof enough. Journalism turned on Howell Raines and his hapless deputy, Gerald Boyd, with such manic enthusiasm that the *Times* stampeded itself into running an account of the Blair fiasco that filled four pages and verged on a parody of its own sense of self-importance. A few years later, the paper turned itself into a pretzel over Judy Miller, the "Miss Runamok" of the CIA leak scandal.

The Big Screw's hardware is driven by software of a sort. These are the narrative templates into which fresh events can be squeezed to provide a satisfyingly familiar story. An editor at *US* magazine I know once analyzed a year's worth of celebrity cover stories in rival *People* magazine and discovered, or so he thought, the archetypical story arc: Once on top, X fell into the gutter because of (1) drugs, (2) booze, (3) greed, (4) heartbreak, or (5) other, and now he/she is painfully scrambling back from despair.

Try as they might (and they don't really try all that hard), journalists can't help replaying these scripts: Martha Stewart's best friend ratting her out on her stock sale, a rich woman dying during a face-lift, a phony doctor who entombed a woman at his home in New Jersey after a botched operation, a Mafia daughter begging a federal judge to let her fiancé out of stir for a few days so they can be married in church, a badly burned fireman going home from the hospital amid cheering comrades, postmortem testimony about a chauffeur shotgunned to death by a pro basketball star, a murder-for-hire defendant who tried to enlist her mother and the mom's gay boyfriend in a scheme to beat up her husband. All these classic scripts were on offer in the *New York Post* in late winter 2004—in a single day's paper.

None of this is to suggest that journalism is incapable of giving readers important information or that the worst excesses shouldn't be discouraged. But having scrutinized newspapers, news and opinion magazines, and TV news for a half century, I can testify that the essential nature of journalism has barely evolved. Technology and taste have drastically improved the look of magazines and newspapers, and satellite transmission has revolutionized the presentation of TV news. And there is certainly more celebrity fluff. But the fundamentals—the attitudes that govern the craft—are remarkably constant. The Big Screw keeps on turning.

The editor riding the Big Screw labors in the fog of journalism. Available information is often fragmentary, contradictory, misleading, or simply wrong. Cloaked threats abound, often that the enemy—the competition— is about to break your big story. Subordinates can be brilliant, but they can also be craven or reckless, reliable with nothing much at stake, hopeless in crisis. Or they can have hidden agendas. It's easy to reach sound decisions and show good character when nothing much is at stake. Making the hard calls under pressure is the real test.

We are craftsmen, not professionals, no matter how many schools of journalism award however many graduate degrees. To be a journalist is to participate at a safe remove—except when covering a war—in the messy life of the times. For all the Arrows to Toyland, my long career in journalism was simply an education in the natural history of human fallibility and folly.

22

THE MARCH OF FOLLY

AS IT HAPPENED, FALLIBILITY and folly engulfed big-time journalism just as I stepped aside. The first wave had been the Jayson Blair fiasco at the *Times* in the spring of 2003, which we had covered aggressively while I was still running the *News*. Then Jack Kelley, the swashbuckling foreign correspondent for *USA Today*, turned out to have been piping stories for years. Then Dan Rather swallowed some dubious documents reporting that George Bush had been grounded by the Texas Air National Guard during the Vietnam War for blowing off his annual flight physical. Just a few months later, my old alma mater, *Newsweek*, had a source melt and was forced to retract an incendiary item about GI interrogators flushing a Koran down the toilet at Guantánamo Bay. The two top editors at the *Times*, the editor of *USA Today*, and a bunch of CBS News producers were buried in the rubble, and Rather was quickly shuffled out of the anchor chair he'd taken over from the beatified Walter Cronkite twenty-four years before. The *Newsweek* Wallendas survived by promising to do better next time.

Then, a federal investigation, demanded by the press, into the leaking of the identity of an obscure CIA analyst enmeshed the *Times*, the *Washington Post*, and *Time* in an intricate and infinitely embarrassing scandal involving the conduct of some of their star reporters. The mess finally engulfed the richest and most famous investigative reporter of all: the untouchable Bob Woodward.

This string of disasters touched off jubilation among conservatives, since most of the offenses took place at bulwarks of the liberal media, and prompted a torrent of hand-wringing, garment-rending analysis from journalism savants. Typically, most of the critiques missed the point.

In the cases of the Blair fiasco at the *Times* and the egregious episodes at

USA Today and the *CBS Evening News,* the people who ran the enterprises had simply been conned. And since every con depends on the mark's hunger for something—whether it's sex or riches or status—the fascinating question is what was it the sophisticated editors at these news operations craved so badly.

At the *Times,* the dirty little secret was that what Howell Raines and his deputy, Gerald Boyd, lusted for wasn't Jayson Blair's scoops but his success as an African-American reporter. Like most big-city newspapers, the *Times* has had indifferent success in finding, nurturing, and keeping minority reporters in a fiercely competitive and predominantly white newsroom. From the day Arthur Ochs Sulzberger Jr. succeeded his father as publisher of the *Times* in 1992, young Pinch put unrelenting pressure on his underlings to diversify the staff. It's said that at one point he even mandated that executive bonuses be calculated in part by the percentage of minority applicants managers wrangled when filling vacant jobs. The grail in such a crusade would be a young black reporter recruited by his editors and polished into a star.

Blair was certainly a likely candidate. A small, unprepossessing fellow, he'd been part of a minority intern program at the paper and had progressed to junior reporter. But he was relegated to fringe stuff, mostly churning out business briefs for the Metro section. The hyperkinetic PR man at the *News,* Ken Frydman, kept cultivating Blair, feeding him a steady diet of boost-the-*News,* slam-the-*Post* fodder. Blair was so receptive that I used to tease Frydman that Jayson was the one *Times* reporter Ken had in his pocket. That Frydman's "pocket pal" could metamorphose in a few months into a page-one scoopster with exclusive stories about the Beltway sniper case was astounding. But it certainly satisfied the need of Raines and Boyd, himself African-American, for a marquee black reporter, despite all the alarms he set off. I'm certain that had Blair been white—and thus not a trophy to display for Pinch Sulzberger—he would have been intercepted before he could disgrace the paper. So young Sulzberger's worthy ambition for his newspaper led directly to one of the most ignominious episodes in the long history of the *Times.*

The marks at *USA Today* lusted for status among their peers. The brainchild of Gannett's hard-charging Allen Neuharth, *USA Today* was ridiculed from its first issue in 1982 as *McPaper,* a colorful mélange of news items and fluff whose signature feature was a rainbow-hued weather map. Over the years, the paper did some ambitious enterprise reporting, especially in the aftermath of 9/11, and turned solidly profitable. Along with the *Wall Street Journal* and the *Times*, *USA Today* is a genuine national newspaper, but when Pulitzer season came round it was hardly mentioned in the same breath. Except when the byline read Jack Kelley.

Kelley had spent his entire twenty-one-year career at *USA Today* and had been nominated for Pulitzers five times by his editors. The judges made him a finalist for the prize in 2001, in part for an eyewitness story of a suicide bombing which turned out to be fabricated. By the time the paper's five-member investigative team got done vetting a fraction of the 720 stories Kelley filed for *USA Today* and grilling him, they concluded that "his journalistic sins were sweeping and substantial." Among Kelley's dubious achievements, according to the paper, were "accounts that he spent a night with Egyptian terrorists in 1997; met a vigilante Jewish settler named Avi Shapiro in 2001; watched a Pakistani student unfold a picture of the Sears Tower [in Chicago] and say, 'This one is mine,' in 2001; visited a suspected terrorist crossing point on the Pakistan-Afghanistan border in 2002; interviewed the daughter of an Iraqi general in 2003; [and] went on a high-speed hunt for Osama bin Laden in 2003."

Kelley's suspicious colleagues had been complaining about his work for years, but they'd got nowhere with the brass, who craved the journalistic gravitas—the sense that *USA Today* was a big-time enterprise—he so readily created for them.

Dan Rather and *60 Minutes II* craved a different kind of journalistic notice. For years, Rather had run a poor third in the evening news anchor race to Peter Jennings and Tom Brokaw, even though his network, CBS, routinely won the prime-time ratings competition with NBC, ABC, and Fox. Rather doubled as a "correspondent" for *60 Minutes II*, which had been spun off the original franchise despite creator Don Hewitt's warnings that standards would be diluted. *60 Minutes II* lagged in the ratings, so both the people who ran the spin-off and Rather himself needed a score. Nailing the president in the midst of his reelection campaign as a wartime malingerer would be a coup and a ratings bonanza.

The story of how Rather and his field producer fell for the suspect Air National Guard documents and stuck to their story was told in excruciating detail in the report of the investigation commissioned by CBS and run by

Richard Thornburgh, a former attorney general of the U.S., and Lou Boc-
cardi, the retired chief of the Associated Press. But buried in the 236-page
postmortem was a revelation ignored in the furor over the report that
exposed the depth of Rather & Company's hunger to be conned.

To authenticate the typewritten documents before the broadcast, Rather's
producer, Mary Mapes, consulted four experts, none a specialist in typewriters and typography. One of them managed to reproduce two of the
documents (supposedly typed on a 1960s IBM Selectric) almost exactly on
her computer using the Microsoft Word program. The spacing between the
letters—"kerning" to typographers—and those cute little subscripts—"19th"
and so forth—were faithfully replicated. This was powerful, if not irrefutable,
evidence the documents were at best re-creations and likely fabrications, a red
flag that would have caused any investigative reporter at the very least to keep
checking the story. The document specialist urged the CBS crew to consult
the leading authority, not on handwriting and signatures, but on typewriters
and typography, a New Yorker named Peter Tytell. A call was made to Tytell
on the day before the show, but he did not return it until the morning of the
disastrous broadcast, when he was told his services were not needed.

The day after Rather's bombshell burst, Tytell downloaded two of the
documents from the CBS News Web site and quickly concluded that they
had been typed in Times New Roman, a font available only on computers,
meaning the documents could not possibly be original versions of what
they purported to be. The day after that, Tytell broke the news to CBS
brass, but the network stuck to its defense of the broadcast for another ten
agonizing days.

Lusting for a score, Mapes and her team failed to pursue the one expert
who could have saved their jobs and reputations. Instead, she and Rather
broadcast the story and defended their report to the bitter end, taking *60
Minutes II* and both of them right over the cliff.

Journalistically, *Newsweek* was the least culpable in this sorry cavalcade, but
its blunder, too, was misunderstood in the inferno of recrimination that
engulfed the magazine. The *Newsweek* Koran story was actually a squib, a
short item in the upfront Periscope section. Periscope has been a *Newsweek*
staple for a half century or more. It was originally a compendium of scooplets
—exclusive, or supposedly exclusive, items designed to give the magazine and
its readers the sense of being insiders. The reality was otherwise. There was

never enough stuff to fill the section, and on closing day the editors routinely squeezed the bureaus, especially the Washington bureau, for "Peri" items, offering a bounty of $25 or $50 for each.

An item had to be about something or somebody vaguely important. It had to seem newsworthy, appear to be true, and essentially be uncheckable. A prototypical "Peri" item might read:

> Pentagon planners are about to sign off on a plan to relocate a battery of Titan missiles across Turkey so that the weapons can be targeting on Iran as well as the Soviet Union. The message won't be lost on the mullahs who rule Tehran.

Ben Bradlee, who was *Newsweek's* Washington bureau chief in the '60s, had no use for the section. "If the items are true, they deserve to be real stories in the magazine," he used to say. "If they're not true, they don't belong in *Newsweek* at all." But Periscope always turned up among the most popular features of the magazine in reader surveys, and it has survived to this day.

It's easy to understand how the *Newsweek* editors tumbled for the Koran item. It was about something important, it was newsworthy, and seemed to be true. It came from a government source who had proved trustworthy in the past, it jibed with earlier reports of Koran abuse at Guantánamo, and officials had not shot it down when *Newsweek* reporters ran it past them before publication. Best of all, the thrust of the item was essentially uncheckable: it reported that the incident would be mentioned in some upcoming military investigative report. Who knew when that would come out? If the report ultimately mentioned the episode, *Newsweek* could claim credit for a minor scoop. If not, who would remember?

Then *Newsweek* was caught in a textbook example of a truth editors live with every day: anything in the paper, even a tiny item, can jump up and bite you in the ass.

A Muslim demagogue used the Periscope squib to foment deadly riots. Pushing its own agenda, the White House decided to hammer the magazine for irresponsibility; and *Newsweek's* reliable source turned squishy. The resulting uproar focused on the fact that the magazine had used an anonymous source for the item. This, in turn, led to endless, ponderous debates on the vices and virtues of anonymous sourcing, as ingrained in American journalism as the adverb.

The fact that *Newsweek*'s source was anonymous was *irrelevant*. Had the item been attributed to "Deputy Assistant Undersecretary of the Army George McClellan," the result would have been the same once McClellan confessed he was no longer sure he knew what he was talking about. The problem was that the source welshed on his tip, not that he was nameless.

In a fetching irony, less than a month after the Koran fiasco, Deep Throat, the ultimate anonymous source in the annals of American journalism, outed himself in the ultimate pop journalism magazine, *Vanity Fair*. Throat turned out to be a retired FBI official named W. Mark Felt, who had mixed motives for leaking leads to Bob Woodward while Woodward and Carl Bernstein were hounding Richard Nixon over Watergate. Felt was trying to protect the agency from Nixon and also get back at the White House for passing him over for promotion after J. Edgar Hoover's death. His motive in coming forward now was to sell his story to raise college money for his grandchildren. Felt's coming out prompted the inevitable debate about whether he was a hero of democracy or a traitorous rat fink. But nothing could obscure the fact that journalism could never have toppled Nixon without an anonymous source.

Woodward had enjoyed an unblemished reputation from the day of Nixon's fall. Over the next thirty years, he turned himself into the most prolific and successful journalist in America, with a series of insider books on everything from the death of John Belushi to the secrets of the Supreme Court. Technically, he was an assistant managing editor of the *Washington Post,* but he rarely came to the news room. Instead, working with his own staff of researchers on a floor of his big house in Georgetown, he produced a blockbuster book every couple of years, with key chapters appearing first in his newspaper. During the second Bush presidency, Woodward became the adminstration's designated chronicler, first with the post-9/11 *Bush at War* and then with *Plan of Attack,* the story of what was supposed to be the cakewalk to victory in Iraq.

The flap over the leaked identity of Valerie Plame, the CIA operative, showed journalists at their worst—at once sanctimonious and craven. And it became a surrogate for the sharper-edged issues of whether the Bush administration had misled the country into the Iraq War and whether the press had heedlessly bought the Bush line that Saddam Hussein had weapons of mass destruction threatening the U.S. and his neighbors.

Plame was the wife of Joseph Wilson, a onetime U.S. diplomat in Africa, who, at his wife's suggestion, was sent by the CIA to Chad to look into claims that Saddam had tried to buy nuclear materials there, reports cited by Bush in the run-up to the war. On his return, Wilson discredited the Bush claims in an op-ed piece in the *Times*. Soon afterward, some of the Bushies pushed back, gossiping to reporters that Wilson's wife had gotten him the Chad gig, and thus, inadvertently or not, identifying her as an agency operative. Among the recipients of the leaks was one of the *Times*'s stars, Judith Miller, an aggressive, opinionated investigative reporter who specialized in terrorism stories. Miller was close to a number of administration hawks and had done a series of brink-of-war pieces on WMDs in Iraq that the paper later had to disavow when none were found.

The federal special prosecutor investigating the Plame affair pressed Miller and others who got leaks to testify but they refused to disclose their sources. Then Bush ordered his people to waive confidentiality and free the reporters to speak up. This was good enough for Matt Cooper of *Time*, Tim Russert of NBC, and others, but not for Miller, who maintained that the releases were coerced. She vowed to go to jail rather than burn her source—who turned out to be Lewis "Scooter" Libby, a top aide to Vice President Cheney—and Pinch Sulzberger threw the authority of the *Times* behind her, prompting the paper to run more than a dozen editorials backing Miller as a heroine of principled journalism.

Miller was no heroine to many in the *Times* news room, who resented her pushy style, her closeness to powerful male editors (including Howell Raines before his fall), and her defective prewar WMD stories. With much fanfare, Miller went off to jail. But after a couple of months of eating gruel and sleeping on a skinny foam mattress, she had her lawyer reopen talks with Libby. Lo and behold, Scooter granted another waiver of confidentiality remarkably like the one Miller had spurned a few months earlier. But this time she snatched it and trotted over to the grand jury after a martini and steak laid on by a beaming Sulzberger.

A few weeks later, she suddenly discovered one of her notebooks and returned to the grand jury for more testimony. By now, relations between the quondam heroine and her paper had turned toxic. The *Times* prepared a long account of the case, but Miller refused to answer many questions from reporters from her own paper or share her notes. And she contributed a long personal account that raised more questions than it answered. Eventually the special prosecutor indicted Libby, not for violating any secrecy statutes in naming Plame—because he hadn't—but for telling too many different versions of his story to the grand jury. Miller resigned from the paper under a pall of bad feeling and worse suspicions from her ex-colleagues.

A key element in the case against Libby was that he was the first to identify Valerie Plame, who technically worked under cover although her name appeared in her husband's *Who's Who* entry and she'd posed for a picture for a *Vanity Fair* piece on him. All during the investigation, Bob Woodward turned up often on Larry King's TV show to hold forth on the case. (As it happened, he didn't think much of it.) Then, months after Libby's indictment and Miller's resignation, Woodward suddenly came forward and rather sheepishly admitted that he'd gotten a Plame leak from an administration official even before Scooter had whispered the magic words to Judy Miller. Woodward not only had neglected to tell the special prosecutor about this wrinkle in the case, he hadn't mentioned it to Larry King's viewers, the readers of his newspaper, or even, until recently, his editor at the *Washington Post,* Len Downie. He said he had thought it was all just Beltway gossiping.

So in barely two years, the *New York Times,* the *Washington Post, USA Today, Newsweek,* and CBS News, along with Howell Raines, Gerald Boyd, Judy Miller, Dan Rather, and even Bob Woodward—some of the greatest institutions and leading figures of the American press—all had their reputations tainted and their stars tarnished. Journalistic scandals are cyclical—both the *Times* and the *Washington Post* had been burned before—but this latest flare-up was either a colossal run of bad luck or the symptom of something much more serious, a malady deep in the bones of American journalism.

Indeed, it can be argued that the glamorization of Bob Woodward and Carl Bernstein—Woodstein, as they were called—was the first step down the path American journalism finds itself on today. Throughout most of my long career, it never occurred to me or my colleagues that what we did was glamorous, sexy, or even remotely interesting to civilians, to nonjournalists.

Stories about journalists and journalism were always among the least read in newspapers and magazines. When I first met Rupert Murdoch in 1977, not long after I'd put him on the cover of *Newsweek,* he said, "I'll bet that was one of the worst-selling covers ever." And he was right.

But a fairy-tale transformation turned bug-eyed frogs into handsome princes and gorgeous princesses. Here was stolid, dough-faced Bob Woodward up on the big screen in Hollywood's version of *All the President's Men* played by Robert Redford, and scruffy Carl Bernstein incarnated by Dustin Hoffman. (Bernstein has the distinction of being portrayed by two of America's greatest stars; Jack Nicholson was Carl in the movie made of Nora Ephron's tale of their marriage, titled *Heartburn.)* After that, television took over. Soon newspaper and magazine journalists started turning up not only on Sunday morning public-affairs shows like *Face the Nation* but also all over cable news and on *Entertainment Tonight.* Now, a whole subset of the Internet is filled with media-obsessed bloggers, who gossip and critique newspaper columnists and other inkies as if they were movie stars. And there is the deification and demonization of women editors like Tina Brown (who had her own cable show for a while) and Anna Wintour of *Vogue,* the focus of the chick-lit best seller *The Devil Wore Prada* that was leveraged into a movie starring Meryl Streep.

Given all that, it's no wonder journalists and their editors feel they're competing in a new world that often feels more like show business than news business. The main imperative for performers is to get noticed and stay top-of-mind. Journalists increasingly recognize the same pressures and act accordingly.

But the fundamental cause of the crisis of confidence gripping mainstream journalism today is technological. The scope and ingenuity of the Internet have turned much of the news and information peddled by newspapers and magazines into a commodity. Every Internet portal gives the user an instantly updated headline digest plus all sorts of financial and lifestyle giblets every time he or she logs on or refreshes the page. Cable news does the same twenty-four-hours a day and supplies an endless parade of opinionated analysts and blowhards. So does news and talk radio. Every day, more bloggers chip in more information and misinformation. ("Opinions are like assholes, everybody's got one," one of my old city editors used to say dismissively. But today, assholes with opinions are the stars of the "blogo-sphere.") One can easily spend a few minutes at the computer monitor a few times a day and stay up on the basic elements and nuances of the day's news without ever looking at a newspaper, which is precisely what a growing number of younger people do.

How does a prosaic newspaper or magazine get noticed in such an envi-ronment? By calling attention to itself with exciting scoops and other dra-matic coups and by packaging the goods with brassy flair—journalism as entertainment. The masters of this kind of stuff have long been trained on London's Fleet Street and its outposts in Australia. So it makes sense that Americans increasingly find Brits and Aussies putting out their favorite papers and magazines. Murdoch started it when he bought the *New York Post* and staffed it with his minions. Then Si Newhouse imported Tina Brown and poached Anna Wintour from me at *New York*. And when Tina left *Vanity Fair* for the *New Yorker*, Newhouse replaced her with Graydon Carter, a Canadian who affects the look and manners of a British toff. My two successors editing the *Daily News*, "New York's Hometown Paper," were Brits.

British editors bring distinct craft and a different sensibility to American publications. But they can't really be expected to reverse the trend that's run-ning against American newspapers and magazines. "They're really cosmeti-cians at the mortuary," one old editor remarked to me the other day.

If American newspapers and news magazines falter, the consequences will be profound and dangerous. Because the truth—known to everyone in jour-nalism, whether they admit it or not—is that nearly all the reporting done in American journalism is done by newspapers and a handful of magazines and the Associated Press. Radio, TV network and local news, the morning shows like *Today*, the TV magazine shows, cable TV news, and the bloggers get their leads, ideas, and much of the detail they broadcast from newspa-pers. Thin as most broadcast news is today, it would be unimaginably flim-sier without the foundation print journalism provides. Scant as it may be, investigative journalism, particularly local, would all but disappear.

What to do? The Next Big Thing in newspapers is already happening in London, where most of the broadsheet papers have morphed into tabloid size. Trying to differentiate themselves from the gaudy tabloid *Sun* and *Mirror*, the "quality" papers call themselves "compacts," a euphemism that can't disguise the truth. The venerable *Guardian* has spent a ransom converting into a slightly slimmer and longer tabloid format borrowed from some German papers. Most of the great American provincial newspapers are broadsheets, among them the *Washington Post*, the *Chicago Tribune*, the *Los Angeles Times*, the *Dallas Morning News*, the *Boston Globe*, and the *San Francisco Chronicle*. All are struggling to hold onto circulation, and the itch to convert is likely to intensify over the next several years, although the sheer bulk of advertising in American papers complicates the decision. In the fall of 2005, the *Wall Street Journal* turned its European and Asian editions into compacts.

But even such radical steps won't solve the fundamental problem: the older readers are dying off and the younger ones are glued to their computer keyboards. The *Times* and some other metro papers attract millions of online visitors to their Web editions. But none of them except the *Wall Street Journal* can get many online readers to pay. With its specialized content, the *Journal* has signed up hundreds of thousands of paying subscribers to its Web edition. The other papers are unlikely to be able to follow suit however hard they try and however little they charge.

Few people recognize it, but the red state-blue state divide of the Bush years and the almost theocratic tone of politics and policy discussion contribute to the slackening interest in conventional, noncelebrity, noncrime news. The underlying rationale for readers to follow news about politics and national and local issues is so that they can make informed judgments on election day. But Bush and his followers—and to some extent his liberal Democratic opponents—seem to make their decisions based mostly on dogma and doctrine. On issues ranging from the war in Iraq to abortion, fetal stem cell research to private Social Security accounts, religious considerations and free-market theology call the shots. What's the point of mastering the intricacies of Social Security reform or the merits of fetal stem cells versus adult ones in the papers if leaders are deciding these questions like medieval scholastics counting angels on pinheads? Readers understand this and skip to the TV listings.

The political climate will likely change, but not the trend running against newspapers and general-interest magazines. Still, the automobile never quite killed off the railroads, although it drastically changed their economic role. Both radio and the movies managed to adapt to rampant television. So it stands to reason that print journalism in some hybrid form will survive the Internet. But the troubles of the last few years plainly foreshadow what's in store for journalism.

Slowly but inevitably, print journalism will become a medium for the educated elite, who need and use accurate information and informed opinion. The rest will get their news bulletins from radio, TV, cell phones, and the Yahoo home page. For the same reason, the evening news on TV will be shunted from the networks to cable, where it can serve its niche audience.

I never expected to end the story of a life devoted to print journalism on such a lugubrious note, but the signs are all pointing in the same direction. As Stanley Walker liked to say, "Better to know the truth than not."

ARROWS TO TOYLAND

NOT LONG AFTER I retired, I was invited to give the commencement speech at my alma mater, the Bronx High School of Science. I knew the graduates were too sophisticated for the usual follow-your-bliss, reach-for-the-stars Polonius harangue, so I decided to offer them some hard-won advice rummaged from my mixed bag of a career—to give them my own Arrows to Toyland. Modified a bit, here they are:

Before you're important, conduct yourself as if you are, because someday you will be.
Dress with care, think clearly, and try to express yourself with wit and precision. The woman or man you will become is already there just waiting to emerge.

Treat each task—no matter how trivial—as if it matters, because it does.
Or a task just like it in the future will turn out to matter a lot.

Always be on time—for work, for appointments, for anything.
Geniuses can get away with keeping other people waiting; the rest of us can't.

Never miss work because you feel sick, unless you literally can't pick your head off the pillow.
Take two Advils and get going.

Don't lie. And always admit when you don't know the facts or the answer.
"I don't know, but I'll find out" is what to say.

*Never do or say anything that you can't bear reading about on the front
page of the* New York Times—*or the* Post, *for that matter.*
Never write anything in a memo—and especially an e-mail—that
couldn't be published without embarrassing you. When you have sensitive
things that must be said, say them face-to-face. If you don't trust the person
you have to tell it to, keep it to yourself.

*Never leave the payroll sheets—or your income-tax return—in the office
Xerox machine.*

*Actions matter more than motives, and actions are more important than
the process that leads to the action.*
Getting it right is the most important thing.

*No matter what people tell you, many decisions don't have to be made—
and shouldn't be made—until the last moment.*
If you wait long enough, many problems solve themselves. When people
pressure you, remember there is almost always a little more time to tease out
the right thing to do.

*Develop a small circle of people whose judgment you trust to help you
make close decisions.*
The group should be a blend of bold and cautious thinkers with a lawyer
in the mix and a common denominator: high analytical intelligence. I assembled such groups at every publication I edited. If you let the discussion run its
course, such groups will invariably identify the weakness and danger of any
proposed course of action. Like focus groups, such ex-coms won't infallibly tell
you what course to take, but they will always steer you away from the rocks.

*When you've made a hard decision—to take a job or quit a job, to stay with
this person or not, to buy a house, to hire someone for an important job, to
change careers—judge it by how you feel when you wake up the next morning.*
If you feel buoyant, even if tingly with anxiety, you've made the right
choice. If you feel heavy with foreboding, you've made the wrong decision.
If you've made a mistake, don't be too proud or embarrassed to change your
mind. The most important thing is getting it right.

Over a long career, you're sure to suffer betrayals—and petty slights—by bosses, colleagues, and subordinates, some by people whose careers you nurtured. Don't take it personally.

At *New York* magazine, the twin doors to my office were almost always opened to the news room, and staffers knew that they could drop by to talk about anything at any time. When I left for *Esquire,* one of my deputies who hoped to succeed me planted himself at a desk right outside my empty office and bragged to the *New York Observer* that he was demonstrating how accessible he was to the staff. He didn't get the job. When I was fired from *Esquire,* another of my deputies who lusted for glory plunked himself in my seat less than an hour after I'd vacated the chair and started giving orders to the staff. He didn't get the job either.

Julie was infuriated by these careerist gambits, but I laughed them off. In fact, I was famous for forgetting all sorts of slights and stunts that should have offended me. That's baseball, as the players like to say when something goes wrong.

Finally, and most importantly, understand and respect the role that chance plays in our lives and careers.

This is a sensitive one because all of us like to think of ourselves as purposeful creatures moving surely and inevitably toward our goals. But, in fact, the world is full of connections invisible to us that play a profound role in our destinies.

People often get jobs not because they're more qualified than dozens of other applicants but because they happen to have an interview on the day that somebody else quits, creating an opening.

A man and a woman never meet, until one night in a bar downtown they are introduced by friends who have no idea the two live in the same apartment building. They fall in love and marry.

Years after you've encountered a man or a woman, he or she is instrumental in helping or harming your career, and you don't learn about it until much later.

More than we'd like to admit, these hidden links shape our lives every day. The trick is to be able to capitalize on chance and survive mischance.

If you do, you might last long enough to write a memoir.

ACKNOWLEDGMENTS

Just as an editor at *Newsweek* once unfroze my fingers on a pesky cover story by saying, "Relax, kid, it's only a twenty-five cent magazine," my wife, Julie Baumgold, said the magic words when I was dithering over this book. "Just write it for your children," she said. If Julie is the book's godmother, my old colleague and friend Pete Hamill is the godfather—a meticulous editor as generous with encouragement as he is with his time and talent.

Other friends and former colleagues—Tom Baer, Jack Schwartz, Richard Babcock, Peter Goldman, and David Hirshey—read the manuscript for accuracy, fairness, and fidelity to what we experienced together. And my smart and beautiful daughter, Lily, offered the most cogent and unsparing critique of the text. For all their efforts, any errors or inadequacies are mine alone.

My gratitude also goes to Amanda Urban, who wouldn't stop until she found a home for the book, and to John Oakes, who provided it.

Amelia Island, Florida
March 2006

INDEX

20/20, 199–201, 252

The $64,000 Question, 75

A

ABC News, 190, 199

ABC Sports, 190

abortion, 121

Adams, Frank S., 80, 85–86

Adams, Joey, 213

agoraphobia, 151

Agrest, Susan, 205–6

AIDS, 214

Albee, Edward, 116

Alexander, Bernie, 12–13

Alexandria Quartet, 303

Ali, Muhammad, 229

Alien, 196

All the President's Men, 173, 315

Allan, Col, 292–295

Allen & Co., 238

Allen, Jenny, 219

Allen, Michael, 276

Allen, Tim, 261

Allen, Woody, 187, 260

Allison, Fran, 52

Alsop, Joseph, 148, 187–88

Alsop, Stewart, 130

Alzheimer's disease, 151, 255

The American Dream, 116

Ancier, Garth, 234

Annenberg, Walter, 237

Antunes, Xana, 293–294

Arledge, Roone, 190, 199–200

Armstrong, Joe, 203, 205, 206

Aronowitz, Alfred G., 93–94, 106

Assad, Hafez, 163

Atkinson, Brooks, 80

Atlantic Monthly, 223, 225, 286

Auchincloss, Ken, 185

Auletta, Ken, 226

The Australian, 208

Automobile, 237

B

Babcock, Dick, 254

Baden, Meyer (Michael), 65

Baer, Tom, 57, 179, 204, 225, 238, 253, 274, 280, 295–6

Bahrenburg, Claeys, 251, 253, 257, 265

Baldwin, Hanson, 80

Baltimore Sun, 122

bar mitzvah, 17–19

Barry, Jack, 76

baseball cards, 19, 41–42

Baumgold, Julie. *See* Kosner, Julie Baumgold

Beame, Abe, 114

the Beatles, 106

Beene, Geoffrey, 248

Bellow, Saul, 169–170, 260

Bennack, Frank, 252, 254, 265

Berendt, John, 203

Bergdorf Goodman, 236

Bergen Evening Record, 87–88

Berger, Meyer, 80

Bernstein, Carl, 173–74, 312, 318–19

Bernstein, Lester, 125–27, 131, 137, 153, 197, 268

Bernstein, Ted, 81

Bessette, Carolyn, 277–78

bipolar disorder, 151

Black and White Ball, 161

Black, Cathie, 218, 265, 271

Black, Roger, 206, 258

Blair, Jayson, 303–304, 307–308

Blanco-Fombona, Lourdes, 128

Blany, Shirlie, 115–16

Bloomberg, Mike, 303

Bloomingdale's, 209–210

Blum, David, 214

Blythe, Will, 266–267

Bott, Johnny, 104, 283

Boyd, Gerald, 304, 308, 314

Boyle, Bill, 277, 298

Bracker, Milton, 80, 88

Bradlee, Ben, 139–40, 144, 154–155, 161, 188, 191–192, 311

Brady, Jim, 203

Brenner, Marie, 213, 219, 249

Brinkley, William, 131

Brokaw, Tom, 309

Bronx Home News, 85

Brooklyn Eagle, 85

Brophy, Daniel, 67

Brothers, Joyce, 75

Brown, Tina, 239, 242–45, 254, 268, 273, 315–316

Browne, Arthur, 277, 279, 285, 295, 301

Bruno, Hal, 127

Bryant, Nelson, 115

Burden, Carter, 178–79

Burstein, Larry, 233, 261

Bush at War, 312

Bush, George, 285, 307, 312

Bushnell, Candace, 260

Butterfield, Alexander, 156

C

Calder, Iain, 297–299

Calloway, Cab, 34

Campbell, Bob, 176

The Campus, 62–68, 75–84, 88

Cannon, Jimmy, 93, 141

Capote, Truman, 161

Capron, Paul, 93

Carey, Hugh, 211

The Carolina Israelite, 94

Carr, William H.A., 93, 95–96, 101

Carroll, John, 108

Carson, Rachel, 26

Carter, Graydon, 316

Carter, Jimmy, 125, 231

Casa Johnny, 27

Casotto, Robert, 56

Catcher in the Rye, 116

CBS magazine group, 201

Chao, Stephen, 234

Chappell, Russ, 126

Cheever, John, 254

Chicago magazine, 254

Chomanan, Kriangsak, 184

The Chronicle, 122–123

Chrysler, 266–67

Church, Millicent, 67–68

City College of New York, 58–68, 75–84

Clift, Brooks, 125

Clift, Eleanor Roeloffs, 125

Clinton, Bill, 227, 246, 260, 264–65, 303

Clurman, Dick, 198

Cockburn, Alex, 214

Cohen, Bobby, 249

Cohen, Claudia, 249

Cohen, Elliot, 26

Cohen, Selda. See Levin, Selda Fisher

Cohen, Walter, 28–29

Cohn, Roy, 212–13

Colasuonno, Lou, 293

college, 57–69, 72

Collins, Nancy, 192

Collins, William, 237

Columbia, 57–58

Commentary, 26

communism, 106

Conde Nast, 243

Conde Nast Traveler, 273

Cook, Bill, 135

Cooke, Michael, 301

Cooper, Art, 267

Cooper, D.B., 134–36, 221

Cooper, Matt, 313

Cops, 234

Cox, Archibald, 155

Cox, Tricia Nixon, 157–58

Cox, Wally, 232

Coz, Steve, 299

Crawford, Cindy, 260

Creatures of Habit, 250

Crewdson, John, 108–9

Cronkite, Walter, 138, 200–1, 307

Cruise, Tom, 259

Cue, 205, 209

Curtis, Charlotte, 104–5

D

D-head, 80–81

Daily Mirror, 85

Daily News, 85, 249, 281, 285, 298–302

Daly, Michael, 211, 214, 218, 254

Darin, Bobby, 56

Davis, Alvin, 88–89, 92, 94, 98, 101, 107–08, 112

Davis, Milton, 24

A Day in the Life of America, 218

de Borchgrave, Arnaud, 128, 162–63

de Menil, Francois, 257

Dean, John, 156–57

DiCaprio, Leonardo, 262

Deep Throat, 312

Dehornois, Jacques, 216

Denson crop, 133

Denson, John, 133

Derow, Peter, 179, 195–196

DeSapio, Carmine, 213

designers, 262

The Devil Wore Prada, 215, 315

Dewey, Thomas, 137, 147, 298

Diamond, Ed, 153–54

Diffie, Bailey, 75

Diller, Barry, 234

divorce, 29, 192

Dog World, 241

Dollygrams, 113

Dombrow, Oscar, 50, 53

Downie, Len, 314

Downs, Hugh, 199

Doyle brothers, 97–98

the draft, 117

Drasner, Fred, 224–26, 271–72, 274, 284, 290, 292

Driscoll, David, 27

Dudar, Helen, 112, 123

Dufty, Bill, 107

Dumont, Allen B., 51

Dunn, Martin, 293, 300–302

Durrell, Lawrence, 303

E

Eckman, Fern Marja, 112

Economist, 130, 224

Edward VIII, 41

Elliott, Osborn (Oz), 132, 136–38, 141, 145, 149, 153 154, 159, 161–65, 172

The Ends of Power, 191

Engle, Bob, 156, 170

Entertainment Tonight, 315

Ephron, Nora, 104, 315

Ervin, Sam, 156

Esposito, Meade, 114

Esquire, 251–54, 257–69

Evans, Harry, 264, 271–273

Evans, John, 190, 232–34, 273

Evans, Joni, 173

Express, 292–293

Exquisite Form, 69

F

Face the Nation, 315

FACT FROM OPINION, 130

Fairchild, John, 203, 212, 248–49

Farrar, Margaret, 81

fashion, 215–16, 262

Fast Company, 286

fatherhood, 117–19, 217

Fay, Ed, 278, 285

FBI, 107–9, 140

The FBI Story, 108

Felker, Clay, 177, 180, 206, 249, 273

Felt, W. Mark, 312

The Final Days, 173, 176

Fisher, Annalee. *See* Kosner, Annalee Fisher

Fisher, Belle. *See* Robbins, Belle Fisher

Fisher family, 5–7, 23–37

Fisher, Freda. *See* Levenberg, Freda Fisher

Fisher, Selda. *See* Levin, Selda Fisher

Fleming, Karl, 134–35, 221

Ford, Gerald, 169

Ford, Richard, 260

Forst, Don, 205

Frankel, Max, 154

Freedom of Information Act, 109

Friday, Nancy, 229

Friedman, Bob, 101

Fromme, Lynette Alice (Squeaky), 169

Frydman, Ken, 308

Funhouse, The, 131

G

Gallagher, Buell G., 66

Galotti, Ron, 260–61

Garment District, 16

Gibson, Althea, 279

Gilbert Hall of Science, 46

Gillette, Joan, 113

Gilman, Max, 110

Gingrich, Arnold, 252

Giuliani, Roody (Rudy), 298

glasses, 10

Golden, Harry, 94

Goldman, Peter, 123, 125, 131–32, 137–38, 145, 150, 157–58, 173, 191

Goldwater, Barry, 137

Gonzalez, Elian, 279

Goodstein, Les, 280

Goodwin, Dick, 141–42

Goodwin, Michael, 280, 285, 296

Gore, Al, 285

Gore, Larry, 69–70, 73

Gore, Lesley, 118

The Gospel According to the Son: A Novel, 294

Gotbaum, Victor, 211

Gottlieb, Robert, 244, 250

GQ, 253, 258, 262

Graff, Herbie, 49

Graham, Donald, 265

Graham, Katherine, 1–2, 127–28, 131, 159, 161–67, 177, 184, 188, 195, 197–98, 215, 247, 273, 294

Graham, Phil, 127–29, 163

Granger, David, 267

Greene, Gael, 112

Greenwich Village, 110

Gross, Michael, 211, 258

Gross, Milton, 93

The Group, 128

Grove, Gene, 104

Grunwald, Henry, 158, 170–71

Guccioni, Bob, 215

Guest, Cornelia, 249

H

Haddon, Briton, 130

Haden-Guest, Anthony, 215

Halberstam, David, 182

Haldeman, Bob, 191

Haley, Alex, 181–82

Hamill, Pete, vii–x, 105–6, 114, 209, 211, 266, 271, 283, 292, 295–96

Hamilton, Alexander, 92

Hamilton, Murray, 108

Harper & Row, 237

HarperCollins, 237

Harper's Bazaar, 203
Harriman, Averell, 114
Harris, Joel Chandler, 101
Harris, Lou, 137
Hayes, Harold, 199, 252
Hearst, Patricia (Tania), 169–70
Heartburn, 315
Hemingway, Ernest, 106
Herald Tribune, 85
Hewitt, Don, 309
Hills, Rust, 266
Hirschfeld, Abe, 293
Hirshey, David, 258
Hitler diaries, 220–22
Hoffman, Dustin, 315
Holiday, Billie, 107
Holmes, Larry, 230
Hoover, J. Edgar, 106–7, 109, 312
Hoving, Tom, 200
Howard, Lucy Anne, 5
Howdy Doody, 11
Howe, Irving, 132
Hughes, Bob, 199
Hussein, King, 163
Hussein, Saddam, 313

I
Information Please, 75
Interview with the Vampire, 259
Irving, Clifford, 220

J
Jennings, Peter, 309
Jerome, V., 83
JFK: The Man and the Myth, 128
JHS 115, 50
John Paul II, 196
Johnson, Edward, 20
Johnson, Lyndon, 139–40, 146
Jones, Laurie, 206, 215, 254
Journal-American, 85
journalism, 75, 144–45, 155, 284–86, 306–9
    future of, 319–22

minority reporters, 312
scandals, 318
Judaism, 6, 17–19

K
K-head, 80
Kalb, Bernard, 63
Kalb, Marvin, 63
Kelley, Jack, 307, 309
Kelley, Kitty, 176
Kelly, Keith, 303
Kempton, Murray, 92, 107
Kennedy, John F., 127–128, 130, 138–40, 142
Kennedy, John F., Jr., 277–78
Kennedy, Robert, 146–48
Kessler, Fran, 263
Kidman, Nicole, 259
Kihss, Peter, 80
King, Larry, 314
King, Martin Luther, 103, 130, 136
Kingsley, Pat, 259
Kirschenbaum, Walter K., 83–84
Kissinger, Henry, 172
Klein, Joe, 214, 226–227, 246, 264
Kline, Nathan, 151
Knauss, Melania, 229–30
Knopf, 250
Kobakoff, Rich, 74
Koch, Ed, 212
Kohut, Phil, 33
Kornbluth, Jesse, 211
Kosinski, Jerzy, 182–83, 185
Kosner, Alice Nadel, 81–82, 85, 88, 97,
    109–10, 111, 117–22, 148–152, 156, 158,
    165–166, 179–181, 183, 192, 206, 224
Kosner, Annalee Fisher, 6, 12–13, 17, 28–29,
    37–39, 41, 43, 49, 53, 68, 119, 120–121
Kosner, Anthony, 52, 121, 166, 193, 197, 217,
    224
Kosner family, 5–7, 12, 23–37, 182–83
Kosner, John Robbins, 118, 119, 166, 175, 193,
    197, 217, 224
Kosner, Julie Baumgold, 3, 93, 177, 179–181,

183, 191, 193–197, 203–204, 206–207,
212–213, 216–217, 219, 223, 225–226,
229–232, 236, 239, 248–251, 257–258,
262–263, 268–269, 281, 321, 323
Kosner, Lily, 217, 223, 231, 239
Kosner, Sidney, 20–22, 25–26, 41, 44–46, 87,
166–67
Krall, Marty, 280, 299
Kramer, Michael, 211, 219, 226, 246, 275, 278,
285
Kravis, Henry, 241, 242, 248–49
Krenek, Debby, 275, 279–80, 285, 294
Kristol, Irving, 132
Kroll, Jack, 131
Kujau, Konrad, 221
Kukla, Fran and Ollie, 52–53

L
La Ronde, 154
Lacroix, Christian, 236
Lady Sings the Blues, 107
Langer, William, 26
Lansner, Kermit, 132–36, 159
Lash, Joseph P., 112
Lasky, Victor, 128
Lauren, Ralph, 216
Lawrence, David, 223
Leavitt, David, 266
Leibowitz, Annie, 259
Leno, Jay, 260
Lerman, Leo, 244
Lerner, Max, 92
LeRoy, Mervyn, 108
Letterman, David, 260
Levenberg, Freda Fisher, 25
Levenberg, Lou, 25
Levin, Donald, 34–36
Levin, Nat, 29–30, 32–33, 36
Levin, Selda Fisher, 28–29, 120
Levine, Izzy, 80
Libby, Lewis (Scooter), 303, 313, 314
libel laws, 76
Liberman, Alexander, 243–44

Life, 130
Limbaugh, Rush, 303
Lindsay, John, 149–150, 157
Locke, Richard, 244
Lodge, Henry Cabot, 137
Long Beach, 30–31, 34
Long Island Press, 85
Lord & Taylor, 71–72
Luce, Betsy, 94, 138
Luce, Henry, 130
Lucky Pup, 52
Lyons, Leonard, 70

M
M-head, 81
Maccioni, Sirio, 255
Macmillan, 241–242
Madonna, 260–61
Mailer, Norman, 3, 162, 178, 229–231, 251, 294
Manchester, William, 140
Manning, Gordon, 132
Mapes, Mary, 310
Maples, Marla, 230
marriage, 109, 193–94
Martin, Steve, 187, 261–62
Martz, Larry, 145
Marx toys, 46
Mason, Alice, 231–32
Maurer, Gilbert, 252
Maxwell, Robert, 241, 271
McCabe, Gibson, 159
McCarthy era, 83, 106
McCarthy, Gene, 146–47
McCarthy, Joe, 212
McCarthy, Mary, 128
McClellan, George, 312
McDonnell, Terry, 253, 258, 260
McGavin, Darren, 70
McQuillan, Harry, 242–43, 245
Mehta, Sonny, 249
Mencken, H. L., 107, 122
Merrick, David, 103
Meyers, Chuck, 81, 89

Midnight in the Garden of Good and Evil, 203
military service, 117
Miller, Judy, 304, 314
Mirabella, 237
Mirabella, Grace, 237
Mitchell, John, 156
Moffitt, Phil, 252
Monet, Jack, 87
Monroe, Marilyn, 106
Morgenthau, Robert, 212
Morrisroe, Patricia, 211
Mortimer, Lee, 69
Moses, Robert, 112
movies, 39–40
Moyers, Bill, 159
Moynihan, Pat, 197
"Mr. Peepers' Nights", 232
Ms. magazine, 218
Mubarak, Hosni, 163
Mudd, Roger, 200
Murdoch, Rupert, 177–179, 190, 203–22,
  233–44, 273, 293, 319–320
Murray, Charles, 235
Museum of Modern Art, 15
Music Vendor, 110

N
Nadel, Alice. See Kosner, Alice Nadel
Nation, 26
National Enquirer, 178
National Star, 178
NcNamee, Wally, 156
Neuharth, Allen, 265, 308
New West, 1/8
New Weston, 137
New Woman, 237
New York City, 211–12, 214, 217
New York Herald Tribune, 177
New York magazine, 177, 203–22, 229–39,
  241–55
New York Post, 85, 88–89, 91–112, 178, 237,
  272, 295–96, 306
New York Times, 79–86, 313, 321

New York Times vs. Sullivan, 77
New York University, 58
New Yorker magazine, 26, 245
Newhouse, Si, 243–44, 250, 268, 316
News of the World, 208
Newsday, 85
Newsweek, 1–3, 125–59, 171, 224, 314–16
Nicholson, Harold, 263
Nicholson, Jack, 229–30, 319
Nicholson, Nigel, 263
Nixon, Richard, 147, 155–59, 173, 235, 255,
  307, 316
Noll, Chuck, 210
Nouvelle Society, 212
Nova Scotia mine collapse, 98–99

O
Observation Post, 73, 82
Observer New York, 297
Onassis, Jacqueline, 243
OP, 84
opera, 20
Opotowsky, Stan, 93, 99–100, 106, 122–23,
  136, 290
Orphan's Day, 34
Oswald, Lee Harvey, 139–40
Owen, David, 235
Owen, Steve, 27

P
The Painted Bird, 182
Paley, Bill, 201–2, 205
parenthood, 117–19, 217
Parker, Maynard, 221, 246–47, 264–65, 268
Pataki, George, 290
Pearlstine, Norman, 229
Peer, Elizabeth, 161
Pegler, Westbrook, 107
People magazine, 172, 308
"Periscope", 314–15
Personal History, 128
Phillips, McCandlish, 80
Pileggi, Nick, 211, 219

Pinkerton guards, 72
Pitt, Brad, 259
Plame, Valerie, 312–314
Plan of Attack, 316
Podhoretz, Norman, 26, 132
Pogrebin, Robin, 263–64
Polansky, Dave, 66
polio, 10–11
Posnansky, Nina, 182
Powell, Colin, 65
Prato, Gino, 75
Premiere, 237
Presley, Elvis, 185
Primary Colors, 227, 264–65
Private Eye, 205
Progressive Labor Party, 84
Proulx, Annie, 260
P.S. 173, 49–50
psychiatric therapy, 151–52
Pulitzer Prize, 293, 313

Q
Quill, Mike, 14
Quiz Show, 77
quiz shows, 75

R
Radical Chic, 204
Raftery, Tom, 279–280
Raines, Howell, 304, 308, 313, 314
Random House, 264, 273–74
Rather, Dan, 190, 311, 313–14, 318
Rauh, Joe, 108
Reagan, Nancy, 255
Reagan, Ronald, 255, 307
Redford, Robert, 319
Reeves, Richard, 226
Reilly, William, 241–42, 245, 247, 252, 254, 255
Reynolds, Frank, 200
Rice, Anne, 259
Richardson, Elliot, 155
Ritts, Herb, 259

Rivera, Geraldo, 200
The Roaring Eighties, 211
Robbins, Belle Fisher, 16, 26–27, 37, 38, 39, 43
Robbins, Sam, 16, 26–27, 36–37
Robeson, Paul, 6
Rockefeller, Nelson, 114, 137, 147
Rodino, Peter, 156
Roe v. Wade, 121
Roehm, Caroline, 212, 241, 248
Roeloffs, Eleanor. *See* Clift, Eleanor Roeloffs
Rolling Stone, 203
Roots, 181
Rose, Charlie, 296
Rosen, Jake, 83
Rosenthal. A. M. 63
Rosenthal, Irv, 64, 80
Ross, Harold, 244
Ross, Irwin, 112
Rubinstein, Howard, 205–6
Ruby, Jack, 139

S
Saal, Hubert, 131
Sackville-West, Vita, 263
Sadat, Anwar, 163
Salembier, Valerie, 265
Salinger, J. D., 115–16, 265
The Sandbox, 116
Sanders, Jacquin, 126
Sandman, Charles, 157
Sann, Paul, 92, 103–104, 114
Saturday Evening Post, 130
Saturday Night Massacre, 155
Saturday Review, 201–2
Schiff, Dorothy (Dolly), 48, 92, 100, 106, 113–14, 123, 178
Schnitzler, Arthur, 154
school days, 9–12, 49–57
Schorr, Bernard, 63
Schwartz, Jack, 70, 76, 85, 117, 192
Schwartz, Tony, 176, 192, 211, 219
Scott, Hugh, 157
The Sea Around Us, 26

Seinfeld, Jerry, 260
September 11th, 289–93
Seventeen, 237
Sex and the City, 260
Shaffer, Sam, 157
Shapiro, Avi, 309
Shaw, Irwin, 27
Shawn, William, 115, 244
Shine, G. David, 212
Shuman, Stan, 238
Siemaszko, Corky, 290
Simmons, Henry, 135
Simon & Schuster, 173, 175, 176
Singerman, Marty, 238–39
Sirica, John, 156
Sixty Minutes, 172, 199
Sixty Minutes II, 313–14
Smith, Buffalo Bob, 11
Smith, Ed, 175
Smith, Gene, 93
Smith, Liz, 172, 174, 225
Snyder, Dick, 173, 175–76
Soap Opera Digest, 237
Sokolsky, George, 107
Soybean Digest, 241
Spiegel, Pat, 80
Spinks, Michael, 230
Springsteen, Bruce, 170–71
stamp collecting, 47
Steinbrenner, George, 212–13
Steinem, Gloria, 83, 218, 172, 177, 223
Stempel, Herb, 75–77
Stern, 221
Stern, Henry, 65
Stevenson, Adlai, 52, 71, 114
Stewart, Jimmy, 108
Stewart, Martha, 303, 304
Stone, Marvin, 223
Stone, Sharon, 261
Stone, W. Clement, 127
Stoopack, Murray, 50
Strom, Robert, 75
Stuart Little, 26

Sullivan, Ed, 69
Sulzberger, Arthur Ochs (Pinch), 308, 313
The Sun, 122, 141, 208, 235
Sunday Daily News, 271–81, 274
Suskind, Richard, 220
Swanson, Gloria, 107

T
Talk, 243, 261, 268
Taylor, John, 211, 247, 248, 254, 258, 266
technology, 319
Teed, Dexter, 102
television, 50–53, 75
"The Term Paper Artist," 266–67
Thomas, Evan, 141
Thomas, Norman, 141
Thompson, Hunter, 150
Thompson, Jane, 71
Thornburgh, Richard, 310
Thurmond, Strom, 137
Tidyman, Ernie, 101
Tillstrom, Burr, 52
Time, 1, 116, 128–30, 136, 139, 144–45, 147,
   154, 158, 170–71, 175, 224, 233, 286, 307
Times of London, 235, 244
Tolson, Clyde, 106
Tracy, Arthur, 70
trading cards, 41–42
Traub, Marvin, 209–10
Travolta, John, 261
Trevor-Roper, Hugh, 221–22
Trigere, Pauline, 248
Trippett, Frank, 126, 132
Truman, Harry, 137, 147
Trump, Donald, 212, 229–30, 249
Trump, Ivana, 229
Tufo, Peter, 179
TV Guide, 237
Twenty-One, 75–77
Twenty Questions, 75
Tynan, Kenneth, 103
Tyson, Mike, 229–30
Tytell, Peter, 310

U
Underhill, Jake, 126
U.S. News & World Report, 145, 223–27, 286
USA Today, 265, 307–309, 314

V
Van Doren, Charles, 77
Van Doren, Mark, 77
Vanden Heuvel, William, 147
Vanity Fair, 243–45, 254, 268, 312, 314, 316
Vecchio, Pat, 149
Versace, 262–63
Victor, Ed, 263
Village Voice, 178, 291
Vitale, Alberto, 273
Vogue, 215, 237, 315
Volcker, Paul, 235

W
Wagner, Bob, 189–90
Wald, Dick, 199, 201
Walker, Danton, 69
Walker, Stanley, 289, 318
Wall Street Journal, 130, 291, 309, 317
Wallace, David Foster, 260
Wallace, George, 134, 154
Wallace, Henry, 137
Wallendas, 131–32, 143, 150, 307
Walls, Jeannette, 258–59
Walters, Barbara, 199–200
"The War on the Cops", 207–8
Warren Commission, 140
Washington Heights, 6
Washington Post, 1, 127, 145, 154, 173, 191,
    192, 264, 307, 314, 317
Watergate, 154–59, 191, 312
Weaver, Sigourney, 196
Wechsler, Jimmy, 92, 105–8, 114
Welch, Jack, 303
Weldon, Fay, 263
Westwood, Vivienne, 262
Weymouth, Lally, 214–15, 268
White, E. B., 26

White, Timothy, 260
Whittle, Chris, 252
Weitz, John, 248
Williams, Carl, 230
Williams, Edward Bennett, 176
Williams, Garth, 26
Williams, Serena, 279
Willse, Jim, 293
Wilson, Earl, 69
Wilson, Joseph, 313
Winchell, Walter, 39, 69–70, 106–7
Winners and Sinners, 81
WINS, 130, 227, 286–7
Wintour, Anna, 215–17, 237, 249, 315–16
Wolfe, Tom, 177, 204, 244
Women's Wear Daily, 203, 212, 231, 248
Woods, Rosemary, 156
Woodward, Bob, 173–76, 307, 312, 314–15
World-Telegram & Sun, 85
World Trade Center, 287–91
World War II, 6, 9, 14

Y
Yiddish, 6, 18, 25, 149

Z
Zabel, Bill, 238
Ziegler, Ron, 157–58
Ziff, Bill, 234
Zuckerman, Mortimer, 223–27, 249, 271–74,
    278–302,